The Idea of Principle in Leibnitz and
The Evolution of Deductive Theory

by JOSÉ ORTEGA Y GASSET

SOME LESSONS IN METAPHYSICS

THE ORIGIN OF PHILOSOPHY

THE REVOLT OF THE MASSES

MAN AND PEOPLE

MAN AND CRISIS

WHAT IS PHILOSOPHY?

MEDITATIONS ON QUIXOTE

HISTORY AS A SYSTEM

CONCORD AND LIBERTY

MISSION OF THE UNIVERSITY

THE IDEA OF PRINCIPLE IN LEIBNITZ AND THE EVOLUTION
OF DEDUCTIVE THEORY

JOSÉ ORTEGA Y GASSET

THE IDEA OF PRINCIPLE IN LEIBNITZ AND THE EVOLUTION OF DEDUCTIVE THEORY

TRANSLATED BY MILDRED ADAMS

W·W·NORTON & COMPANY·INC·New York

All rights reserved. Published simultaneously in Canada by
George J. McLeod Limited, Toronto.

Library of Congress Catalog Card No. 66-18068

SBN 393 01086 4

PRINTED IN THE UNITED STATES OF AMERICA

1 2 3 4 5 6 7 8 9 0

Contents

6   CONTENTS

Preliminary Note

THIS BOOK was written by Ortega, almost all of it in Lisbon, in the spring and early summer of 1947. He planned to finish it in the autumn and then give it to the printer.

Its first title was *El principialismo de Leibnitz y algunos problemas anejos* (Principalism in Leibnitz and Some Related Problems); but later, after using some of its paragraphs in the "Prologue" to the Castilian version of *El Collar de la Paloma* by Ibn Hazm (Madrid, 1952), Ortega gave it the title *La idea de principio en Leibnitz y la evolución de la teoría deductiva* (*The Idea of Principle in Leibnitz and the Evolution of Deductive Theory*) with the announcement that it was going to be published by the Hemeroteca Municipal of Madrid. They had agreed to celebrate the tercentenary of the birth of Leibnitz with the first Spanish edition of the "Essays," which appeared in the *Acta Eruditoreum*, Leipzig 1688–1716, presented with a preliminary study by José Ortega y Gasset. Some sheets to this end were printed in 1948. Ortega then revised the first draft in part, and added some pages and notes. Nevertheless, various obligations took him from this work, and delayed its finishing. On his account, the homage to Leibnitz was not performed.

Among the author's unpublished papers there appeared the originals of the study as it is now published. Its editing was not finished, for in the text he announces a second and a third chapter (pages 157 and 159) which were never written.

We added as Appendices the discourse "Concerning Optimism in Leibnitz," written for the opening of The XIX Congress of the Spanish Association for the Progress of the Sciences, celebrated in San Sebastián in 1947, and some pages on the Renaissance, which Ortega had interrupted and set apart from the study.

The exceptional significance of this book—because of its length, its subjects and the manner of treating them—and what it has of novelty in Ortega's intellectual trajectory gives it a preeminent place in his philosophic production.

The Compilers

The Idea of Principle in Leibnitz and
The Evolution of Deductive Theory

1

The Idea of Principle
in Leibnitz

KNOWLEDGE, whether formal or informal, is always based on the contemplation of something according to a principle.[1] In the sciences, this process becomes formalized and converted into a method or a calculated procedure whereby the data on a problem are related to a principle which "explains" them. In philosophy this is carried to an extreme, which tries not only to explain things on the basis of their principles, but also requires those principles to be "ultimate" in the sense of being root principles.

The fact that we customarily call these root principles, these "most principle" of all principles, "ultimate" shows that in our intellectual life we move habitually within an intermediate zone which is not pure empiricism or an absence of principle, nor is it in the area of root principles; these seem to us remote, far out at the limit of the mind's horizon, representing a goal still to be achieved, a point not yet reached. Inversely, at other times, we call these "first" principles. Note that when we say this, or think it, we tend to move the head slightly upward. This is because, even when we call these principles "first" rather than "ultimate" we still do not bring them close to us but regard them as distant, although now in a vertical direction.

As a matter of fact, we set those principles as high as possi-

1. To avoid possible confusion it must be remembered that in both English and Spanish the primary meaning of "principle" (Sp. *principio*) is "origin, source, beginning." A secondary meaning is "fundamental truth, law or motive force." Either set, or both, of these meanings can be read into the text of these chapters at various points [*Translator's note*].

ble: in the sky, and at the zenith. This is a relic of our Indo-European and Semitic (i.e., Hebraic) tradition, the tradition of peoples whose religion is shot through with the brilliant and the starry, for whom the gods are made manifest in the planets and the meteors. Always the same, we see them at the greatest possible distance. They appear, then, as both necessity and aspiration. The other forms of knowledge range across the intermediate zone which extends from the place where we normally and spontaneously are, a place made up of vaguely generalized facts, to that last line of the horizon where the root principles lie hidden. Philosophy, which is intellectual radicalism or extremism, is determined to reach by the most direct path that last line of the horizon where the ultimate principles abide; therefore, it is not merely a form of knowledge that, like others, is drawn from principles, but philosophy is a formal exploration directed to the discovery of those principles.

From this it follows that philosophers as a group may be designated as "men of principles." By the same token, it is in truth surprising that of them all, Leibnitz appears to us as standing out in a very special sense as the "man of principles" par excellence.

Our reasons for attributing this special characteristic to Leibnitz are the following: first, he is the philosopher who uses the greatest number of principles *sensu stricto*, that is to say, the greatest number of general principles. Second, he is the philosopher who introduces the greatest number of new principles into philosophical theory. Third, we see him in his writings constantly citing one or another of those principles. If in reading him we are not satisfied with understanding what he says, but give attention to the way he says it, if we study his prose stylistically, scanning its features, then we cannot fail to see the almost voluptuous manner with which he draws a principle forth from the depths of a paragraph, displays it, brandishes it, making it shine like a rapier, and addressing to its myriad reflections a look of enormous delight, like that which escaped Achilles, disguised as a woman, when Ulysses, disguised as a merchant, drew from his box a sword. And fourth because, as we shall see, knowledge, for Leibnitz, depends on principles in a sense more serious—and more paradoxical—than anyone before him had supposed.

Let us make for ourselves a list of Leibnitz' principles:

1. The principle of principles.
2. Principle of identity.
3. Principle of contradiction.
4. Principle of sufficient reason.
5. Principle of uniformity or the harlequin principle.
6. Principle of the identity of the indiscernible, or principle of differentiation.
7. Principle of continuity.
8. Principle of the better or of the expedient.
9. Principle of harmony or rule of law (principle of symmetry in modern mathematics).
10. Principle of the least effort or of the optimum forms.

Except for the second and third, all the principles in this list were originally set forth by Leibnitz, which does not mean that in the philosophic past they had no prehistory. All human activities, being part of history, have their prehistory.

The aggregate of previous statements we can call the idea of principle in Leibnitz, his "principle-ism." But now the matter begins to become complicated. Into this aggregation we must introduce these objections: first, in stating his principles Leibnitz usually finds formulas which are full of grace and verbal effectiveness; but the fact that he uses several expressions for a single principle, and that the terms are almost never precise—whereas in the rest of his concepts, he is precise to a high degree—produces in the student of his works a most curious uneasiness of which the first reaction, informal, of course, but sincere, might be this: Leibnitz plays with principles, he loves them, but he does not respect them. Second, although the essential core of knowledge is, for Leibnitz, orderly thinking, he never set himself seriously to put the tangle of his principles in order, never arranged them in a proper hierarchy, never established subordinate relationships, never coordinated them.[2] Because of this, his principles float at undetermined altitudes of the theoretical system, and their relative rank, which is so decisive for a principle as such, never appears clear. Third, and as a matter of greater substance, Leibnitz insists again and again that it is both appropriate and necessary to prove principles, or try to prove them. Very well, but one usually understands by principle something which neither can be proved nor needs to be, but is the very thing which makes all proof possible. Does this not mean that Liebnitz disdained principles, and that of all the philosophers, he was the least devoted to them, least "principle-ist"?

The two series of statements above stand in sharpest contrast with one another. Note that in each series the one which is stated last is not, like the others, of a more or less external character; on the contrary, it is a doctrinal thesis, and one might even say that it is internal and even visceral to the doctrine. So we are left, then, perplexed at this dual, changeable attitude of Leibnitz toward principles.

2. Take, for example, the passage in *Die Philosophischen Schriften von G. W. Leibniz* (C. J. Gerhardt, Berlin, 1879), Vol. II, 56, and Couturat, *Opuscules et Fragments*, pp. 402 and 519, in which the principle of sufficient reason is stated as merely corollary to the purely logical principle, according to which the predicate is included in the subject in every true proposition.

2
What a Principle Is

In the abstract, a "principle" is that which, within a given order, is found before another thing. If A stands before B, we say that B follows A, and that A antecedes or precedes B. When the order is rectilinear, but not infinite, we can say of two elements that one is the precedent or principle of the other, the other being that which follows or the consequence. But in the finite linear order there will be one element which has no precedent or principle. All others are consequences of that element. Within the order, then, this will be a principle in the root or absolute sense, it will be a first principle. The elements that precede those that follow them, but are in turn preceded by others, may within the order be called "relative principles." At first sight, only the "absolute principle" will, strictly speaking, be regarded as a principle. But note that the abstract notion of principle rejects that assumption since its identifying characteristic is "being found before another." The essential feature of a principle is, therefore, that something follows it, not that nothing precedes it. In this way the notion of principle is as valid for the absolute as for the relative, and valid, moreover, for orders which are not of the finite rectilinear type; for example, for an infinite rectilinear order in which there is no first element, or for a circular order in which each element also comes before another, but is impartially first, intermediate, and last.

With the notion of the abstract firmly in mind, let us now move toward one of its concrete forms. Let us, for example, see what "principle" means in the order which is *traditionally* called "logical." In the traditional sense, the logical order is made up of a multiplicity of propositions, both true and false. To simplify, let us deal only with the true ones. These true

15

propositions form an ordered whole. This order is rooted in the character of truth which the propositions display. In view of this, they are so ordered that one follows another, except that here the "following" becomes more specific; the truth of one follows the truth of another. That is the principle of the truth of this, and this is the consequence of that. Our language in this case subtly emphasizes the "follow" and says that one proposition (that is to say, its truth) is followed by another. In this way, moving backwards, we reach a level at which *not one but several* propositions appear which do not follow each other nor do they follow any antecedents of themselves; they are therefore independent of each other and have neither precedent nor principle. These are the principles of all the others. They are, therefore, absolute principles. They are the principle of identity and the principle of contradiction. Some would add the principle of the excluded middle, which Brouwer's work now puts in grave question.

Now then, from the above there rises spontaneously the question of why the order has a final element, why it ends. The answer is clear. Since each true proposition receives its character of truth from the one before it, and so on successively, the series must have an end or it would remain completely empty of truth. There must be a beginning and in it there should already be *all the character of "truth,"* which will flow through and fill the entire series, which will "make" all the other propositions true. This, at least, is the traditional opinion in regard to the logical order.

After this a second question surges forth: why, in place of a first element that begins the order or the series, does it happen that there must be at least two coordinates in the logical order? Traditionally, men did not think about this. It was taken for granted and accepted as the most natural thing in the world. By the same token, we are not at the moment anxious to resolve it.[1]

1. The scholastics, for example, Suárez in *Disputationes metaphysicae* (I, Sec. II, 3), establish the need for at least two principles since the

On the other hand, it is important to note that, in view of what has been said, the logical order appears to be made up of pairs of propositions, one of them being the *principle* of the other, which in turn is its *consequence*. Each proposition of each pair forms, in turn, a pair with another of which it is the consequence, or of which it is the principle. *Every* logical proposition—except the first ones—is at once principle and consequence. This gives the logical *corpus* its perfect continuity. There is in it neither leap nor *hiatus*. When we say that one proposition is the principle of another, we could vary the expression, without this changing the idea, and say that the one is the *basis* of the truth of the other, and that the latter is founded on the former. Also, in place of "principle" or "basis" we can say *reason*. The principle of the truth of proposition B is the reason A. The logical order is articulated in the "play" of *reason* and *consequence*. Finally, in place of the "reason" we can also say the "proof" of a proposition.[2] This accumulation of synonyms is not superfluous, because their similarities are, strictly speaking, only partial, and each of these words signifies a different side or aspect of the same thing. In certain cases we will gain greater clarity by using one rather than another.

Now then, a simple inspection of the logical order as a whole reveals that in it the character called "truth" has a double value and because of this it becomes equivocal. *Within* the logical *corpus* every proposition is true because it has its "reason" or its "proof," which is another proposition. So that "to be true," "to be the consequence of," and "to be 'proven'" are all the same. But at the end of the series we find ourselves with propositions—the "first principles"—which are not in turn "consequences," which are not "proven," which do not have

---

syllogism has three terms and there are only two with one principle. But this does not justify having more than two.

2. Even though nothing of what has been said up to now is especially *Leibnitzian*, it is advisable to warn that *Leibnitz* accepts this equivalent meaning for the terms "reason" and "proof." (*Nouveaux essais sur l'entendement humain*, Vol. IV, Chap. II.)

"reason." What does this mean? Undoubtedly it means one of two things: either these are true in a sense different from the one that up to now has been established, or they are not true. If the former, we will have the "principles" of the logical order as true propositions with a truth which is neither "reason" nor "proof"—propositions that have no foundation and are therefore neither reasoned nor reasonable. This new form of "being true" is usually expressed by saying that they are "true in themselves," that is, not for any "reason"; that they are self-evident. And now we have two meanings for the word "true," each completely alien to the other: truth as reason, and truth as evidence. In place of evidence men have usually talked of "intuition" (thus Descartes). It should be added that, strange as it may seem, although the whole of human knowledge has been made to depend on evidence, not until Husserl (in 1901) did anyone seriously occupy himself with giving that word a controllable meaning. But this is not important now. It is more important to be aware of the serious situation presented by the existence of two opposing kinds of "truth": the one reasoned, proven, based on evidence, and the other unreasoned and unreasonable, spontaneous and immediate. But neither is this important now. On the other hand, it is vital to note that this doctrine of "first principles" as "truths *per se notae* or evident," implies the conviction—which is the traditional one—that first principles must be true of themselves, for it is considered that they are the ones which must transmit truth, must breathe truth into the entire series of their consequences. If not, whence can these consequences derive the attribute that makes them true?

Now we must face the second possibility: that the "first principles" might not be true. This does not, of course, imply that they are false; it says only that they are indifferent to their own truth, that they can not be false, but they need not *by themselves* be true. What, then, can they be? Remember the basic law of the logical order, which in this respect coincides with any "good order": that every element follows another element and is, in turn, followed by another. This is all that the law says. In it something is a principle because from it another something follows. The substance of the principle is, therefore, not that something else does *not* precede it but, I repeat, that something follows it. In this case the decisive thing is not what it may be *in itself*, but that it have consequences; therefore, that it be the *reason* for something else, that with it another proposition could be proven. In this sense, what constitutes a principle is not its own truth, but the truth that it produces; not its inherent "egotistical" condition of being true in itself, but its transitive "altruistic" virtue of making other propositions true, of rousing within them the character of "truth." This condition is what we previously called "relative principle," and this is common to all propositions, *even if there were no first principles*. There is nothing strange, nothing extravagant about this. In the series of causes and effects, which is a projection of the logical order over and above the real order, there is no first cause, and yet each effect finds its reason in an antecedent fact.

In this doctrine, therefore, it is enough that first principles need not be true, but are simple "admissions," free assumptions which are adopted not for any reason of interest in them, but rather *in order* to "bring out" their consequences, in order that they may be the *reason* for what follows, in order to *prove* a whole world of propositions which can be derived or deduced from them.

The time has come to leave this question still undecided in order to confront just as energetically the two meanings of the logical principle which derives from the articulatory law governing the logical order, namely, the pair called "reason and consequence," "foundation and founded"—in short, *principle* and *proof*. This linkage, this nexus, permits us to place the accent on one term or the other; to put it in a somewhat battered phrase, either the important thing is to "prove," or else the important thing is that the principle be true.

With this slight and elementary preparation we can now return to the enigma of Leibnitz' attitude toward principles, although our return will have to be a very large roundabout.

3
Thinking and Being,
or the Heavenly Twins

PHILOSOPHY is a certain idea about Being. A philosophy that breaks new ground brings forth a new idea of Being. But the curious thing about this is that every innovating philosophy—beginning with that great innovation which was the first philosophy—discovers its new idea of Being thanks to its having previously discovered a new idea of thinking, that is to say, an intellectual method previously unknown. But the word "method," although adequate for what I am hinting at, is a grey and flabby expression which does not convey strongly enough all of the seriousness or the basic nature of the notion which it attempts to express. The word "method" seems to suggest that the philosopher introduces certain modifications into the operation traditionally called thinking which would tighten the screws of its mechanism, making it more precise and ensuring its efficiency. This is not what I want to say. It is something much more significant. A new idea of thinking is the discovery of a way of thinking radically different from those previously known, although it retains this or that *part* which it has in common with them. It is therefore equivalent to the discovery of a new "faculty" in mankind, and it is to understand by "thinking" a reality different from any previously known.

Accordingly, one philosophy differs from another not so much, or primarily, for *what* it says to us about Being as by its *way of saying* it, by its "intellectual language"; that is to say, by its way of thinking. It is lamentable that the expression "way of thinking" should be understood as referring to the doctrines, to the content of dogmas in a thought, and not, as its grammatical structure would require, to differences in the process, in the actual operation of thinking.

This matching of a certain way of thinking with a certain idea of Being is not accidental; rather, it is inevitable. By the same token, it is not important whether or not a philosophy explains the method by which it operates. Plato, Descartes, Locke, Kant, Hegel, Comte, and Husserl devote a part of their philosophy to expounding their method, their new way of thinking; they give a preview of the biceps with which they will lift the enormous weight which is the problem of the Universe; but this does not mean that those who do not do the same thing are less methodical, or that they also may not have their own method. When we study their dogmas, we discover easily enough in what their method consists. But although it does not matter whether or not a philosophy proclaims its method, it is a bad sign if, on holding a philosophy against the light, we fail to see clearly, as though in a piece of filigree, just what its way of thinking is.

A consequence of all this is the practical advice that in order to understand a system of philosophy we must start by setting aside its dogmas and by trying to discover as precisely as possible just what that philosophy understands by "thinking," or to put it in terms of the vernacular, we have to find out "what they are up to" in that philosophy.

Now then, what did Leibnitz understand by thinking? One can seldom state in a few words what constitutes a way of thinking, a method. Nevertheless, with Leibnitz this can almost be done—and not by accident. One can, in fact, answer the question of what Leibnitz understands by thinking in one incisive phrase: to think is to prove. What we said in Chapter 1 serves well enough to give this aphorism an initial approximate meaning. But it is essential that we get closer to its full significance. For that it is necessary to take into account what philosophizing meant in Leibnitz' day.

4
Three Positions of Philosophy
with Respect to Science

THE POSITION OF PHILOSOPHY in the modern era is very different from what it purported to be in the ancient world. We are not speaking now of the essential difference between modern life and the life of ancient times, which is obviously enormous. We are looking only at one very specific factor in which the two sets of circumstances differ.

In Greece it was philosophy that invented knowledge as a form of precise thinking which compels men to see that things *must be* as they are, and not otherwise. It discovered necessary thought. In so doing it was fully aware of the radical difference between its own way of thinking and others existing around it. What other forms of mental attitude toward Reality were in sight? Religion, mythology, poetry, and the Orphic "theologies." In all these "disciplines," thinking consists of thinking plausible things, which perhaps are, which would appear to be; but not of thinking in terms of necessities, of things which are not dependent on our recognition of them, but which, once comprehended, impose themselves inescapably on our minds. This first-born philosophy regarded all those other intellectual attitudes toward the world with utter disdain.[1]

1. To complete the picture, however, it is advisable to note that there was one mental activity outside of philosophy which the philosophers of that period did contemplate with a certain respect: medicine, which was represented in certain parts of Greece by "semisecret societies," above all, the Society of the Aesculapians in Cos, to which Hippocrates belonged. The quotation in Phaedo makes of a Hippocratic aphorism the classic point of departure for calculating the relationship between philosophy and medicine.

Philosophy as thinking in terms of necessity was *the* knowledge, was *the* learning. Properly speaking, there was no other, and for its purpose it found itself alone in confronting Reality. Within its ambit the sciences began to be distilled as particular aspects of its "way of thinking." They busied themselves with *parts* of Being, with particular themes: spatial figures, numbers, stars, organic bodies, and so on, but the way of thinking about these things was philosophic. Hence, Aristotle still calls the sciences *fragments* of *knowledge* or topics—ἐν μέρει λεγόμενα.[2] Modern men of science must swallow, willy-nilly and once and for all, the fact that the "strict" character of Euclid's science was merely the quality of "strictness" as cultivated in the Socratic schools, especially in Plato's Academy. Now, all those schools were occupied chiefly with ethics. It is obvious that the Euclidian method, the exemplary "strictness" of the *more geometrico*, originated not in mathematics but in ethics. Whether it would have had better luck in the one than in the other is another question.[3] The sciences, therefore, were

2. It is curious that Dilthey, in his first period, should think that the sciences originated outside of philosophy, in techniques and as a reflection of them. In his second period he corrected this opinion. But as Dilthey never talked idly, it is best not to toss his original opinion lightly overboard. Let this reservation be set down here, but not developed.

3. Thus Solmsen, a disciple of Jaeger, in *Die Entwicklung der Aristotelischen Logik und Rhetorik*, 1929, pp. 129–30. Hardly were the sciences born when the phenomenon of specialization appeared. I am alluding, not to the fact that every man involved in a discipline would confine his attention to it, but to specialization in the way of thinking. As though it were a living thing, each science tends to withdraw into the requirements of its own subject. This automatically produces a modification of the general method corresponding to the need of each science. Thus mathematics pays no heed to the problems of reality. This leads it to employ only those principles which suffice for its deductions. Hence it has no interest in the principles properly called first; toward the top it is closed off with respect to the universality of philosophy and, consequently, closed off on all sides with respect to related disciplines. No one seeks a unity which would permit a common derivation of number, space and body. Arithmetic, geometry and stereometry are separate. This undoubtedly permitted considerable refinement of the method peculiar to every science. Aristotle's *Posterior Analytics* are reflections on this stage in the sciences. But nothing shows better what

born as particular aspects of the philosophic theme, but their method was the same as philosophy's, modified to accord with their fragmentary nature.

Philosophy's position in the modern period, even if considered only in its relation to the sciences, is completely different from the earlier one. During the 16th Century and the first two-thirds of the 17th Century the mathematical sciences, including astronomy and mathematics, achieved a truly prodigious development. The broadening of their themes was accompanied by a growing refinement of their method, and this in turn was followed by great material discoveries and by really fabulous technical applications. These moved not only with complete independence of philosophy, but actually in conflict with it. The consequence was that philosophy ceased to be *the* knowledge, *the* learning and saw itself only as *one* knowledge, *one* form of learning confronting others. Its theme, given its range and its universality, can still pretend to some primacy, but its way of thinking has not evolved, whereas the mathematical sciences have gone on modifying what philosophy originally taught them, and out of this they have made what are, in part, new ways of thinking. Philosophy, therefore, no longer stands alone confronting Being. There is another court of inquiry, a different one, which is busy searching out the truth of things in its own way; that way is exceedingly precise, superior in certain aspects to the traditional philosophic way. In view of this, philosophy now regards itself as one more science, with a more important theme but a clumsier method. In this situation it has no choice but to emulate the sciences. It wants to be a science, and for that reason it

the real situation was than the fact that Plato's Academy cultivated two forms of mathematics: one, the specialized, the mathematics of the mathematicians; the other, philosophic mathematics (dialectics). And all this culminates in the final detail that, as Proclus shows us concretely, it was Plato himself who, praising unitary science as the only knowledge in the full sense of the word, suggested the special mathematical method to his students of mathematics—to Leodamas, for instance, Proclus shows us both methods in this text, side by side (Proclus, *In Euclidis*, 211, Fr. 18).

cannot rest content merely with looking at the face of the Real; it must at the same time be looking at the exact sciences. Thus it ceases to be governed exclusively by that Reality which is its theme, and, in some degree, it takes its orientation and control from the sciences. Because of this, modern philosophy has double vision; because of this, modern philosophy is cross-eyed. This whole period can be documented simply by recalling Kant's well-known formula in his prize dissertation of 1763 entitled *Enquiry into the Distinctness of the Principles in Natural Theology and Morals*, "The true method of metaphysics is at root identical with that which Newton introduced into natural science and which there had such fertile consequences." [4]

This text can be taken as representative of innumerable others which can be adduced since Descartes. Moreover, it has the advantage of showing us how that adaptation of philosophy to the way of thinking used by the exact sciences is in its turn a process whose variations are a function of those produced in the evolution of those sciences. This makes it possible for us to locate each philosopher at a predetermined point in the series, as we shall soon do with Leibnitz. In effect, while Descartes and Leibnitz are oriented toward pure mathematics, because the physics which they themselves were helping to create *did not yet exist*, Kant's generation immediately fell in with the consolidated triumph of that physics which Newton symbolized. Hence, Kant disdained pure mathematics but kept one eye on physics, which was destined to build itself into a *regina scientiarum*. The text cited above is also interesting in that it was written by Kant when he had ceased to be a follower of Leibnitz and was finding himself without a philosophy. He was bent on discovering one, and in this quest we find him obsessed by Newton's physics as an ideal of knowledge. At that time Kant had no clear idea as to whether or not the quoted formula expressed the possible. By the same token it exposes the "scientific" snobbism which characterized

4. *Untersuchung über die Deutlichkeit der Grundsätze der natürlichen Theologie und Moral. Zweite Betrachtung.*

the philosophy of that period. Seven years later Kant would publish his famous dissertation, *De mundi sensibilis atque intelligibilis forma et principiis*, in which he achieved that adaptation of philosophy to physical science which he had postulated.

But since an idea never stands clear unless it appears between two others that, in one way or another, limit and shape it, the modern position of philosophy, with its rear-guard marked off by its ancient position, demands that we set it in relation to the present position, which is already a future position, a future in which we exist because we are its seed. It is clear that to do this here we must limit ourselves to the utmost sobriety of terms.

Once philosophy became habituated to keeping one eye on the exact sciences, even to envying them—especially physics because in it precision seemed to preserve in knowledge something appearing to be Reality—it continued to do so. As in the past, it still looks to physics, but now it finds that physics, in turn, has a way of thinking which is very different from that of Newton's physics, and in general, from what is called "classical physics." This innovation, which is most profound, has nothing to do with the theory of relativity. That theory represents the ultimate development of "classical physics." If Galileo could have been entirely faithful to his own way of thinking, with which he established the *nuova scienza*, he would have arrived at Einstein's physics. The Galilean way of thinking, to which Galileo had to be faithful, is that which in a marvellously clear way states his definition of the new science; this had to consist in "measuring everything that could be measured and putting in shape to be measured that which cannot be measured directly." He could not comply with this imperative for three reasons: first, because in his day procedures for measuring were crude and let escape certain combinations of phenomena which would have forced him to revise the principles of his mechanism, making them more concrete; second, because even if he had more precise measurements available, the mathematical techniques which would have allowed him to formulate and manipulate them did not exist; and third, because both of these circumstances made it easy for Galileo to expound his own definition of physics without going deep enough. This definition implies that all the integrating concepts of a physical proposition must be concepts of "something measured." Now then, only variations can be measured (Galileo knew very well that these in turn can only be measured relatively as between one and another). But variations are an expression of "forces." In physics "force" is not a magical notion; it is, strictly speaking, a "principle of variations," and therefore, by nature, measurable. Thus space and time, in order to enter the area of physical concepts, must cease to be geometric magnitudes in order to become measured magnitudes. But to measure them is to measure variations and, consequently, to introduce dynamic concepts. "Measured space" and "measured time" imply forces. This is what relativistic mechanics consists of—a simple effort to make the initial idea of physics compatible with itself; by the same token, it is merely the basic fulfillment of the program, of the way of thinking of classical physics.

Galileo never reached this depth of understanding. He thought that geometric theorems were inherently valid for physical phenomena, that they were a priori nothing more than "physical laws," so elemental that physics could assume them. His idea of inertia comes out of this. In Galilean inertia the straight line as such, as a geometric entity, constitutes a physical reality. It is a "force without force" which acts magically. Relativistic mechanics is the reduction of straight lines, physically magical, into dynamic curves which are physically real.[5]

5. Galileo deduces the notion of inertia as the boundary line of the law of falling bodies, considering the inclined plane to have zero inclination and thus to be converted into a horizontal. It is the "law of permanence and perseverance." It is known that in Galileo this law has few applications. It was Newton who raised it from "humble condition" to no less than the first rank among the *leges motus* (laws of motion) which are the axioms of his physics. To do this he had to affirm an absolute space, which is equivalent to the apotheosis of geometry. Newton is, I think,

The profound modification of the way of thinking in physics, and of physics with respect to "knowledge," is rooted in two characteristics which are completely alien to the theory of relativity as such; first, for more than half a century physical theory has been progressively converted into a system of statistical laws. This means laws of probability above all those closest to the expression of events. Therefore, physics today does not speak of the "real Being" but of the "probable Being." What probable Being really means has not yet been adequately explained, although it is clear enough for our present purposes that the probable Being *is not* the real Being, is not

---

the first to call inertia a "force"—*vis inertiae*. Remember that the general theory of relativity starts by noting that the inert mass may be considered as weight, and vice versa. Mach was the first to relate inertia and gravity, considering the former as an influence of the sidereal masses. Originally, the metric field was a dynamic space. Geometry penetrates relativist physics more deeply than it does the physics of Galileo and Newton, but the reason for this is that geometry, having been previously swallowed up in physics, had become dynamic. Thus Reichenbach could say that the theory of relativity is summarized in a "causal theory of time and space." And the surprising thing is that— except for the relativity of simultaneity—that was the Leibnitzian theory of space and time (Reichenbach, *Die Philosophie der Raum-Zeit-Lehre*, 1928, p. 308). On the other hand, there is this: the concept of inertia was extraordinary beyond measure. It does not provide an originating force, but the extension of a pre-existent force. It came, then, to be something like a "force without a force," something intermediate between dynamism and nondynamism. And it is curious that when it appeared in the theory of relativity as interchangeable with gravity it transmitted its nondynamic aspect to the latter, and with it to all physics, edging the mechanics theory toward abandonment of the idea of force. The result is that, as dynamism penetrates all the physical concepts, physics ends up by becoming indifferent to it and contenting itself with presenting phenomena through a system of pure numerical relationships, a "configuration" of metric values.

For Leibnitz, the concrete space in which phenomena appear to us, which he calls "extension," is a "system of positions." These positions result in—we might better say that they are—dynamic relationships between the fundamentals which are "forced." It cannot then be said that "things," i.e., forces, exist in space if that implies a space which antedates them. Concrete space, extension, springs from the actuating forces and is a manifestation of their activity. Being dynamic, the system of positions is continually changing, it is movement, and it cannot disasso-

Reality. But up to now knowledge was understood to be thought in which Reality is more or less present. Second, if knowing is the presence of Reality in thought, not only must there have been something real before the thought, but the thought—that is to say, what has been thought—must consist of something *similar* to reality. Similarity means partial identity. This similarity, which must exist so that there may be knowledge linking what is thought and what is real, may be greater or less. For Aristotle the similarity was almost *complete*, because what was *important* in the thing, namely its essence, entered into the thought and was within it. Therefore he could say that "the mind or the soul is in a certain way all things." Similarity, in the Aristotelian idea of knowledge, was stretched to mean "identity of that which is important." Only

---

ciate itself from time, which in Leibnitz represents that system of dynamic relations in its consecutive aspect. The absence of separation between space and time is thus built into Leibnitz more basically than into the theory of relativity, which associates space and time only insofar as they are measured. The fact that different forces appear successively in the same position allows us to form an abstract concept of that position, which thus becomes a mere "place." The system of places is abstract or geometric space, which is also—and hence newly abstract—a border case of concrete space insofar as it is a system of unmoving positions. Leibnitz will say that it is "ideal."

Clumsy as so brief a description may be, it may give an idea of what space was for Leibnitz. Nevertheless, it lacks one whole side of that idea, which cannot be summarized so lightly. I refer to the purely phenomenalistic character which space has for Leibnitz. Reality, properly speaking, is alien to space. The intelligible world of the monad is not extensive. But we have no knowledge of that world which is both concrete and clear. We have only a confused notion of it. This confusion as to what is genuinely real, this *minus* of intelligibility, is imagination. The world of the phenomenon—and with it space—is an imaginary world. This must not be taken only in its negative sense as concerned solely with our limited and inadequate information about the real. That distortion of the real is not merely subjective but is rather the objective way in which unlimited and authentic reality is represented in a limited framework. What is imaginary, although less than real, is founded in reality. And this, which has value for concrete or phenomenal space, also has value for "ideal" space. The "idea" of pure geometric space also has its foundation *in re*. But this is what I cannot here make crystal clear, because it would oblige us to set forth the most complicated concept in the entire Leibnitzian doctrine—the concept of phenomenon.

the accidents remain unassimilated. We are not interested now in whether or not Aristotle was right. His idea of knowledge serves us here only as an outer boundary in establishing a gradation of similarity, starting from the point of maximum similarity. The correspondence of similarity which constitutes the idea of knowledge therefore permits gradations. The oil portrait of a person is similar to him, although it has only two dimensions while he has three. In this case similarity ignores entirely a part of reality—its third dimension—and, nevertheless, the picture is similar, it does "resemble" the sitter, not because *all* of the sitter resembles the portrait, but rather because everything in the portrait is identical with *part* of what is in the sitter. If we consider the picture as a *series of elements* (the pigments) and the body of the sitter as another series of elements (his visible areas), we encounter a similar congruity in both series, for *each* element of one series *corresponds* to an *identical* element in the other. A pencil portrait of the same man cuts out more parts of his reality but maintains the identity with some of them; its relationship with the object is still one of similarity. But it is clear that if there is to be a relationship of similarity, there must be at least a minimum dose of *identity* between image and model, between thought and reality.

If we form a *corpus* made up of physical propositions as a group and call it "physical theory," we will find that in modern physics the propositions which make up that "physical theory" do not have a similar relationship with reality, that is to say, that *no* proposition of physical theory corresponds with reality, and even less, does the matter stated in any physical proposition *resemble* something real; in colloquial terms, what physical theory tells us, its content, has nothing to do with the reality of which it speaks. This is startling, but in any admissible schematic form, there it is. The only contact between "physical theory" and reality is that the former permits us to predict certain real facts, which are the experiments. According to this, modern physics does not, therefore, pretend to be the presence of reality in thought, since thought, in "physical theory," does not pretend to be in a similar relationship with reality.

Herman Weyl gives graphic expression to this strange characteristic of physical science, which has become completely manifest in modern times, by representing "physical theory," the inner *corpus* of physical propositions, with this figure

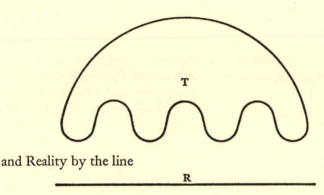

and Reality by the line

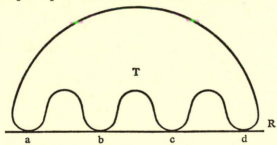

If we superimpose the one on the other we find

that T does not coincide with R except at points *a*, *b*, *c*, and *d*. These points are the experiments; but the remaining content of physical theory—the other points of the figure, those within its area—does not coincide with the points of Reality. Hence, there is no similarity whatever. There is no correspondence of identity between the contents of the interior points of the theory and the parts of reality. What must be compared with the parts of reality are not the parts of the theory but the whole of it. Their correspondence is guaranteed by experiments, not by similarity. What sort of correspondence is this? The way of thinking practiced by "physical theory" begins by enclosing that theory within itself and creating in its imaginary ambit a whole world—a system, an order of series—of objects which bear no resemblance to real phenomena. That imaginary intratheoretical system, by the very fact that it is imaginary (like all mathematics), manages to be unequivocal. This makes possible an *unequivocal* comparison between the order of imaginary objects and real phenomena; one that discovers whether these latter allow themselves to be arranged in a system or series isomorphic with the former. This unequivocal comparison is experimentation. When its result is positive, a correspondence that is dissimilar, but not unambiguous, remains established between the series of imaginary objects and the series of real objects (the phenomena). Between the objects of one series and the other there is no likeness; therefore, the correspondence is dissimilar. The only bit of similarity is the order between both of them.

When we leave overcoats in a theatre cloakroom, we are given numbered checks. A check does not look in the least like an overcoat but the series of overcoats corresponds to the series of checks, so that each specific check corresponds to a specific overcoat. Imagine, then, that the cloakroom attendant has been blind from birth and can read the engraved numbers on the checks only by the sense of touch. He can distinguish between them or, what is the same thing, he knows them. When he touches a check and finds its number, he then runs over the series of coats and finds the coat which corresponds to the check, and this is possible despite the fact that he has never seen a coat. The physicist, then, is the blind cloakroom attendant in a material universe. Can one say that he *knows* the coats? Can one say that he *knows* reality? Even at the beginning of the century the physicists—Thompson, for example—were saying that the method of physics is limited to the construction of mechanical "models" which show us clearly the real process that manifests itself only confusedly in phenomena. In modern physics there is no room for models. What physical theory says, transcends all intuition and admits only of analytical, algebraic representation; it confirms that when, subsequently, "quantum" mechanics, faced with its completely new theme "to go back and begin all over again," had in the process passed once more through the childhood stage of theory, it had to turn again to making models for itself (Bohr's atoms). But the speed with which this stage was passed and its transition to a theory even less open to intuition than the "metric field" of relativity, shows better than anything else the pressure of the modern way of thinking in physics.

We find ourselves facing a form of knowledge totally different from that which this term signifies in its first, spontaneous and full sense. Physicists themselves called this blind knowledge "symbolic knowledge" because instead of knowing the real thing, it recognizes its sign in a system of signs or symbols.

No "theory of symbolic knowledge" has yet been constructed which solves rigorously enough the question of the extent to which this can be considered authentic knowledge. It is nevertheless evident that, whatever its other advantages, it cannot pretend to be exemplary when the model of knowledge is being sought.

So physics, on the one hand, renounces all talk of Reality and contents itself with probability, while on the other, it renounces all pretense of being knowledge in the sense of the existence of Reality in thought.

With this the position of philosophy is radically modified as compared with that in which it found itself during the modern period. Physics, the *regina scientiarum* for centuries, has been rendered problematical as far as knowledge is concerned. (Problematical, let it be well understood, not as physics, not as "science," which today it is more gloriously than ever.) Hence, to the two reasons set forth as responsible for that problematic aspect, one would have to add those originating

in quantum mechanics, which, by making that problematical-
ity more concrete, make it even more profound; I am referring
to the "principle of indeterminism" and to the fact which
motivated it. What is of less importance, as Planck said, is that,
as no attribute is left for matter except to occupy a place in
space, according to the "principle of indeterminism," it remains detached, without *ubietas* (Leibnitz would say), and
therefore as if it had passed from being matter into being a
"soul." This would be a novelty in what is known rather than
a modification in the manner or meaning of knowing. The
serious thing is that "indeterminism" is the opposite of what
tradition considered knowledge to be. But it is even more
decisive that the indeterminate character of the material element arises because the experimenter, observing a fact, does
not observe it, but fabricates it. Now then, there can be nothing more contrary to "knowing reality" than "constructing
reality." The most unavoidable *a priori* of all is that of reality
with respect to its knowledge.[6] If, on trying to know reality
A our knowing creates another reality *B* which takes its place,
the knowledge we thus acquire will always lag behind Reality,
retarded with respect to it, and it will be like the greyhound
which, instead of running down one hare, prefers to race after
a continual series of new hares, thus condemning itself to
catching none of them.

This is typical of science today.

In such a situation it is understandable that philosophy has
no interest in being considered as *one* science.[7] It therefore

6. This is the difference between the real and the possible. The possible that we imagine—and therefore invent—can be present in our thinking but, as we shall see later, this makes it highly arguable that to think
the possible is *sensu stricto* to know (Cf. Aristotle, *Categories*, 7 b 24).

7. Even less interest, of course, in whether others regard it as science.
It is not the man who philosophizes but philosophy itself which detaches itself from the others. It does not need them, as does poetry,
which is essentially a matter of speaking to another and needs that other,
even an anonymous and indeterminate other. Nor is it, like science, in
need of collaboration. Philosophy is not a form of speaking to another,
but of talking to oneself. It is not a business of sociability but a need for
solitude. Philosophy is a form of playing Robinson Crusoe. This is

ceases to look wall-eyed and with envy at the sciences. There is no reason why it should aspire to imitate them in its way of thinking. It is cured of its scientific snobbery. More than that, it will try to become as different as possible from the form of theory which characterizes the sciences, because it has no choice but to go on trying to be knowledge in the sense of presenting reality to thought. Therefore it returns, as in ancient days, to confronting the Real in its *modo recto* without oblique deviations.[8] It is obviously modifying the ancient way of thinking profoundly. It might even be considered that its ancient way of thinking gave birth to the sciences, i.e., that the first-born philosophy was "too scientific." In its method it must be more genuinely faithful to its mission, to its destiny, and accept what there may be of the tragic in this. I am surprised never to have read that philosophy as such arose in Greece—with Plato and Aristotle—as an immediate continuation of the period in which tragedy flowered.[9] When philosophy recovers its position of independence with respect to the sciences, it must see with superlative clarity that it not only differs from them in its way of thinking, which is knowledge

---

especially so because the philosophic Crusoe does not live on a desert island but on a "deserted island" where previous inhabitants have all died. It is an Island of the Dead, of dead philosophers, the only companions whom philosophy in its solitude needs and will traffic with. See in Aristotle's *Topics* how "there is no need for the philosopher to bother with others in order to philosophize" (VIII, 1155 b 7).

8. In 1911, Husserl was still insisting that philosophy should be "*strenge Wissenschaft.*" (See his famous article in *Logos* entitled *Die Philosophie als strenge Wissenschaft.*)

9. Nietzsche wrote a magnificent essay on *Philosophy in the Tragic Period of the Greeks*, but the very title shows that he did not see the problem. Those pre-Socratic Greeks undoubtedly created a primitive form of philosophy but they were not yet philosophers. They belonged to the "tragic epoch" and therefore they themselves were, almost *sensu stricto*, tragedians and the authors of tragedies. But philosophy is the very thing that follows the tragic attitude, which consists in the fact that tragedy is accepted and one remains within it, confronting it. Philosophy lives tragedy to its very root, but does not accept it, instead struggles to dominate it. This antitragic struggle is the new tragedy, the philosophical one. About the relation between these two periods, I hope to write soon.

whether it likes it or not; not only for its theme, that is to say, for the very special *content* of its problem, but because of something prior to all this, namely, because of the character of its *problem as such*. According to established rules, science is preoccupied with problems which are, in principle, solvable. Therefore, these are problems which are relatively, tractably problematical; problems which, when they emerge as such, are already half-solved. Hence, the scandal produced in mathematics when an unsolvable problem is encountered. But the problem which stimulates philosophical effort is limitlessly problematical, it is an absolute problem. Nothing guarantees that it will be solvable. If a scientific problem happens to be unsolvable, it is abandoned. Science exists to find solutions. These are indispensable. Sciences are sciences because they achieve proper solutions. But philosophy is not like that. Philosophy does not exist nor is it recommended for finding solutions, but rather for the inexorable nature of its problems. Scientific problems are those which man sets for himself when he is in that mood. Philosophic problems pose themselves by themselves, that is to say, pose themselves to man whether he wants this or not. It follows that philosophic problems are not assigned to philosophy as physical problems are to physics, but are independent of the methodic treatment to which they are submitted.

Today, then, philosophy must enunciate its purpose in terms which are the inverse of those used by Kant in the phrase cited earlier, and say: "The method of philosophy is, at bottom, approximately the opposite of the method of physics." [10]

10. This has nothing to do with the question of "*ciò che è vivo e ciò che è morto*" in the Kantian doctrine. Although Kant said that and thought it, the truth is that his philosophy necessarily bears very little resemblance to the method of Newton. Note that again and again, and almost in the same words, Kant contrasts the method of philosophy with that of mathematics; that is to say, for various reasons he considers it erroneous to orient philosophy toward these sciences, just as we, for other reasons, believe it necessary to keep it at a considerable distance from physics. Kant very specially dedicates the first section on methodology in the *Critique of Pure Reason* to dissassociating philosophy and mathematics. For example, we read there: "From all that has been said

This sketch of the present-future situation into which philosophy has moved does not pretend to give a clear idea of it, but only to say what is strictly necessary about it in order to contrast it with the former situation, which thus remains clear in outline and precisely limited. Otherwise the modern position would appear to be the only possible one—and therefore definitive—and then one would not be treating of a position in which philosophy found itself, but of one that would be confused with philosophy itself, like something definitive and exempt from conditions arising out of the situation. Nothing human is outside a "field of forces." The historical position is in effect a field of force in which the forces are the predominating intellectual tendencies.[11]

Another question, which for some years has clouded the exemplary character of physics, emerges from the variable nature of its doctrinal content, which has accelerated so much and so importantly in recent years. One gets the vague impression that the variation in physical theories, far from upsetting their continuity and validity, is actually strengthening them; but this unstable aspect of physical knowledge has not yet been clarified, nor is it probable that its clarification will come from the physicists. That a science is "true" for the very rea-

---

it follows that it is completely inadequate to the nature of philosophy, above all in the field of pure theory, to strut about with dogmatic stride and adorn oneself with the titles and ribbons of mathematics, an order to which philosophy does not belong, although it has reason to hope that a brotherly union can be maintained." For Kant, then, it is fundamental and important not only to avoid orienting the philosophical way of thinking toward the mathematical way of thinking, but also to establish its formal counterposition. The entire *Critique of Pure Reason* can be summed up in this formula, enunciated in one form or another many times throughout the whole work and appearing in its final pages: "All rational knowledge is such either by originating in concepts or in the construction of concepts; the first is called philosophical, the second mathematical." These formulas probably caused no less *shock* among Kant's contemporary readers, most of them followers of Leibnitz, than does the phrase of my text to which this note refers, when read by a modern student educated in Kantianism, positivism, and so on.

11. Not only intellectual, of course. But now these alone are of interest to us.

son that its doctrine is changeable, flies in the face of the traditional idea of truth, and can be cleared up only by renewing *a radice* the general theory of truth itself and by making us see that, as this is a human matter, it is affected by man's condition, which is that of being *mobilis in mobile*.[12]

With this we have formed a threefold series of "historic places" where we can locate the different philosophies, so that a simple reference to any one of them gives us certain basic characteristics to be expected, and above all, certain tacit suppositions concerning each doctrine. Because each situation is, moreover, not static, but in its turn constitutes a process, a movement in an ordered direction. This appears with exceptional clarity in the modern period, within which Leibnitz' thought emerges.

12. On correcting the proofs of this page—February, 1948—I read a communication from Dr. George van Biesbroeck, attached to the Yerkes Observatory, Williams Bay, Wisconsin, making known the first results of his observations of the 1947 eclipse of the sun, made in South America. Unlike those of W. W. Campbell, of the Lick Observatory, which produced the most impressive confirmation of the theory of relativity, these made now do not refer to stars which are very near the sun but to others which are as distant as several times the sun's diameter. The displacement of its images should therefore show a minor curvature of space and light. Measurements confirm this curvature; but at the same time they modify it, for it turns out to be so much greater than was foreseen in Einstein's theory that one is forced to attribute the greater curvature to other and different factors. So it is not at all improbable that we may be on the threshold of a far-reaching reform to which the theory of relativity will have to be submitted and one cannot now predict how much of it will stand up.

(November, 1950. One must also note here the discovery, announced a few weeks ago, that the accepted computation of the speed of light now appears to be erroneous.)

5
The Reign of Physics Begins about 1750

FROM THE END OF the 16th Century to the end of the 17th Century, philosophy sought its discipline in the exact sciences, which during this period advanced gloriously with triumphal rapidity. Two stages in their trajectory can be clearly distinguished. During the first, progress occurs in pure mathematics. During the second, mathematics managed to reduce phenomena, "realities," to pure theorems, and was converted into physics. In this transformation the character of exactitude was modified, but continuing the meaning it had in pure mathematics, that is, keeping its tendency there.

The creation and development of physics is without doubt the most important event of history, *sensu stricto* human history. Even those who believe that man also has a superhuman history must recognize this. This judgment is not influenced by enthusiasm for the spectacle of an almost prodigious adroitness—in this case of an intellectual adroitness. We are not talking of the spectacular skill that is manifest when we watch the functioning of the superb mentality of the great men who have been creating physics. Physics is not *only* a circus act, not just acrobatics. It is one of man's essential needs. In this place I cannot express what this means except by stating it in an irritatingly laconic form. It would go something like this: man is an unadapted animal, existing in an element which is foreign to him, hostile to his nature, namely, this world. In these circumstances his destiny implies, not exclusively but to an important extent, his intention to adapt the world to his essential needs, precisely those needs which prevent his own adaptation to it. So he must exert himself to transform *this world,* which is foreign to him, which is not his, which is not in harmony with him, into another and related world where his desires may be satisfied—man is a complex of desires that are impossibilities in *this* world—in short, in what he can call *his* world. The idea of a world in harmony with man is called *happiness.* Man is an unhappy being, and by the same token, his goal is happiness. Hence everything that man does, he does *in order to* be happy. Now then, the only means man has for transforming this world is technique, and physics provides the possibility of an infinite technique. Physics is thus the *instrument* of happiness and the development of physics is the most important event in human history. By the same token it is basically dangerous. The capacity to construct a world cannot be separated from the capacity to destroy it.

The two stages in the "modern" evolution of the exact sciences are unequivocally separated by a single event—the publication in 1687, of Newton's principal work, *Philosophiae Naturalis Principia Mathematica.* Nevertheless, the chronological caesura between those two stages considered as "historical periods" does not coincide with the date of that publication. The reason is simple: the historical is above all the collectively historical, and to the universal human collective one must first refer periods and epochs. Well then, in order to transform an event in the intellectual order from a personal or group basis into a collective event—therefore into a historical force—considerable time must elapse. The collective is always a usage, and usages are slow to establish themselves. In 1687, Newton's science was his personal opinion. Certain other men, the "Newtonians," began at once to adopt it; in other words, the personal opinion of one man became the personal opinion of a certain number of men, of a group of people. But what is decisive in an idea is the step from being a personal or multipersonal opinion to being a "public opinion," i.e., an opinion prevailing and predominant in the collectivity—in this case, the collectivity of European intellectuals. One must, then, wait for more or less time until an idea becomes "public opinion," until it *becomes customary* to think that way. Since the collec-

tive is, as we said above, a matter of usage, for creative individuals it is always laggard; for them it is perennially anach-
ronistic and relatively archaic. This truth, which obviously
is not empirical but *a priori*, I call the "law of the lagging attribute," an essential aspect of historical reality. *Because of this*
history is inexorably slow. Only by experience can one arrive
at approximations of the truth which it enunciates. The older
Greeks knew this, since the *Iliad* cites as a hoary adage this
profound saying: "The mills of the gods grind slowly." The
gods are fate, they are history.

So we must advance the date of the gap between those two
stages and thereby speed up greatly the coming of the New-
tonian doctrine into a historical force. The causes of this speed-
up are so clear that we need only allude to them. This is the
point in time when all the European minorities—save the
Iberian Peninsula, which remained secluded in the "Tibetan-
ism" imposed on it during the reign of Philip IV—form a
single collectivity and live, moreover, in a state of hypersensi-
tivity, alert to all scientific progress.

One bit of data simplifies the search for the date when
Newton begins to "reign"; this is the publication in 1738, of
Voltaire's *Elements of Newton's Philosophy*. This indicates
that Newtonism before that date was only the opinion of
groups representing a "program for the conquest of power."
But it also suggests that one need add only a few more years
to fix accurately enough the date of its conversion into European intellectual usage. For although it was true that "*Monsieur
tout le Monde a plus d'esprit que M. de Voltaire*," it is no less
true that "*l'esprit de M. de Voltaire faisait l'esprit de tout le
monde*," and particularly in this case when he was proposing
to make all-out propaganda on behalf of Newton's ideas, i.e.,
to transform controversial, or ignored, opinion into public
opinion. Consequently, we can say that the second historic
stage in the evolution of the exact sciences begins around 1750.
What a coincidence! That was the year when Kant was 26
years old—the age at which every thinker normally begins to
develop his own thinking. It would be Kant who would draw

the philosophic consequences from the orientation of philosophy in Newton's science.[1]

The last great figure of the first period is Leibnitz. His philosophy is therefore not *oriented* in physics. It could not be, because he himself, together with Newton, is one of the creators of physics. He belongs to the same generation as Newton (1642–1727). The exceeding richness of his thought makes us uneasy even today, as though we were in the presence of an extra-human hyperlucidity, of an ever-phosphorescent soul, which, creating entire sciences while travelling in a stagecoach, kept him from ever giving systematic expression to his hypersystematic ideas.[2] Leibnitz lived in perpetual conflict with Newton. This polemic became one of the most awe inspiring battles between giants that has ever occurred on this planet, and it is a shame that this remarkable display of intellectual fisticuffs has not yet been reported in a manner worthy either of its doctrinal or its "human" side. This last is also extremely interesting, for in it we see that of the two men it is Newton who has always had a "good press," whereas Leibnitz has always had a bad one, starting with that genius of journalism, Voltaire. The matter is the more scandalous[3] since in that polemic, as we can now see, Leibnitz "upheld the right" in most of the differences which arose. And he upheld the right to a degree which, I repeat, seems almost superhuman. With a clairvoyance that gives one goose flesh, Leibnitz anticipates what has come to be, in our time, the newest pure mathematics

1. On what prevailing historical ideas are, and the lag in spreading so important an idea as that of Copernicus, see my lecture *En torno a Galileo* (*Obras Completas*, Vol. V) [Published in English as *Man and Crisis*, W. W. Norton, 1962].

2. It would be important to study the frequent lack of adequate correspondence between systematic thought and the fragmentary, ragged expression which the circumstances of life oblige one to give it. The case of a genius like Leibnitz offers an extreme example, but a study of this lack in men of lesser stature would also show how hazardous throughout history are the conditions in which thought is made manifest.

3. Whoever knows even a little about human affairs knows that to have a "good press" is in itself a bad sign.

as well as the most modern physics; it must be noted that it is *Leibnitz, of all the past philosophers, from whom came the greatest number of theories current today.*[4] Today is, of course, not tomorrow.

4. The comparison of Leibnitz with Newton also offers a priceless opportunity to clarify the precise difference between the philosophic man and the scientific man. As both are of the same importance in their respective fields, we can superimpose one figure on the other and then we see that, while the whole of Newton coincides with Leibnitz the comparison leaves Leibnitz with a certain extra stature.

Remember that the first principle of modern physics is not one of Newton's *leges motus*, but the principle of minimal action, which Leibnitz was the first to consider and which he called the "principle of the shortest routes" or of "the optimum forms."

6
Back Over the Road

LET US TRY not to lose the thread of our discourse.

We began—this plural is not pompous, I am not being pompous, it is a true plural, the reader and I—I because I began with a certain statement, and the reader because in reading me he accepts a dialogue with me, agreeing for the moment to the exposition and development of my thesis in order to reply later to whatever part of it he pleases, be it in writing, be it in conversation, be it in the privacy of his meditations.

We began, I say, with the fact that Leibnitz, of all the philosophers, appears to us as par excellence the "man of principles." But then we noted another aspect of his intellectual doctrine in which he appears to be disdainful of principles. This contradiction aroused our minds to a conscious effort to eliminate it or at least to understand it completely (Chapter 1). It obliged us to form for ourselves an idea, however imprecise, of what principle is. Then we find that, at least in the logical order, i.e., the order made up of "truths," the term "principle" was divided into two distinct meanings—relative principle and absolute principle—to which two values of the notion "truth" correspond: truth as proof and truth as evidence. The preference for one value or the other was an indication of two ways of thinking (Chapter 2). Now then, philosophies are different in the measure in which their "ways of thinking" differ. The proof of this cannot be provided in this study except, as in the case of Leibnitz, by extracts from proof referring to other cases. But the whole truth can only be set out in a complete history of philosophy.[1]

1. I hope soon to be able to show in detail the truth of this assertion in two exceptional cases which, being exceptions, can be as valuable in themselves as proof for all the rest of the philosophies, as is the proof for n plus 1 in the complete induction of mathematics.

What is the "way of thinking" of Leibnitz? We respond dogmatically: for Leibnitz, to think is to prove (Chapter 3). Why and in what particular sense did Leibnitz understand thought to be this? This whole study is concerned with the answer to this question, which must be given step by step. The first step consists in showing that in his day that "way of thinking" was already pre-formed. This led us to examine the character of the philosophic period in which Leibnitz emerged, and for this purpose we distinguished three great periods in such a way that the middle one, which is the "modern" period and that of Leibnitz, would stand out clearly. The result of this was our discovery that the most important component of philosophy's modern position vis-à-vis the ancient and the present is the extraordinary development achieved by the exact sciences in that time. Philosophy must take account of the way of thinking of those sciences, that is to say, it must consider itself as a science (Chapter 4). But during that period there was not only a glorious development in the exact sciences, but in mathematics this development produced a radical innovation: its conquest of the world of perceptible "realities" as constituted in physics. This divides the modern era into two stages with the division point marked by the conquest of the Western mind by Newton's system of physics. In the second stage, philosophy is "fixed" on physics. In the first, with mechanics not yet sufficiently established, philosophy is oriented in pure mathematics. Leibnitz is the great figure—chronologically the last and doctrinally the extreme—in this orientation (Chapter 5).

Now we will see what happens in pure mathematics when Leibnitz begins to cogitate, what innovations he, as a mathematical genius, introduces into the exact sciences, and what repercussions all this has on his philosophic way of thinking.

7

Algebra as a "Way of Thinking"

SHORTLY AFTER 1500, creative effort in the field of mathematics came to life in extraordinary fashion. It will go *in crescendo* without interruption up to our own time. This does not mean that the rate of increase is not marked from time to time by periods which can be described as flood tides.

It is enough to cite certain names to see the rising trend: Tartaglia (1500–1557), Cardano (1501–1576), Pierre de la Ramée (1515–1572), Benedetti (1530–1590), Vieta (1540–1603), Stevin (1548–1620), Galileo (1564–1642), Kepler (1571–1630), Cavalieri (1591?–1647), Desargues (1593–1662), Descartes (1596–1650), Fermat (1601–1665), Roberval (1602–1672), Torricelli (1608–1647), Pascal (1623–1662), Huygens (1629–1695), Wren (1632–1723), Hooke (1635–1703) and Newton (1642–1727).

This list of names would seem at first sight to betoken a vast expansion in mathematical *materia*. But this is of no interest at this point. What is important to us in the evolution of mathematics is the list of advances in its *form;* particularly those that represent radical changes in the mathematical way of thinking or method. On that assumption the list can be cut drastically. We need focus on only two names preceding Leibnitz: Vieta and Descartes.

Vieta was a great practical mathematician but his most important invention did not take the form of progress in the extension of his science, but an apparent step forward in the technique of arithmetical notation. No more, no less. It was a piece of nothing. This "piece of nothing" is called algebra.

The invention of algebra provides an ideal opportunity for

clarifying certain vital aspects of historical reality. One need only compare in some detail the way this looked to Vieta himself and to his contemporaries with the aspect it offers us today. I am not going to attempt this, however, because it is irrelevant to our theme. I will say only that to Vieta and his times algebra meant merely a more convenient process of notation, with certain immediate and substantial consequences for the solution of problems which this brought with it. Not until later did men see clearly the more obvious gain which the creation of algebra would bring in terms of both general progress and progress in method: it makes possible the orderly form of analysis, i.e., of deduction; thanks to this, arithmetic, which since the time of the Greeks, had remained far behind geometry (still the prototype of the mathematical way of thinking), now caught up with it in a single leap and went far beyond it.

If, on the other hand, we look at the same event from the vantage point of today, we see it clearly and simply as the most decisive step in the modern evolution of mathematics; here modernity does not stop, as in what we called the "modern position" of philosophy, on a date when the contemporary or present begins, but comes straight on to our own day; from Vieta we move smoothly on to Hilbert.

Biologists, talking about organic evolution, cite cases of *orthogenesis*. This occurs when an organ, arising tentatively in one species, appears in a chronological series of them, unfolding without vacillation, deviation or retreat, until it is established in a final, complete form. The organ has advanced —has "evolved"—in a straight line; it is *orthogenesis*. Well then, in the evolution of mathematics, Vieta's invention initiated an orthogenetic development which has lasted until today. Even more, it is as though algebra was born as a program which has been completed, literally, only now. For Vieta it was the mathematics of numbers—*Logistica numeralis*—which was expressed in figures (*species* = signs), transferring itself into *Logistica speciosa*. For Hilbert, mathematics is explicitly a science of signs and not primarily one of numbers or magnitudes. History has taken Vieta at his word and, in a manner which would have frightened him, has confirmed that word literally.

We express numbers by means of words or graphic figures which we call "ciphers," for example, *one, two, three* . . . 1, 2, 3. . . . Obviously, neither the word nor the cipher is the number. They are only its representatives. By means of these we present numbers mentally to ourselves or to others. Well now, whenever we purposely use one thing *in place of another*, as representing another, we have converted the one into a *sign* or *symbol* of the other. When *aliquid stat pro aliquo*, we have a significant or symbolic relationship. In this sense, words and ciphers have always been the *signs* for numbers. But note that each word *one, two, three* . . . and *each* cipher 1, 2, 3 . . . is the sign of a single number; therefore, we need as many signs as there are numbers. The fact that the words in turn all result from a combination of a small number of sounds, and the ciphers all result from only ten figures, i.e., 0 to 9, does not prevent each word and each cipher from being a unique body; 289 is a figure completely different from 2, from 8, and from 9. When there is the same number of signs as the things which they sign-ify or designate by those signs we say that the sign is a *name*. Thus, 4 is the individual name of an individual number. This brings with it so close a relationship of sign and thing that the function of signifying is reduced to a minimum and its usefulness is reduced to saving us mental effort, thus avoiding the necessity to spell the effective intention of each number. When I read 5932, I do not need to examine every one of its units; I do not need to fabricate the number in my mind. Therefore, the difference between the number and its cipher, or name, does not affect it in the slightest, does not modify in the least the relationship of our minds with the object "number." Hence, as there is a relationship of one to one between number and cipher, we can say that for the purposes of our intellectual or conscious concern with numbers, the cipher is the number and not its sign.

If, on the other hand, I say: let x be a number equal to the

number b plus the number c, the situation is completely different. However many changes I may ring on the isolated x, or
on b, or on c, I will not recognize in them any number. That
is to say that x, b, and c are not individual names of individual
numbers. I use each of them as representing *all* numbers, taken
singly; or to put it another way, as representing *any one* number. One after another, *all* numbers may be this *"any one of
them."* So Leibnitz will define algebra as the *Mathematica
Numerorum Incertorum*—the mathematics of undetermined
numbers.[1]

The distance that appears here between the representative x
and all the numbers it represents is enormous; x is not the name
of any number, nor is b or c. Here the sign has a new power.
It allows a single figure—x, or b, or c—to present us with an
infinity of numbers. For algebra is an arithmetic which, in
place of occupying itself with numbers themselves (we said
that cipher = number), occupies itself *only* with their signs *as
such*. (Algebra uses numbers in secondary fashion to express
coefficients, powers, and divisors, but these are never the numbers with which it is concerned.[2])

But with all this we have gained nothing. On the contrary,
we have lost ground. The name or cipher sets up before us a
determinate number, not to be confused with any other. Now
when it is proposed that we see numbers in x, b, and c, we feel
momentarily seasick, dizzy. (Remember the "algebraic *shock*"
of our childhood.) That dizziness is a good thing; it means
that we are entering another world on a higher plane and that
we are beginning to suffer mountain sickness.

But what we said above was not only that we must see
numbers in x, in b, and in c, but something more precise: that

1. *Die Philosophischen Schriften von G. W. Leibniz* (C. J. Gerhardt,
Berlin, 1890), Vol. II, p. 59.
2. Vieta himself uses a still more complicated notation in which letters, numbers and geometrical names play a part. Thus he writes the
equation $A3 + 3BA = D$ like this: *A cubus + B planus in A3 aequatur
D solida*. Descartes gave it approximately its present form. (See *H. G.
Zeuthen, Geschichte der Mathematik im XVI und XVII Jahrhundert*,
1903, p. 98.)

x is a number equal to the number b plus the number c.

This a very different matter. Because then x, which is the sign for any number whatever when it stands alone, becomes a determinate number when put into an equation; x, for example, has become 6. Let us ask ourselves again what we have gained by this circumlocution, because we began with x as an indeterminate number in order to arrive at 6, which is a determinate number. We might have saved ourselves the trip. But let us recognize that 6 is not *actually* a determinate number, for it does not tell us in what its determination consists, or how or for whom it is determined. It is an isolated entity, like the figures we see in a vision, and in fact the Greeks saw it as two series of points:

$$. \quad . \quad .$$
$$. \quad . \quad .$$

and because of this they called it the oblong number. A number alone is an object figurally determinate but not mathematically determinate. Nevertheless, we call it mathematically determinate because arithmetic can always *discover* its determination for us by saying $6 = 5 + 1$, where $5 + 1$ is the determination of 6. But then it means the same if we write $x = 5 + 1$.

Thus in order to ensure that 6 moves from being only potentially determinate to being so in fact, i.e., to make its *determinate character* explicit and patent, we must put it into an equation. But *ipso facto* we perceive that this formula allows for the determination of all numbers merely by substituting 5 for n, which represents "any number whatever," when we say that $x = n + 1$.

Once more let us ask ourselves: "Is this expression not more complicated than 6?" Undoubtedly; but it provides us with something highly important: *6 is only* the name of a number, whereas the formula defines it for us. To name a thing is not the same as knowing it. The formula, on the other hand, serves us as both the name and the definition of the number. It is named *by means of* the definition, which is ideal for a name.

Each one of the letters a, b, c, x, and z represents all numbers, and by the same token represents none. One might say that they represent "pure numerosity." But in order to do this some of them must enter into combination with others. What are these combinations?

Algebra is made up not only of signs which are letters and which represent numbers, but also of signs which represent *relationships* and of signs which represent *operations*. The relationships are those of "being equal," "being greater," and "being less." The operations are adding, subtracting, and so on. These operations are limited to creating conditions in which the relationships of "being larger" or "being less" exist. To add is *to make* something greater; to subtract is *to make* something less.

The algebraic formula consists in defining or determining the value of a letter through its equality, its being greater or its being less, as compared with the value of other letters. In this way the meaning or the notion which each letter represents is also defined with respect to the others by the notions of equal, greater or less. A letter by itself has no value, it means nothing, or, more exactly, it means the pure compromise by which we force it to acquire a determinate value, a precise meaning, entering into certain relationships with others to which the same thing happens. *In the equation, numbers determine themselves, that is, they define each other mutually. It is a system, a small universe, within which each thing—each literal sign—is determined by all the others.*

So we have the following: the cipher presents us with a ready-made number having a mysterious genesis which it does does not reveal. It confronts us like the sight of a real object which we see without knowing of what it consists. We handle it with practical certitude but with theoretical irresponsibility. In algebra the letter, precisely because it has already been drained of all specifically numerical significance, must *make itself a number* in our eyes by becoming part of the formula which is the equation. This gives us the definition of a number; before presenting us with the ready-made number it gives us its genesis and its inner meaning, it always makes it explicit and clear that the number consists purely of relationships of equality, of more and of less.[3]

The cipher shows us each number, first, as if it were a thing in itself, and later, as being also something equal, greater or less as compared with another.

We can therefore sum up the progress which algebra as a way of thinking represents by saying:

First, it shows that the number consists purely of relationships.

Second, in algebra the number appears replaced by its definition, which makes the algebraic way-of-thinking method consist of a chain of definitions, that is to say, of pure deduction.[4]

Third, the most important consequence of the first and second is that it obliges us not to interpret the number except *in terminis,* that is, in terms of its definition, which frees it *in each case* from its infinite, confused, and uncontrollable value and makes it logical. In algebra, arithmetic tends to become the logic of the number.

These three qualities are those that characterize present-day mathematics in its purest form, at least the mathematics which we might call *canonical.*[5] All of later mathematics is anticipated in Vieta's invention, because it is there that the *method* which will make it possible begins to function. The method, the way of thinking of modern and contemporary mathe-

3. In his correspondence with Tschirnhaus, in 1678, Leibnitz called attention to the fact that Arabic ciphers have the advantage over Roman ciphers of expressing the "genesis" of a number and thereby of defining it. (*Mathematische Schriften,* Vol. IV, pp. 455 ff.)

4. For eighteen centuries there already existed in Euclid's geometry a splendid example of deductive theory. But in geometry deduction is reduced to a nexus between notions. These are not properly deduced, they are not "logical," but intuitive. In Euclid's deductive method a "foreign body" intervenes again and again in the logic; this is *congruence,* which is not reasoning but a method *ad oculos.* Later the reader will find some discussion of this matter.

5. This reservation refers to the intuitionist direction of Brouwer and others, which is still only an attempt, although it goes far enough to pose grave questions regarding the dominant tendency in the modern history of mathematics, which has been a progressive *logicism.*

matics *is*, I say, *functioning* there; but at the same time it is not expressed. Apart from his concrete use of it, Vieta had no clear idea of what that method was.

In the development of that idea of method no new step was taken until Descartes. Although he also was a great practical mathematician, there may have been others of his period who could be considered his superiors in this respect; for example, Fermat.

Descartes, as a matter of fact, took not only one step forward, but two which are clearly discernible.

8
Analytical Geometry

I SAID THAT in algebra each number is brought before us by its own definition, and that this definition reveals that it consists exclusively of relations—equal, greater, lesser. Nevertheless, algebra does not employ these relational ideas in all the fullness of their possible meaning: it restricts them to their meaning with reference to numbers, i.e., to quantities or multiples. That they may have a very different meaning when they refer to extensions, for example, to magnitudes—is apparent if we think about it. Two magnitudes superimposed, one above the other, are equal when they coincide fully; the one that exceeds the other is greater, the one that is exceeded by the other is smaller. Two quantities, on the other hand, are equal when they use the same numerical units, and one is greater or less than the other when this does not happen. The idea of these relations, therefore, is different with respect to quantity and spatial magnitude, in arithmetic and geometry. In extension there are no numerical units proper to it; in arithmetic there is no room for superposition or for congruence. This means that the idea of these relations is not truly an idea, but in every case it expresses a *basic intuition*— that of number and extension. That something is a numerical unit, to which another identical unit can be added, and so on successively, has nothing to do with logic; it is an "absolute fact," which is always certain, which is always clear to us, which is an "intuition." It is also an "absolute fact," also a basic intuition, that magnitude is a continuous thing—it has no parts, therefore, but it can be divided in two and those parts may coincide or one may remain included in the other.

Now we observe in algebra something which has gone unnoticed. It defines every number by making it consist of relations, but it does not define those relations for us; it takes them for granted, that is, it derives them from a basic numerical intuition. Geometry does the same thing, except that it refers us explicitly to intuition as a guide to understanding.

Consequently, we have the fact that relations bearing the same name—equal, greater, less—have different and "irreducible" meanings in arithmetic and in geometry. For this reason both worlds—that of number and that of extension—and both sciences—arithmetic and geometry—diverged in Aristotle's time (Chapter 4). There was no place, save among the formal principles of logic, where any principle common to both subjects might be discovered. For Aristotle this confirmed the reasons which he already had for formulating the law of the "incommunicability of the genera," a law which would leave the intellectual world divided, on a basis of principle and not by accident, into a plurality of sciences wholly incompatible with each other. As long as each science starts from a "basic intuition" it stays shut up within itself, boxed in, its roots constricted, the slave of its intuitive heritage.[1]

Now you will understand what I tried to suggest when I said that each single letter in algebra, while representing all numbers, actually represents none; but it does represent the possibility of a number or, as I prefer to express it, "pure numerosity." That is to say, algebra assumes the basic numerical intuition and is therefore arithmetic, although set up in the most *logical* form possible.

The revelation with which Descartes was blessed consisted in the observation that, although the intuition of number and that of space are mutually irreducible, geometric relations can be represented by means of numerical relations, and vice versa; *in principle*, therefore, whatever differentiates them is immaterial. It is *technically* possible, then, to get the two

---

1. In Aristotle this lack of communication appears in three areas which geometry will later reunite. The sciences of the line, the plane, and the solid are watertight *pragmateías*, each with its exclusive principles.

worlds into communication and construct a common science to act as mediator on their frontiers. The principle of the incommunicability of genera and the plurality of sciences was practically knocked out. There is an identity of correspondence between number and extension. That this might be possible in the concrete case of these two categories opened up a horizon of unlimited possibilities. This was Descartes' first step; it is called analytical geometry.

The exact meaning of the analytical geometry of Descartes is disputed, and with good reason. I have given the minimal interpretation in which both objective areas—number and space—are neither confused nor subordinated one to the other. This is what is important and sufficient for our theme.

Leibnitz, although so "optimistic" and so conciliatory, was at the same time almost as vain as Descartes and in temperament, considerably more "difficult"; [2] he customarily dealt mercilessly with Descartes. As for analytical geometry, Leibnitz flung in Descartes' face that there is no such analytical method, that space cannot be reduced to number; rather, that for his numerical creations he starts from spatial theorems. Obviously, this is to assume in Descartes the same intention which inspired Leibnitz, namely, to proclaim within mathematics the Holy Roman Empire of arithmetic. But it does not seem that this reduction to arithmeticism was Descartes' idea.[3]

The second step taken by Descartes, which is really a fabulous leap, confirms this.

2. History is bound to see clearly and to emphasize inexorably the different—and frequently antagonistic—tendencies which in combination create a character; and thereby a personality. Leibnitz' censures as documented may be the subject of possible historical studies, since the vanity of Descartes and Leibnitz was not fortuitous, but typical of scientific men in the 17th Century, and this typicality, in turn, arises out of certain general conditions of the period which can be defined with some precision. Greater clarification of this matter, with reference to the vanity of the first generation of the 19th Century, may be found in my *Obras Completas*, Vol. V (*"Memorias de Mestanza,"* IV).

3. It was not proposed only to explain geometry by means of algebra, but also vice versa. One usually forgets that algebra was for Descartes an obscure and troublesome science. This refers, of course, to the algebra of Vieta and his successors up to Descartes' time.

9
Concept as a "Term"

ARITHMETIC IS COUNTING. Counting is an intuitive operation, as is its product: numbers. Algebra, we have seen, gives intuitive numbers a second life, converting them by its definitions into something logical. Certainly these definitions reduce numbers to notions of relation—equal, greater, less. And these notions are intuitive, they are the basic intuition of numerosity and, therefore, of arithmetic. Algebra is not independent of arithmetic; it starts from it and in the end returns to it, since the formulas must incorporate numbers, which are not algebraic but rather arithmetical. But midway between the point of departure and the point of arrival algebra gives numbers what I call a second life—their logical life.

But nothing moves so vaguely in the minds of men as that which tries to be less vague, namely, what we understand when we say of something that it is "logical." Logic is a "way of thinking" in which one pays exclusive attention to the pure relations that exist between concepts as concepts, pretending at the same time that what is valid for these concepts is also valid for the things conceived. Later we will see clearly what all this means. Now it is only the first part of that sentence which matters. What I see with my own eyes is not something logical but something intuitive. It is not a concept. But if I say that what I see is a horse, "horse" is a concept. Why? Because it is the sum-total of a definition, because when I have "horse" in mind I also have in mind the different individual components of the selfsame thing that I am thinking. This does not happen with what I see when I am looking at something. In that case everything is conjoined and undivided. The components do not seem to me like separate and distinct components, each *detached* from the others. Intuition, moreover, grasps many other inseparable elements which are not components of the concept horse—various sizes, various colors, various forms of the image. Hence when I see something, I am not sure, strictly speaking, of what it consists. The concept, on the other hand, consists exclusively of its definition. It is that series of "notes," of ingredients, which the definition displays like the parts of a machine. *In this sense* the concept is always identical with itself, and I can handle it safely. It is a coin that has a precise value, on which I can confidently rely; it is not, like vision, a jewel that is worth much, but how much I never surely know, and therefore I can never exactly count on its worth. A concept is a thought that is stamped officially, given a label, put on the inventory. This transformation of the thing seen into the thing conceived is accomplished by means of a simple mental act. In what is seen, and more generally in what is perceived through intuition, our attention *fixes* on one or several elements, that is to say, fixes *itself* on each of them. Then our mind *abstracts* from all the rest that which is obtained by intuition, and *extracts* the fixed elements, leaving the rest. Thus the concept is an extract of intuition. Whether intuition is well or poorly extracted, i.e., whether what is most important in intuition is extracted, is not what interests us for the moment. We are now interested only in what the concept contains of the *extract*, because that is what properly comprises a concept. The Greeks called the mental extract of a thing its *lógos*, that is, its "language," "what is said of it," because words do actually represent those mental extracts. "Table" is the *lógos* of innumerable human artifacts which are very different from each other but which have an identical minimal structure, an identical extract.

Once this operation is performed our mind turns its back on what is seen or acquired by intuition, and no longer pays attention to it but, starting from that extract, holds to it exclusively, applying the "logical" principles of which we will speak later in this study, puts that concept into relation with others which are no less extracts than it is, noting whether there is identity or contradiction between them or whether the one is included in the other; a new conceptual unit is formed from two concepts which are not contradictory, but compatible, and thus successively the mind spins a web of pure concepts which is precise and coherent. We call that web of "extracts" a *logical theory*, and what we have been doing has, since the time of the Greeks, been called "thinking logically."

Out of all this, what I want most to underline is the fact that once the concepts, sufficient for the theme in hand, have been prelogically extracted from intuitions, logical thought incorporates them within itself, and its statements refer exclusively to those concepts; these thereby become the "things" of which a logical theory speaks. If I use the name "horse" to designate certain animals which win prizes in the races, which have carried on their backs Alexander the Great, the Cid, and the picador in the bull ring—objects regarding which I have had innumerable and widely divergent intuitions—the meaning of the name is theoretically uncontrollable, although it enjoys a degree of *practical* control sufficient for certain activities of life, which are very different from "thinking logically." Its meaning is uncontrollable because, used in this way, the name represents those innumerable intuitions, the content of which has not been completely inventoried because, among other reasons, it is inexhaustible. If, on the other hand, I use the word "horse" as the name of the definition of this animal given by zoology, its meaning is *limited*, it is a *limitation* of the original meaning, which was un-limited, in-finite, un-defined, diffused, and confused. The word that Aristotle uses to express the idea of concept is "that which is limited."—ὅρος, *hóros*. *Hóros* is something that stands out in the landscape, something that is raised high and, by the same token, attracts attention, makes itself conspicuous. The corresponding word in Latin is *terminus*. *Hóros* and *terminus* were the piles of stones and later the markers which separated fields and delimited the property of each owner. As the Greeks, with their deep sense of living, created a god for everything important, they deified these

dividing markers, which also stood at crossroads to differentiate roadways. The god of delimited boundaries and right
roads—the right road is called "method" in Greek—was
Hermes, a very ancient god, older than Apollo. But the curious
thing is that, as a divinity in a very old religion whose gods
were underground, Hermes was at the same time the god of
dreams and the *psicopompo* god who guided souls and led
them beyond death to repose; therefore, the god of the "right
road," or the means of salvation. He was the god of the knowing and the god of deceivers. (Plato, in his day, will show the
Sophists that only he who knows the truth knows how to
deceive.) Inasmuch as the erect stones which first represented
the god suggest lively, virile sex, the ithyphallic Hermes was
sculptured on them. The Romans, who in matters of property
did not jest, considered stone dividers sacred and charged a
god with the exclusive task of guarding boundaries and upholding limitations—*Terminus* he was called. And as Jupiter
was the god of the State and had to guard the frontiers of the
Roman nation, they made him a *Jupiter Terminalis*. By the
same token, when anyone was cast out of Roman territory he
was said to be ex-terminated. The Latins translated the *hóros*
—the "limited" of Aristotle—as *terminus*, and the Scholastics
had the good sense to keep it. We ought to go back to this
expression when we refer to logical concepts, because "concept" by itself means a good many other things.[1]

Terminus* is therefore thought as it is delimited by our
minds; that is, thought which establishes boundaries for itself,
which makes itself precise. Now I think that the metaphors I
used earlier when I called the concept a thought which is
given a label, made official, inventoried, will be understandable.
Let us make of *terminus*, the dependable guarantee of property, the instrument for ensuring the propriety of what we
say. Logical thinking uses terms, and therefore should normally talk *in terminis*. Leibnitz recommends this incessantly,

---

1. The relationship between the words *termino* and *signo* will appear
to us later.

and that recommendation originates from the greatest depths of his way of thinking.[2]

2. To define is therefore, as Aristotle tells us, to exchange names for concepts: δεῖ δὲ τὸν ὁριζόμενον λόγον ἀντὶ τῶν ὀνομάτων ἀποδοῦναι (*Topicos*, VI, ii, 149 2). In the *Physics* (I, 1, 184 b) τὸ ὄνομα ἀδιορίστως is opposed to λόγος which διορίζει.

10
Truth and Logicality

OUR DEFINITION of the concept has a second part, the one which begins with "pretending." Let us now go back to it. The idea was that a concept must be of such a nature that what is valid for it will also be valid for the things conceived in it. This quality of the concept has in itself nothing to do with the concept as a *term*. Thus it is manifest that, as is common with the Hermes and all the forms of gods concerned with boundaries—Janus, for example—a concept has two faces. With one face the concept pretends to tell us the truth about a thing; this is the face which looks upon reality, hence outside of itself, outside of thought; this is its face *ad extra*. With the other, the concept is limited to its own mental content; this is its face *ad intra* of thought. With the former the concept is not sufficiently true, not a matter of knowledge. With the latter the concept is more or less precise, strict, unequivocal, exact; it is more or less *lógos*, more or less logical or fit so that the logical operations may function with precision. The result is that the logicality of a concept is a different thing from its veracity. In Dante, the Devil—Prince of Deceit —says to Pope Sylvester:

Forse tu non pensavi chi'io logico fossi! [1]

The inverse of this—whether a concept in order to be true does not first have to be logical—is a different question. Let us leave it at that.

My interest has been above all to point out that the concept is only logical, that is, that it only serves to enter into logical relations, to the extent that it is a "term." It is not its truth or

1. "Perhaps you did not take into account that I too am logical!" (*Inferno*, Canto XXVIII, lines 122–123).

its validity with regard to things which makes a thought a logical thought, a *lógos*, but its precision and its exactness. The truth of a concept comes to it in its relation to things; therefore, from something external to it. This is the concept's extrinsic virtue. On the other hand, its precision, its unequivocal character, is a virtue which the concept itself has or does not have as a thought, and without relation to anything extrinsic.

So truth and logicality are two different properties of the concept, and this is not saying merely that what is appropriate for one is appropriate for the other. If there is a bias toward the first of these, the tendency will be that the extract of sensible things, which is the concept, resembles these as closely as possible. But as sensible things are always confused and diffuse —in short, inexact—for the sake of logicality, the concept which has the least possible resemblance to things is preferable. Consequently, we are talking of two interests which for the moment are antagonistic. So much so that it led to this tremendous event: knowledge was born—and hence philosophy and the sciences—when for the first time there was discovered a kind of thinking which could be characterized as exact. This discovery arose out of a desire to know certainly and precisely what the things around us are, things among which man moves as one lost. But the result was, *ipso facto*, that exact thinking, precisely because it was exact, was not valid for the things surrounding man. And then that monstrously paradoxical thing happens by which the effort to know turns itself inside out, and instead of looking for concepts which might stand for things, exhausts itself looking for things which might stand for exact concepts. These things which meet the measure of concepts were called Being by Parmenides, Ideas by Plato, Forms by Aristotle. Almost the whole history of ancient and medieval philosophy is the history of certain concepts about things which go in search of the things conceived through their agency.[2] And this mad pursuit continues (at least in

2. This is seen literally among the disciples of St. Bonaventure, educated in Augustinianism and hence in Platonism. It is very moving to

part), for if we leap to the other extreme of scientific history, to the present day, we hear Einstein telling us: "Mathematical propositions, insofar as they refer to reality, are not valid, and insofar as they are valid they have no reference to reality." [3]

It is very important here to identify these two separate and antagonistic forces battling ceaselessly in conscious thought, thus producing a perennial drama of ideas, because we are studying a form of philosophy which, like all modern philosophies, is oriented toward the way of thinking of the exact sciences, and we have been describing the very moment in which the exact way of thinking is going to suffer the most radical change since that which initiated its first establishment; a change which, toward the peak, consists in carrying interest in the logicality of a concept to an extreme, and consequently, creating concepts that are still farther removed from things. Presumably, it is the modern conviction, which in this respect comes down to our own day, that if exact traditional thinking was not valid for things, it was not because it moved away from things as it *became exact*, but, on the contrary, because it was not sufficiently exact, not logical enough. Do not, then, find it strange that at this point in our study we must pause at every step to clarify the factors on which the problem hinges.

----

follow Mateo de Aquasparta (1235–1302), who goes laden with his science and asks himself if there is anything for which it will have value, anything to which science will belong, for example, "*Quaestio est, utrum ad cognitionem rei requeratur ipsius rei existentia, aut non ens possit esse objectum intellectus.*" That is to say, man asks himself if the object of knowledge may not be nothingness. (*Quaestiones disputatae de cognitione.*)

3. Einstein, *Geometrie und Erfahrung.*

11

The Concept in Pre-Cartesian
Deductive Theory

WHAT IS the traditional way of exact thinking up to the time of Descartes? Let us try to describe it clearly, even though this means that we must make a long detour through the history of philosophy and mathematics.

Faced with a multitude of different things our attention, I said, fixes on certain components which they have in common. Those that assume a triangular form, for example. In each of them we see whatever looks like a triangle and we disregard every other aspect. Thus we obtain the extract "triangle." The triangle that forms part of each of those things is not a distinctive triangle, or to put it another way, it is not that each thing contains a triangle of its own *other* than the triangles of all the others. They all contain the same triangle because, since we have disregarded everything else in them, we have disregarded everything which differentiates, diversifies, and multiplies them, for example, the fact that one is here and the other there, or that they are of this or that size. The extract triangle with which we are left is both here and there, indifferently and simultaneously. It is ubiquitous because it is always the *same* triangle wherever it is.[1]

1. Fixation, abstraction, and extraction may be carried out by looking at one thing alone, and it is not necessary for these operations to be directed to a deliberate search for something in common. We disregard the white color of a billiard ball and extract its spherical character, or vice versa. But *ipso facto* its spherical quality is revealed as able to be colored successively in an infinite variety of tints; its whiteness can assume the most diverse forms. That is to say, its common qualities emerge just as though we had planned them beforehand. Aristotle says that although we form a concept of the sun by looking at only one sun, once it is formed it refers to an unlimited multitude of possible suns.

The triangle, an extract of many concrete things, turns out to be a unique thing, certainly an abstract thing—I prefer to say an extract. But in spite of being abstract it is still a thing. The reason lies in the fact that we acquired it *only* by fixing on certain components of concrete or real things and disregarding the rest. It is, let us say, a real part of a real thing. The triangle is there, in this place or another, as are things; hence in any place or in all places, only with complete indifference toward each place in particular and toward all of them as a group. It is, for example, in a drawing on a blackboard. Do not tell yourself that this drawing is not exactly a triangle, but something trianguloid, more or less triangular. By fixing our attention on it and disregarding the rest, our imagination believes that it has succeeded in omitting from consideration in the trianguloid figure anything over and above a triangle. This "exact" imagination is what Kant, in mathematics an ardent partisan of the ancient way of thinking, called "pure intuition." We shall meet with this further on. But however pure an intuition may be, even though it be the very purest intuition, it will always be the case that what is there before us is a thing as a thing. By this we mean to say that while we will have taken away many ingredients of the concrete thing in order to get our extract, it is beyond question that we have not for our part put anything into it. Since it comes out of the thing it is a thing.

The ubiquity of the extract triangle carries with it the fact that it resides at one and the same time in an indefinite multitude of things, i.e., it forms an abstract part of them. This permits us to say of each of these that "it is a triangle." The extract has enabled us to formulate a proposition. If this is a true one we will find ourselves in possession of an item of "knowledge," i.e., of a necessary thought about the thing. Now then, is it true that this △ is a triangle? Whether it is or not will depend on whether the nexus between that drawing as the subject of the proposition and the predicate triangle has an unquestionable foundation, *basis* or *reason*. That nexus expressed by the word "is," consists of an identification which we have established between the drawing and the thought "triangle." That identification pretends to be true. In order to transform the pretension into a lawful title, its basis must be set forth.

The triangle is an abstract unique thing which we have extracted from many concrete things. When, reversing our operation, we look at it in *relation* to this multitude or diversity of things, a new quality is born in it—it becomes in fact "the one in the many." Extracted by means of an abstraction which sought what was *common* in that multitude—hence a commonal abstraction—it is natural that we can attribute it to each one of those many things, and to "all" of them. This aptitude of the one for being attributed to the many is what, in a word both unintelligible and absurd, is customarily called "universality." Aristotle, who originated the idea which that word tries to express, does not use any one equivalent name for it. On the contrary, he uses three different words. We owe it to the Scholastics, who on that point were scholastic in the bad sense of the adjective.[2] The relationship between the unique abstract thing and its many concrete aspects, which is what now interests us, is called by Aristotle "that which is said with regard to all" (*tò legómenon katà pantós*). The Scholastics translated this—and this time correctly—as *dictum de omni*. This aptitude for being "universal" converts the intuitive extract into a *concept*.

I have insisted that we call the concept a *"term"* for only one reason, because, or insofar as, it is a delimited, definitive, and exact thought. But I pointed out that a concept has other aspects or characteristics. We have already seen one—its claim to truth. Now we see another—its universality. But this universality of the intuitive extract, faced with many concrete or individual things, is not an authentic universality. That is why Aristotle was not satisfied with the *dictum de omni*, which for him is *only one* of the three salient meanings of the concept's universality. Now we concern ourselves with the first.

2. Strictly speaking, we owe to Boethius the term *universale* as a translation of καθόλου.

For the traditional way of thinking this poses a grave question. Note that we are in the primary operation which is going to lead to knowledge and science; hence, at a decisive point on which everything else will hinge.

The question of why our proposition "that △ is a triangle" is true confronts us with two requirements. First, out of the intuitive extract triangle, now having become a germ of concepts through its aptitude for universality, we make a logical concept, a "term," by giving its definition. Only then can we decide whether or not △ is actually a triangle. The other requirement is this: granted that we now have the triangle transformed into a logical concept, can there be a logical relationship between it and the drawing △ or any other concrete real thing? Or, to put it another way, can anything be predicated of individual things? Or, to make the question more pointed, in the funereal schoolboy syllogism which, since our adolescence, has announced to us the incontrovertible death of Pedro, there is proof only when the minor premise—Pedro is a man—is true. I ask not whether that proposition is true or false, but something more elemental, namely, if it is a proposition which belongs in the class of "logical propositions."

Let us give further attention to the first requirement. When in view of many things we tried to find out what was common to them, and by abstracting the common element we extracted the triangle, we did not know that our operation was controlled in advance by a decision to look at the multitude of things from a specific point of view, namely, from what they might have in common with regard to forms. Had we chosen another characteristic, for example, color, we would have arrived at the common denominator of "whiteness." Now we recognize that, actually, while we were finding that many things coincide with triangularity, we were rejecting others because they diverged and went off by themselves to join other groups—that of the square, that of the circle. The triangle extract and its group reject the "square" extract and its group, and so on. This does not happen between "triangle" and "white." There is nothing obviously incongruous in that tri-

angular things may also be white, but squareness and triangularity are manifestly incongruous. The reason is that all
these incompatible extracts—triangle, square, circle—have
come to life in the same respect, shape. They stand opposed
among themselves for the very reason that they are common
members of a much broader commonalty, established by the
extract "shape" which holds them all together. On the other
hand, they are not opposed to colors because these have nothing to do with shapes, because they belong to another group.
Shape makes up part of the extracts triangle, square, and circle,
as these form part of certain multitudes of things. The extracts
appear at different levels. For if we rise from triangle to shape,
we can also descend from triangle to equilateral, isosceles, and
scalene. Extracts constitute a hierarchy. Each one contains the
one immediately above it, and as the same thing happens to
that one, each extract contains those above it or they form
part of it, while it contains none of those below. This is the
relation—or implication—of containing and contained, which
makes it possible to establish the hierarchy of genera and
species. The traditional way of thinking is to think in terms
of genera and species. But this, and nothing less than this, is
what will change in the new method of exact thinking, and in
what I am saying I am impelled to clear up the difference between old and new.

The generic extract forms part of the specific extract. To
get the former we do not need to look at the concrete things
around us. It is in the species, as the species resides in the
things. The genus is therefore neither more nor less an intuitive thing than is the species. "Shape" is found in the drawing
△ , as the triangle is found in this drawing and in many other
things, but with one difference: being already an extract, it
comprises only that on which our attention has *fixed*, and
therefore the number of its components is limited; moreover,
we know which ones they are. The triangle is a thing previously inventoried. We cannot say the same of individual concrete things, because these we have not *made* ourselves, as we
made the extract, but they present themselves to us spontane-

ously with an infinity of components which we cannot control. Hence, we cannot define, and de-*termine* the individual things, at least in this way of thinking which proceeds by means of the commonal abstraction and stays with the "common thing," abandoning what is different in individual things. These are in fact in-*finite* and in-de-*terminable*, or irreducible to *terms*.

Let us keep in mind that in all this business of obtaining extracts and setting them into hierarchies as genera and species we are determined to know, and to know is always to know, or try to know, something definite. Let us, therefore, choose a specific example and say that we want to know the thing "triangle," confident that once we know it we will have knowledge, however incomplete, of triangular things.

The first knowledge of the triangle that we can grasp consists in defining it. So we say: *A triangle is the figure formed by three straight lines which intersect each other, two at a time*. What do we gain by replacing the intuitive extract "triangle" with this definition? First, we discover that it is a composite of parts, and moreover, that it is an organic whole of which the parts are parts because they are articulated, because they serve certain functions. In outline, the triangle comes to be like an animal or a machine. Nothing of this appeared by itself in our intuition. The definition is the result of an anatomical operation which we perform on the intuitive extract. Plato again and again compares definition to the carving skill of the cook.

Second, those parts or pieces are presented to us separately. There are two of them: the "figure of straight lines" and the "three which intersect, two at a time." [3]

3. Here one sees that the definition does not present us with the parts which we call "components," which would be all the points of the integral straight lines of the triangle, but only with the functional parts (organs). Actually those three points, the only ones which are shown as separated (although implicitly in the notion "two intersecting straight lines"), are the only ones which perform an essential function in the triangle as such. Besides the parts, the definition of a triangle brings in the numbers "three" and "two," the presence of which in this intui-

Third, those parts are intuitive extracts of a higher order—that is to say, more simple or elemental—in the hierarchy of genera and species. In this hierarchical order the more elevated or elemental part is the "figure of straight lines"; this is the genus. We understand the thing very well. On the other hand, the other part, "three which intersect, two at a time," is arcane to us, we do not understand it. Neither do we understand many pieces of a machine when we see them taken apart. It is precisely this hermetic quality which shows us that this is an articulation, something which exists solely to be joined with another piece or pieces and thus to form a whole. Let us first put it together. Its meaning is automatically clarified. The part that articulation plays comes in the expression "straight lines." Now we see that the second part serves the function of differentiating the triangle from other rectilinear figures. To that end it produces a division in the extract "figure of straight lines," leaving only the case of there being three intersected, two at a time. Thanks to that *difference*, the genus "rectilinear figure" is narrowed down to the species "triangle."

We are saying all this about the definition as a result, but now we must ask ourselves how we arrive at it; that is to say, insofar as our operation is concerned, what does defining mean?

Now we will forget individual concrete things for the time being. We do not have to deal with more than the abstract things which are intuitive extracts—triangle, and so on. In producing this last extract we said that it emerged at the same time as other extracts on the same level: "square," "cube," "octahedron," . . . , "circle," "cycloid," "ellipse," . . . ; that is to say, we find ourselves again confronting a multitude or a variety of abstract and intuitive things. In order to find out what a triangle is, we search, with a new commonal abstraction, for what all those extracts have in common; thus we fashion the extract "closed figure." But this does not help us

---

tive geometry is evidently an intrusion. For the sake of simplification we omit this from consideration.

to distinguish the triangle from any of the other extracts. It therefore remains completely indeterminate among the others. In view of this we seek to *differentiate* it from at least a goodly portion of those things. This is an inverse operation whereby we separate a group into one or various sections. In this case we divide the group of "closed figure" extracts into two groups: those which are "rectilinear closed figures" and those which are "curvilinear closed figures." With this we have achieved an initial *determination* of the triangle which locates it in the smaller group of rectilinear figures. Now it is confused only with the square, the rectangle, the hexagon, and so on. There it is in its most intimate group, in its "proximate genus." All that is lacking is to seek a new determination which will differentiate it from other rectilinear figures. To find this difference we must check over all the rectilinear figures one by one and determine for each what differentiates it from the others. This is "enumeration." In this traditional way of thinking one can never be sure that the enumeration is complete. It furnishes us with only a practical certainty. With this reservation we manage to discover the *particular difference* of the triangle, which is its three straight lines intersected, two at a time. Adding this differentia to the genus the extract triangle is left fully determined; that is to say, it is converted into a defined concept, a term. Definition, then, is a double operation which looks up for the nearest group and immediately separates the thing defined from the other things included in the group. Thus the thing defined remains as a composite which has been segmented into its parts, i.e., into the relatively simple elements which make it up: its genus and its difference. Leibnitz called these simple elements by a legal term—necessary conditions. To define is to take apart, and this in Aristotle's time was called *analysis*, the reduction of a composite to its simple elements, of a whole to its parts. Note that in the defining process no logical operation intervenes. Its result—the concept as a *term*—is now something on which logical operations may be performed. All our analytic activity has been performed on the intuitive materials of the extracts; we have done nothing more than compare one with another intuitively, retaining what is common among them and differentiating some things from others within their group. We have proved *nothing*, nor had we reason to. This is not a mere nominal definition, because we have the defined thing before us and what we have done is to describe its active parts. Each will be compared with the thing "triangle" and we shall see whether or not they coincide.

Let us repeat once more that logical operations can be performed only on concepts. With our definition, and the earlier ones which it took for granted as realized, we have fabricated the concepts. *In the mode of exact thinking, according to the Euclidian-Aristotelian tradition, the fabrication of the concept, which is the definition, consists of nothing more than specifying the parts of an intuition as such.* And there is no reason to give oneself great airs when the mathematical definition assumes the aspect of what has been called a "genetic or causal definition," as when one says of the cone that it is the surface created by the rotation of a right-angle triangle on one of its sides which is not the hypotenuse; or the most modern one, which it is not necessary to adduce. This operation to which the triangle submits is not in the least logical; it is purely intuitive and in some respects manual. It describes a ceramic fabrication which any idiot can produce. One takes a lump of clay, thrusts into it a right-angle triangle cut as thin as possible from tin or cardboard, turns it, then takes it out and pours into the hole a semifluid material capable of drying without sticking to the clay. After a time the block of clay is broken and the cone appears "defined with a genetic definition." Meanwhile logic was locked out and sent packing. The genetic definition, like the nongenetic, merely describes the operations we perform on the intuited thing. Every definition is genetic, including the one which in the ordinary sense is considered purely nominal since it engenders the concept from a name, which is a thing like any other, and gives rise to a natural science which busies itself with names as zoology does with animals.

The prelogical character of the definition is not usually seen with any clarity, for we speak of defining when the greater part of the concepts of a discipline or theory are already formed and have automatically constituted its particular conceptual hierarchy of genera and species, which makes them enter into the relations of containing and contained, or implication; this is certainly a logical relationship. But this assumes that these definitions have already been formulated, whereas what we are now discussing is not their resultant—the concept —but the very operation which fabricates it.

The definition, then, generates a concept from a thing, precisely stating the components of the former. These in turn are concepts, so that a definition does no more than transfer us to other definitions until we reach the final ones, which are limited to naming the ultimate intuitive elements. Thus the definition of the triangle transfers us to those of the figure, the angle, straight line, line and point. The saving of intuitive effort which these transfers provide for us is no small matter, but the beauty of the definition does not consist in this economic advantage. There is also in it an element which is not transference, but a new intuition which the definition invites us to acquire; it is not that of line, nor of straight line, nor of three straight lines, but of the intersection of these, two at a time. This does not appear in any of the definitions before that of the triangle.

But once more let us not forget that what we want is to know the thing "triangle." What does the definition give us as knowledge of a thing? For the moment nothing we would not already have in the intuitive extract. What adds to our intuitive traffic with the thing is only its breakdown into parts. This is something, but it is not a material increase in our knowledge. The gain comes from the fact that when we isolate one of the two parts of the "triangle"—that which we call "figure of intersecting straight lines"—we are automatically presented with a whole series of "theorems" and "corollaries," that is to say, of true propositions which have been demonstrated from the lines and angles. The concept *triangle* is a species of the genus "figure of straight lines which intersect," and everything which is true for the genus is also true for the species. We are now glutted with logic. With the definition we not only have what the concept "triangle" is—it does not matter what the ancients may have said of the thing "triangle" —but all of a sudden we have a whole series of properties which this thing has and which neither intuition nor, at the moment, definition discloses to us. Already this is knowing no small amount about the triangle. It is a knowledge which comes to us from a level above it, and as the triangle is the least complex closed figure, and itself stands very high in the geometric hierarchy, that earlier knowledge clearly cannot be very great.

12
Proof in Deductive Theory
According to Aristotle

A DEFINITION is an operation that both names and describes. Its outline is this: I call what is before me "triangle," and what is before me comprises such and such parts. It makes no sense to require proof of such a proposition. It is merely an assertion. It tells me that something *is* thus, but not that it *must* be thus. It does not express necessity. It cannot and need not be proved. What is said can only be compared with what is seen. "Compare" can, if you wish, be called "verify." This is also true of the primary definitions of the discipline—those of the point, the line, the angle. The definition is the formula which makes analytically explicit the intuitive knowledge of what a thing is, a knowledge which to me was already implicit.

But having once defined the triangle I come automatically to realize that if I prolong two of its lines beyond the point where they intersect each other, they form an external angle which is equal to their internal angle. This, in the first place, is not the triangle, but merely one of its properties; in the second place, it is not a simple assertion, but an essential truth. Hence it is, in its most typical value, a bit of "scientific knowledge" which is beyond dispute.

That property is, of course, not exclusive to the triangle. It is common to "all straight lines which intersect each other." The result is that it is inadequate to call it the property of a triangle since it is not the triangle's private and exclusive property. The triangle has this property because it belongs to the group or *genus* of "straight lines which intersect each other." With respect to the triangle, then, it is commonal property. A commonal property is a rounded square. Let us then, in place

76

of property, say "generic characteristic." But this very thing which is a generic characteristic of the triangle becomes the authentic, exclusive and private property of the genus "straight lines which intersect each other," hence it is missing from other lines—those that are curved or that do not intersect. This means that the genus is not one in the absolute sense but only in relation to its inferior; but of itself or for itself it is a species. Every authentic property is private and specific. Thus the equality of its angles to two right angles is a specific property of the triangle. The reason is this: we saw that the concept and the extract "triangle" were together a composite of two parts; one was the genus, the other the differentia. The genus can be isolated from the differentia, but the differentia cannot be isolated from the genus because the result would be unintelligible. Well then, the properties of the concept's independent part are predicated as "generic characteristics." Its "properties," on the other hand, belong to it as a whole—ὅλον, *hólon*.

Scholastic terminology calls the attribution to the species of the "generic characteristic" a "universal" predication because it is in fact valid for all the species of the genus. But it also calls "universal" the attribution of a "property" to the species, for example, the angular sum of two right angles to the triangle. Why, if this pertains only to the species, and the species is a "singular thing"? The cause of this error is that the species, in turn, is valid for a great number of individual concrete things to which it bears the relation of the "one in the many." I have referred previously to this triple ambiguity in the word "universal," which in any case is of itself unintelligible.

The same word is used to express three completely different relations: first, that of "one among many," or extension of the concept; second, that of part to whole (genus or species), or comprehension of the concept or implication; and third, the characteristic of the property to the species, which is a relation of consequence to principle.

Now, as I said earlier, it is clear why Aristotle had no word corresponding to the term "universal" which, confused and equivocal, served as a war horse in all the great battles of medieval Scholasticism.

With perfect appropriateness Aristotle gave those three distinct relationships three different names: first, κατὰ παντός *kata pantós;* we might say universal predication.[1] Second, καθ'αὐτό *kathautó;* we might say general predication, since it is from the genus to the species. Third, καθόλου *kathólou;* we might say, as did Aristotle, catholic predication. In Latin we would say *de omni, per se* and *quoad integrum.*[2]

It seems to me that the term *kathólou,* one of the most important and genuine in all of Aristotle's doctrine, is not very well understood despite its clear definition in the Aristotelian text,[3] and the example adduced therein, which is the equality of the angles of the triangle to two right angles, as a property

---

1. Through weakness in the face of tradition. Strictly speaking, we ought to say "commonal predication." The relations of "one in many" is what logistics calls "class." A "class" is a group or mass of individuals with a definite property in common. This presumed "universal" is only one commonal aspect of class. Russell wanted to reform the old logic radically by elaborating a logic of classes but he failed, as he was bound to, and had to found it on a logic of relationships.

2. In spite of the fact that Aristotle makes a distinction between those three relationships and gives each of them a name, he will make the same slip as the Scholastics did when they almost always used *kathólou* for all three. But in Aristotle this has two causes: one, purely linguistic, which is the difficulty of converting the other two terms into adjectives; the other, a matter of substance—the difference between the extensive and the comprehensive relationships of the concept—which Aristotle, although he saw it, could never master, as is well known, and he is constantly jumping from one to the other. This duality is the great defect of his logic and the reason why it remained static for century after century. The reform of logic since the end of the 19th Century has been a matter of clarifying and mastering the difference between those two relationships. As Aristotle understood the κατὰ παντός informally, in the end the three "universal" relationships seemed to him identical *a parte rei.* But when in his logical explanations some more concrete matter forces him to it, he distinguishes very well between the arithmetic universal and the κατὰ παντός, catholic whole. Thus *Posterior Analytics,* I,5,74a 30–31, οὐ γὰρ ᾗ τρίγωνον οἶδεν, οὐδέ πᾶν τρίγωνον, ἀλλ' ᾗ καθ' ἀριθμόν. That is to say, "this way one does not know the triangle in its essence (in its ὅλον), nor in all its species (in their implications or *generality*), but only in its arithmetic 'universality.'"

3. *Posterior Analytics,* I, 4, 73b 26 to the end of the chapter.

predicated of the triangle. Note that the problems of universal predication refer principally to proof. In the case of "property" this is verified by bringing the integral (specific) concept of the subject into the reasoning, not as in the generic predication or *per se*, in which only the part that represents the genus intervenes. But this proof, which allows generic characteristics to be attributed to the species, is not only, as the Scholastics recognized, less perfect than the *catholic* proof or the proof through the species itself [4]; it assumes rather that those characteristics have previously been proved catholicly of the genus, which for this purpose reveals its more authentic character as species. There is, then, no proof more basic than the specific, or truer than the catholic, which here does not mean a profession of faith but a literal interpretation of Aristotle, using his very own words. He, or at least his disciples, were not satisfied with the positive word but used it in the comparative and the superlative, asking, for example, for a more catholic proof, a most catholic proof.

In all this the precise difference, as between the pre-Cartesian way of thinking and that which, with progress and constant refinement, has dominated the exact sciences since then, is still hidden. Therefore, we have no choice but to touch for a moment the nerve center of the question.

With the proposition "the sum of the angles of a triangle is equal to two right angles" we have a typical example of knowledge, that is to say, of necessary thought about things. It is a true proposition, with a necessary truth. This character comes to it from *proof;* it is a proved catholic truth. In what does that which we call proof or demonstration consist? Let us look at it in this concrete case. In order to prove the stated proposition we isolate a part of the definition of triangle, the most generic part—"straight lines which intersect each other," i.e., angles. We take the triangle apart or disarticulate it into

4. The scholastic *secundum quod ipsum* is not sufficiently emphasized in the *per se*, and moreover it does not stress the decisive note, which is not the *ipsum*, indiscernible from the *per se*, but the wholeness of the concept, the *hólon*.

simple angles, thereby making the triangle disappear. Faced
with simple angles we find that we already know a good deal
about them, namely, the true propositions or theorems which
determine the properties of angles *when they enter into relation with each other*. These relations consist in being equal, or
being greater than another, or being less than another. They
regulate our operations with angles: to equalize them, add
them, subtract them. The triangle, *as a plurality of angles*, is
not in the least new with respect to the concept "angle," which
is its genus. To demonstrate, then, consists in showing that
the new is the old, the already known; that to talk of the triangle is *the same* as to talk of angles, and that, consequently,
the new proposition is a *tautology* of the earlier or generic
propositions. The new proposition is true *because* it says the
same thing as those already known, because it *tautologizes*.
To make this clear one has only to break the triangle down
into its angles, to *reduce* the composite to its relatively simple
elements, the concrete to its abstractions. It is merely a case of
identification. This thinking in terms of reduction from the
composite to the simple, and this seeing that the new is identical with the old, with the *a priori*, is analytical thinking *a
priori*. This is not intuitive thinking. It installed itself in the
definite concept—or term—"triangle" and there found nothing
more than the previous generic concept "angle." It limited itself to recognizing then, that *angle* is implied in *triangle*, that
the triangle contained the angle and was resolved into or reduced to it. There was no need to *go beyond* the definition
or the concept of the triangle. This reducing of the composite
to the simple, the concrete to the abstract, the new to the old
or *a priori*, is called *deducing*. The proof *deduces* the concept
"triangle" from the concept "angle."

But this is not enough for proof. We must take a second
step, very different from the previous one; we must see what
happens when the theorems or *general* laws concerning relations between angles are applied to a *determinate* (specific)
case, namely, when it is a matter of three angles whose straight
lines intersect each other, two at a time. In the generic concept

"angle" and in its laws, the number of angles which will enter into a relationship is not *determined*, is not foreseen, nor is any condition of its straight lines other than that they intersect; nor is it foreseen that the angles are three in number, nor that the straight lines intersect each other, two at a time. This, with respect to those *a priori* truths, is completely new. The second mental operation which completes the proof consists in *applying* the general law about angles to the case *determined* by the new condition.

Because of the confusion to which I have referred previously, the ancient logics do not bring out sufficiently that the concept has two extensions. One consists in its validity for a number of individual entities which are numerically distinct—its numerical or quantitative extension. The other consists in its validity for a multitude of specific entities—its generic extension. This is its properly logical extension. Thus, the concept "angle" refers to an infinite number of forms or "species" of angles before whose differences it is neutral or indeterminate. The species-genus relationship is asymmetrical, irreversible. The species contains the genus; the genus does not contain the species, but rather its undetermined possibility. From this the genus can be recognized in the species, but the species as such cannot be recognized or identified *in* the genus. *In this way of thinking the species is something new with respect to the genus.* To get its concept, one has to *get away* from the generic concept and *add* something unforeseen to it.

This makes the proof or demonstration consist in joining together two mental operations which are completely distinct: the analytical *a priori* thinking by which we recognize or identify "triangle" as "angle"—the species in the genus—and the *thinking by addition* of the new condition which creates the species—to be three straight lines intersecting, two at a time. Analytical thinking is an operation both inter- and intraconceptual. And the second? Obviously not. We have not extracted the new condition out of any concept; it was born spontaneously from our intuition which, amid the infinite forms of angles, imagines the unique case of three straight lines intersecting each other, two at a time. This intuition creates for us a new concept *irreducible* to the generic concept of the angle. By an activity *external* to the earlier one we insert or add this new generic concept "angle," and departing from it *as from a new principle* which we add to the generic principle, the proof emerges, automatically and without further ado. It is born, then, from the *priori* which is the angle, *plus* the new-born *priori* which is the specific condition or determination. This *plus* declares that our second thought is not *a priori* analytical but *a priori* synthetic. Thanks to this we *deduce* the proposition about the sum of the angles of a triangle.

But it is obvious that this second *deduction* is one in a very different sense from the first. It did not consist in deducing, in identifying the triangle with the angle—a purely inter- and intra-conceptual relationship—but rather in *adding* to the concept "angle" a new intuition which crystallizes in a new concept. Between the concepts "angle" and "triangle" an intuition interposes itself.

If from the generic concept "angle" we could, without the intervention of any new element of intuition, deduce or derive —that is, formulate—the concept "triangle," we would have a deduction *sensu stricto*, a purely analytical operation between concepts, and hence a purely logical operation. We would have deduced the species from the genus. *But in this way of thinking the species cannot be deduced from the genus.* Instead of this we have had to "deduce" it through an intuition, a synthesis of the angle with a new condition. The equality of the angles to two right angles is true for the triangle with an *a priori* truth; but this *a priori* is nothing like an analytical, conceptual, or logical *a priori*. It is an intuitive *a priori* which adds itself to or *synthesizes* the analytical *a priori* of the genus with respect to the species. The proof or demonstration, as a process of reasoning or a way of thinking, becomes a centaur of analytical thinking and synthetic thinking.

This invites us to take careful note that if we set the expression "analytical thinking *a priori*" against the expression "synthetic thinking *a priori*" we commit a terminological impropriety, because we are using the same term *a priori* with two different meanings—one logical, the other intuitive; therefore, our terminology "analytical thinking *a priori*" and "synthetic thinking *a priori*" is for various reasons not a little misleading. The expression "analytical thinking *a priori*" is a redundancy. All analytical thinking is necessarily *a priori*. These, then, are synonymous. Let us abolish the term. But all synthetic thinking is, as such, *a posteriori* (*a posteriori* of an intuition is understood). If it happens that, nevertheless, it can take on the character of *a priori*, this will be through some consideration external to its synthetic character, so external that to say "synthetic *a priori*" is to state a paradox. The external consideration is this: in intuition we synthesize or add to the intuition of angles the determining intuition that they be three and that their straight lines intersect each other two at a time. On the basis of this mental act, which is mere synthesis, we form the new triangle concept, synthesizing with the old concept "angle" the new intuitive condition, now formulated as a concept. From the resulting concept "triangle," which is the *integrum* or whole—the *hólon*—we now deduce the propriety *analytically*, hence *sensu stricto* "*a priori*." In the expression "synthetic thinking *a priori*" the intuitive and not the conceptual will be tacitly understood in the term "synthetic," and the analytical or conceptual in the "*a priori*." The coupling of this characteristic, so foreign to the condition of "synthetic," should therefore be expressed by the copulative word "and." We should say "synthetic and *a priori* thinking" (in place of "and notwithstanding *a priori*"). This is the term which expresses adequately what happens when we prove a proposition in pre-Cartesian geometry.[5]

5. The great similarity of these terms to the famous Kantian "synthetic judgments *a priori*" should not lead to identifying them too quickly; rather, it is well to tie them to the strict meaning with which they have emerged in our development. But it is clear that by this road, after many turns, we would reach the question which Kant poses. And what was said above is useful then, in that it shows vividly the

Now let us give the synthetic element of proof a rest and proceed to illumine the background of its *a priori* element, because we have still to clarify its most important aspect, that which motivates these long considerations of the pre-Cartesian way of thinking; but we must not forget that, although we have referred incidentally to Aristotle, it is not his theory of method or logic that we mean to define, but rather the actual way of thinking which Euclid employed. Hence, in talking of proof I did not talk of the syllogism. It is false to say that Euclid would normally proceed by way of syllogisms; this is not only because they fail to appear *in forma* in his *Elements*, but because very frequently his arguments are not transformable into syllogisms. The way of thinking of Euclidean exact science is, in substance, the same as the philosophic way of thinking from Aristotle to Descartes. As Aristotle usually takes examples for his logical theory from contemporary mathematical sciences, one might think that his philosophy also, like that of the moderns, is oriented toward their method. But the relationship between philosophy and mathematics was very different then. The similarity of method arises, as I indicated much earlier, from the fact that mathematics learned the fundamentals of its method from philosophy. As its theme—the extension of magnitude (the discrete quantity or number showed itself more intractable)—when once learned could be spun out further, a retroactive effect of its method on the philosophical method was certainly produced; but, of course, this was of a very secondary character. This seems to me to be the actual traditional situation between the two disciplines.

The proof, in a strict sense *a priori*, of the propositions about the triangle consisted in deducing its truth (by an act of analytical thinking) from the truth which other anterior or generic propositions possess. Hence the truth of the former is transmitted from the latter. The argument *a priori* is only

---

character of the enormous paradox contained in the term "synthetic judgments *a priori*." That paradox stirred Brentano's bad temper to frenzy and because of this, with the sharp wit of a great pamphleteer, he calls them "synthetic prejudices *a priori*."

Juanelo's waterworks [6] or an aqueduct through which the truth of the previous general proposition flows to the specific or later one. It is, then, a received truth. *Logical proof by itself does not engender the character of truth which a proposition has.* This reaches it from on high, swooping down like the dove of the Holy Spirit.

But the same thing happens to the truth of the previous proposition. We are always being referred back to an antecedent truth. With this we find ourselves facing three possibilities: first, that the regression backward and upward does not end, but that one proposition transfers us to another, and that to another, and so on indefinitely; second, that on arriving at an earlier proposition we find it proved by another later one (the demonstration would be circular); third, that at the end of a limited number of mental steps we might reach one or more propositions which might need no proof but might, nevertheless, be true.

The first possibility solves nothing for us. An infinite series of propositions in which one derives its truth from another never arrives at the primary truth. The second is, as primary truth, impossible *in this way of thinking* through genera and species based on commonal abstraction; it is the circular proof which, when it manifests itself, constitutes one of the great logical sins, the *circulus in demonstrando,* which is vicious. Only the third, *in this way of thinking,* seems to provide a solution.

Let us recognize without delay that this solution of traditional logical thinking is the most illogical of the three possibilities; since the truth in exact thinking consists in proving, the result is a fantastic illusory truth, while the real truth comprises certain propositions which cannot be proved, which are truths *per se notae* or evident; and note that what is *per se*

6. Juanelo, a 16th Century engineer, was so distressed by the practice of sending innumerable water-laden donkeys to supply Toledo that he built a tower (probably also powered by donkeys but more efficiently) to raise the needed water from the river to the city's summit. This tower appears in several paintings showing Toledo in that period [*Translator's note*].

notum in them is not only their particular content, what they say, but their character of truth. We have then a duality of meaning in the notion "truth," and that duality is a plain contradiction. This is what is illogical. Add that hitherto thinking in the sense of exact or scientific thinking—επιστήμη (*epistéme*)—meant proving; now it happens that thinking in the sense of proving is only a secondary form, and derived from thinking in another and more primary form, which is the opposite of proving and which we will call *evidencing*. Proof is "reasoning," and to prove is to reason. Well then, the kind of thought used for thinking out the primary propositions does not reason, and is therefore irrational and illogical.

As is noted, we have reached a point at which we complete the loop begun in Chapter 1. This means that everything introduced between those earlier paragraphs and the present moment has been set forth as inescapable preparation, so that we can now begin to talk of what is important to us in this study. When we asked ourselves what thinking was for Leibnitz we proclaimed—although sketchily—that for him, to think was to prove. Throughout the preceding pages it may have seemed that this was not peculiar to Leibnitz, since all philosophy before him, from Aristotle on, repeats a hundred and one times, as he does, that science is proof.

But now we will see that this was not so,[7] and that will be when our formula about Leibnitz begins to assume its real significance.

7. The abridgement of the term "science" in Aristotle is surprising because the result is that it does not coincide with "true knowledge," with νοεῖν (*noeîn*), which already means only knowledge that is proved. This is not possible without fundamental premises which are not proved, but are knowledge; so that "science" is, for him, a fragment of itself, something incomplete, an abstract side—and by the same token inseparable from the other side—is complete "knowing." This, as is all too well known, is a matter of the difference between νοῦς (*noûs*) and διάνοια (*diánoia*).

13

Logical Structure in the Science of Euclid

As we have seen, the specific or catholic proof assumes in one of its aspects—the proof from the genus—that it is analytical or *a priori*. But the generic proof in turn assumes that it was proved specifically. Thus, working backwards, we reach a first proof that is clearly specific, but of which the proving genus does not need to be proved in turn, but is true in itself without going further. This is equivalent to saying that a science must begin with one or more unproved or unprovable first propositions which are, nevertheless, more true than those which follow them and are based upon them, since the truth of these latter propositions is derived only from the primitive and innate truth of the first propositions. These are called "principles," not only because one *begins* with them but also because the others, which are called "consequences," *follow* them. That these two characteristics of the principle—being the beginning and being followed by something—are different will become evident when we observe that in science there are many other principles which appear at all levels in the body of its doctrine and which are therefore very far from being the origin of the discipline and first in its structure of theory. Now we are talking of first principles, or *principia maxima*.[1] The other characteristic of the principle, which is to emphasize most strongly that in this traditional way of thinking science *needs* many other principles—which, nevertheless, are neither first nor maximal—and that *this* is what differentiates it from the Leibnitzian way of thinking, is in a certain

1. Hence the meaning which the word "maxim" has acquired in our Western languages when used as a noun. Thus "moral maxim."

sense the whole purpose of this study.

The first book of Euclid's *Elements* begins with a series of propositions which are divided into two classes. Some are definitions—of the point, of the line—in which nothing is affirmed about the thing, but it is presented or exposed or explained. The others are propositions which affirm with the character of necessary truth certain ways of behavior of those defined things, *once they are already defined*. Euclid calls these κοιναὶ ἔννοιαι (*koinaì énnoiai*), which we might translate as "common knowledge"; Aristotle called them *axioms*. Euclid adds three which he calls "postulates"; these we shall disregard because they are not relevant to our theme. More definitions appear in the books which follow, and new axioms in some.[2] The famous postulate of the parallels is not included among the pos-

2. It is not proposed here to study Euclid as an individual historical fact, but only that part of his method which is representative and of permanent influence until Descartes (in the teaching of some countries— England, for example, it has continued as a school text), although the subject would be far more suggestive than might be generally supposed. Euclid belongs to the first generation which flourished after the death of Aristotle; hence to the one in which Stoicism was born. This is not to say that Euclid was a Stoic (he had been educated in the Academy), but that both Stoicism and his own work sprang from the same ambit of historical tradition. The term κοιναὶ ἔννοιαι reveals it. In Aristotle ἔννοια is a vague word which has not yet crystallized into a *term*, and it means the informal idea or notion of something, whether or not it be true. In Euclid, as in Zeno, it means "true knowledge" which appears spontaneously in every man, and whose truth, therefore, needs no proof, but is the origin of possible demonstrations. With the adjective κοιναὶ it becomes a most important term in the Stoic doctrine, where "communities" replaces "all men." In Aristotle this adjective has two very different meanings; one, the same as above; the other, propositions *common* to various sciences. I deal with this second meaning later. The dispersal of definitions among various books, the appearance of the famous "postulate" among the definitions, the difference of meaning between the first five axioms and the rest of them, along with many other things, produce the impression that Euclid's work—for so many centuries the prototype of exact thought—is nevertheless a work which reveals a certain degeneration in purity of method and which assumes other earlier works whose exposition is outlined much more clearly. It is known, moreover, that our Euclidean text contains additions and perhaps suffers amputations performed on it up to the time of Theon of Alexandria, who lived in the 4th Century A.D. It is thus a text eroded by the currents of six centuries.

tulates in the *Elements*, but constitutes the last definition (number 23 in some texts, 25 in others, and 35 in the one used [in Spain] as a student text until recently).

In order to see with perfect clarity what that tangle of definitions and axioms represents insofar as they are the elements of the Euclidean "way of thinking," it is advisable to lay bare its logical structure by means of a schematized expression. In this way we will expose the form of "deductive theory" in the Euclidean sense, and we can then compare it, part by part, with the form of the deductive theory which, originating with Descartes, is canonical today.

I have already said that definitions adduce "abstract things" whose constituent characteristics they make explicit; these are the point, the line, the straight line, the surface, the angle, and so on. We are going to represent these things by lower case letters, for example, the point will be a, the line b. The characteristics of each of those things which the definition shows as separate we will represent by capital letters and a plus sign, which only indicates their bringing together in order to integrate the concept of the things. Thereupon Euclid's way of thinking, beginning with definitions, can be formulated thus:

Let there be these classes of things:
$$a = A + B,$$
$$b = C + D,$$
$$c = E + F, \text{ and so on.}$$

Those abstract things, remember, are intuitive extracts which the definition breaks down into their components. The concept does no more than discover an intuition in which the thing *itself* is. Hence, one starts from things and definitions which show their components *taken from them*.

Now let us turn to the axioms. Let us choose those axioms that represent their different *logical* characteristics, rather than concern ourselves especially with their particular content.

Axiom I. Things which are equal to a third thing are equal to each other.

Axiom II. If to equal things we add other equal things, the totals are equal.

Axiom VIII. Magnitudes which coincide with each other, that is, which fill exactly the same space, are equal.

Axiom IX. The whole is greater than its parts.

Axiom VI. Two magnitudes, each twice another magnitude are equal to each other.

In these axiomatic phrases we observe the following characteristics:

First, they are propositions which, once understood, demand forthwith to be considered as necessary truths. Hence, they are true in themselves, and not by virtue of reasons of proofs.

Second, the predicates of all of them express relationships into which things enter, which are thereby converted into equals, greaters, lessers.

Third, Axioms I and II differ from the rest in that they speak of things, whatever they may be, whereas VIII, IX, and VI speak only of things which are magnitudes.

Fourth (connected with the preceding), in Axiom I there is talk of equal things, but equality has not been defined. In Axiom VIII, on the other hand, what is to be understood as equality is defined; but in so doing, it is made to consist in a relationship which is valid only for things that are magnitudes and not for any things whatsoever.

To these observations we will add only a final reference to the famous postulate which appears as a definition. The "Definition-Postulate-Axiom" expresses it thus: lines parallel or equidistant are straight lines which, being on the same plane and being prolonged both ways, are never able to touch.

This "definition-postulate-axiom" differs from other definitions in that they describe only a thing which is evident in intuition, whereas the definition-postulate-axiom defines nothing, but affirms what is going to happen with two straight lines, namely, that not only are they equidistant in this intuition—which could still be valid as a definition—but they must be so. This, then, displays the character of a necessary truth, and in this it is like an axiom.

But definition-postulate-axiom differs from axioms in that the latter back up their truth with the intuition which we can have of them at any moment, whereas the postulate enunciates a form of behavior on the part of straight lines which no intuition can confirm. There is no intuition of the infinite.[3] Note, then, that Euclid's postulate is somewhat hybrid—between definition and axiom—something which is neither truth by reasoning, like the theorems, nor by evidence adequate for its own affirmation like the axioms. It seems certain that Aristotle did not know this, strange as it may appear. But if he had, it would have given him splitting headaches. In his logic and in his methodology there were, as we shall see, no means of recording the *class of truth* which pertains to this postulate.[4]

3. The famous fourth proof of the subjectivity of space which Kant formulated is an extraordinary *lapsus* on the part of the great master. "Space," he says, "is represented as an infinite magnitude which is *given*" (Kant's emphasis). . . . "Therefore it is the originating representation of space, an *intuition a priori* and not a concept. . . ." What lies between those two phrases and has been omitted is not material to us now, but it is, and very importantly, elsewhere in this study. It is clear that infinite space is not *given* to us in any intuition, but only finite spaces of one size or another. What adds that extra sense of infinity to intuited finite space is recognizing that we can broaden all given intuition beyond itself. But obviously that cannot be done by intuition itself, but only by the understanding, which creates the concept or law of unlimited reiteration in our amplifications of space. Far from having the infinity of space given to us, then, we must fabricate it for ourselves, and with no small effort; first, by successive amplifications of intuition, and then by means of the concept that our own activity in broadening it is not limited by any intuition; a concept, therefore, which denies this and declares that the totality of space can never be an intuition. The infinitude of space proves, then, exactly the contrary to what Kant pretends; it proves that space is not mere intuition, but in the final analysis it is a concept formed with intuitions—and not with only one—but transcending them by virtue of the most conceptual principle, which is that of sufficient reason. Because the concept of infinite space is in fact founded on the idea that there is no reason for any limit in our successive amplifications of finitude or, as Leibnitz would say, that the indefinite progress of the amplifications *habet ipsu rationis locum*, is valid as sufficient reason for its infinitude. The *lapsus* of Kant, it is clear, makes good sense. It was his intention to deny that our notion of space would be an Aristotelian concept obtained by commonal abstraction, and his era did not yet know another form of concept.

4. The notion of postulate, αἴτημα (*áitema*), is uncontrollable in Aristotle. It signifies what is evident to the teacher but not to the pupil. Let it be said in passing that many things in the Logic of Aristotle are

Deductive theory of the Euclido-Aristotelian type consists in deducing (that is, demonstrating analytically or from the genus) propositions which start from principles whose truth is evident. Although Aristotle dedicates many more pages to studying demonstration, this way of thinking places all the burden of theoretical truth on principles, and recognizes only now and then that these are *truer* than their consequences, that is to say, than the reasoning which produces consequences.[5] This conversion of truth into terms of quantity amazes us, because it is not a matter of credibility, which can be more or less probable, but of the fully established truth. The process of quantification becomes diaphanous, nevertheless, if one remembers that in this kind of thinking there are two classes of truth—that which is proved, or rational truth, and that which depends on evidence. This latter is assumed, and is the basis of the former; therefore it is the truer.

---

hard to understand because of the accident that the Greeks of his day did not "see" science in books but in its scholarly presence as a dialogue between teacher and pupil. The very name of "mathematics"—teachings—shows this. That we still call a science a discipline is a vestige of it. Axiom XII is the reciprocal of the postulate of the parallels. The difficulties which its understanding created were the reason why, for centuries, many people considered it a postulate. It surprises me that the most recent and exact studies of the foundations of mathematics declare too quickly, *referring to Euclid*, that the postulate of the parallels is only one more axiom. From the present point of view, as we shall see, this is clearly so; but this is because the present notion of axiom is very different from the Euclidean. I have nowhere seen an appreciation of its hybrid character, and of its difference from the axioms because of the intervention of infinity in it; but this means nothing because I have not seen many things. That distinction seems to me so obvious that I would be surprised to find that it had not been made before. By the same token, I would be grateful if the mathematicians would give me some bibliographic guidance on it. The three postulates which Euclid formulates as such are charged with stating the homogeneous condition of infinity proper to space, and two of them reiterate its basic rectilinear structure, which the definition of the parallels already establishes. Together with this, then, they constitute what we, from the present point of view, would call "restrictive Euclidean axioms." So that Euclid called it definition, the moderns, postulate, and his contemporaries, axiom. It was, therefore, no mere whim of mine to call it what in truth it is, definition-postulate-axiom.

5. πιστώτατον (*pistótaton*): the most worthy of credit.

14
Definitions in Euclid

THE FOREGOING shows us with the clarity of an anatomy lesson the principles of a science—in this case geometry. Now we will get to the bottom of them, not in order to scrutinize their particular content as would a geometrician but to clarify fully for ourselves their general function as principles in the economy or organism which is a deductive theory. This is all that interests us, because this study deals with what a "principle" is in order to determine precisely what it was for Leibnitz. Was it the same for him as for Aristotle, or was it something different? This is our real question.

We have the following: deductive theory requires two classes of principles, one that defines for us the elemental things of which everything with which we are going to deal with is composed; another that defines for us the relation in which those things can be. These relations are reduced to three: things that are equal; one thing that is greater than another, and, conversely, one thing less than another.

Definitions consist in giving names to the components of each elemental thing. Those components *are not* in turn defined, but we must discover them in intuition; the name acts merely as a peremptory indicator so that we will look for it in intuition. There is no guarantee that the elemental thing— point, line, straight line, angle—will be adequately defined, that is, broken down into its actual components. Nor is it guaranteed that those components, as they appear to us in intuition, will be something precise, unequivocal. The definition, then, in creating a term, i.e., a defined, precise concept, does not—as definition—guarantee its precision, but hands us on to the doubly irresponsible precision of intuition. I say "doubly" because intuition does not guarantee either that the components are the right ones or *precisely* what each component is.

Let us take an example. The first definition of Euclid announces: "A point is that which has no parts and no magnitude." That we are given two definitions for the same thing in place of one is already suspicious. But let us go on. The second definition announces: "A line is that which has length, but no breadth." This does not tell us what either length or breadth may be. But we can infer it: to have no breadth is to have neither magnitude nor parts; therefore, in accordance with the first definition, to be made up of points. That is to say, the second definition relegates us to the first, which is even more elemental, or to put it another way, these two definitions present us with two classes of elements which we are going to deal with later: the class of "points" and the class of "lines." The elements of this second class are composed, then, of elements of the first; hence it is a "class of classes." This mental process continues in the definitions which follow, with no further novelty than the introduction of concepts which the definitions do not define—equal, greater, lesser—and which are transferred to axioms. The important thing is that all the elemental things imply the first class—the points. What we say about their definition will, then, be valid for all that follows.

In view of this, let us go back to the first definition of the point: a point is that which has no parts. It we understand this definition as an expression of something logical, i.e., of a determinate concept whose meaning is sufficiently determined, thereby allowing us to confront the defined thing with no possibility of confusion, we must reject it *a limine*. For it does not permit us to distinguish the point from innumerable other things which, like it, have no parts—the soul, for example, or God, or the syllable,[1] everything which has no extension and is "that which isn't." This failure makes us fall back on the second definition of the point—that which has no magnitude.[2]

1. Aristotle, *Categories*, VI, 4b34.
2. This second definition is, of course, an addition, inserted very late in the classic Euclidean text.

We are no better off. As logical formulas both definitions are impossible, but their very crudeness reveals that we should not regard them as terms or logical concepts, but as mere indicators of something intuitive. Both definitions take for granted (and by dint of assuming it, fail to express it) that we are about to speak of the extensive, the spacious, the continuous magnitude—however you want to call it—and more concretely, they assume that we have it before us, that we see it. They also assume that we see what we see as a whole, and that we divide it into parts. They assume that with one of these parts we measure the whole, and they propose that we search for a part so small that it already has no parts and cannot be measured with another part because it is smaller than any other. All this implies a good deal of geometry before we begin. But let us accept it all. Even so, the definition does not permit us to accept the point as something determinate, because it transfers us to intuition, and in intuition every given point has parts and some magnitude. When we are going to say that "this one there" is now the point we are searching for, "this one there" gives birth, becomes fruitful, and from its belly sallies forth an infinite number of points into which the single one has been magically converted, i.e., into what least resembles *one* point.

But this inadequacy of the definition is not the interesting thing.[3] What is interesting is that Euclid does not make use of this definition in his work, even when that work is wholly occupied with points, when all the figures already imply them and at times are explicit about some of them, such as the intersection of two straight lines, the vertex of angles, the equidistance of parallels which are parallel from point to point, the center of the circumference and its intersection with the

3. As is well known, Aristotle (in different works) proposes two opposite routes for arriving at the first geometric concepts: the one which begins with the point, from it to the line, from that to the surface, and so on; the other which starts from the solid and arrives at the point as the extremity of the line. In present day geometry, which is stricter, the point is defined as a "precise place."

tangent, and so on.[4] On the other hand, if Euclid had set forth his method and formulated the theory of his theory, it would surely, given certain variations, have coincided with Aristotle's doctrine about science. Because of this the book begins with 23 or 25 definitions. This contradiction is understandable if we note that these definitions define "things," that is to say, they transcribe their composition into names, and limit themselves to that. Now then, when the defined thing is as simple and as close at hand as the point, the line, the angle, and so on, it is, for all practical purposes, the same whether one has the thing itself before one, or its definition, and it does not matter if the definition is inadequate.

In saying "for all practical purposes" we have introduced into our mental progression a concept which has a foreign aspect. Geometry is pure theory. What is the significance of "practice" in theorizing? Nothing less than this: all theory, except the theory of theory, is a practice. Geometry *produces* its theorems without need to think about *how* it proceeds, without necessarily taking into account what is the logical form of its theorizing. This is what I call—and it does not seem inappropriate—proceeding practically, like a geometrician. Now this distinction between reflecting on theory—or the theory of theory—and the *practice* of theory, shows us a science with two different aspects, one superimposed on the other.[5]

This reminds us that there is room for another explanation of the aforesaid contradiction, an explanation which we cannot make at the moment without babbling in confusion, giving it only the value of a mere possibility. It is as follows: once philosophy discovered a theoretical plan, the Greek mathematicians, in producing their science, behaved (without real-

4. Leibnitz, likewise, notes that the Euclidean definition of straight line is erroneous, but fortunately he also makes no use of it.

5. For me, this theoretical practicality is characteristic of the great creator of science as contrasted with the philosopher. The greater part of the sciences have been engendered in a state which we might call "theoretical somnambulism." Later on, apropos of Newton, I will explain this a little better.

izing it) according to the method which mathematics demands; this coincides in part with the philosophical method; hence exact science could be constructed with its aid and under its discipline. But in another good sense the actual method which gives mathematics its peculiar theoretical virtue is different from that of philosophy. This is the reason, for example, why Plato in the *Theaetetus* makes Theodorus say that he has retired from philosophy and is busy only with mathematics.

This hypothetical duality which I suggest would have caused a curious mixture or interpenetration of the two ways of thinking. The philosophical way, defined and announced by the philosophers, was placed like a carapace or *camouflage* over the actual way of the mathematicians, who had not reflected on what was peculiar to their method. This combination would have lasted up to Descartes, who freed the mathematicians from their Aristotelian shell. The philosophical *camouflage* of mathematics, not operating in the reality of mathematical production, would nevertheless have had a substantial influence on it; that is, a negative influence—and we shall soon see why—that of impeding the expansion of mathematics, obliging it to pretend that it was thinking about "things," and that it thought about them by the abstraction of what is common, in terms of genera and species.[6]

I could do no less than anticipate this, though even now it may not be well understood, because I must make it clear that out of this contradiction—namely, the principal definition is not used, and, nevertheless, it must be made clear

---

6. I cannot accept Solmsen's diagnosis when he says in the work cited (*Die Entwicklung der Aristotelischen Logik und Rhetorik, 1929*): "The Apodicta of Aristotle, which is nothing but a methodology of mathematics, and which is constantly and on every side oriented in the practice of those sciences. . . ." Neither does the Aristotelian theory match exactly the practice of those sciences, nor is this same practice found in the time of Aristotle, especially in what is most important to him, which is the common character or property of the principles. And the fact is that some of the most interesting things in Solmsen's book are the places where he brings in concrete data on the still fluid state of mathematical practice.

despite its obvious state of disorder—it is possible to provide another inverse explanation.

Let us assume that instead of defining the thing "point," which is, or now pretends, "to be there" by itself, we define x to be in no way determined by itself; therefore, it is not anything which "is there." What x may be, we are going to determine ourselves, this time abstractly, i.e., not by trying to reproduce a reality which existed prior to our definition, but on the contrary, by creating it *with* our definition—*a nihilo*, as it were. In this case x will consist exclusively and unquestionably in what we wish to make it reveal; in view of this, x will be a pure concept of our own, with no mystery about it, without any possible inadequacy between it and its concept, since our concept antedates it and is going to create it, establish it. Having agreed to this, let us say: x is that which has no parts.

Now the situation has changed completely. That definition can *not* be inadequate, because it makes no pretense of being adequate to anything, because it does not wish to define a thing, but to make a mere visible sign, x, the basis for a pure concept. This definition does not pretend to be—nor can it be—a truth. Truth about what, if there is nothing previous to it that one talks about and to which one refers? It is, if you wish, a purely nominal definition. It makes no difference if, in place of x, we choose any other sign whatever—*a* or *z* or even the sign *point*. This word as used here does not mean the thing "point" but the concept "that which has no parts." We can then say, with a meaning which is radically different from the earlier one: a point is that which has no parts. It is enough that in geometry, whenever we have to speak of a point, we do it with reference to something—no matter what —as having no parts; that is to simply say, we do not attribute to it any predicate which implies "having parts." Now it does not matter to us that the soul, God, and so on, may be things without parts, because now the soul, God, and so on, will be for us neither more nor less than "points."

This definition is arbitrary—that is, independent in respect to something which may be anything at all—but once it is given effect, we lose our freedom of choice with respect to it, and we engage ourselves not to use the sign point in our theory, except when it refers to something which, in fact, has no parts. As a result, this definition defines not a thing which existed earlier, but rather our own subsequent mental behavior.

Nor do I assume for one moment that Euclid would have believed that he had given this meaning to his definition of the point. No, he defined it, with perfectly good faith, in the Aristotelian sense of defining things by way of genera and species. But it is a fact that he does not make use of that definition as such, and it is also a fact that he always behaves toward what is called "point" by attributing to it an absence of parts, *despite the fact* that all the points he sees and all those that he imagines have parts.

At the beginning of the book he defined the thing "point," which, as a thing, is indefinable and is something contradictory, therefore, impossible; but in the rest of his work he behaves as if his definition had been nominal and arbitrary, that is, carrying it along without worrying whether there could be things of this kind or not. Everything happens, then, *as if* Euclid, beneath the *camouflage* of an essential definition (of a thing), was using only a nominal definition of mental, or purely logical, behavior. With this we end the present episode: the nominal definition gives us a concept, which will not be of any one thing, but which, on the other hand, is truly and strictly a *term;* therefore, exact and unequivocal; therefore, logical *sensu stricto* (Chapter 9).

It was useful here to take this step in advance, but once having taken it we must relegate it to the background of our present horizon, so that, without intervening actively in what follows, it remains clear as a term in contraposition to what is the official Euclidean-Aristotelian definition, insofar as it is a *principle* of pre-Cartesian deductive theory.

15
"Evidence" in Euclid's Axioms

THE DEFINITIONS that Euclid framed must enunciate truths because they are *principles*, they are the primary sources and they give forth truth. Their truth is not existential, that is to say, they do not posit existence, do not say that there should be the things they define; but although they are not mere indicators of intuitions to be realized by us, it is clear that—contrary to the opinion of Aristotle—they do suppose these existences. But it is certain that the definitions explicitly posit only consistencies, they say what the thing consists of.

But we can do nothing with the things and their composition which the definitions set before us, nor can we say anything geometrical about them. In order to do this we must bring in principles of another type—the axioms.

Let us proceed as before. Let us examine, as an example, one of the axioms among those cited.

Axiom VIII says: Magnitudes which coincide with each other, that is, which fill exactly the same space, are equal.

What does that mean? Provisionally, it is *also* a definition like the others. The only difference is that it does not, as they do, define a "thing," but rather a "relation." A relation differs, above all, from a thing in that, besides the rational moment itself, at least two other things intervene. When, as in the present case, it is a matter of relation which we find *in the things* themselves, the relation pertains to the same ambit of *thing-ness* or "reality" as theirs, and hence it will be not a thing but something *thing-like*.

Axiom VIII defines the relationship of equality in a more peremptory way; it says that the things called "magnitudes" coincide, that is, that they fill exactly the same space. Let us put aside here, in parentheses as it were, our surprise at being suddenly brought face to face with "magnitudes," something which certainly has not been defined for us previously. The axiom gives us to understand that it deals with "somethings that fill space"—therefore with extensions—and declares that *if* the space they fill is the same, then those magnitudinous somethings acquire the property of being equal. That is to say, equality here means "perfect spatial coincidence," the sameness of space which two or more things exhibit. It is clear enough that equality is something thing-like. The axiom-definition makes it consist of something which is seen with the eyes.

But on hearing this most people, giving themselves ridiculous airs of being in the secret, hasten to make it clear that the equality of which geometry speaks is not the kind which can be seen with the eyes; that equality is only approximate, whereas Euclid states, textually, that the coincidence or congruence of two straight lines must be "exact." To which I reply with no less celerity by asking where Euclid gets that coincidence in which equality consists if not from the act of seeing. But the know-it-all is already prepared, and he answers me without hesitation that it is drawn from that internal vision which is intuition and not from external ocular vision. Then I have no choice but to launch the first assault against this term, especially since it is very important to me.

In previous pages I have used it frequently in view of the inveterate use which is made of it in the theory of science. I once said in passing that no one before Husserl had achieved such a controlled clarification of so decisive a term. But I did not say that his definition would be sufficient, nor am I now going to develop the problem of intuition in its entirety. From now on we have no choice but to elucidate this problem in successive assaults. This is the first.

I would ask the know-it-all to tell me what, according to him, is that intuition from which Euclid extracts the *exact* coincidence which he calls equality. The fact is that Descartes and Leibnitz, more modest, were content to talk rather of imagination than of intuition. To each of them *intuitus* means precisely the most purely conceptual or intellectual mental act, that is to say, the act farthest from intuition in the sense which the smart boy gives it. Imagination is not a vague entity but a trustworthy personage which can be captured; it is in fact the internal or non-ocular vision which we have of our own imaginary world. Ocular vision presents us with the forms of things as it chooses. Over these forms we have very little power. To animate or modify them takes a great deal of effort on our part and in many cases this is all in vain. But ocular visions, after they are over, leave in our minds their "doubles," which are images. Images reproduce vision, but freeing them of many of their characteristics. They are normally less vivid and less detailed; but on the other hand, within certain limits, they are always at our disposal; within those limits we can call them into being, we can modify them, we can break up their forms and combine them at will; in short we can transform them. Imagination is the kingdom of transfiguration or metamorphosis, which in turn is an attribute of the gods. This malleability and docility of the image is due to its reduced vigor, its tenuity. It gains with what it loses, but it loses with what it gains. The image is docile because it is asthenic, frail, spectral.[1] *The image, because of its greater tenuity, is unquestionably less precise than is ocular vision.*

Imagination is a marvellous tool for the geometrician. It is the equivalent of always having something like a blackboard in one's own head. At any moment we can imagine a horizontal straight line at whose median point we introduce another straight line slightly inclined toward the first one, thereby forming a minimal angle on its right side. Then, merely by an act of will, we raise that straight line and see with our inner eyes—those imaginary eyes of our imaginary world—how the angles forming as it rises are successively greater until they reach a "certain point" at which the angle

---

1. Thus Aristotle, literally: ἡ δὲ φαντασία ἐστὶν αἴθησις τις ἀσθενής: "Fantasy is an asthenic sensation" (*aesthenés*) (*Rhetoric*, I, II).

is greatest; then the line begins to descend on the other side, making angles which in turn are successively smaller. In what I have just said there is an impropriety: it is false that we see the straight line reach "a certain point" at which it forms the maximum angle which is a right angle. That point does not stand out, it is not a "certain point." The most we can say, in order to state precisely what we see, is that there is a "group of points," whose outline is blurred; on passing through this the line forms a right angle. The "certain point" is in reality a small galaxy of points, what we might call a "geometric quasiplace" within which, in fact, we know exactly that the "certain point" lies. Note that we gain the right to affirm that we know this exactly *because* what we thus know is itself inexact and only approximate.[2] What appears most clear in intuition is first the increase and then the decrease of the angle which the straight line forms, first on one side and then on the other. The very thing that what we cannot see clearly—far from it—is the right angle itself; it was in order to see this that we had to imagine all that business of a figure and its movement. There is no doubt that by making an apparatus out of fine metal and drawing straight lines under a microscope we might be able to determine by *ocular vision* with much greater precision that "certain point" at which the straight line becomes perpendicular. Nevertheless, geometry was created out of those imaginings and not by means of these pieces of apparatus.[3] Hence, the role in geometry of both ocular vision and "interior vision," or imagination, cannot be referred either to precision or "exactitude." The tools of precise measurement, the rule and the compass, do not serve geometry better than the drawings on

2. Let me record, because it echoes what has been said, that when I was a boy the bull-ring reports of *La Correspondencia de España*, giving an account of the goring suffered by a bullfighter, said that "the horn produced a wound of little more than three short inches."

3. And not because it has not been tried. Remember the geodesic measurements which Gauss undertook a century and a half ago in order to resolve doubts about a theorem.

the blackboard; these in turn do not serve the *ratio geometrica* directly either, but they do serve imagination, and it is this, in the final analysis, which *serves* reason directly.

But the know-it-all does not yield to this; he will say that intuition, the origin of exactitude, is neither ocular vision nor imagination, but *pure intuition*. We owe this concept to Kant. It is one of those hyperbolic concepts which appear in philosophy, and for the very fact that they are hyperbolic they enjoy the best of good fortune, are installed on the thrones of theory as legitimate rulers, and hang on for centuries and centuries before abdicating.

Intuition is a genus which has many species. One is ocular vision, another is imagination. So nothing is to be gained by setting up vision in opposition to intuition. But one pretends, at least, that "pure intuition" is another species of intuition. While vision and imagination are both sufficiently identifiable psychic phenomena, we have no identity card for pure intuition. We do not know in what dimension of the mind it exists, nor what its attributes are. We have only its name, which aims to be a concept but does not achieve this because it is a rounded square. All the species of intuition which can be recognized and seized upon are impure, i.e., imprecise and inexact, while we understand this word to mean something which is opposed to pure intellection, to the *intuitus* of Descartes and Leibnitz. The latter, perhaps, might be truly pure; perhaps there might be an "intellectual intuition," which Kent proposed as a problematical concept, essentially superhuman, but which Fichte and Schelling brought into this world and humanized.

But in traditional Euclidean geometry, intuition is treated not as intellection, but as vision; a certain kind of vision, ethereal as you like, but vision. Now then, there is no such thing, and there is nothing more to be said if by *pure* intuition one understands pure *intuition*. In Kant the purity of his idea of pure intuition refers to its object rather than to the intuition. Intuition of space is pure, in his judgment, because on perceiving an extensive thing through intuition—impurely but effectively—we abstract from it everything that is not space and attend solely to pure space. This is the true meaning of this term, but that is not to say that it has meaning. And here ends the first assault.[4]

Let us now turn to Euclid and his "equality," which consists of the vision of the coincidence between two lines, which we call a *thing-like* equality. This is in fact imprecise and only approximated. Against it the know-it-all leaps up in front of me. Let us settle this question: considering the exactitude of which Euclid's geometry is capable—now I am not talking of all "Euclidean geometry"—does it matter very much that its equality is inexact? In the expression "that *exactly* fills the same space," let us substitute "approximately" for "exactly," and let us always do the same thing in the rest of the theory wherever that word is used, or others implying its idea. Then the point becomes a "group of points within vague limits"; consequently, the straight line will have a certain vague thickness, like a fluorescence of points, like a tube of neon gas, and so on. Will the theorems of that geometry thereby cease to be true, *exactly* true? Obviously not. Furthermore, *if* Euclid's geometry—as unquestionably happens in its historic form—defines equality by handing us over to intuition, his theorems will possess exact truth only if the things of which he speaks are understood to be *only approximated,* and vice versa; if by a line one is to understand *exactly* a line, and by equality, *exact* equality, then Euclid's geometry is only approximate. The reality in that one is as good as the other, for in both cases Euclid's geometry has enough validity for all the uses for which it is destined. And if it is not valid for some of them, like the great cosmic distances or the subatomic minima, this is not because Euclid's geometry is either exact or only approximate, but because it is *Euclidean* geometry; that is to say, for reasons which are completely foreign to the present theme and which we will briefly mention later. Without going into the question now we already see its negative side clearly:

4. The *lapsus* of Kant to which I alluded earlier in this book is due to the hyperbolic character of this concept.

that exactitude is the task neither of precision in measurements nor, therefore, of intuition. In the end may the result not be that there is nothing exact in the Universe, except exact speech—ἀκριβῆ λέγειν—(*akribê légein*)—or logic. In which case exactitude would be a matter for conversation although not, perforce, for café talk.

16
Aristotle and the
"Transcendental Deduction"
of Principles

Axiom VIII defines equality as a relation, but that is what makes it an axiom. Besides discovering for us what equality consists of, it affirms that this is a relative or relational quality which magnitudes possess; and it is as if it said that every magnitude is equal to some other magnitude. I insist that we do not know officially what magnitude is, but it goes without saying that pertaining to it are the "classes of things" appearing in previous definitions—therefore the line, the straight line, the angle, and so on. The problem remains unsolved, the enigma of the point which, having no magnitude of its own, is the thing of which magnitudes are composed. Later, they will say that exact thinking consists in not thinking what is contradictory, even though we have here the exemplary science which has been valid for 20 centuries as the prototype of exact thinking, of logical thinking, and whose first principle from which all the rest derive is a contradiction which injects itself into the entire body of the doctrine. The point is an element of the line, the line of the surface, the surface of the solid. This gives rise to innumerable paradoxes. Axiom VIII, itself, immediately poses this one: that it is not valid for points because, since these have no magnitude, they cannot be geometrically equal, and if they are not equal, neither can their components be—the lines, surfaces, and so on; that is, the magnitudes.

The question is most serious because all the other axioms except Axiom X, *insofar as they are understood geometrically*, imply that notion of equality. Axiom X, as is well known, is not one of Euclid's; it was introduced later, and in the system of Euclidean axioms it represents a foreign body. The others define and affirm other relations of magnitudes: inequality, being double, one being the half of the other; in short, having that relation of the part to the whole on which the relations of being greater and being less are founded.[1] But, as I have said, these latter do not interest us for their particular content, and this observation as to the lack of order between axioms and definitions has, in showing how they clash with each other, no other purpose than to bring out this most obvious warning: that the axioms define relations between some things which have been previously defined without reference in the least to relations into which those things are going to make them enter. Now a very precise meaning—I do not say it is the principal one—can be understood in my phrase: "the traditional way of thinking defines magnitudes as things," *not* as relations. Each magnitude is an absolute reality which is in the concrete thing, belonging to it and therefore absolute. The magnitude in itself is not equal, greater or less than another; these relational qualities follow as a mind compares it mentally with other magnitudes.[2]

1. At the same time some axioms regulate certain operations with magnitudes which we can permit ourselves: adding, subtracting, and so on. But in this study it is neither possible nor useful to clarify and discuss what is an "operation" in geometry, and more generally in mathematics.

2. Even so, one would have to distinguish the degree of proximity in which those relational qualities can be attributed to it. For Aristotle, only equality and inequality are naturally harmonious. To be greater and less is not only a relation, but is in turn a relative relation; that is, it is relative to the unity of measure which is chosen *arbitrarily* and which therefore cannot assign a value to any natural property. Hence, one thing compared quantitatively with two others can at the same time be greater and less. Well now, the quantity which a thing has in itself, and not *secundum dici*—the quantity as "thing in a thing"—cannot at the same time be both greater and less; neither can it, therefore, be properly greater or less. The measure is relative to the unity with which one measures, but there is no magnitude at our disposition which in itself, i.e., in its own reality or consistency may be a unity. I suppose—though I have never seen it anywhere—that some Scholastic has

It is not likely that Euclid or anyone else, while this way of thinking prevailed, saw that these axioms included definitions, because their role was not this but another, in a certain way the opposite. What was most evident in them was their condition as truths needing no proofs, manifest in themselves; in short, *first principles*. Their importance in the organism of the deductive theory is, then, incomparable. It would appear natural for maximum and detailed attention to be dedicated to the analysis: first, of the concrete meaning of the content or *dictum* of each of them; second, of what that aspect of indubitable truth, of "truth in itself" which they offer us, consists internally. But, false though it may seem, this has never been done. The first has had almost no attention, the second very little, never getting to the basic question: the origin of that strange "truth in itself." Even that little which has been done was all done by Aristotle, but if the number of pages he devotes to demonstration in both *analytical* works is compared it is surprising how few he devotes to the principles of demonstration. It is as though the very matter which in this case had to be explained—the existence of truths *per se notae*, that is, truths which once understood are already true and without further ado—dissuaded thinkers from its investigation, as if any attempt to undertake this might seem to be the equivalent of trying to prove it, and therefore somewhat contradictory. Although he was less of a genius, less fundamental than Plato, Aristotle is the very opposite of cunning. He goes straight at problems like a bull to a red rag. More than this, for him all philosophical investigation starts with an enthusiastic and passionate search for problems, a kind of preliminary choosing of the bulls to be fought, an operation called *aporética* or "questionnaire."

But in the matter of discussing or analyzing the character

---

drawn forth the consequence which this permits: for God, who has the corporeal Universe completely in view, quantities are absolutely greater or less, because then there is a true unity of measure, namely, the whole Universe, in relation to which magnitudes are arranged *per se* as greater or lesser parts.

of "truth" connected with principles he was more than a little deficient, and he seems to us always a bit confused. Because the fact is that he sees the problematical aspect of this truth, and he sees that it is necessary somehow to discover its basis, even though this may not take the shape of a formal demonstration. And actually that is what he does, but always in a hurry, with the air of one who would not want to stop to face the question. *It is in fact false to say that Aristotle does not prove the truth of the first unprovable principles.*[3] What happens is that this proof does not turn on the particular content of each principle, but on the general character of its truth, that is, on their condition as principles. His proof of these can be stated in an amusing tongue-twister. It would go like this: principles are true not because they might be true, but because they have to be true, because it is necessary that they be true. The expressions which he actually uses any number of times are these: there must be truths which are unproved and unprovable because otherwise science, that is proof, would be impossible.

Few things reveal better and more deeply what history is, than the fact that not until Descartes—and in a methodical way, not until Kant—was any attention focussed on this thought, which is incomparably the most important in the Aristotelian doctrine, for principles depend on it and everything else depends on principles. It can be formulated equivalently as the "principle of principles," therefore as the first principle of knowledge—and through this of things—the "principle of the possibility of knowledge," or of "that science must be possible."[4]

3. Despite the attacks against those who demand that everything be proved,—attacks which are altogether too numerous and frequently insulting for them not to reveal that there is a bad feeling toward the matter and that there is something wrong with it. We will soon see something of this.

4. This does not mean to say that Kant, and much less Descartes, would see even from a distance that Aristotle had already formulated the "transcendental deduction"—thus Kant names this argument—of principles. I refer to the fact that without presuming on what is already in Aristotle, they practiced it.

That Aristotle occasionally entertained this thought is beyond question; it is no less certain that, in spite of having
done so, he did not stop to face up to it, did not reflect on it,
and did not notice that out of it burst a "way of thinking"
which was *basically* different from his own and from that
current in his time. This means in effect—and raised at least
to the third power—a total inversion of his doctrine: first,
because it makes truth about Being depend on what is *true
only* for thinking;[5] second, because the reality or true actuality of knowledge is founded on its possibility, and for
this way of thinking it is absurd that the "act" should be
founded on the "capacity"; third, because it annihilates the
ancient idea of deductive theory, turning its back completely
on what was understood by principle. If this is "proved"
because it makes science possible, that is, because consequences
are derived from it, then it is these which prove the principle.
With this we have a vicious circular proof, a *petitio principii*
which in this case is titular.[6]

Now then, the reform which Descartes initiated, which
Leibnitz developed, and which has been established for nearly
a century—hence the *modern* idea of deductive theory—consists formally in committing that *petitio principii*. Long ago,
a principle was that which imposes itself by itself and which
neither can nor has to ask for anything. So the difference be-

5. Being consists in what the first principles say and what is derived
from them. But if it should result that those first principles are true,
because thinking needs them to construct its science, this means that
from the first principles we do not derive Being as it is in itself, but
that we manufacture it *ad usum Delphinis*, to the measure of our knowledge. Which is pure Kantianism.
6. A good example of how, in Suárez, seriousness, limitation and caution go hand in hand can be seen in the fact that where in his *Index
locupletissimus in Metaphysicam Aristotelis* he reaches the proof of the
principle of contradiction, he says simply, curling up like a hedgehog,
that "in these five chapters there is nothing that offers any special usefulness." His companion of the Fonseca Order, on the other hand, gives
this argument great importance (*Com. Conimbricensis in 4 Metaph.*,
Quaestio 16). Suárez despises this attitude of Fonseca in giving importance to a proof which goes only *per extrinsecum medium* (*Disp.* III,
Sec. II, 9).

tween one way of thinking and the other, turns on what is understood by principle. From here on, since our theme is that very "principle-ism" of Leibnitz, we must follow all these twists and turns.

According to ancient epistemology that which is the principle for thinking: πρότερον πρὸς ἡμᾶς—*próteron pròs hemâs*—is *not* the principle for knowledge (thinking the real), but thinking must discover what is the principle for the real: πρότερον τῇ φύσει—*próteron tê physei*—and that will be the authentic principle for knowledge. The ancients started their thinking from Being, while the moderns, beginning with Descartes, start their thinking from thought, from "ideas." Hence Descartes initiated a new philosophy, and with it a new age, when he said these words in his *Remarques aux Septiemes Objections* (I copy from the version that his friend Clerselier gave in 1661): "*La maxime 'Du connaître à l'être la conséquence n'est pas bonne,' est entièrement fausse. Car, quoiqu'il soit vrai que pour connaître l'essence d'une chose il ne s'ensuive pas que cette chose existe, et que pour penser connaître une chose il ne s'ensuive pas qu'elle soit, s'il est possible que nous soyons en cela trompés, il est vrai néamoins que 'du connaître a l'être la conséquence est bonne,' parce qu'il est impossible que nous connaissions une chose si elle n'est, en effet, comme nous la connaissons, à savoir, existante si nous concevons qu'elle existe, ou bien de telle ou telle nature, s'il n'y a que sa nature qui nous soit connue.*"

17

The "Implicit Axioms" in Euclid—
Common Axioms, and
"Proper" Axioms

WHAT MAY BE EVIDENT in Euclid's Axiom VIII is not well understood, and even less so is what constitutes his evidence. What is clearest in it is what it has as definition and not as axiom, while its definition of equality is not properly a definition but a warning of the intuitive signal by which we will recognize that two magnitudes meet in the relation of equality. But here there is nothing evident except what is at most a tautology: I call equality the coinciding of two magnitudes; if I now add that two magnitudes which coincide are equal I add nothing, for this is equivalent to saying that "two coinciding magnitudes are coinciding magnitudes." The meaning has to be squeezed to get anything like an axiom out of this. Thus, I came earlier to surmising benevolently that this means that every magnitude is equal to some other magnitude. But granting that this may be the meaning of the axiom it contains no evidence of it, and even less is there evidence originating from intuition.[1]

It is not evident because it implies too many things which do not appear in it and are, therefore, not evident in it. To attribute to every magnitude a possible equality with some

---

1. Leibnitz modifies this axiom of Euclid by breaking it down into a definition and an axiom as such. . . . "*Definitio: aequalia sunt quae sibi substitui possunt salve Magnitudine. Axioma identicum: unumquodque (magnitudine praeditum) sibi ipsi aequale est.*" *Die Philosophischen Schriften von G. W. Leibniz* (C. J. Gerhardt, Berlin, 1887), Vol. III, p. 258. Leibnitz prefers the algebraic notion of substitutability to the intuitive idea of coincidence.

other one—that is, its possible *coinciding* with another—assumes attributing to every magnitude the possibility of being *transported* from where it is to the position in space where the other one is, and thus being *superimposed* on it. In fact Euclid's *Elements* are constantly performing transpositions or displacements and superpositions. Nevertheless, we are not told anywhere how or why these two operations are possible —because they certainly are operations, no more, no less, in the same sense as are adding, subtracting, and so on, except that the former are specifically geometric. Why are we not told this? Because it is judged *too* evident a thing that every magnitude can be displaced and superimposed on another, the result being equality or inequality. But, then, *superposition* is an axiom, and Euclid in his work does in fact use various axioms like this which are not enunciated and which, therefore, have in modern times been called "implicit axioms."

What one does not see is why these remain implicit while others are as explicit as though in a glass coach. Only one explanation comes to mind, namely, that the possibility of displacement and superposition seems even more evident than the expressed axioms, that it enjoys the position of arch-evidence. In fact, we can take this as an outstanding example of what is called evident, so that what results from its evidence will be valid for the rest of the axioms.

Thus, we have Axiom VIII implying the "axioms of displacement and superposition"; therefore, it is not as much of a *first* principle as it pretends to be. It drops in rank, but are these implicit and implied axioms as evident as they are at first judged to be? In their turn they make quite a few assumptions, for example, that a magnitude when moving through space in the process of displacement is not deformed. This assumes that it is rigid (a new axiom on the rigidity or lack of variation in the figure), and it also assumes that the space through which it passes and that to which it is taken are homogeneous with respect to the initial one; hence, an axiom concerning the homogeneity of space.

The more these mutually interdependent axioms appear to be first principles, and therefore unproved and unprovable according to the traditional way of thinking, the deeper the level of their implication. Now then, Poincaré noted in his study *Des Fondaments de la Géometrie* that displacement and superposition are no more than secondary theorems, and therefore it is easily proved that they belong to one of the highest and most purely logical (i.e., least intuitive) disciplines in all mathematics, the transformation groups. Arch-evidence and arch-truth "in themselves" become a modest result of logical proof.

This is enough to take away prestige from every idea of the principle as evidence and thus to put in question the character of having truth of its own, not received from proof, which gave it the rank of *first principle*. Here we begin to see that this rank and this condition, apparently absolute, are very relative, and that, therefore, yesterday's principle becomes today's mere theorem; that is to say, in the scale of the theoretical hierarchy the principle rises and falls, it is mobile, it is like a Cartesian demon of doubt.

Given the clarity with which the case presents itself, the possibility of displacement and superposition affords an excellent opportunity to investigate how a logical truth, i.e., one founded on reason or proof, can for centuries and centuries be considered as evident. In this case the evidence is made from what is most contrary to it, from the condensation and, as it were, the *impasto* of a mass of proofs; from clear reasoning about spatial relations, so elemental that it did not occur to man until recently to convert them into problems, to theorize about them, to prove them. But as this question does not affect our theme we put it aside, leaving it barely touched upon.

In order to simplify the orderly progress of our study, which in itself is already complicated enough, I have managed to concentrate in the analysis of a single axiom all the questions and the sides which pertain to the general condition of all of them. Nevertheless there is one point in the Euclidean system of axioms which is not clear unless we compare some of the axioms with others, for example this Axiom VIII with Axiom I.

Axiom I says "things equal to the same thing are equal to each other." As can be seen, this expresses a specific property which enjoys the relation of equality—that of being transitive, passing from two terms to another two when one of them is common. The thing in itself is of no interest to our theme. On the other hand, the indication that the term "equal" is used here, although equality has not yet been defined for us, puts us on the alert. This alert is intensified when we observe that in the axioms which follow, up to Axiom VIII, there is also talk of equal or unequal without previous clarification of these relations. The definition of equality finally emerges in Axiom VIII, which we have already studied. How is this explained?

At first sight it is a very simple matter. Axiom I speaks of equal things, but does not speak especially of *magnitudes* or of quantities continuous or extensive. It is an axiom which has the same value for these as for numbers or discrete quantities, and perhaps for anything else in the Universe.[2] The relationship of "equality" attributed to these things is not magnitudinal, it is not geometric, but is more generic. In Axiom VIII the generic meaning of equality narrows down to its specific extensive or geometric meaning. There are, then, two classes of equality: equality between any things whatsoever and equality between spatial things. This in turn shows us that among Euclid's axioms two classes must be distinguished: those which are valid only in geometry, because they refer to continuous magnitudes, and those which have a common character.

Here we must inevitably adduce a long quotation from

2. For Duns Scotus equality and inequality are no less than transcendent (*Opus Oxoniense*, lib. I, dist. 19, quaest. 1 n. 2). Aristotle seems to think the same (*Metaphysics*, IV, 4, 1005 to 22). But it is extremely difficult to give precise Aristotelian meaning to these words. They are in contradiction to what follows.

Aristotle. In the first book of his *Posterior Analytics* he says: [3] "Among the principles of which the demonstrative sciences make use (*deductive theorems*) some are peculiar to each science and others are common, but *common in the sense of analogous,* their use being limited to the genus which is the province of the science in question. For example, the definitions of line and straight line are principles; common principles are propositions such as "if two equal things are subtracted from two equal things the remainders are equal." But the application of each of these common principles is sufficient —ἱκανόν, *hikanón*—when it is limited to the genus in question, *because it will have the same value* even if not used in its universality but applied—in geometry, for example—to magnitudes alone, or in arithmetic, only to numbers.[4] The context of the three preceding chapters in Aristotle's work, and the example which by chance he adduces, and even the first part of the paragraph, make us understand without hesitation that these common principles are the axioms. I say this because the second part of the quotation, where the logical function [5] of the common principle is set forth concretely, is imprecise and rather *flou.* Attending exclusively to this we would gather that a common principle, such as that used here as an example, *can* be an axiom or a principle of a science, but

3. 1, 10, 76 to 37 ff.
4. This paragraph from Aristotle was translated by G. R. G. Mure in 1931, for the Oxford English edition of Aristotle's works, as follows: "Of the basic truths used in the demonstrative sciences some are peculiar to each science, and some are common, but common only in the sense of being analogous, being of use only in so far as they fall within the genus constituting the province of the science in question. Peculiar truths are, e.g., the definition of line and straight; common truths are such as 'take equals from equals and equals remain.' Only so much of these common truths is required as falls within the genus in question; for a truth of this kind will have the same force even if not used generally but applied by the geometer only to magnitudes, or by the arithmetician only to numbers" [*Translator's note*].
5. Exactly the same uncertainty appears in another canonical place when he talks of principles—and here he refers *specially* to none less than those that concern contradiction and the excluded middle (Metaphysics, IV, 3, 1005ª 24).

that it is *enough* to use it narrowed down to the genus with which one is concerned—to magnitude *or* to number. But this is not at all what Aristotle is thinking and has made clear to us in Chapter VII. In his judgment the common principle *cannot serve* to prove anything in geometry or in arithmetic. The reason is that the term "equal," which is a logical genus, divides its meaning between two logical species: equal in space and equal in number. *These logical species are what Aristotle calls genera.* Hence, it leads to error to say that for proof it is *enough* to narrow the common principle down into its own principle—ἴδιον—(*idion*) "idiot," and to base this affirmation on the fact that both forms of the principle *have the same value or do the same thing* ταὐτὸ γὰρ ποιήσει. This last is a plain error. The duplicity of the concept *equality* divided between two species would render illogical the syllogisms or proofs created with the common principle as major premise, since they would in many cases combat paralogisms or *quaterniones terminorum.*

We have reached the point of neuralgia in all this way of thinking. This consists, as we have already said,[6] in starting with things of the senses and extracting from them by commonistic abstraction concepts which are made up of what there is in each one of them in common with others. This gives the concept its commonal pseudo-universality of the "one in the many," or κατὰ παντός—*katà pantós*. On the other hand, the content of the concept originating in *each* sense-perceptible thing continues to be sense-perceptible, whether it be an extract or, as is customarily said, an abstract. On these "sensible" or "sensual" concepts the commonal abstraction acts again and finds, for example, that some of them anew contain something in common. The concept of the common element among other concepts is called a "genus" and the others are called "species." To be a genus or to be a species

6. It would not make sense to try to develop here all the questions which the traditional Aristotelio-Scholastic method poses. Our titular theme is limited to the way of thinking in the exact sciences.

is a relation between concepts as such,[7] and therefore logical.[8] This means that the characters genus and species are merely relative. The genus results when the common element is isolated from the species. *Hence, it leaves outside itself a part of what constitutes each species.* For these, all the truths would be valid that are valid for the concept which *in each case* we consider a genus. When we attribute to a species those truths *peculiar* to the genus, we are speaking "in general," and this operation is called "generalization." *Nor is it, then, generalizing to attribute to the genus the truths peculiar to the genus without attributing them to the species.* From this it follows that to generalize *is not* to know the species, because these, if they communicate or participate in the genus, may also differ from it among themselves. Triangle, square, circle all participate in the genus "lineal figure," but the whole— ὅλον, *hólon*—of each one cannot be reduced to that genus, and they differ among themselves—the triangle has three angles, the square has four, and the circle none. The species are intractable toward the genus, they escape from it, they are not anticipated in it, but each one adds something new, and this new part is always a return to beginning from the principle.[9] Hence, the genus cannot be a principle of the species. These cannot be deduced or derived from it. Aristotle should not

7. This is the great step which Aristotle took beyond Plato. In Plato there is no relation which is only logical, but this is existential of itself— ontological. But the reader who is little versed in ancient philosophy should disregard this question.

8. Nothing makes clearer the degree of ontology in Aristotelian logic than that a relation as purely logical as this one, has in his doctrine a value of reality rather than being conceptual.

9. The scholastic manuals of the present day, for example, Gredt, do not want these figures to be species, but they do not give convincing reasons. See in Aristotle the species of the number. Father Urraburu, rather, once more expresses the character of absolute novelty which the species provides when he says that "the differences are added over and above the common notion" *per modum extraneae nativae.* One cannot better emphasize the foreign, newly arrived character of the species with regard to the genus. (*Ontologia*, 1891, Vallisoletti, p. 154.) The idea and the expression are, of course, in Suárez and in Saint Thomas.

have called it "genus," because this word suggests generation and the Aristotelian genus is sterile because so is the general abstraction from which it arises.[10]

Under these conditions, in what concepts does a science, that is, a deductive theory, begin? This is the question for the basic truths of science, and what has been said shows us that these cannot be "general principles." Each species is condemned to retire within itself and, therefore, to be the beginning of itself. Thanks to containing the genus within itself, it can draw predicated or generic "universals *per se*" from that genus. The only properties to be deduced from it are those which are valid for other species of which it is the genus. This tells us once more that the true knowledge or proposition must always be originally a specific or catholic truth. This will necessarily happen with the first principles of a science, or with its *most* general principles. The result is a paradox inherent in this way of thinking, the general principles of which may not be generic, but rather logically specific, and besides, they may not be general or properly common—κοιναί.

But this difficulty arises; the species is a genus to which a difference is added and synthesized. This would lead to a situation in which, if the first concept of a science—the definitions and axioms—must already be specific, other earlier ones that are its genus would be assumed. This would mean that that science is only a derivation of another and more "general" science, and so on successively. *So there would be only a single science, a single body of knowledge, a "universal science."* This happened in the Platonic doctrine and this has been happening—at least thematically—since Descartes.

But in the Aristotelian-Scholastic way of thinking the opposite occurs. There the sciences begin with specific principles, each of them shutting itself up within itself, cutting off communication with the collaterals and looking down proudly on any other science which might seem "more general." This is clearly no whim, it is the result and the inevitable limitation

10. Aristotle takes the term from Plato, in whose doctrine and way of thinking—the dialectic—the genus actually generates the species.

of the common character of sense-perceptible things which is the Aristotelian way of thinking.

The "first" concepts—ἀρχαὶ πρῶται—of each science are the highest species to which that thinking carries the matter—πρᾶγμα. This is what circumscribes and shuts each science up within itself, hence it is called *pragmateía*.

Thus one understands the drifting, the *flou*, of those expressions in which Aristotle teaches us what the "common principles" are. On the one hand, the axiom "if two equal things are taken from two equal things the remainders are equal" seems to be equally valid for continuous and for discrete quantities, for geometry and for arithmetic. In the face of these, a principle would be truly general, since no reference to species is made in it. But by the same token, it could not be a principle either of geometry or arithmetic. That would be equivocal. Because the concept of equality used in it is uncontrollable in this way of thinking, that is to say, it does not correspond to any sense-perceptible intuition, it cannot be found in any *thing*.

Thus, we have the following strange situation—strange but consistent with this intellectual style. A generic concept of quantity exists, and Aristotle defines it in Book V of his *Metaphysics*,[11] but that concept in itself is inoperative. Geometry begins with the concept of "magnitude"—μέγεθος—*mégethos* or continuous quantity; logically speaking, therefore, with a species. Why is it the only one qualified to acquire true propositions? Because in this order it is the *ultimate common factor* which the general abstraction can find in sense-perceptible things. Pure generic quantity already rejects sensation: *pure quantity is not yet a "thing."* The same thing happens, in turn, with number, although this irritated Aristotle considerably because he seems to want it applied for its own sake to magnitude in any of its forms. The point is already like a unit, two points are like a straight line, and so on. We are in the decisive regions of this way of thinking which with him are always shadowy and not at all pellucid.

11. *Metaphysics*, V, 13, 1020ᵃ 6.

So it is that, out of those specific catholic concepts, "magnitude" and "number," a first principle for two lonely sciences is produced. As the most general species is actually within each of these, Aristotle will call them "genera" par excellence.[12]

How unclear things are here one gathers from the attitude of Suárez toward the concept of quantity *in genere*. Without accepting it, he defends as best he can the sound meaning which the Aristotelian definition *can* have *if it is not* taken as such, but rather as "*per illam descriptionem magis explicat quid hoc nomen 'quantum' significat, quam quid* proprie *et secundum suam essentiam quantitas sit*" (*Disp*. XL, Sec. I, 5). But before doing this, in order that there be no doubt, Suárez roundly denies occupying himself with the generic concept of quantity,[13] and makes it clear, as though shedding some-

---

12. And indeed they are for his doctrine insofar as they are "genera of the real," but they are not—nor in his doctrine—insofar as they are logical concepts.

13. *Ibid.* Preamble: "*quamvis autem ratio quantitatis abstrahi soleat a quantitate continua et discreta, ad maiorem tamen claritatem et brevitatem* non instituimus *disputationem de quantitate in communi sumpta, qua vix potest eius essentia et ratio in ea communitate declarari.*" Suárez had nothing of the genius about him, but he is one of the most serious thinkers who ever lived. He treats problems in depth, in the measure that scholastic rule permits him; therefore, in every decisive question he fails to enlighten us, but he exhausts all the possibilities of what he discusses, examining them in minute detail, with exemplary grace and immense calm; he adduces and analyzes all divergent opinions, and all this with marvellous lucidity. These qualities make of him the teacher *par excellence*. And this he has been—teacher of teachers. To him Leibnitz owes both his clarity and his solidity. Again and again he acknowledges the mastery of Suárez, for whom his respect is unlimited. It has been said that he was also the teacher of Descartes, because the publication of his *Disputationes Metaphysicae* was completed in 1603, and in the following year Descartes entered the Jesuit college of La Flèche, recently created as an advanced pedagogical institution determined to offer every novelty and to be *à la page*. He was there until 1612. It is doubtless very possible that Suárez' book circulated there very soon, although its divulgence seems very rapid for those days. Descartes quotes Suárez sometimes. But I must say that I do not find in Descartes the least trace of anything peculiar to Suárez, although the latter's innovations follow the thread of the Cartesian revolution closely. This makes me think—without committing myself to it—that Descartes read

thing which weighed on him, that in the book of the *Categories*, where he does not deal with merely nominal definitions, Aristotle also ignores them and *statim illum divisit incontinuam et discretam.*

The result of all this is that the "first" concepts of a science —the definitions and the axioms—are therefore, strictly speaking, logical monstrosities. Each one is, in turn, its genus and its species, since the authentic genus has no life of its own and is jumbled in the species, availing itself of the fact that genus actually plays a part in every species. Thus we get humped concepts carrying a genus on their shoulders like camels bearing their generic burden on which they feed. This can be seen very clearly in the axioms.

In the series of axioms which Euclid demonstrates (let us now leave out his "implicit axioms"), we saw that there are two classes. Now we understand their difference perfectly: some are actually common at least to arithmetic and geometry; others are exclusively and specifically geometric. But this duality reveals a lack of theoretical beauty in Euclid, because the truth is that the common or properly generic axioms function only when specific axioms are transfused with them. In order to convey their logically strict efficacy one must picture them as plastered against each other, interpenetrating and forming a homogeneous dough. Only thus are ἱκανοί

---

him when he had already constructed his own system and, moreover, that he read him badly, for he was as bad a reader as he was infrequent. On the other hand, it does seem that he studied logic in one of these two Iberians: Fonseca (*Institutionum dialecticarum, libri* VIII, 1609) or Toledo (Adam: *Vie de Descartes*). The case of Leibnitz, then, is very different because, in addition to his teaching skill, Suárez influenced Leibnitz' own doctrine deeply and concretely, and even in the most personal of it, as happens with the concept of "representation," which supports and gives coherence to his whole philosophy. Apart from the eminent qualities of Suárez, his influence as an incomparable teacher during the 17th Century is due to a most simple fact which people either ignore or, among the few who do know, usually forget, namely, that the *Disputationes Metaphysicae* was the *first treatise on Metaphysics that ever existed,* since the metaphysical books of Aristotle, the father of the infant, could not, for innumerable reasons, be considered as such.

(*hikanoí*) efficient or sufficient. To formulate them separately is an impropriety which, like many other things, reveals in Euclid a great "theoretical" carelessness and a great disinterest toward philosophy, which go perfectly with a great feeling for the *practice* of mathematics.

The matter is not, as it might seem, without importance, and because of this I had to underline the *flou* of Aristotelian expression which is dangerous for his particular doctrine. Because *if* common or generic principles could behave that way in a science, one would have lost nothing less than the distinctive character of science with respect to "demonstrative thinking"—ἀποδεικτικός λόγος—as compared with other forms of thought. This distinction was Aristotle's greatest discovery. In fact, if the common principle is used by itself—without being restricted by other specific axioms—thought ceases to be logical (scientific) and is converted into analogical (dialectic) thought while the common principle ceases to be a principle and is transformed into a "common place" or τόπος (*tópos*). From a rigorous science we end up with a vague topic; neither more nor less. So this was no light matter. Aristotle makes this clear in the first part of our quotation.[14]

Definitions, axioms, reasonings must move into the hermetically sealed ambit of a *genus* (first species in my interpretation). Only thus are they scientific. Hence, along with begging the question (*petitio principii*) and the paralogism, the third capital sin in the Aristotelian-Scholastic logic is the passing over to another genus μετάβασις εἰς ἄλλο γένος (*metábasis eis állo génos*).

14. It is worth noting the surprising fact that Aristotle does not anywhere define his idea of the *topic* in spite of the fact that this is the pivotal point in his "dialectic" and his "rhetoric." But Alexander, in his commentary on the *Topics*, preserves for us an admirable definition of the *tópos* attributed to the great Theophrastus. "The *tópos*"—he says—"is a certain principle and element from which we derive principles for *this or that subject* by means of a discursive analysis of it ἐπιστήσαντες τὴν διάνοιαν. The *tópos* is determining as circumscription περιγραφή (*perigraphé*) but undetermined with respect to each particular subject." (Alexander: *Topics*, 5, 21, 26.)

The pre-Cartesian way of thinking is characterized, then, by being thingist, commonist, sensual and idiotic.[15] Hence, its principles must be uncontrollable intuitive pieces of evidence drawn from sense-perceptory intuition. Hence, they can hardly be "general" and they continue to remain ascribed to the small clod of a pseudogenus without being able to go beyond it to others or to raise themselves to a higher generality or commonness.[16] Finally, its principles can never properly be called "first," since in the whole discipline which they inaugurate there will appear a host of new principles— the definitions and the species—which are as fully principles and as surely first as they are. I have not had time to say earlier that in pure Aristotelian orthodoxy the so-called principles of Euclid are not sufficient for a theory unless there are watertight compartments in it; the surface vis-à-vis the line must have its private principles, and the solid vis-à-vis the surface, and so on, that is to say, geometry in its turn is divided into three *pragmateias*.

Consequently, we have a way of thinking which insists very much on proof, which is proud of its syllogisms, but the fact is that each science is composed of so many principles that they are scarcely less numerous than the proofs. As "principle" means that "to think is to evidence," it now becomes transparently clear why I have set this up in opposition to the Leibnitzian way, if that can properly be characterized as "to think is to prove." [17]

15. This is not a matter of "stirring uprisings against Aristotle and his followers." There was no choice but to talk of him, because he shows the anatomy of the way of thinking in the exact sciences of his time, which for us is the interesting thing. To talk of Aristotle is a complicated thing, for there are many sides to his genius, some of them better and others worse. Thus in the matter of *idiotism* a magnificent but ill-fated intention shows through, as against the defect of the Platonic "generalizations" which never attain knowledge of the "things out there." Because of this, Aristotle demands that which is "peculiar to each thing," the *idiotic*.

16. What was said before refers to this negative influence of the philosophical method in Euclid's time.

17. Statistics should have been worked out for the number of principles which intervene in the Aristotelian *corpus* or in any treatise on

Abundance robs principles of prestige as it does princes. Those principles which Leibnitz introduced and handled seem to us numerous; so many are they that I have ventured to call him a "principle-ist." But in comparison with the pre-Cartesian doctrine his stable of principles is infinitesimal. Nevertheless, there is no impertinence in that characterization of Liebnitz, for he understands by principle something much more pure and lofty as an element in deductive theory. Aristotelianism calls anything a principle—ἀρχή or πρῶτον— even the simple empirical definition of any thing whatsoever.

The *Prior Analytics* expounds the theory of the syllogism. This theory is, in fact, the first example of deductive theory which man ever worked out in detail. It is a prodigy, and in 24 centuries it has hardly had to be retouched. But by the same token, it has been the cause of an illusion from which the human mind has also suffered for almost as many centuries. The perfection of the theory whose theme was the syllogistic form—hence, a *formal* deductive theory—was confused with its application to the sciences; that is to say, with the attempt to elaborate deductive theories on *material* themes. And then the situation changes completely; science is not only syllogism and proof, but before and rather more than this, as we have seen, it is the acquisition of principles which will make the syllogisms possible. In the formal theory of the syllogism this functions in a vacuum—which is a way of not functioning properly—because what is interesting in it is its *pure* form of functioning, and not its concrete and full functioning. In place of actual concepts, the judgments that are premises and conclusions are replaced by signs, as in algebra —*S* is *P;* all *S*'s are *P*'s; some *S*'s are not *P*'s, and so on. Syllogistical logic is in fact an algebra of concepts. It was the primogenital algebra. In it the conditions are defined which those concepts would *have* to have in order to be substituted for the *S*'s and the *P*'s so that the syllogism may function

Scholastic philosophy. With the cynicism peculiar to the impassive character of numbers, the hypertrophy of principles in that intellectual method would have been made manifest.

with precision. But how to obtain complete concepts to meet these conditions?

To this end the logic of the *Prior Analytics* has to be completed with a methodology wherein we are told how one arrives at the concepts which are the principles of the syllogism. This Aristotle does in his *Posterior Analytics*. Together, the two works yield a theory of science.[18] But this second part is not a deductive theory of principles—although some parts of it may be—nor is it in any sense at the level of the first, which does not mean that it, too, may not be awe inspiring. In Aristotle even error and inadequacy are luminous.

But, as I have indicated several times, this is not a matter of explaining what Aristotelianism is, but of taking from him only what can be considered as for the common good of philosophers and men of science in the generations that followed up to the time of Descartes. Take into account the fact that Aristotle's logic and his methodology—not his philosophy, of which we have said not a single word—are immediately adapted to general use in scientific life. It is the first *koinón* or intellectual *lingua franca* to be created in the Occident.

18. It seems that the chronological order of his output is reversed. The *Posterior Analytics*, although retouched later, shows residual signs of a state in the evolution of Aristotelian thought which precedes the wisdom of the *Prior Analytics*. The *Posterior Analytics* are closer to the dialectics of the *Topics* and the *Refutation of the Sophists*, works in which the predominating influence of Plato still endures. On all this, see the cited book of Solmsen.

18

Sensualism in the Aristotelian "Way of Thinking"

HAVING MADE THESE RESERVATIONS we have a right to arch our eyebrows high in surprise that Aristotle devoted no more than one unfinished page to the question of how those concepts which are principles are to be identified. Nevertheless, the process of arriving at concepts is for him the most important mental faculty of knowledge, more important than science or the proof which science assumes; in short, it is the most authentic and powerful form of knowing.

This is a matter of exact thinking, of a unique capacity to engender *necessarily true* propositions. This requires the greatest imaginable acuteness of intellect and it creates a conflict within the duality of dimensions—truth and logicality—which Chapter 10 made us distinguish in the concept. For the first, the concept must be valid as a concept of the being of things; for the second, it must be exact or, as we said, a *finite term*.

In Aristotle's time the "youthful character" of thought had reached the degree of maturity which makes it capable of being truly knowledge, that is, thought about what things are. It was only then, and not before, that the sciences were created. In Greece, that condition of maturity was the flower of a single day, because politics erupted that same evening, that is to say, it was made a truly political matter, and when politics is truly politics (it is the nature of politics to be violent), it becomes a destructive force; or, to put it more precisely, politics, preoccupied by its very nature with preserving one thing alone—I do not say what—destroys all the rest. It has always been this way ever since man existed.

Changes in the Hellenic world crushed the maturity of Hellenic thought at the moment when it was really about to take
shape. What went before had been only preparation, education, *Vorspiel und Tanz.* Among the effects of political
changes—rather modest at the moment but more lamentable
in the long run—was the fact that they brought about the
loss of books. This happened recently in Europe as it happened in Greece upon the death of Aristotle. The preservation of his pragmatic [1] books is traditionally due to pure
chance, thanks to the arrival in Athens—at the very moment
when they were about to disappear—of the first "dictator"
who had ever appeared in the Occident and also the most
"elegant" one who ever existed—Publius Cornelius Sylla. He
took possession of the books and carried them off to Rome.
On the other hand, the books of Aristotle's three disciples
disappeared: those of Theophrastus, whom Aristotle himself
is said to have called "well spoken," Dicearcus, Aristoxenus,
and the latter's disciple, Estratón. Not one of them was a
genius, but by the same token, I believe that they must be
considered the purest representatives of the maturity of Hellenic thought. That these were already "political" times is
demonstrated by recalling the permanent controversy between
Theophrastus and Dicearcus, despite their fraternal relations
as fellow students, as to whether or not the intellectual should
intervene in public life. This theme is perhaps the most typical
one in every "time of troubles" when human affairs are not
going well.

All this is only a symptom, suggesting that Hellenic thought
settled into its maturity with Aristotle, felt itself competent,
and by the same token, desired urgently to know what were
the things about it. Aristotle was a man of science, and a

---

1. This is what I call those works which are not, on the one hand,
books of logic and dialectic, nor on the other "literary work" like his
dialogues. I hope some day to occupy myself with this matter: *Disap-
pearance and Preservation of Books as a Historical Category.* The richness of content and the succulency of this theme, which looks so dry,
is beyond description. The case of Aristotle is particularly illuminating.

philosopher *because* he was a man of science.[2] His reform of Platonism consisted in declaring that it was urgent to acquire knowledge of the concrete things which "are there" and which surround us on all sides.

When Plato wants to know a thing that is close to him, his first action is to run off in the opposite direction, separate himself from it completely, go beyond the stars, and then, coming back as from a "supercelestial place," he sees what can be said with meaning about the things of this world which are so meaningless. This Platonic *flight in order to approach* seems to me the most inspired invention of a theoretic nature which has been produced on this planet; nothing else can even be compared to it. Athough we are not writing a history of philosophy, or even a history of the idea of knowledge, the transcendent importance of this Platonic invention is such that I must allude to it at times in paragraphs to come. Because, no doubt about it, "modern" science is Platonism on the march. I consider it most healthy for everyone occupied with intellectual activities to consider carefully, now and again, what that original Platonic procedure means and the quality of genius it implies.[3]

Plato's method is basically paradoxical, as every great philosophy perforce must be. Aristotle and his time adopted an opposite method, which coincides with public opinion and common sense. He thinks that the truth about things is found in maximum proximity to them, and this maximum proximity

2. Although it has not been formulated up to now, the fact that every original philosopher creates his philosophy *for* something else may stand almost as law in the history of philosophy. I mean to say that he does it in order to found another human discipline. At times this is, in turn, an intellectual discipline, a science. Thus, in Descartes, it appears very clear that his philosophy is the shortest road to the establishment of physics. In Aristotle he deals first of all with founding biology, and after that cosmology and mathematics. In Plato, on the other hand, the proposal is to found a practical, not a theoretical discipline: Politics as public morality, and so on.

3. It has nothing to do with the value of this invention that Plato, in order to arrive at it, had to accept many assumptions, toward many of which we must take a most negative attitude since they seem to us errors and defects.

of mind with reality is sensation. *This is the fundamental noetic faculty in the Aristotelian doctrine* and in the period which follows it. Hence, one is forced to categorize this way of thinking as sensualist. It is true that, in my judgment, we slightly pervert the Aristotelian meaning of this first contact of mind with thing when we translate αἴσθησις as sensation. Current psychological terminology gets in our way. The Aristotelian notion of "sensation" is much broader than the present one, and we must find synonyms for a whole series of terms now in use. Sensation is the *sensation* of color or of sound; but it is also the *perception* of an individual thing, and it is also the *appearance* of movement and repose, figure and magnitude, number and unit.[4] Sensation is exactly like the mental function by virtue of which we say in front of a figure on the blackboard: "This is a triangle." This means that to distinguish *a* triangle from *a* square is a matter of our sensation. In fact, on the last page of the *Posterior Analytics*, where Aristotle is going to tell us how we know principles, he starts by considering sensation as the capacity to discern, to distinguish or to judge.[5] Finally, Aristotle will not stop until he

4. *De Anima*, III, 1, 425ᵃ 14.

5. In the *Ethica Nicomachea* there is opposed to sensation or particular sense—seeing, hearing, and so on—a "sense with which in the mathematical arts we judge that this ultimate figure (concrete, individual figure) is the triangle." Except for the parentheses, which I added to make interpretation easier, I take the translation from Pedro Simón Abril (*La Ética de Aristóteles*, 1918, p. 262). Simón was a magnificent translator and those words render the meaning of the text perfectly. Nevertheless, where Simón says "we judge," Aristotle says "we feel," because here actually it is "to judge." And I have not forgotten to take into account that *Topicos* I, 5, 106ᵇ 23 is tied in with *Topics*, II, 4, 111ᵃ 19. The fact is, then, that sensation in Aristotle exercises a certain number of intellectual functions which are usually attributed exclusively to reasoning and to the rational faculty or understanding. This is a judgment, although pre-predicative. It would be clarifying to compare it with the analysis of perception which Husserl makes in the last book prepared for publication *before* his death, *Erfahrung und Urteil*. This shows how almost everything that definite judgment may enunciate, making it explicit, is already in perception in modified and abridged form. Without realizing it, Husserl does no more than develop fully, with that minutia and rigor which are his virtues, what Aristotle is thinking in abbreviated form up to the point at which the title of his

affirms that sensation is a form of knowledge: γνῶσίς τις— *gnôsis tis*.[6] As we are occupied now only with the theory of knowing, it seems to me best that we translate the term *aisthesis* as "sense-perceptible or sensual intuition." Nowadays this is necessary for active understanding. We are not caught in the ridiculous psychology of the last century which handled mental phenomena as though they were inert matter. With Aristotle everything must be understood verbally. Sensation is not "something there," but a feeling, a *taking account* of this color, of this sound; or inversely, it is the color coloring *me* and the sound sounding to *me*. "Sense-perceptible intuition" is the first "taking account," or understanding, or perceiving. Hence, I have called it the *noetic* faculty. I have added that it is the fundamental faculty and this gives it a lift. Nevertheless, the thing seems to me simple and obvious, although I have not enough space here to do more than summarize it. My idea is this: the "purest" intelligible—νοητόν— *noetón* which the mind can conceive is something of which we have already *taken account* in sensation, and *in itself, it is nothing more*.

Aristotle contraposes sensation and *lógos* as two distinct forms of knowledge, by *lógos* meaning concept, especially in its explicit form which is definition. But the truth is that in his psychology he establishes a marvellous and obvious continuity between the mental function "feeling," which he presents as inferior, and that which he considers as being on a higher level, the thinking out of principles. The former is common to all animals, the latter would be an attribute of man.[7] But, on the other hand, he insists repeatedly on estab-

---

book *Experience and Judgment* might be translated into Aristotelianism as *Sensation and Logos*. A text less quoted than it deserves to be, and which is conspicuous enough in *De Ánima*, III, 9, 432, says: "There are two different faculties in the soul of animals—I mean in their discernment—τῷ κριτικῷ—which are the work of reasoning and sensation." This is a weighty text.

6. *De Generatione Animalium*, I, 23, 731ᵃ 33.

7. He says of animals that not only are they—like plants—active in engendering but καὶ γνώσεώς τινος πάντα μετέχουσι, τά μὲν πλείονος, τά

lishing, as he had to, that thought never thinks without images, which, in turn, are nothing more than a precipitate of sensations. Strange as it may seem, this relationship between images and *lógos*, which has been officially held to be necessary, has never been studied with the care that it warrants. What is the precise role of the image in the *lógos* and what service do other mental activities perform in it?

It does not seem that there could be the slightest doubt. In sensation we "take account" of it, we "take it into consideration" or we understand it as an individual sense-perceptible thing. One part of this is stored in the imagination (memory or free fancy). In either of these—for the case is the same —the mind fixes on certain components and passes over the rest of them in silence. This is an effect of our attention. Aristotle does not know what "attention" is but that does not matter here. After a similar fixation and abstraction has appeared in many sensations or images, one becomes aware of the identity of those *ABCD* components which, therefore, appear as common to them. This awareness does not modify their sensual character in the slightest. That they appear as common is a relational quality which we add to them, but this neither takes anything from them nor adds anything to them. We already have before us the first universal. But not because they carry the "burden" of the universal and of genus do they cease to be *ABCD*, exactly the same as they were before—as sensual characteristics of a thing. The operation of comparing in order to discover the common element and the differential *is not a new form* of "taking account," of understanding; nor is it a more intelligent operation. To a certain extent it is mechanical, an exercise in transferring whatever gets our attention—also not intelligent *in itself*— from one sensation to another. What is understood by comparing and "generalizing" continues to be what is understood by sensation, and all these operations from which the universal results are stupid in themselves, existing on account of

δ'ελάττονος, τὰ δὲ πάμπαν μικρᾶς αἴσθησιν γὰρ ἔχουσιν, ἡ δ'αἴσθησις γνῶσίς τις. (*De Generatione Animalium*, I, 23, 731ᵃ 31.)

sensation, which up to now is the only intelligent and discerning activity there is.

The great crisis in this whole process should be the moment
when the sensual extract *ABCD, charged* with representing
or exercising the role of universal and of genus—hence the
lógos—referred in a *new way* to the individual thing with
which sensation regulates contact for us, and appears to us
as manifesting and revealing the *Essence of the thing.* Then
it becomes the *lógos of the Essence*—λόγος τῆς οὐσίας—*lógos
tês ousías.* What "sleight of hand," what act of illusion has
been operating, by virtue of which the thing—"that there"
before me in sensation—has been converted into an Ens,
into something which *has a Being,* into something to which I
attribute a special existence and a special consistency? In this
study we are not trying to define doctrines, but different
"ways of thinking," and we have strictly avoided any ontological problem. But we cannot forget that those are ways
of thinking about Being. Does this oblige us to get into the
wasp nest of ontology? I think not for the moment. For our
present purposes the following is sufficient: in his dealing with
the sense-perceptible things which surround him, man is
chained to them like the slave to the bench in the galley. In
this he does not differ from animals or stones. But like the
galley slave chained to the bench, "both hands on the oar,"
he can imagine that he is freed from the galley, lying in the
arms of a princess or on the distant native soil where he
spent his childhood. This ability to imagine himself freed
from the galley, this *imaginary freedom,* means *ipso facto* an
actual *freedom to imagine* in the face of sense-perceptible
things, in the face of "that there" to which he is chained.
Sensations are precipitated as images which are a memory of
those sensations, hence memory-retentive images; but with
these memory-retentive images as ingredients, man can construct new, "original" and, in the strong meaning of the word,
fantastic images. Thanks to imagination—and note that this
consists only of "freed" sensations—man can, in the face of

the web of sense-perceptible things in which he is imprisoned, fabricate for himself a world of imaginary things; or to put it another way, a structure of fancies organized into an imaginary world.

I said that he can fabricate a world in this way, but that is not exact: he can fabricate innumerable worlds in this way, i.e., imaginary worlds. The sense-perceptible things among which he is prisoner do not constitute a world. They are not things, strictly speaking, but the "business of life," some articulated into others to give a pragmatic perspective. They are converted into things when we free them from this perspective and attribute to them a *being*, that is, a shape and substance which is their own and alien to us. But then they are presented as *being in* a world. They are not isolated, they are not this and this and this indefinitely. Now one, then another, without sufficient connection with the former one, and so on without end, but forming a world which is already pure fantasy, which is the great phantasmagoria. Such a world is imaginary; I mean to say that there is none if there is no imagination, and that it is not, nor can it be, given to us as another thing. Things are "given" to us in some kind of a world. If animals do not have a world it will not be, as is often said, because they lack reason and are nonrational, but because they lacked sufficient imagination. But imagination is famous as the "mad woman of the house," the irrational faculty in man. It would be amusing if, on investigating things more closely, it should appear, when all is said and done, that what defines man best is not his so-called "rationality," but his positive irrationality or phantasmagoricism, because it happens that the former *assumes* the latter, that is to say, that *reason is only one way among many in which imagination may function.*[8] But let us leave the question undecided. The urgent thing is to note that those imaginary worlds can be referred to things, or vice versa, these things to each of those worlds. This process of reference is called *interpretation.*

8. See "Ideas and Beliefs" in *Obras Completas,* Vol. V, p. 375.

Hence, we have this: mankind is free to interpret those things into the midst of which he is fated (i.e., not freely) to be introduced.

In saying that man can form "original" images let this be understood as meaning every image which is not just what sensation deposits in the memory. To focus on an image in regard only to certain components *ABCD* is already to form an original image. Here originality is reduced to dispensing with some parts and keeping others; the image is abstract or extract. It is no less original than the centaur, but in another direction; it is no less phantasmagorical.

We can interpret as a god the "thing there," which is this river on its tranquil course. By this we mean the river of an imaginary world of gods, or a divine world, and what we have done is to *invest it with divinity. We talk (lógos, légein)* of things *insofar* as they are gods—we *theo-logize* or *mytho-logize.* This is a form of interpretation. In the same way we can refer things to a world which is made up of imaginary elements, each of which has these characteristics: it is identical with itself, it is not in contradiction with others, and it enters into various relationships with them without thereby losing its identity. Of the "thing there" interpreted *as an* element of this world—hence possessing those characteristics—we say that it is an Ens and that which appears to be identical, and so on, in each of these we call the *Essence of this Ens.* *Chance provides* that those characteristics of the *entia* coincide with the characteristics of the sensual extract called *lógos* or concept. This makes our talk of *entia* or *onto-logy*—philosophy, science—become logical talk. The *logos* of the myth is not *sensu stricto lógos* because it is not logical or exact talk, but mythology is a "desire to talk," though certainly a marvellous desire to talk, so much so that it is pure desire to talk about the marvellous as such.[9] This is enough *for our present theme.*

9. That I call mythology the "desire to talk" does not mean that I have the desire to talk but that it is the expression with which Aristotle himself designates a saying which is neither true nor false, which is what

Note in what has been said that the transformation of the sensual extract *ABCD* into the *lógos* of the Being of a thing, into a notion, a concept, a definition and a principle is also a new function or charge or magistracy, which descends on it but does not in the least modify its content, does not make it different from what it was when we fixed on it, abstracted it, and extracted it in modest and sensual sensation and imagination. We arrive, then, at concept and principle without the intervention of more than these three mental activities: sensation-imagination, attention-inattention, and comparison. But of these we have said that "paying attention" and "comparing" are like mechanisms and not primarily intelligent, since they operate only on what is understood in sensation. So that the only activity which by origin is intelligent, the only "taking account" or "taking into consideration," is sensation, especially when freed in the form of imagination.[10] Aristotle establishes a supreme faculty of the mind which is charged with "being in charge," with "taking into account," with "making contact" or "touching"—θιγγάνειν—*thingánein*—the intelligible—νοητὸν—*noetón;* it is reason, intelligence or νοῦς (*noûs*). "Intelligence is made one with the intelligible when it touches it, and thus understands"—νοητὸς γὰρ γίγνεται θιγγάνων καὶ νοῶν ὥστ ταὐτὸν νοῦς καὶ νοητόν.[11] But the famous *noetón* or intelligible does not consist of more than that primitive sensual extract or imagination. The result is that intelligence understands nothing new, except what sensation had previously

---

mythology is. It is for the λόγου ἕνεκα λέγειν, which means "talking for the sake of talking," or *orationis gratia*, as Bessarion translates it. Tricot turns it into *Plaisir de parler* (*Metaphysics*, IV, 7, 1012ª 6). Remember that Bergson attributes the *fonction fabulatrice* from which myths emerge to *homo loquax*.

10. The canonical text in which Aristotle declares that sensation has as its object *what is going to be a "universal"* is this: καὶ γὰρ αἰσθάνεται μὲν τὸ καθ'ἕκαστον, ἡ δ'αἴσθησις τοῦ καθόλου ἐ τίν, οἷον ἀνθρώπου, ἀλλ' οὐ καλλίου ἀνθρώπου. (*Posterior Analytics*, II, 19, 100ª 17). Although a final point is missing, the comment of St. Thomas, *Sensus est quodammodo et ipsus universalis*, and what follows is masterly (*Posterior Analytics*, II, 19, lec. 20).

11. *Metaphysics*, XII, 7, 1072ᵇ 21.

understood. Because of this we said that this was the first *contact* of the mind with the thing. But now it becomes apparent that it is also the last contact, and therefore the only one; this obliges Aristotle, when referring to the relationship between intelligence and the intelligible, to use the same metaphor that we employ for sensation—*contact*. Now we understand all the exemplary coherence of Aristotelian thought when he repeats untiringly that the intelligence cannot understand, cannot think, without images.[12]

It is notorious that Aristotle disposes of the definition of his concepts of passive and active intelligence, or agent, in a few paragraphs of his third book, *On the Soul,* and that these paragraphs have, up to now, been unintelligible. The text of his treatise *On the Soul* has been treated most soullessly by fortune. But besides this there is reason to suspect that Aristotle tripped here by wanting to bring his psychology, which is a natural science, into line with his theology and his ethics. Of course, this desire to bring psychology into accord with these disciplines was not arbitrary, but on the contrary, was inspired by an admirable sense of *systematic responsibility,* which is a definitive obligation of the philosopher. System for him is a duty. In place of system we might say "continuity." Continuity between God and the natural order was necessarily established. Counting downward, man is here below in continuity with the animals, the animals with the vegetables, the vegetables with the minerals. Continuity on an upward trend was lacking; natural man lacked that which would at the same time be something divine. Aristotle needed to make thought divine—apart from many other motives which he had as a Greek intellectual—and this, made difficult by the assumptions of his psychology and of his theory of knowledge, led him to a violent solution, reached confusedly at the

12. The reason why Aristotle calls the intellection of the intelligible a "contact" goes deeper than all this, and was not clear to Aristotle himself, although he suffered from it precisely because it came to him as imposed by the whole mental tradition of the Greeks. It cannot be stated here, because that would send us back to the dawn of Greek thought.

last moment and "from outside," by including a power in man—the *noûs poietikós*—which in its residual state had not been foreseen, and which almost turned Aristotelianism into pantheism. But the truth is that the *noûs* or Intelligence has nothing divine in it which sensation did not already possess. The metaphor of the Stagyrite which depicts the intellectual agent as a light, is hardly a metaphor, because it signifies the power of making manifest the meaning of concepts; that is, that we take account of them, that we understand what there is to understand—as light makes manifest the colors of Nature. But the fact is that the content of the concept is already manifest in sensation or sense-perceptible intuition, and if it were not there it could not be in any other mental power. So that it is absolutely not a metaphor insofar as the light—the authentic, not the metaphoric light—is the sensation of light or the illuminating light which actually opens for us the great panorama of things. And to *take account of the light of day* is the most intelligent operation in this "way of thinking." [13]

That all this may not have been understood in this way arises out of a strange bigotry which the abstract has always aroused, as if abstraction were somehow a magical—or at least alchemic—operation capable of giving that which is abstracted a new nature different from that which it had when it was concrete. To abstract would be to transmute the copper of the concrete into the gold of the abstract. But we already saw in Chapter 9 that this is not so. This bigotry toward the abstract is complicated by bigotry toward the universal, which is the false common universal. It is not necessary to say that both bigotries, like all others from the Occident, came from Plato, who has been the Mississippi of bigotry. Nothing is to be gained by this, and everything is besmirched because to differentiate man from the other animals by citing their various capacities to abstract and to generalize is not a good method. Even if this were true, man and animal would still remain separate, contrary to the methodological norm of continuity which counsels us to differentiate without separat-

13. *Topics*, II, 7, 113 to 131.

ing. This is Aristotle's custom, as it is in Leibnitz on a more conscious level.

The opacity of the Aristotelian formulas which refer to intelligence or reason has given rise to innumerable interpretations, divergent among themselves and none satisfactory insofar as they pretend to coincide with the text. The one which I offer leans *a tergo* on all the texts of Aristotle which, as is well known, are highly contradictory on this subject, and for this reason it may have a certain value as an interpretation. But in this matter it avoids clinging to what Aristotle believed the power of thought to be, but includes a critique which tries to show what is the form of the Aristotelian theory if his assumptions are carefully thought through to the end. Let it be said to the credit of Aristotle and to the discredit of us, his critics, that we have been able to profit by some of the most important and decisive investigations which have been made in philosophy during this century with reference to abstraction.[14]

14. I allude to the previously cited studies by Husserl. But I differ from Husserl in detail since at the end of his admirable analysis of abstraction (the theory of the wholes and the parts, and of objects which are concrete or abstract) it is not finally clear whether the "species" is or is not the same as the "abstract moment" of the individual object. (See *Investigaciones Logicus,* translated by Manuel García Morente and José Gaos [Revista de Occidente, 1929], II, 115.) If I abstract from this paper everything but its whiteness, this automatically ceases to be the whiteness of *this* paper, and hence *this* whiteness, as *this* is not taken as substitute for the nonexistent word which would name the shade of its whiteness which is before me. One does not see what there could be in the intentional act with which I *fix* the whiteness, relating myself to it, which is capable of individualizing that whiteness. Husserl falls into the same complication as the Scholastics for whom, in short and taking another turn or so, the "species" when it lost its individuality (in Husserl's terminology) had to take on the new character of generality and through it of universality, should at least be *fundamentaliter et in potentia.* The basic abstraction, I repeat, does not modify the abstract in the least, does not transmute or transubstantiate it, and even less does it endow it with universality. The only thing it adds to the moment of extract is solitude. But with this it is enough for all other logical and ontological functions it is going to serve. It would coincide with Scholasticism, then, in recognizing two classes of "species," the sense-perceptible and the intelligible, as if the sense-perceptible, as "abstract mo-

My exposition also enjoys an excellent background. It coincides in part with that of Themistio—commentator of the 4th Century A.D.—which inspired that of St. Thomas Aquinas. According to this, passive intelligence, which in his sense is the most proper and controllable understanding, would come to be one and the same thing as imagination. But in Aristotle imagination does not differ materially from sensation, except for a reason which does not affect our subject, namely, that sensation requires a pre-existent extra-mental object whereas imagination does not. The difference is very important, and fruitful for many purposes, some of which Aristotle himself did not envisage, but it is innocuous and useless in any effort to explain intellection. It cannot be said that St. Thomas Aquinas is a "mystic" thinker when he was capable of resting his case on an opinion so close to extreme sensualism.

My interpretation corroborates superlatively the fact that the next two generations of disciples of Aristotle went on understanding his doctrine in this way, progressively until they reached the end, as if an internal force within the doctrine, superior to any personal inclinations or talents, made these conclusions inevitable. In these first peripatetics the hallmark of Aristotelianism is revealed, and it is clear that Aristotle himself, above all the man of science, functioned also as a thinker who was fundamentally naturalist and secular.[15]

---

ment," were not intelligible, and the same one which is later going to be called intelligible. I cannot accept that *sunt alterius generis* (St. Thomas, *De Anima*, Art. 4). The truth is that the term "intelligible"—νοητόν—so unfortunately used by Plato and Aristotle, ought to be shelved, precisely in order to use it in another sense, at once more serious and more lively, precisely because one must at last resolve to do what never has been done, incredible as it may seem, and that is to ask oneself peremptorily why there is in the Universe something—whatever it may be—which obliges us to call it "intelligible"; hence, in what does the intelligibility of the intelligible consist, *a parte rei*.

15. Let us say briefly what it is that happens to the doctrine of the *Noûs* or Intelligence in that very Lyceum, thanks to the directors of the school themselves, the heirs of Aristotle, in the next two generations.

Theophrastus, a faithful copy of his teacher, finds difficulty only in the notion of intelligence. He does not understand what passiveness is,

That such a man should have been converted into the official philosopher of Catholicism is one of the strangest and most confusing events of world history. In saying this I do not

---

nor the agent come from outside, nor the relationship between the two of them. In order to make the notion of intelligence correspond with the rest of the doctrine he considers it necessary to recognize movement in the soul, that is to say, to reduce it to material or physical reality. Thus, he takes the first step toward extreme corporeal naturalism, which is the ancient classical form of "materialism." Atomism was always an aberrant form in Greek thought. Theophrastus brings the psychic even closer to the physical. Hence, he makes the human soul homogeneous with that of animals, from which it differs only in degree of perfection. *He does not believe it possible to distinguish between imagination and intellection.* (See the principal texts brought together in Zeller, *Die Philosophie der Greichen*, 1921, IV, pp. 847–851.) Meanwhile Aristoxenus will frankly reduce the soul to a resultant harmony between corporeal functions.

Dicearco, a fellow student of both of them, insists that the so-called soul is reduced to a harmony between corporeal elements—heat, cold, humidity, dryness—therefore that μὴ εἶναι τὴν ψυχὴν (the soul does not exist). This is ἀνούσιος (unreal, unsubstantial). It is nothing apart and distinct from the body. He denies immortality. *There is not a superior part of the soul—the rational or noetic—different from sensations.* (Sierbet: *Geschichte der Psychologie*, 1884, t. II, 164. Quoted in Lactancio, Inst. VII, 2, 13.)

Estratón succeeded Theophrastus as director of the Lyceum. In him corporeal naturalism advanced much further. Every effective cause is inseparable from matter, and in that sense is material. Therefore, the soul, the psychic functions, are movements in matter, as much sensation as intellection. One need not talk of one part of the soul—reason—as different and separate from the body. The soul is, therefore, a capacity *of* the body.

But the most interesting and decisive thing in which this whole process ends is Estratón's idea according to which sensation inversely implies intelligence, so that it is from now on the essential psychic function. It makes no sense to distinguish between reason and sensation. There is no more than *one* noetic function, which is "taking account" or "taking into consideration." Intellection and the different senses are reduced to particularizations of that single function in view of the particularization of objects. Hence Tertullian says of it in *De Anima*, 15, that with Dicearco "*abstulerunt principale, dum in animo ipso volunt esse sensum, quorum vindicatur principale*"; this is exactly what I maintained when calling sensation in Aristotle the fundamental noetic function because it will now be clear that my thesis does not consist solely in affirming that intelligence is reduced in Aristotle to sensation but that sensation at the same time is reduced to intelligence. (The manner used by Tertullian to state Dicearco's thesis is clearly inadequate

mean by a single whisper to detract from the abundant pro-
ductiveness of his garlanded genius.[16]

---

because he had to take it from some Stoic. Hence he calls the soul, and
the intelligent factor in the soul, *principale*—that is to say—τὸ ἡγεμονικόν.
The most direct doxography is Plutarch *Adv. Colot.* XIX, 1115; Sexto
Empirico, *Adv. Logic.*, 1, 349, and *Hypotyp.*, II, 31, important under-
linings in Simplicio, in *Arist. Categ.* 8ᵇ 25 and Nemisio, *De Natura
hominis*, II; Migne, XL, p. 537.)

I did not want to take into account earlier that intelligence in
Aristotle has still another function which is constitutionally opposed
to seeing the universal, namely, the *noûs praktikós*. The "practical reason" is charged with understanding, with *seeing* the most unique case.
Thus formally in *Ethica Nicomachea*, 1143ᵃ 36: καὶ γὰρ τῶν πρώτων
ὅρων καὶ τῶν ἐσχάτων νοῦς ἐστί. This singularizing reason is estimative;
it distinguishes the best from the worst in order to decide our actions.
But the fact is that this function is entrusted to sensation in animals and
the *passus* where Aristotle says so (*De Generatione Animalium*, I, 23,
731ᵃ 24) is the one cited earlier where he declares that sensation is a
way of knowledge (see Zeller, *ibid.*, pp. 915-19). Anyone who, in interpreting and attesting Aristotelian thought, leaps like a bullfighter over
the fact that it was so understood by his immediate disciples and his
successors in running the Peripato is a . . . good bullfighter but a bad
historian of philosophy.

16. Referring to this very problem of the role of sensation in knowledge, and the *obstacle* to knowing God that it sets up, Gilson says:
"*Ici comme ailleurs, la tentation était forte, pour les Chrétiens, de
suivre la ligne de moindre résistance et de chercher dans le platonisme
les principes d'une solution. Ce n'est pas ce qu'a fait saint Thomas. . . .
Il se déclare d'accord avec Aristote et avec l'expérience pour affirmer
'qu'en cette vie nous ne pouvons former aucun concept sans avoir eu une
sensation*" (*L'esprit de la philosophie médiévale*, 1932, deuxième série,
p. 44). I have high regard for M. Gilson, whose work, insofar as it is
expositive, has taught me a great deal. But at this juncture, I must say
that Mr. Gilson does not illumine anything for us with this way of
justifying Aristotelianism for the sake of Catholicism, because we do
not see that to be a Platonist is an easier *task* than to be an Aristotelian,
nor most of all, can we admit that for Christianity this poses a serious
dilemma in view of which Christians must be either Platonists or
Aristotelians. This is an arbitrary dilemma, as is shown by the simple
fact that in 1300, William of Ockham had already been born and that a
Franciscan as was Mateo de Aquasparta, he is neither Platonist nor Aristotelian, and that he systematizes Nominalism, thanks to which "Christian philosophy" lived vigorously for two centuries more, generating
from it modern philosophy most gloriously. But this was not the only
solution for Christian philosophy. The truth is that with these mental in-
tolerances, what would have been a genuine and original Christian philosophy has remained stillborn, and with it humanity lost one of its
highest possibilities.

19

Essay on What Happened to Aristotle with Principles

Now LET US GO BACK to where we paused with arched eyebrows at the fact that Aristotle devoted, at most, only a single page to telling us how the principles [1] were obtained.

Do not be surprised at the frequency with which I underline the fact that a certain author or a certain school—or the whole past—has failed to carry out a task which should not have been abandoned. Do not waste time accusing me of seeing only the holes in the Gruyère cheese. Such attention to deficiencies is not a matter of character or propensity; it is an essential part of a great new task involving our knowledge of the Universe, which must be completed and which I shall attempt to define in this study. [2]

Consider the importance which principles have in this "way of thinking." Almost half of a *pragmateia* is composed of them, because this method needs to seize upon a new principle at every step. Here deduction is short of breath. Moreover, principles are a form of knowledge of greater importance than proofs, the truth of which depends on principles. It, therefore, does not seem excessive to reiterate our surprise at Aristotle's attitude toward the means of arriving at principles despite the fact that he created a whole science which is nothing less than the basic one for searching them out.

Let us refer first to the axioms or principles called "common." As they are so few in number, he could collect and compare them as he compared hundreds of political institu-

1. In the *Posterior Analytics* and in the *Metaphysics*.
2. See also in my lecture on Leibnitz before the Association for Scientific Progress the necessity for a *dis-teleology*. [Appendix 1 of this book.]

tions or, to make a closer comparison, as he himself notes, "a great effort was made to bring the *tópos* together." He should have studied them one by one in order to see in what mutual relationship they stood, if coordinated, if arranged in a hierarchy.[3] Above all, he should have considered at greater length how they leap to the mind and what comprises that strange truth of theirs called evidence—so explosive, so like the crack of a pistol shot. Aristotle did none of this. On the contrary, we have seen him, when he was dealing with axioms, let them swing vertically, rising and falling from their generic form to their specific form, an oscillation which permitted me, with a view to what I shall say later, to categorize them as the demons of doubt or little devils of Descartes. Now then, as long as this way of thinking is dominant, not one step more will be taken to settle the question, although thousands of pages have been laid waste over this matter. This is a good example of the essential sterility of Scholasticism.

But in Aristotle, while not justifiable, it is in a way explicable. Compare the uninhibited attention which he pays to principles that are definitions with the minimum attention he devotes to axioms. This is due most of all to the fact that Aristotle has his own idea of the definition and its function in the device which he has just invented and of which he is justifiably proud—the analytical syllogism. About axioms, on the other hand, he has no proper conception unless it be the uneasy conviction that he ought to restrict their application to "genera" (what we call species). This poverty of ideas about things as important as axioms arises, in turn, from the fact that Aristotle encountered them before inventing his logic and, hence, before adopting his idea of science (*epistéme*) as analytical proof.[4] Because Aristotle was dialectical before being, like the Devil, logical. The dialectic—*Topics, Refuta-*

3. Only in *Metaphysics*, IV, 3, 1005^b 33, does he say that the principle of contradiction is by nature the principle of all the other axioms.

4. In the *Topics* the analytical and the apodictical syllogisms travel in convoy, but this is not yet the syllogism of the *Prior Analytics*. This difference gives us the approximate date of the *Topics*.

tion of Sophisms and the first version of his *Rhetoric* [5]—is the first appearance of the theory of thought or ratiocination in Aristotle while he was still an academician. We might say that this is his proto-logic. This is where he stumbled over "common knowledge or admissions" and over axioms.

We cannot develop here the difference between Aristotelian dialectic and the scientific or apodictical, especially logic. It is too rich and delicate a theme for us to begin now. It is enough to say that dialectic is not a technique of science. Science is inescapably the work of a man alone, for the simple reason that thinking—and not just repeating mechanically that two and two are four—is a task which cannot be performed unless a man is alone with himself.[6] Dialectic is the technique of discussion with others, or dialogue; it is pure conversation, it is socialized thought. In it arguments do not pretend to be unalloyed truth, but only to have a certain formal structure of truth. This argumentative reasoning also starts with principles, but these do not necessarily have to be true. It is enough that to most people they appear to be true, that is to say, they are ἔνδοξοι—*éndoxoi*, opinion—prevailing in the community; therefore, governing principles or "public opinion." [7] The community within which they rule may be that of the "world in general" or better, that of the sages. In this latter case, it can be either directly the public opinion of the learned or that of a pre-eminent sage who *rules* within their community, who exercises in it the social function called "authority."

5. The *Rhetoric* which we have is much later and presupposes the *Prior Analytics*.

6. In normal conversation, what is said and heard is understood only in its "usual meaning." Not only is a word a usage, and therefore a social action, but so also is its "meaning" or "idea." The system of verbal usages which is language corresponds to a system of intellectual usages, of "notions" or "opinions." Usage engenders in the individual habits which are mechanized mental life. The science of words, or linguistics, must be founded on a previous "theory of saying." If it were not the habit to say certain things, the language, or instrument by means of which we say them, would not exist. I hope to clarify this in my book *Man and People* [W. W. Norton, New York, 1957, Chaps. XI and XII].

7. On collective laws in force see my *Obras Completas* [Consult the Index].

Science, germinated in the Greek colonies, established itself in Athens. It is a daughter of the "city." Athens is the Agora, the gymnasiums, the *symposios* or banquets; places and occasions for endless talk.[8] Hence, science must be established in Athens not so much in the form of a book as of a colloquium, which is not solitude but may engender it; that is to say, it adopts as a way of manifesting itself an external form which is adapted to the "city" and which is most inadequate for science. From this comes the equivocation inherent in the first technical term, the one it has in Plato: *dialectic*, which means "way of thinking" and at the same time discussion, logomachy. Even Aristotle, when writing his *Topics*, finds himself in this Platonic situation. This does not mean that he has not already developed a great part of his own doctrine, hence para- or anti-Platonic. But Platonism continues to be the foundation on which he advances and from which he will continue to stand free.

Plato believes in a unitary knowledge which embraces everything—philosophy—and to the day of his death he believes that this knowledge is produced collectively, by talking together. It is not a literary accident that he writes dialogues, nor is this due solely to his eagerness to project or objectify science in the image of Socrates, who was an unmitigated chatterbox and an enemy of the book. Until his death Plato regards science as a social function and, moreover, a collective creation in which the whole "city" participates, although this requires a special collective organ—what the Romans would call a *socialitas* or association—charged with its promotion. *For this reason* he founds a *school;* from then on and until it dies out, Athenian philosophy preserves this form of living, of Being, which is the social aspect of the schools.[9]

8. "Without 'talk' in the Agora and *symposio* the Greek is incomprehensible," Burckhardt says (*Historia de la Cultura Griega,* I, p. 70. Translation by the Revista de Occidente).

9. This is not a matter of surmise. Proclus (pp. 16–19, Friedlander edition which Solmsen cites) says literally that the mathematicians immediately before Euclid and whom he popularizes, "living together in

But Aristotle was a stranger, born in the border region of Hellas where little was known about the great fact of the "city." He was therefore prepared, regardless of Plato, to discover a great truth: that science is solitude. Plato himself was obliged from time to time to recognize that certain intellectual operations must be carried out by "the soul alone with itself." From and within this solitude the man of science deals with other men of science, dead or far away, and equally solitary. All of Aristotle's great books begin with a dialogue between him and other philosophers, "ancient" or far away, whose doctrines raised questions for him. Aristotle discusses the *pro* and *con* of every doctrine with them. This is what he calls *aporética*, the way, according to Aristotle, in which every book of philosophical science should begin. It is the starting point which science chooses in order to establish itself and, therefore, before establishing itself. The *aporética*, then, is a disputatious conversation between solitaries which takes place within a man alone in solitude. It is like an absorption of society into a solitude, into an individual. The man of science starts from prevailing opinions—direct or from "authorities" —*in order to* reach the point of finding and deciding on the authentic principles of his discipline. In this, unavoidably his first preoccupation, the science is dialectics, and hence in *Topics* science appears as one more species of the genus "discourse." Once the man of science has discovered the principles of his discipline, he withdraws from the social plane, ceases to heed or listen to *others,* and vanishes into basic solitude.

Taking the whole of Aristotle's dialectic as a historic reality it would represent a pseudomorph in which the lonely stranger from Macedonia encounters the sociability which is the essence of Athens, and tries to adapt himself to it. Therefore two things characterize his activity: absorption of that which

the Academy, made their investigations in common." These are the men with whom Aristotle lived while he was Plato's pupil. In the foundation of Plato's school the precedent set by the Pythagorean association also had influence; this had been a secret society with a character at once religious, scientific, and political.

is alien and the adaptation of himself to it. But Aristotle has too much native genius to stop at that. The more accurate picture is that from the very *first moment* of imbibing Platonism, he begins at the same time to adapt to it and to oppose it. In the *Analytics* there is nothing from the past except in the relentless measure imposed on us by the law of continuity which applies to all things human; it is very much his own creation, in which the Stagyrite discards his adopted mask—dialectic—as the larva its cocoon.[10]

But this was the origin of a great evil, the effects of which lasted up to the time of Descartes. What was done was done. How to re-do it from the new point of view? Furthermore, the dialectic of the *Topics* was not an error; it was an inadequacy stemming mostly from mixing very different things. It studied correct thinking and was therefore rational, but it was not true, only plausible. That kind of thinking is not true, either because it is not absolutely true (which does not imply that it is false but only that it is problematical), or because it is only probable, or because it is true thinking insofar as it is formulated; therefore, it is not true *yet*.[11]

This final task of the dialectic is of exceptional transcendence. It consists plainly and simply in providing the method

10. Aristotelian dialectic, although derived from Plato, is already a concession to the social environment and accepts the occupation of disputation—arguing for the sake of arguing—in a form which its teacher would have found difficult to accept.

11. Aristotle enumerates three uses for dialectic: for the mental gymnasium, for discussion, and for the exact, i.e., the philosophical sciences (*Topics*, I, 2, 101ᵃ 25). This last use, as heterogeneous as the other two, is in turn divided into two functions: one, to discuss the *pro* and *con* of problems as such—hence of problematic judgments—which is the *aporetic;* the other, to identify and decide upon nothing less than the principles of the sciences. This disposition of the *Topics,* so crassly "Athenian" that it would not have surprised us to find it in Isocrates, for example, presents a hodgepodge which could not be put in order except by writing a new and completely different work. Aristotle was not disposed to do this. In 1833, Brandis maintains *"dass die Topik anders ausgefallen sein wurde, wenn Aristoteles nach vollender Analytik sie ausgearbeit hatte."* (*Reihenfolge der Bucher des Organons,* 252 ff.; quoted in Maier, *Die Syllogistim des Aristoteles,* II, 2–78, n. 3, 100.)

for arriving at principles. That an operation of this importance should suddenly appear mixed in with others is so absurd that we must unhesitatingly attribute it to some peculiarity or "secret" of the Greeks, or at least of the Athenians. *When an action which is not unique to a single individual, but appearing with normal frequency in a people, seems to us irregular—i.e., incomprehensible—we must consider it as touching on a fundamental assumption which inspires that people basically, as an inherent preconception by which they live, and by the same token, as the most natural and obvious thing in the world for them.* The soul of a people is made up of these things which for others are "incomprehensible." The aggregate of them includes specifically—for it can be reduced to precise lists—the Hellenic, the Roman, the Spanish, the Castilian, the Basque, and so on.

The *Topics*, then, a work so marvellous in itself, was probably the reason why Aristotle would never treat in depth the problem of how axiomatic principles are arrived at, and could not distinguish—in any part of his work that I remember—what their function in knowledge is as compared with that of definitions. He contented himself with setting them up in opposition to definitions to the extent that they are *common.* But we have already seen that for him, especially, they are not common either, but must be narrowed down to the "genus" delimited by definitions.

It is my hypothesis that Aristotle had his first lively and energetic encounter with axioms when he was collecting his "commonplaces," and they presented themselves to him as conjoined and confused with the *éndoxoi* or "prevailing opinions." That is why the word "axiom" appears very seldom in that work and then only in its last part.

In Chapters X and XI of the second book, Aristotle explains the "*tópos* or place of similitude" and the "*tópos* or place of addition." There was talk there of the more and the less, but referring to quality rather than quantity. Hence there is talk, not of equality but, more generically, of similitude. But the fact is that, however disguised they may be by this qualitative aspect, we recognize there various axioms of Euclid. Their expression is so generic that the Euclidean axioms could be *deduced* from those "topics." [12] Nevertheless, none of this transpires nor is it seen even faintly in the text of the *Topics*. It is in later works where we discover—and even this is not expressly stated—that the discovery of principles is a task for dialectic thinking supported by sensation. This is a tremendous thing, but Aristotle does not deserve any special consideration on this account.

It is an enormity that the principles of exact thinking originate in thinking as inexact as is the dialectical. Dialectics is the realm of induction, that is to say, of experience and analogy. Note that for Aristotle analogy is a kind of second-class thinking, an *ersatz* of the authentic; it does not give us the truth about Being but rather grants us only a "Being—something like—as." It comes very close to being nothing more than metaphorical thinking. It is well to underline this here, for we shall soon see how for Descartes thinking by analogy becomes that which is really logical and exact. There is no room for peripeteia or major upset. Modernity inverts the traditional (Aristotelian-Scholastic) "way of thinking," putting the feet up and the head down. In doing this the moderns think they are putting things in their proper places because, in their opinion, the Aristotelian-Scholastics thought with their feet. Outside of formal logic they were incapable of creating a deductive theory that was truly deductive; therefore, they were incapable of exact thinking. This is because they were empiricists and sensualists. Because of this, they thought with their feet and not with their heads, i.e., being empiricists, what they called head was only feet. It has been too often forgotten in our time that the Descartes-Leibnitz-Kant line of thinkers conducted a most impassioned battle against sensualism and empiricism.

12. For example, 115 to 117. The *Dialectic* is a *formal* theory, like logic, but as it is the part of Aristotelian doctrine which is least studied, its structure has not been schematized nor has its formalism been compared with that of logic.

Experience, *empeiría*—ἐμπειρία—is a word which in Greek, as in Latin, stems from the root *per*. Words, like plants, stem from their roots. *Per* is found also in the Germanic languages, but in the form of *fahr*. Hence, experience is termed "er-*fahr*ung." This root belongs to a "verbal field" and a corresponding "pragmatic field" which are extremely curious.[13] It is found in Armenian and in Sanskrit. It is, then, a very ancient Indo-European root which reflects a very ancient life experience (*vivencia*).[14] Meillet and Ernout, with their unsurpassed linguistic-phonetic precision, pay little attention to etymologies. These require a semantic sense as well as phonetic knowledge, and that is a philosophic talent which, like all talents, one either has or has not. The strict etymological method consists in the coming together of two points of view which are completely different from each other, but which permit us to create two series of things which must be parallel. One is the series of phonemes which for thousands of years goes on producing a root; this is the phonetic series. The other is the series of situations in life which those phonemes have continued to express: the meanings; it is the semantic series and it is the decisive one. Nevertheless, in this method the phonetic series plays an *indispensable* role. The character of almost physical law which the phonetic law possesses is a precision instrument which enables us to control our semantic arguments from the outside; it is their guarantee.

Ernout-Meillet speak of the root *per* in the word *peritus*:

13. See in my next book, *Commentary on the "Banquet" of Plato*, the chapter in which I will set forth my *theory of pragmatic fields and verbal fields*. (See *Obras Completas*, Vol. IX, p. 749.)

14. According to a friend of his the author coined the word "*vivencia*" as the exact equivalent of "*erlebnis*," used by the German philosopher Dilthey, which is usually translated as "experience, occurrence, event, adventure." After some delay the Royal Spanish Academy recognized "*vivencia*" as a Spanish word, and in 1956, defined it in the *Dictionary of the Castilian Language* as: "Used of an experience which is consciously or unconsciously incorporated in the personality." It is difficult to translate into English except as "life experience" [*Translator's note*].

qui a l'expérience de; d'où "habile dans." [15] This is "expert,"
and often with the passive meaning of *éprouvé* (tried, ill-
treated by life). The nearest group, they add, is the Greek
around πεῖρα (*peîra*), which means "proof, trial," and which
has its corresponding Germanic *fara: action de guetter,* danger." And in fact just before this they were concerned with
the term *periculum,* where *per* appears again, meaning first
essai, épreuve and soon afterward "risk." This is our *peligro*
(danger). Note that the meaning of "experience, proof, trial"
is generic and abstract. *Guetter* and *peligro* are more concrete, which is very often an indication that this last meaning
is the older or more primitive.

And in fact *péiro*—πεῖρω—appears again when Ernout-
Meillet take up the word *portus,*[16] port and door. *Portus* and
πόρος (*póros*) mean the "way out," the pass that we discover
when walking through the mountains. Probably that meaning
of "way out" is older in the sense of "walking on land" than
the maritime one, which means the *passage* through a reef and
the *entrance* to an inlet, and is therefore called *port.* The road
leading to the port, *portus* or way out, is the *opportunus.*

But with this new stratum of words and meanings surrounding *portus,* we have entered into a conception which is very
far from being abstract and colorless: experience, proof, trial.
On the other hand, we find the semantic link in it. The
semantic reason (exact prototype of what I call "historic
reason") is, according to Descartes and Leibnitz, like every
other reason a *chaîne* between that convolution of abstraction and the concrete, dramatic intrinsic experience of *periculum.* The new idea, which will clarify the whole series for
us, is that in *per* one was *originally* concerned with a journey,
with walking through a world when there were no roads, so
that every trip was more or less strange and perilous. It was

15. Ernout-Meillet: *Dictionnaire étymologique de la langue latine,*
1939, p. 756.
16. I am not repeating here what I said about the etymology of this
word in my "Prologue to a Treatise on Hunting" (*Obras Completas,*
Vol. VI). Put what I am now saying with that.

154 THE IDEA OF PRINCIPLE IN LEIBNITZ

travelling through unknown lands without previous guidance, the ὁδός (hodós), without the μέθοδος (méthodos or guideline).

Experts in semantics know well that the oldest verifiable meaning of a word is not, on that account, the most ancient in point of fact, that is to say, the (relatively) "originary" one. But they do not pay attention to the fact that the "originary" meaning persists as latent and can suddenly be recognized in more recent forms of the word, including the most modern. That is to say, the root from which these words derive can revive in full vigor at any moment. With this we have the paradoxical but unquestionable fact that a word today can recover a meaning which is more like the original, and therefore far older, than all the most ancient now known; that is, those accepted up to now.

I will give you an example of this which will show at the same time how I came to clarify for myself the etymology of all this "verbal field" which is so important in the theory of knowledge.

I was reading Paracelsus, the miracle-working doctor who, as is well known, was a fraud but was also a real personality. His idea—very typical of those early 16th Century men in whom the intellectual Renaissance [17] culminates, ambivalent minds in which the substance is still medieval but with *modern* anxieties fermenting in it—his idea, I say, is that knowledge must absolutely be founded on experience or *erfahrung*. But as I read, I realized that Paracelsus uses this word in a sense which was unknown in the language of that time—not very far from today's—but in a sense which he encounters *reviving* in it, namely, *er-fahren* is to travel, "land *fahren*," to walk the earth. Knowledge must be founded on traveling, going to see things personally, there where they are, with one's own eyes. Nature is a "codex" which it is necessary to read while "peregrinating and vagabonding through it" (*peregrinisch und mit landtreichen umkeren*). *Fahren* in the German language nor-

17. It is well known that the artistic Renaissance began earlier and went faster than the intellectual one.

mally means "to travel," especially to travel in a vehicle; our contemporary meaning postulates exclusively another earlier meaning of traveling on foot. In fact Paracelsus set forth on the road—on *hodós*—with the deliberate intention of employing a "way of thinking," a *méthodos*, and dedicated himself to traveling in order to see. On journeys one sometimes encounters "dangers," from which a way out must be found, *portus* and *euporías*. On journeys one sees many things. Hence the Arabs called their travel books "books on going and looking." Empiricism, or experience, is then an actual "going and looking" as a method, a thinking with the feet, which is, according to the moderns, just what the Scholastics did.

Ernout-Meillet recognized that *per* is "to traverse"; in Greek πείρω (*peíre*); in Sanskrit, *piparti* ("make to pass," "save") and *paráyati* ("make to traverse"). On the other hand, *portus* gives us *transport*. All that is lacking is the decisive advance of discovering in *per* the "walking in order to travel," walking through unknown or unfamiliar lands. This is the "primary" intrinsic experience which ordains this whole galaxy of phonemes and semantemes. And this comes to life after millennia, in Paracelsus in the 16th Century, when it is no longer found in Greek or Sanskrit. Note that these retain from the intrinsic experience of *viajar* (traveling) only the most vivid and dramatic moment, the *atraversar* (traversing), the *pasar* through a difficult spot—difficult to pass or difficult to find, in short, "to pass the ports." This contraction of a meaning which first indicated a general reality—here "to go on a trip"—to a single one of its outstanding moments is normal.

It seems clear to us, then, that the Latin phonemes *per* and *por* and the Greek περ (*per*) and πειρ (*peir*) come from an Indo-European word which expressed this human reality: "to travel," apart from its eventual termination, and transcending its performance—therefore, of removing to a distant determinate spot—is to take a trip, *to be traveling*, "walking through the world." Then the significance of "to travel" is what happens to us while we are doing it, and this is chiefly a matter of encountering curious things and passing through dangers—*prouver et éprouver*. In omitting from the idea of travel its objective *ad quem* (trip *to* Rome), there remains that vague sense of *errare* and *vagare*, whose roots have many times been substituted for *per*. Thus *perrero, qui a l'époque impériale remplace peragro, percurro.*[18] Is there not ground for suspecting that the prefix and preposition *per* is exactly the same as the old root *per? Vagar* (to wander) is, in its oldest accepted meaning, as it is today, to walk from here to there, but without a predetermined goal. Finally, the German *fara*, like *guetter*, is close to *gué*, which is the Italian *guado* and the Spanish *vado*. But these do not exist without the *paso* (pass) *portus* or *póros* through which those who travel must pass. *Vadus* is also *wat* in German.[19]

This linguistic episode gives us a much more concrete understanding of what empiricism and experience are, more alive and philosophically important than all the epistemological definitions of those terms. Nevertheless, what we have gained from it will not become apparent until, in another paragraph, we make our first contact with the modern way of thinking, which is the one that accuses the Scholastics of sensualist empiricism, of thinking with their feet.

But now it is going to be very useful to us.

In the modern method the definition of a thing is the last step taken in the cognitive process. In Aristotle and among the Scholastics this is where a beginning is made. It is not strange that to the moderns this seems as though they have their heads in their feet. For Scholasticism the definition is a starting point, and so are axioms. Neither Aristotle nor the Scholastics ever knew how to differentiate between the function of axioms and that of definitions. Their elements are difficult to distinguish, notwithstanding the obvious difference in their terminology.

A definition is a principle for a syllogism, for ratiocination.

18. Ernout–Meillet, *ibid.*, p. 309.
19. The danger included in the idea of *gué* persists in *guet-apens*.

It is, then, the principle for deduction, which is purely a logical operation. But it—the definition itself—is not obtained by logical means. It wants to give us the Essence of the thing, that is to say, that in it from which we can enunciate propositions with unvarying or eternal truth. How can we discover, how detect that eternal "essential" fund of things, which do nothing but shift and change and mismatch themselves constantly before us? This is the decisive point in the whole theory of knowledge. On it depends the deductive theory which is science. Well then, the inadequacy of Aristotelianism on this decisive point is outstanding.

A definition is obtained by induction. And what is that? It is observing the individual things which the senses show us and seeing what regularity of behavior they manifest. For example, it is to see whether in this case, and this, and this, two characteristics or components always appear together in the thing observed, e.g. if talking appears frequently combined with having two feet.[20] We can say of *each one* of the things observed that this is a talkative biped, because it does, in fact, exhibit those two qualities. There is no doubt about it. This is an observation of various cases, it is an experience, and it constitutes the first action of inductive recognition, even though there is as yet no reasoning. Animals have this same experience. But in view of this we carry out an authentic act of reasoning and we say: if bipedism and loquacity appear together in the cases observed, we can expect that the *same thing will occur in cases which have not yet been observed.* This is reasoning by analogy, typically dialectic. Its result is a *dictum de omnii:* everything that is talkative is a biped. Now we have a universal proposition in which one speaks of *all* the things that belong to a class, to the class of the "loquacious," which we designate with an *L.*

In order to arrive at this we have drawn the analogy be-

20. The example is imaginary but, if my memory serves, the case which Aristotle discusses in the *Parts of Animals* about the correlation between long life and having no bile is identical in structure. I do not include it because it is more complicated grammatically.

tween a *few* cases and *all* cases. This is an anticipation on our part, for we have not observed *all* the cases, nor can we ever observe them. We have, then, transcended the experience which makes us recognize individual things *a posteriori* of seeing them. Now, anticipating these, we say *a priori* that *all* the *L*'s will be *B*'s (bipeds). Let us designate with the exponent *i* the unobserved cases of *L* and with *o* the observed ones. The mental operation which we perform is this: if all the L^o's are B, will the L^i's be B? This takes the logical form of a problematical proposition:

$$L^o = L^i$$
$$B \quad XB$$

In order to make the X which is alongside the B disappear, that is to say, in order to be able to say that the L^i's will *also* be B (this is anticipation based on experience), we need some reason, therefore some new principle. Inductive reasoning does not function by itself, it does not reach a conclusion as induction. It demands to be completed with some principle which is not induction. Otherwise we will have what we kept hearing in our childhood: "Because I once killed a dog they call me dogkiller." Once is the same as a thousand times. The distance to *all* which claim to be *infinite* is the same.

The reason that L^o may be B is clear: experience. This has shown us that *all* the L^o's were associated with B. This *all* (the cases observed) is correct; it coincides with its significance. Those that are this kind of *all* can be counted, but the ALL L^i is an ALL which can neither be counted nor verified. This is not a matter of facts; it expresses something which is not numerical but has rather the character of necessity. The reason that L^i may be B is that it has to be. But as the definition is a principle, it cannot itself be based on a principle. The result of this is a great fallacy. A definition is always arbitrary if it is properly a definition, that is, if it does not relate to a "simple reality," assuming that there is such a thing.

Experience, and hence induction, lets us find out only that things frequently behave in a certain manner, that they are *accustomed* to be that way. This is enough for certain rough requirements of our practical life, which is satisfied with knowing the "habits of things." But if we cut experience loose from judgment and affirm out of hand that the L's are B's— hence that every L is a B—we have greatly exaggerated the role of induction, our thinking has become hyperbolical, and the concept of essence or definition, far from being an understanding, is no more than a "costume novel."

In cases like this, irretrievably lost, our dear Suárez, like Aristotle, likes to pull the body of San Isidro [21] out on the street to see if it is raining on the definition which is not waterproof. In this case the body of San Isidro is the *lumen naturale* or *noûs*. Induction would serve only to clear away the confusion of things and facilitate the "intellectual vision" of the necessary unity which the two attributes L and B form. It is not explained to us, nor has this way of thinking the means of explaining what comprises that "intellectual vision," that explosive "intellection" or *lumen naturale*. This is the *virtus dormitiva* of knowledge. In the same way Suárez explains the basis of axioms.[22]

21. San Isidro is a famous and popular saint of Madrid to whom people for centuries have prayed when they wanted rain, or did not want it [*Translator's note*].

22. Recalling the somewhat harsh reference to Gilson (p. 143, note 1) and to show that in this matter one would have to cover a good deal of ground, I will say now that while the *lumen naturale* is in Suárez, as in St. Thomas, an ultimate fact—and therefore somewhat irrational—for St. Augustine, on the contrary, it constitutes a tremendous problem which, as he should, he sees himself obliged to take apart, building out of it because of that a wholly admirable theory: "illuminism." Gilson will say later that St. Thomas took the more difficult road and St. Augustine the easier one. St. Augustine was much more of a philosopher than St. Thomas, as is shown by his resolute attack on ultimate problems. But he was not, nor could he be in his day, an unsurpassable *administrator* of the Greco-Arabic-Gothic philosophic heritage which is what St. Thomas was. In this sense it is understandable that the Church—not Catholicism—would have preferred St. Thomas, because the Church is a State, and States have always, with some reason, preferred good administrators to geniuses. Geniuses are always disturbers, and dangerous. Every great creation is on its reverse side a cataclysm. The proof of this is the first creation—that of the angels. What a mess that was! There is perhaps another more substantial reason for the Thomism of the Church, which is this: philosophy does not, as

Empirical induction, exaggerated by analogy into *one* argument, would be the way to arrive at principles. But reasoning by analogy does not work; it has no authentic basis, and in order to counterfeit one, the *deus ex machina* of the *lumen naturale* or *intelligence* is dragged out. A supposedly exact and deductive way of thinking, which shows so little refinement in the most important intellectual operation, thus shows in the search for principles that it does not understand them, and it is precisely the teeming multitude of principles which it tolerates that strips them of validity as such and makes them of little moment.

Because it is fictitious, illusory, and arbitrary, the functioning of analogy, which would make induction complete—as it is complete in contemporary mathematics since Poincaré—the one and only source of principles remains the purest empiricism. What is comic in Scholastic concepts comes because they are merely the result of modest experimental observation and thus would be admirably useful because they would always be subject to correction in view of later observations, although they would not be "principles" nor serve for a deductive theory. But analogy brings the bellows of the *lumen naturale* and inflates them, transforming them into

------

is natural, interest the Christian. He does not need it as philosophy. But "to speak of God"—*theologeîn*—does interest him. Well now, in order to speak one needs a language, a system of signs which is common to those who carry on the dialogue. This, for a Christian, is philosophy— a language, a *modus dicendi*, and nothing more. Philosophy as knowledge for its own sake, as truth, does not enter into the question. Thus, philosophy is neutralized and converted into mere terminology. But then it is appropriate that philosophy be chosen as a language, as a habitual means of putting oneself in harmony with God. In the final analysis all philosophy, even as knowledge, remains at such a great distance from its object—God—that even the best one is so incongruous with its theme that everything stays at the same level. What is lacking is that the philosophy-terminology in which one speaks should always be the same for all, as coordinates of reference. Whichever is chosen, then, will depend on secondary qualities: for example, being a good and complete terminology, which is what philosophy is in the seminaries. The complete opposite of a system of questions, namely, a dictionary of terms.

absolute concepts, into *dicta de omni et nullo,* and the paltry notions of sensual and observational origin, blameless in themselves, are obliged, because of this inflation, to be "principles" and to rise aerostatically, like those crude tissue paper figures of men and animals made in the shape of balloons to entertain children at village fairs. Out of this come definitions like the one about man being a rational animal, not much less inept than the one about the featherless biped, but much more regrettable.

During the second half of the 19th Century all the Messieurs Homais,[23] who were predominant in the Europe of those days —and not a few of those we suffer from today are survivors— opposed modern science, which began at the end of the Renaissance with what they called Aristotelian-Scholastic "pseudoscience," attributing its defects to the fact that, unlike Mr. Pickwick, it did not observe Nature. The imputation is most stupid. They had only to read the works of Galileo himself to find out that the very opposite had occurred, and that it was the Scholastics who imputed to Galileo a failure to rely on observation. Galileo's *nuova scienza,* which will become physics, *is not characterized* by observation, but by just the opposite, and, strictly speaking, by nonobservations, as we shall see very shortly. Those who observed, the empiricists, were the others. Taking into account the times and the circumstances, it would be no exaggeration to say that Aristotle was the man who observed more things in all of Nature, including man, his societies and his poetic creations, much more than Darwin, much more than Virchow, much more than Pasteur. But also there was always one or another of the Scholastics, who with normal frequency after the 14th Century, continued to do no little observing. Only the Iberian Scholastics—those of Salamanca, Coimbra, or Cómpluto—failed to do any observing, because they were posthumous Scholastics and behind the times, Scholastics of the

23. M. Homais, the pharmacist in Flaubert's *Madame Bovary,* is a prototype of the pompous little pedant who thinks he knows more than he does [*Translator's note*].

Scholastics, which is no mean accomplishment. This does not mean that in theology as in philosophy there were not among them minds that were noble and egregiously endowed. Individuals cannot be held responsible for the space-time destiny into which they are born. With minds like those of Fonseca, Toledo, Suárez and John of St. Thomas—to name only a few of them—disposed to function in another direction, it is very probable that Spain would have been the nation to create modern philosophy and science. Except for a certain number of names—such as Kepler, Galileo, Fermat, Descartes—it is doubtful that outside Spain there were men as well endowed for thought as those mentioned above. There is not, then, any intention to belittle, in the slightest, full recognition of their great gifts.

On the contrary, it is a matter of sympathizing wholeheartedly with their destiny and by the same token . . . weeping over it.

In all modern philosophy—indeed in the whole exact way of thinking which created modern science (physico-mathematical)—experience has never been given as important a role as it played in the Aristotelian-Scholastic doctrine. Yet in all truth, this judgment can be given too much importance, keeping in mind that in Leibnitz and Descartes—to cite the two names of highest standing in modern philosophy who were at the same time the great creators of mathematics and physics—experience is the only notion about which they are confused. They do not know quite what to do with it, nor what precise role to entrust to it in formulating exact knowledge.

The defect in the traditional method is thus, on the other hand, the excessive and inappropriate importance which it grants to experience. This excess is what obliges us to class it as empiricism in a pejorative sense. Because the deductive theory depends on principles, they make experience responsible for producing them. This is what cannot be, for experience is the antiprinciple. If one tries to make experience in general into *the* principle of knowledge, as some Positivists (not Comte) attempted, this will not be through experience, but by virtue of some *a priori* reasoning.

This reveals the confused idea that this way of thinking has of "principle," which gave place to what the moderns fought so fiercely. According to them this begins by confusing the *principium essendi* with the *principium cognoscendi*. The fact is that Aristotle distinguishes perfectly between the "first for us" and the "first in reality." He has his reasons, by no means to be disdained, for asserting that the principle of knowing should be the principle of Being. Quite so, the moderns—Descartes, Leibnitz, Kant—will say to this, yet this does not relieve us, but rather enjoins us to settle accounts beforehand with ourselves and, since this is a "first for us," to develop and analyze the order which this creates, even though we may think that it is provisional and that the order, which will ultimately be regarded as correct, is the one which begins with the "first in Being." Once this admirable distinction is made, there is no use to leave it at that, instead of going straight to the heart of the matter and examining it to see why this distinction is there and in what it consists. Aristotle, according to the moderns, was obliged to construct a philosophy with a double perspective: one perspective which explains the order of thinking just as thinking, or subjectivity—the appearance of the world when it is seen as simply *ordo et connexio idearum*—beyond which appears the need for the other perspective, in which the world is seen as *ordo et connexio rerum*.[24] Aristotle saw this task but he left it essentially incomplete, and modern philosophers have had to finish it. This incompleteness was the reason why Aristotle never had a clear notion of what "principle" is. The element of duplicity in the terms which he uses to dominate it reveals this. Principle is ἀρχή (*arkhé*) and πρῶτον (*prôton*). *Arkhé* is "the most ancient" with which the process of reality, *origin*, began. It is a term which the "physiologers" of Ionia may perhaps have already used and it appears when one seeks the genesis of natural phenomena. It is a heritage from prephilosophic ways of thinking—of

24. This, for example, is what Hegel does in his *Phenomenology of Mind*.

Genealogy, of Cosmogony—in short, of the Myth, which is a formal *arkheo-logía. Arkhé* is the "ultimate for us," the farthest away or most distant. *Prôton* is originally the "first for us," the nearest, from which we depart to go to the far away. Since "what is *common* to all *arkhai* is to be the first," [25] (the first in an order, it is understood), one must not stop with this common, generic, and abstract attribute of "principle." This "must" is not a whim of mine; it is an imperative imposed by the Aristotelian doctrine, as we have seen, when it insists that we consider as "real," that is, as concrete, only what is specific, peculiar to it (*idion*). To put it another way, among the things or somethings which are principle simply *because* they are first in an order, one must decide on the one which is principle in the best and most appropriate sense. In short, one must decide in favor of *one* of the two orders—that of ideas or that of realities—in order to invest it with the character of *absolutely* first. What will be principle in this absolutely first order will be "principle" by *antomasia* and *appropriately* so. As for knowing, we are not at liberty to choose because knowing is a subjective act, our own doing and nothing more, but it is the order in which the objective order, the order of Being,[26] must manifest itself. *For* a *cognoscente*, therefore, the "absolute" order is the *ordo idearum*. Absolute does not mean that it is the only one, nor the most important or decisive, but that the adjective will refer *exclusively* to the notion of principle. This is a matter of deciding what should be considered as "absolutely principle" or as "principle in the absolute," which does not determine in advance that what may be "absolutely principle" must be the absolute *simpliciter*, for example, the absolute in the real or absolute reality.

The *proper* concept of principle must be principle in the order of knowing. Out of its meaning in that order comes the

25. *Metaphysics*, V, 1, 1013ᵃ 17.
26. I use the terms "subjective" and "objective" here in order to be easily understood, with the value which it is customary to give them today, in contrast to the one they had in Scholasticism. The inversion of meaning does not in the least modify the exposition of the problem, which I set forth *from the point of view* of Aristotelian-Scholasticism.

one that it has in the order of Being. To affirm with respect to the notion of principle the absolute precedence of the *ordo idearum* as compared with the *ordo rerum* does not imply any idealism. Thus Descartes proclaims this view and, nevertheless, it is not idealistic. But in proclaiming it one can be even less idealistic than Descartes, namely, not at all.

Aristotle's language quoted above is a weighty passage. Read that whole first chapter of Book V in *Metaphysics* and you will see that it summarizes and brings out the result of the detailed induction which precedes it. This, in Aristotle, is the natural goal of the mental activity which coalesces into a definition. It is, then, nothing less than the definition of principle. We have seen that it is, in terms of Aristotle, improper because it says the common and not the right things about principle. But even if taken as an abstract (generic, common) definition, it is not felicitous. It says that "the character common to all principles is to be the first from which Being, or generation, or knowledge derives." Let the reader be sincere with himself and ask himself what, in this definition, lingers in his mind as the most decisive aspect of principle. I do not think there is any room for doubt; it is the importance of its primordial character. It is undeniable that in this definition there is a second matter of importance: to be that *from which* other things emerge. The expression that Aristotle uses most frequently when he refers to principle is not a noun or an adjective but a mere bit of syntax, an adverbial particle: ὅθεν (*hóthen*), "from whence." [27] Principle is "that from whence. . . ." This particle does not make the least allusion to the idea of primordiality, but on the *contrary*, enunciates the idea of posteriority or subsequency. It states "something *x*, from whence *y* follows." It is a magnificent algebraic expression, it is a function. A function is a "thing" for which there is no place in Aristotle's logic. But let us leave this extreme behind. Faced with the primordial element, the "from

27. In Spanish the word *principio* means both "principle" and "beginning." Ortega implies here that Aristotle may have used the word "principle" as "beginning from whence" [*Translator's note*].

whence" reveals the importance of subordination, the subsequent or the posterior, that is to say, according to this, principle is not something first but simply something which another thing follows, *from whence* another thing *follows*.

At the beginning of this study we already saw that there were two faces of "principle," inseparable from each other but each distinct from the other. No one can think of one without juxtathinking [28] the other, [29] and, nevertheless, it is of decisive importance that greater attention be given to one face or the other; indeed, I could even say that thinkers are divided into two classes: those who adhere to the belief that principle is "the first," and those who emphasize more strongly that principle should be "that from which other things follow." Now, that affirmation of mine takes on a meaning which is clear, concrete, and fruitful because, in spite of the fact that Aristotle identifies principle by means of the particle "from whence," the truth is that he always sees it in its primordial aspect, and this entails enormous consequences.

To understand it let us imagine the inverse case, which will be no waste of time because it will be the Leibnitz case and we will save ourselves later discussion. Anyone to whom the most important thing about principle is that consequences follow it or derive from it, will have to look for such a principle among concepts or propositions from which, in fact, *many* other truths are derived. It might even be possible that all the truths of a science are derived from it; even more, one might dream that *all* the truths of all the sciences could be derived from a minimum number of principles, so that instead of many sciences there would be only one, a *science universelle* or

28. Ortega, with his love of words, takes the example of juxtapose (in Spanish, *juxtaponar*) and creates in Spanish "*juxtapensar*," which has no proper English equivalent except the awkward "think side by side" or "think together" [*Translator's note*].

29. This is what I call "thinking by addition" about what one actually thinks in each case. Juxtathinking can be analytic or synthetic. On thinking right we analytically juxtathink left. On thinking "whiteness" I synthetically juxtathink "extension," because color cannot show itself without extending over a surface.

mathesis universalis. In this event the most general possible component will be added to principle. Principle is thus, *a nativitate,* a systematic principle or a system for everything. One cannot admit that there could be *individual* principles, that is, *idiotas,* because one then runs the risk that there would be almost as many principles as things, and knowledge would be converted into a duplication of the real, which would make it useless and meaningless.[30] But, as Aristotle held with perfect reason, in demanding the *individual* principle as against the principle which states only the general character of the *common,* he wants to say that this other tendency will lead to the discovery of a *generalization which is not common in character.* So that, paradoxically, it happens that in the matter of principle the one who gives less importance to being "the first" is he who refuses to recognize as principle anything except what in an absolute sense is first. He will not, like Aristotle and the Scholastics, have recourse to distinguishing between the *principles* of infantry and the *first* principles of artillery, a repetitive and redundant expression which in itself proclaims an inadequate notion of principle. Finally, on finding that tradition—the Aristotelian-Scholastic one—has in science made principles teem like mushrooms, squandering them in spite of Ockham's razor,[31] the principle will be established that it is necessary to try to demonstrate principles; clearly, so that they leave off being principles in the sense of truths *per se notae.* This is precisely what Leibnitz says.

These deliberations with respect to the role of "principle," which we have constructed *a priori* from the simple tendency to prefer and to place the importance of subsequence ahead of the notion of principle, are—one after another and point by point—the new and characteristic attitudes in the history of philosophy which will constitute Leibnitz' *principle-ism.*

30. Duns Scotus, in fact, reached this extreme with his *haecceitas,* in which the individual thing is converted into a principle, and the man Socrates is accompanied by his real spirit, the *Socratitas.*

31. This phrase is best explained by Bertrand Russell as referring to a maxim which says: "Entities are not to be multiplied without necessity" [*Translator's note*].

If the reader has for many pages felt himself off the track and not seeing clearly why I made him enter into so many, and such varied, themes, I hope that now he will recognize that these were indispensable if we want to reach a real and masterly comprehension of the subject matter with which this study is concerned. Not that we have yet achieved this with what has been said, but we are now at the level, and at the starting point, which will make it possible for us to achieve it.

We ought to end this long journey in which we have patiently analyzed the traditional way of thinking and the meaning of deductive theory in Aristotelian-Scholastic doctrine by taking matters to their ultimate decisive point, namely, by formulating in exact and clear terms the reason why, in view of what we have said, a form of thinking that is thing-ist, commonist, sensual and *idiota*—cannot have a clear idea of what a principle is, and it is therefore incapable of constructing authentic deductive theories, save for its glorious restoration of formal logic or, more precisely, of the theory of the syllogism. We could do so at once, but not every reader would easily understand it. On the other hand, he will reach it on his own initiative if we leave the formulation of that decisive point until we have begun to explore the opposite way of thinking, which is the "modern" way.

Now I only want to finish showing why Aristotle always moves so hesitantly and clumsily when it is a matter of principles *as such*, especially of the most characterized of principles, which are the axioms.

I said that he had his first decisive, and most vigorous, intrinsic experience of these when he prepared the *Topics* and constructed his dialectic, the first form of his "logic." Dialectical thinking and scientific thinking are mixed together in this work. Consideration is given to each of them equally. Hence "principles" in the dialectic as such—that is, on its level of importance—may be either those that are true or those that are simply plausible. Therefore, he does not explicitly call them principles, but only established and accepted "prevailing opinions." The validity of principle is here a social and not a personal fact, as a genuine scientific principle will be. Hence axioms are presented as no more than ordinary opinions, as commonplaces. It is not a good way to begin dealing with principles. One starts by counting on them, like external facts which "are there" in the public square, in the community, but are not respected nor interesting for their unusual content. They are *idola fori*. Never, it seems to me, was Aristotle cured of this youthful adventure, and from it comes the fact that, with two exceptions, he always speaks of this, that, and the other axiom, citing it as an example and interpreting its superficial aspect, but never going to the heart of its *dictum*. And it is curious that the Scholastics have also inherited this *tic*.

It will be said that before that adventure Aristotle had another which was much more serious and profound: his reception of Platonism and with it his plunging into the most rigorous thinking. How was it that he did not experience there the pure epiphany of principles? Well . . . there it is. Plato's thinking is extremely precise and also it carries with it a requirement for principles of the highest quality, the most general principles which must be so in the most absolute sense. Plato does not divide *the* science into sciences. Science for him is one and undivided. Plato is a Cartesian and a Leibnitzian *avant la lettre*. Very well. But the fact is . . . how shall I put it? The fact is that Plato never achieved a properly set and established doctrine, complete in its *corpus* with well-defined members. *Plato's philosophy is really only a program.*[32] It was certainly so fertile and full of genius that in the final analysis the entire Occident has lived on it up to now, including Christianity through one of its roots. This does not change the fact that Platonism is not properly a doctrine, but rather a doctrinal *magma*. This explains the paradoxical fact that, although this is the intellectual tendency which provides the most direct impetus toward general principles, none of that character appears in Plato. Incredible as it may seem, there is no term in Plato for designating a proposition which is a principle. It is

32. Much more than what the *Dialogues* tells us of it, which is only bits and pieces.

clear that he perceived its function through its effects, but he never reached a clear and distinct notion of it. As this, I repeat, has the aspect of something incredible, it is worth pausing to give it a moment's attention.

Plato did not have the good fortune to find any man to talk with who was worthy of him, and this makes him, despite the mountain range of books written about his person and his works, seem something less than complete; as a reality he is unknown. Only a few simple observations have been made which would help to explain him. One of these, which I merely state but do not develop further, is that Plato, as a thinker and writer, is a surprising mixture of the archaic and the futurist. Aristotle, on the other hand, seems in the chronology of Greek life to represent "modernity." One of the characteristics of the archaic thinker is that he does not speak in "finite terms," he does not hammer them out. His language is not terminology but the current jargon. Hence, there are generally very few of Plato's concepts which *come close* to demonstrating the crystalline character of "finite terms." I would even venture to say that except for dialectic there are, strictly speaking, none. Hence, the difficulty of understanding Platonic thought. Terminology, of course, is a typically cynical "modern" practice.

Time and again Plato uses the word ἀρχή (*arkhé*) which in Aristotle is a term for "principle." But in Plato it *never* has any real terminological value. He uses it exactly as the Athenians used it in the Agora and in their colloquial exchanges. It is the beginning, it is exordium, it is the start, it is the first, it is fundamental, it is the ancient, it is the highest and so on. Like any good word in the living common language it has innumerable semantic variations. On the other hand, it *never* means "principle" with complete and stringent conviction. We shall immediately have a most vivid demonstration of this.

Arkhé—principle—is in Aristotle, as in all later science, that proposition from which reasoning starts. Well now, in Plato that is called ὑπόθεσις (*hypótesis*): supposition, a "provisional admission from which we start." Generally that hypothesis from which we start is too narrow and problematical. Then we seek another broader, firmer one—ἀσφαλής (asphalés)—, less problematical, and so on until we reach one whose usefulness as the point of departure for reasoning appears to be "sufficient"—ἱκανόν (hikanón). That was for him what we will call relative principle, and that *is* the only "term" with which Plato usually expresses its initial function. Curious! Sufficient is the same word that, with some surprise, we found in the explanation of axioms in the *Analytics*. Curious! *Sufficient* is the adjective with which Leibnitz categorizes a principle as more manifestly principle since it proclaims the need for principles—the principle of sufficient reason. It is an adjective which he does not use often because it is redundant. Principle is precisely "that which is sufficient," above all, in his doctrine.[33]

My attention will be called to the fact that I have forgotten the main thing: that Plato speaks of something which is even more than just sufficient, which is ultrasufficient because it is ἀρχή ἀνυπόθετος (*Republic*, VI, 500) *arkhé anhypóthetos*, ultrahypothetical or nonhypothetical principle. Is this not the most explicit expression which conveys the notion of principle? No. Indeed it designates the "thing" called principle, but the word *arkhé* here does not explicitly mean principle. That very expression is the strongest proof of the opposite. If *arkhé* meant principle the adjective "nonhypothetical" was redundant. That this is joined to *arkhé* shows that for Plato the normal *arkhai* were hypothetical, hence not properly principles. What *comes close* to being a precise term in that expression is not *arkhé* but "nonhypothetical," which means or is, and this time I speak more cautiously, the "fundamental" thing. Well now, this word appears only twice in Plato, *both times on pages 501b and 511b of Book VI of the Republic*. As that expression is in fact the one which comes closest to enunciating the precise notion of principle, which in all of Plato's works presents only that ambiguous aspect, it demon-

33. See in the first chapter of this study, p. 13: "The principle of sufficient reason."

strates overwhelmingly the incredible fact that Plato never came to have a *clear and distinct* understanding of the exceptional function which can reasonably claim to be fulfilled in the body of knowledge by what we call "principle" because he would still have to add something about the real meaning of *anhypóthetos*. Strictly speaking, this is the ultimate principle, beyond which no other is affirmed, but which, on the other hand, affirms or affords a basis for all the rest. But this would not be understood as referring primarily to the series of thoughts—hence to the *ordo idearum*—but rather to the order of realities. The *arkhé anhypóthetos* is the reality from which all the rest emerge and from which they acquire their being. By the same token, it serves secondarily as a principle of knowledge in deductive theory. But the basic difference between Aristotle and Plato is brought out forcibly here because, even taking *arkhé anhypóthetos* as a beginning of knowledge, this is not *because it is evident* or true *per se nota* but, on the contrary, because all other forms of knowledge follow it or are derived from it. *In Plato there is nothing, at least openly declared, which may be true because it professes to be evident.* That principle, then, is not differentiated in its character as truth from any other true proposition. It is, therefore, not a principle in the strict meaning of Aristotle. Hence Aristotle could not learn from Plato what in his opinion a principle is.[34]

Principles do not appear as such except when thought is formalized and formulated, when its joints are tightened, when its architecture appears. Platonic doctrine never met any of these conditions. So that, contrary to what one might believe, the apprenticeship of Aristotle to Platonism, far from bringing the young philosopher face to face with the intrinsic experience of authentic, general, and systematic principles, ac-

34. The coincidence between what Plato actually took as principle (in the sense we think of its character), and what principle is *today* in deductive theory, is prodigious, almost incredible. We will prove it in discussing the most recent axiomaticism.

customed him not to perceive them. So much more is he to be admired in that he gave to what he called principles (for example, definitions) the importance that, when all is said and done, he does give them. My idea, then, is that Aristotle on his own account, and later, discovers "something like a principle"—from among principles which not he, but the Scholastics called "evident," irresponsible and haphazardly true principles which pretend to be undemonstrable [35]—in the process of making his great discovery, after the *Topics*, of the apodictical *analytical* syllogism. This is a cart which cannot move unless the two oxen which are the premises are yoked to it. These premises of the syllogisms are, for Aristotle, principles. Given his ontological way of thinking, these logical principles are what they are because they were already principles in reality.

I said that Aristotle did not spend his time solitarily (*singulatim*) with principles, save for two exceptions. We cannot end this outline of his way of thinking without paying some attention to those exceptions.

In Book IV (I) of the *Metaphysics* we find confirmation of the fact that Aristotle did not have an easy conscience over his behavior toward principles. There they were, being nothing less than cement for the sciences, and nobody bothered to reflect on them in terms of epistemology. This *nobody* was Aristotle in particular. The men of science did not have to elucidate them; this would make a question of them, and for the geometrician the principles of geometry are not to be questioned. "There was there," then, a reality—the principles —to become a question for which no discipline, *pragmateia* or science existed. Aristotle, for whom sciences existed only in the plural, had just invented one more, which as a science is merely one among many, but which has the special character of the generality of its subject. While the rest give their attention to various forms of the Real this one scrutinizes the

---

35. ". . . *principia indemonstrabilia, quae cognoscuntur per lumen intellectus agentis*" (Saint Thomas, *Contra gentiles*, III, c. 46; cf. *Summa theol., Prima pars*, qu. 17, art. 3, ad 2; qu. 85, art. 6; qu. 117, art. 1).

Real insofar as it is real, ignoring—in principle—its particular forms.[36] As nothing can be studied, "theorized"—that is, considered regardless of the service it contributes or can contribute to us—unless it is metamorphosed into Reality or Ens, this means that all comprehension of its particular character, its peculiar *entity*, assumes that we already understand what being Ens is—in the abstract. Or, what is the same thing, that the science of the Ens—just that—must come first. Since it is first, there will evidently be competition from the theoretical treatment of everything which in any real sense can be called first. Among these are the "principles of the sciences." And Aristotle then feels a prick of conscience for having never taken the question of these principles seriously. Without very pressing reasons but nevertheless hastily, as always happens when he speaks of the principles of knowing, Aristotle decides that his newborn science of the Ens is the one which should attend to them. He announces the project solemnly, and we lend an attentive ear. It deserves no less. At last Aristotle is going to speak of the principles of the sciences! But once more the Stagyrite limits himself to providing examples. After declaring that the science of scientific principles is the *first philosophy*, he says not a single relevant and important new word about them.

On the other hand, he busies himself in depth, relatively speaking, with two principles, only two—that of contradiction

36. Previously, in his Platonic phase, he had invented another science, which was concerned with a *particular* form of the Real, the most conclusive of all, namely, the First Real, from which, in a certain sense, all the others issue, or at least on which they depend. This First Real, this chief of the line of the Entia, is the Supreme Ens or God, and the science is called *theology*. Later, upon inventing the other science of the Real insofar as it is Real, which eventually would be called *ontology*, Aristotle found two sciences which had to be first in the *series:* two πρώτη φιλοσοφία (*próte philosophía*), one because its subject is the First Ens, the other because its subject is the ens in general. Each had rightful title as they struggled for first position in Aristotle's mind, and the result was that he was a bit muddled. The "tablets" of both sciences were mislaid and mixed together and thus, introduced into each other as digressions, they came down to us with the unrepresentative title of *metaphysical books.*

and that of the excluded middle—which also seem to be principles of all the other sciences but which, for the very reason that they were so general, were not enunciated by the mathematicians of Aristotle's day. They were left in the background, like something taken for granted. On the other hand, the generation previous to that of the first mathematicians, educated or influenced by Plato, begin enunciating those two principles, or at least the one about contradiction. In this third chapter of the fourth metaphysical book Aristotle submits these two principles to the same kind of acrobatics which he made the mathematical axioms perform; he makes them vibrate up and down like springs; he turns them into Cartesian demons of doubt. On the one hand—and more specifically here than in the *Analytics*—he says that common principles or axioms are valid for all the Entia [37] but then he immediately makes it clear that their use is limited to the "genus" with which each science is concerned. With this he once more transfers his attention to each science when he has just said that they *cannot*, that they have no means of giving axioms attentive consideration.

Well now, the two principles of contradiction and the excluded middle, most general with respect to all being, are for that very reason appropriate, specific or catholic with respect to Ens as Ens. That is to say, they are the *special* axioms of metaphysics or ontology.[38] Therefore, Aristotle has no choice

---

37. *Metaphysics*, IV, 3, 1005ᵃ 22.

38. We have, then, the following: contradiction and excluded middle are principles peculiar to the Ens and *therefore* they are *generic* principles of other things. But this implies that Ens is the "genus" of the *entia*. Now then, Aristotle does not admit that Being might be a genus. Its relationship to the rest is very strange. When a relationship is very strange—that is, incomprehensible to him—Aristotle calls it "analogical." And once again we have the fact that *everything fundamental in Aristotle is dialectic* (*Posterior Analytics*, I, II, 77ᵃ 29). I reserve the development of this theme for myself. What I want to underline here is only that on this point of the value of contradiction and the excluded middle it appears very clear, *as much* for the Ens *as* for *entia*, that Aristotle never saw clearly the relationship between his concept of Ens as such and *entia* or things. This is not by chance but, as we shall see, for an important reason.

but to plunge in, examine (?) his *dictum* and ask himself about the aspect which their truth presents. Without this the ontologist cannot take a step, and since for every ontologist there is always an ontologist and a half, there are gentlemen who come forward, plant themselves before Aristotle, and dispute him, refusing to accept the truth of those principles in good faith. Among those gentlemen there was one who was truly, to a superlative degree, one of the most lordly lords who have existed in our Milky Way, son of kings and himself a king, the great Heraclitus of Ephesus. Aristotle referred to him by name but carefully refrained from voicing a similar opinion of him and left to others the responsibility of interpreting Heraclitus in that way.

A whole book would have to be written about Chapters 3, 4, 7, and 8 of Book IV of *Metaphysics* because those chapters, being immediately concerned with its two axiomatic principles, are the essence of philosophy. It is inconceivable, is it not, that this work of meticulous commentary has not been completed? But it is a fact; a fact that includes another, no less inconceivable. Even up to the present time Aristotle's "ontological or metaphysical theory" has not been studied pragmatically, that is, studied insofar as it is *pragmateia*, explaining its theoretical anatomy, revealing its scientific structure. If this had been done, it would have been apparent that Aristotle, without meaning to and without being aware of it, but inspired by the very nature of things, begins his doctrine with an *axiomática*, that is to say, with a system of definitions and axioms. The explanation of the concept of Ens *qua* ens is a "definition." The principles of contradiction and of the excluded middle are both explicit axioms. Aristotle does not quite know why he feels obliged to discuss these. The reason cited above, that is, since they were first, the first science had to concern itself with them, is beside the point and obscure.

We shall find that when he characterized the concept of Ens as analogous Aristotle was right, and was not right. [A note in the manuscript, never developed further, says at this point: "Formalization. Ens is not a commonist but a formalist genus."]

But why did he speak of them precisely in Chapter 3? The previous chapter ended with a consideration of competing principles. These posed the *disputa maxima* with which philosophy began and which, for about a century and a half, did not cease for a minute. The real cannot ultimately consist in contrariety, as those Pythagorean antiphilosophers, Empedocles and others, maintained. The Real must be One: Parmenides; then the Multiple is not explained: Heraclitus, Prothagorus, Democritus, Plato, and Aristotle; the Real must be *One* and *Multiple*, identical and contradictory. This last is what Aristotle says at the end of Chapter 2. Such a thesis cannot be sustained if it is not made precise. Axioms appear when something must be made precise, be made *exact*. The sense in which the Real must be One and the sense in which it can nevertheless be Multiple and contradictory must be interpreted strictly. This is the reason why, on turning this corner and not elsewhere, Aristotle finds himself obliged to discuss the two great principles. This explains the *place*, but the basic reason is otherwise: that there can be no deductive theory unless it begins with a *system of axioms*. *Velis nolis*, Aristotle, without ever recognizing the reason, had no choice but to construct the *axiomática of the Ens*.[39]

Therefore, he begins by stating the principle of contradiction in the form which applies to practically everything. He obviously means that the Ens cannot, at the same time and in the same sense, be and not be; be thus and not be thus. According to this formulation the primary truth of this principle would come from Reality itself. Aristotle does not say this, but he accepts it. Or better, he does not accept it, but under all his deliberation and careful thinking there develops in him that earlier and basic conviction that: first, the Real is as it is, but how is it going to be? second, this is the first truth, the fundamental assumption on which all the rest is based.

39. The same formulation of "principle" is found in Plato and emerges in the *same place* when someone makes the point that the tops which children play with are at once stationary and in movement—the central point stationary, the rest rotating—hence, by reason of the unity of the one and the opposites (*Republic*, IV, 437ᵃ).

What there is in us which we do not ourselves generate *develops* in us through the *people* to which we belong, through our collectivity or village. It is the *people* who generate everything which *develops*, every anonymous operation. That Aristotle does not even try to ask himself the question as to whether that principle in its *real* or ontological meaning is true or not, and *why*, or at least *how*, reveals that this is one of those "incomprehensible" secrets of which a "national soul" is made; in this case the Hellenic soul. Since our own people, throughout the whole of Western development, have been inheriting traits from the Greek people, this has also become, *though by inheritance and not at first hand*, an "incomprehensible" secret of our own "collective soul."

It will be argued against this that before formulating the principle—in 1005^b 14 ff. *et seq.*—Aristotle has already anticipated the demonstration of its truth by saying: "The most solid and enduring principle of all will be the one with respect to which it will be impossible to admit of error. It will have to be the best known, necessary and nonhypothetical." Now then, a principle that it is necessary to accept—ἀναγκαῖον ἔχειν (*anankaîon ékhein*)—in order to understand any Ens is not hypothetical. What is necessary to know in order to know any Ens is necessarily what was already known in advance." [40] These conditions reconcile the principle of contradiction; *ergo.* . . .

Everything in this most famous passage is surprising. In the first place, that nothing less than the principle of all proofs and understanding should be *proved*. In the second place, that it should be proved by showing that it is *necessary in order to prove*, which is equivalent to understanding all the rest. In

40. Compare with the Greek of Aristotle the Oxford translation which reads as follows: ". . . the most certain principle of all is that regarding which it is impossible to be mistaken; for such a principle must be both the best known, necessary and nonhypothetical. For a principle which every one must have who understands anything that is, is not a hypothesis; and that which every one must know who knows anything, he must already have when he comes to a special study" [*Translator's note*].

the third place, that with this "proof" it is still not proved that it is true, but, as an act of supererogation, it is the *most* true of all. In the fourth place, that in proving it there is no attempt to prove that its concrete *dictum* is true, but that it is *necessary* for it to be so *in order* that there be understanding. In the fifth place, that it will then have been proved as a principle of understanding, but not as what it was presented as—the principle of Being. Therefore, that although it may be true for being, it is not true for understanding, but inversely that it is the *principium essendi* because it is proved as the *principium cognoscendi*. But this *principium cognoscendi* can be less than nothing for Aristotle unless it is previously true as a *principium essendi*. In the sixth place, it is surprising that the whole proof hangs on the assumption that there must be understanding, a thing which is exceedingly problematical.[41]

Let us add only one detail. The beginning of that "proof" is a dig at the method of hypothesis which Plato advocated; hence, there appears in it the quasi-term *anhypóthetos* which Plato had invented, a term so un-Aristotelian that Aristotle used it this one time only. It is a *hápax*. Aristotle, who was one of the greatest of human geniuses, did not have to be generous. He was a "reasoner," and very frequently the "reasoners" are perverse and coldblooded animals. For *both* reasons, an astonishing number of mathematicians have taken part in all the bloody revolutions. Aristotle spent 20 years at Plato's side and he spent another 20 years spitting in the eye of Plato's memory.

It is no use saying that in that quoted passage Aristotle does not prove the principle of contradiction, because for him proving is something very different. In previous pages we have seen what Aristotle actually regards as proof. But here it is not only whether or not Aristotle believed that those lines

41. Lichtenberg, a German humorist of the 18th Century, goes into a bookshop. The bookseller shows him various new books, among them a very voluminous one which he offers, saying: "You ought to take this because it is essential for reading the odes of Klopstock." To this Lichtenberg answers: "All right, but . . . as a matter of fact I do not read the odes of Klopstock!"

were what he called proof, but whether that passage, whatever Aristotle thought, is proof or not. There is not the least doubt that it is.

The operation that we call "reading a book" is not complete when we have understood what we believe the author *wanted to say*. This falls short of understanding *what the author said without meaning to say it*, and also, an understanding of what he *has done* willy-nilly with his work and every line of it, because a book, a page, a phrase, are actions—voluntary or involuntary. This, and not the idea of it that the author had is the genuine reality of a piece of writing. We must free ourselves once and for all from what we might call "philological psychologism."

What those lines convey to us is something more interesting and important than if they enunciated a proof which Aristotle had deliberately thought out. They show us that, very much against his will—and furthermore, in that excessive form of the involuntary which is "not taking it into account"—Aristotle had no choice but to prove the principle. The greater part of the demonstration is the definition of principle: absolute principle is a proposition of truth, improbable according to normal apodictical, nonhypothetical but necessary proof. The lesser part says: there is a proposition—that of noncontradiction—the truth of which is *necessary* to the existence of any other truths whatever. The conclusion announces, then, that this proposition is an absolute principle. It is a syllogism. That it may not be the typical apodictical syllogism in the Aristotelian sense, does not deprive it in the least of its syllogistic quality.

But it is not enough to show that a thinker *has done* something he did not do or he did not realize, did not think he had done, but it is necessary then to show how the thing he has done was reflected in his thought. Because to have done something without realizing it, does not mean that this was done under chloroform. Aristotle does not realize that he has proved the principle of contradiction *because* to him such an operation was incomprehensible. In his judgment, principles are what cannot be proved. Moreover, the proof which he achieved is not what he was accustomed to *seeing as* proof. But he was entirely aware that he had done something that came close to this, and hence in later paragraphs—in lines 1006 to 4—he will say: "We have just assumed—νῦν εἰλήψαμεν (*nyn eiléphamen*)—as impossible that the Ens may be and at the same time not be and *through this*—διὰ τοῦτο (dià toûto)—we have shown—ἐδείξαμεν (*edeixamen*)—that this is the surest principle —βεβαιοτάτη (*bebaiotáte*)—of all." This is how Aristotle tells himself what he has just done.[42]

It is interesting to note the vocabulary employed. The phrase seems to be written in English, which is the language for not saying what one cannot avoid saying but does not want to say; the elusive language par excellence. Take note: he does not say "we have just perceived, not yet proved, nor even convinced ourselves or shown our conviction," but instead he says "assuming," that is, "taking as truth," "taking into account that something is thus," as one who, on saying this, expresses a fact and not a law, without, on the other hand, denying that it is a firm and operative law. A typical Anglicism![43] The same thing happens in another difficult spot. Once he had "admitted" the truth of the *dictum* enunciated in the principle of contradiction, what does Aristotle think should then be done with it? Demonstrate that it is true "in

42. This refers to the lines previously copied and it goes on to the end of Chap. 3, which merely reiterates what is said in them.
   Compare the Oxford translation with the Greek of Aristotle which reads, "But we have now posited that it is impossible for anything at the same time to be and not to be, and by this means have shown that this is the most indisputable of all principles" [*Translator's note*].

43. I do not have a good Greek dictionary at hand, but I suspect that εἰλήφαμεν (*eiléphamen*) is a seldom-used form of λαμβάνειν (*lambanein*). The subjunctive is the way of speaking (not only the mood of the verb) in which we express ourselves when "*nous ne nous engageons pas.*" It is the perfect *modus ponendo tellens*, which stops just as it begins, which pulls back what it advances and advances what it pulls back. The British Isles are the subjunctive isles—the isles of "wait and see." And this is, or was, their attraction and their nature, as those of the Spanish world are exactly the opposite. The Spaniard begins by "*s'engager, puis nous verrons.*"

fact" and not just "assumed"? To some extent. He will say
that "on the basis of that assumption he *has shown* that it is
the sounder truth." Aristotle recognizes, then, that he has been
doing something which is "like a demonstration." In his
careful wording there is a distinction between δεῖξις (*deîxis*),
exposition, "making see," and ἀπόδειξις (*apódeixis*), demonstration or proof. But that distinction, practised or carried out in
speaking and writing, was never, as far as I know, formalized
by Aristotle in a definition of *deîxis* which we can compare
with his definition of *apódeixis*. This indicates that *deîxis* is a
vague and irresponsible word in his speech and not a finite
term, as is *apódeixis*. In the *Prior Analytics* it is used to
characterize the *proof* which comes from imperfect syllogisms, like the one I have extracted from these lines,[44] and
the oblique proof *ad absurdum*, like the one we will suggest
later. *Deîxis* means proof, therefore, and Aristotle, without
meaning to, tells us that he recognizes that he has "proved"
the principle of contradiction with a *direct although imperfect
proof*. *Deîxis* is a proof which is not quite a proof, but is a
proof; it is also a subjunctive proof, one of "off" and "on,"
elusive and eluded, but a proof. It is *exposition* as against
demonstration, the light infantry as against the hoplite. In this
swinging, rocking and fluctuating of the word *deîxis*, it is
necessary to determine the meaning of the idea of "making see
or being clear," "making manifest," "bethinking oneself of"
something. Hence, in the *Rhetoric* there is talk of a "proof or
exposition"—in rhetoric there are no authentic proofs—which
consists in illustrating with gestures of the countenance, the
arm, and the posture of the torso; a state of mind corresponding to the matter in hand: sadness, for example, terror or joy.
This is what Aristotle calls ἡ ἐκ τῶν σημείον δεῖξις, demonstration
by signs, demonstration which, as in a monstrance, is exhibi-
tion pure and simple.

---

44. It is curious that just at that stage, next to *deîxis* is one of the
three or four places in this whole work where he again uses *lambánein*
with the *ei* subjunctive. Imperfect syllogisms are "presumed or assumed"
syllogisms.

It was the right thing to make use of the interpretive micro-scope to try to extract from those exceptionally important Aristotelian lines whatever we could of their lifeblood. Now, I believe, we can appreciate the twilight, the shadowy state of thought in which Aristotle sees what he has just done.[45]

This direct exposition or "quasi-proof" of the principle of contradiction is followed by the well-known oblique rebutting or re-arguing proof, which is presented to us as a "proof against another," disputatious and not theoretical. But in truth this is only an expansion of the first exposition, that is to say, of the proof called "transcendental deduction." The expansion consists in showing that *if* the principle is not admitted, the

45. St. Thomas reproduces the text. He accepted the version εἰλήφαμεν for "*accipimus quasi impossibile*" and ἐδείξαμεν for "*ostendemus.*" In this last one, which as a root is perfect, there is a slight error in failing to note that it refers to the past, to having done it already. St. Thomas does not question these lines. To reproach him for that lapse would be impertinent, because for St. Thomas the text of Aristotle neither was nor could be a human achievement floating over history which it is interesting to understand in that whole reality of living action which it was. It would still be five centuries before a "historic sense" would appear and with it an interest in historical reality as such. St. Thomas' attitude toward Aristotle's text was the one that had to be, and the only one then possible—a pragmatic attitude. For him it was solely a matter of doctrine, of understanding whether or not Aristotle told the truth, although with a preconception that this was a treasure of philosophic truth. It is, then, natural that he does not comment on certain passages which, far from being a doctrine, are in Aristotle himself an evasion vis-à-vis a doctrine. If Aristotle was incapable of subconsciously *seeing* in his own words the highly important doctrine which it signified, much less could St. Thomas see it; he is a receiver, the *Angelicus Receptor*, as Ockham would become the *Venerabilis Inceptor*. [See *Sancti Thomas Acquinatis in Metaphysicam Aristotelis Commentaria* (Taurini, 1926), p. 202.] The very brief commentary added by these lines is limited here to repeating what Aristotle says immediately before: 1005^b 26 ff.

Allow me to add a personal recollection. In my Teubner copy of the *Metaphysics*, I found a marginal note on the lines we are now inter-preting, written by me in pencil—forty years ago!—in a seminar about Aristotle conducted then in Marburg by Paul Natorp (died in 1924). It reads thus: "According to Natorp there is a small interpolation here, because it is not *diá toûto.*" This shows that Natorp had, with reason, found the paragraph strange; but that at the same time he had not the least idea of the interpretive problem which the lines presented. I do not think there would be a similar interpolation here.

word would have no defined meaning, but an infinite significance. "If a word does not have only *one* meaning, that is, a unique one, it is worth nothing" [46] in its simple ability to mean everything, in which case conversation would be impossible. (New "transcendental deduction.") Everybody would tell the truth and everybody would be wrong. There could thus be no difference between truth and error. There would be no room for the more or less of truth.

The other proofs are of interest only to the Aristotelian doctrine and they are proofs which leave everyone cold who is not a parishioner. It is necessary that the principle of contradiction be true so that the meaning may be *one*, and this in turn so that "substance" may be possible. Otherwise all would be accident. *A la bonne heure.* And why not? Natural science—physics, biology—occupies itself with nothing but accidents as such.

What must be said in the face of this magnificent argumentation of Aristotle can become clear to the reader only when we have shown briefly the axiomatic way of thinking in present-day exact sciences. But in order to provide a brief sketch and some orientation I will at this point say the following: the fact is that if a word does not have only *one* meaning it is impossible to be understood, to converse. Now then, it happens that, strictly speaking, no word has in itself only one meaning; on the contrary, its meaning floats, it varies constantly from person to person among those who are talking, and even within each of them it varies from moment to moment. This means that, strictly speaking, it is not possible to be understood. How can the one be squared with the other? The principle of contradiction does not apply to meanings which exist; it applies only to immutable meanings which do not exist, and we simply postulate them as notional meanings,

46. Compare the Oxford translation with the Greek of Aristotle which reads, "If . . . one were to say that the word has an infinite number of meanings, obviously reasoning would be impossible; for not to have one meaning is to have no meaning, and if words have no meaning our reasoning with one another, and indeed with ourselves, has been annihilated . . ." [*Translator's note*].

or as a notion of meaning. This postulate becomes precise under specific conditions of meaning, and with those in view we could construct certain meanings which approximate immutability. The combination, the system of these conditions constitutes "exactitude" or "way of speaking strictly." But one of those conditions implies that speaking strictly, while coming closer than anything else, must also be understood as approximate. In the light of this, traditional logic and almost all the philosophy of the past appear to be inverted. They are presented for the purpose of thinking about Reality, but the result is that instead what they constructed was a Reality that engendered something notional by means of definitions and axioms, as today spaces are constructed in this or that dimension. Their thinking was Utopian and in place of knowledge it was imagining, fabricating *desiderata*. Taken thus, they are coherent, like the metageometries. But then their interpretation must be translated into the axiomatic method. So, in the case of Aristotle's metaphysical books one must commence thus; We call Ens that which does not give way to contradictory propositions at the same time and in the same sense. Here the principle of contradiction is not an evident truth which applies to everything, but an arbitrary axiom which determines the behavior of a something exactly. What is exact in it is what it has of the arbitrary embryo. Clearly, the Ens engendered by axioms gives up being of itself a representative of Reality. What may happen is that afterward we may find real somethings which behave more or less in the manner of the axiomatic Ens.[47]

But with all this, we are interested in making it clear that nowhere does there appear the slightest indication to show in what that form of sudden truth consists which would recognize this, as it does other first principles. We are not shown the least hint about what it consists of, what air that manner of knowing the known *per se, per se notum* has, although what the Scholastics will say—that the axioms are known

47. See my study *Notes on Thought* (*Obras Completas*, Vol. V, p. 513).

"solum per hoc quod eorum termini innotescunt" [48]—is sub-
sumed. This formula is like an opium poppy, for it seeks to inject us again with the *virtus dormitiva*. To say that we know
the principle because the terms, when they become known to
us, emanate from the truth of the principles is, on committing
a *petitio principii*, to set the opacity of magic where a greater
degree of transparency would serve us better. But we will
defer full entry into this matter until we find something similar
in Leibnitz, when he exerts himself to give the formula a bit
of good sense. There the discussion will be fruitful, for
Leibnitz made an effort to construct a basis for the idea of a
truth that emerges through the "simple intellection of the
terms." But the Scholastics contented themselves with saying
that, and calling it "evidence." In Aristotle, no corresponding
term exists. It seems to have been his disciple, Theophrastus,
who forged it—giving the word ἐναργής [49] a technical value—
visible, patent, and clear. Cicero translates it excellently with
perspicuitas. Down the centuries—even in our own times—
people have believed in *evident* truth without anyone, as I
have said, taking the trouble to make a bit more evident to
us what that evidence is. That men should have thus behaved
on the most decisive point in the world of theory suggests
that something else, which is very different from all theory
and all intelligence, is moving obscurely behind this.

In fact, we have left for the end what Aristotle's first reaction was as soon as he formulated the principle of contradiction. It is surprising! Because it does not consist in analyzing
the meaning of principle, pondering it, looking at all its
aspects, asking himself questions about it, even though they be
didactic and of minor importance. Nor is he moved now, as
he will be later, to "explain" and demonstrate it. No; the first
thing he does, having barely stated it, is to turn his back on it
and get nervous, almost frantic, over some irritating people,
real or imaginary, who have the audacity to question the
principle, to poke around in it, or frankly refuse to accept it.

48. Which is what St. Thomas says in commenting (p. 201), Chap. 3.
49. Empirical Sixth (*Adv. Math.*, VII, 218).

Aristotle loses his head—a thing he does very rarely because, as I said before, he is a cold-blooded animal. Why? Is there anyone who believes that the real can both be and not be, be thus and not be thus, as Heraclitus is *supposed* to have done? Heraclitus *would say* this—Aristotle replies—but just because someone says a thing does not mean that he believes it (thinks it with credence or believingly). That is, Aristotle does not limit himself to declaring that in his judgment Heraclitus made a mistake, but he accuses him of saying what he does not think, that is, that he lies. And he calls "uncultured" (*apaídeusía*) the others who have doubts about that principle or who demand that it be clarified. He says that if they do not admit it, they cannot even talk, but are vegetables, melons— *phytón*.[50] How far we are from the elusive and unctuous English subjunctive which Aristotle will adopt later! Because, take note, until now he has not said a single word about the content of the principle, but has merely enunciated it. Already he gets angry!

That is the trouble with "evidence." Something is "evident" to one—*one*, as the great painter Solana always said in place of *I*—therefore, it is true and beyond question for one who does not know how or why it is true. We find this in ourselves as an absolute and inexorable fact from which we cannot extricate ourselves; it forms part of us; strictly speaking, it is as oneself. Oneself, the *I* or person that each of us is, also holds for us that character of absolute fact, inexorable and impossible to eliminate or expel. *One* cannot dispense with *one*. Our *I* is our unavoidable destiny. But here is the *other*, a fellow creature, denying what is "evident" to us, what is like *our very selves*, and then we feel the denial of the principle "evident" to us as if it were the denial of our very selves. We feel ourselves "annihilated." This provokes in us an emotional electric discharge of hatred and terror, as if we saw that

50. In an identical situation, when expounding the principle of his physics—that there is a first immutable prime mover—he will bluntly call "imbeciles" ἀρροστία (*arrostía*) those who still ask the reason for its immutability.

someone was pulling the earth out from under our feet and making us fall into the horror of an infinite vacuum, of an awful Nothing. If this "evidence" were an intelligible and intelligent quality which the principle possesses, we would not get so angry nor feel consternation and animosity toward the fellow creature who "does not believe in what we our-selves believe"; on the contrary, we would laugh at him and amuse ourselves by destroying his erroneous belief with a multitude of well-honed reasons. But the reaction of Aristotle, like that of anyone else in a similar situation, has nothing to do with our intellectual and cognitive side, but is emotional and frantic. The fact is as paradoxical as it can be, for it hap-pens that at the very time when the great principle of knowl-edge is involved, the least reservation or objection to it moves men instantly from theorizing to the opposite pole of them-selves, to passion and anger.

Such paradoxes are normal in history. Everyone who has raised any objection or has denied this principle or that has encountered opposition, not from this or that scientist disposed to discuss the matter quietly with him, but from the whole of society united against him, pointing fingers at him, full of rage and at the same time of secret panic, as if he were a rebel, an insurgent, an "enemy of the people," an incendiary, an atheist. That is to say, the reaction is of the social type, and although it may be produced in an individual it originates in the "collective" depth of his person. Hence, it exhibits the characteristics of a religious protest, of fanatic passion. Reli-gion has a side in which it is the "religion of the city," a col-lective and not an individual faith.

At this point in his work, which is the most notable work in philosophy, Aristotle did not behave philosophically. Philosophers cannot get angry, because then the order of the Universe would be upset and everything would go to pot. There is a race of people who live in the deserts of New Mexico and belong to the group of tribes called "Pueblo" by ethnographers. These are the "Zuñis." Their whole civiliza-tion is inspired by the principle of sweetness and serenity.

Miss Ruth Benedict studied their way of life and she tells us that in Zuñi culture the order of the Universe depends on the priests fulfilling their spiritual duties strictly, and that the first and foremost spiritual duty of the Zuñi priest is not to get angry. If he were to get angry the world would tremble. The author relates an anecdote which aroused real emotion, at least in me: "One summer," she says, "a family I knew very well had given me a house to live in, and because of certain complicated circumstances another family claimed the right to dispose of the dwelling. When feeling was at its height, Quatsia, the mistress of the house, and her husband, Leo, were with me in the living room when a man I did not know began cutting down the flowering weeds, which had not yet been hoed out of the yard. Keeping the yard free of growth is a chief prerogative of a houseowner and, therefore, the man who claimed the right to dispose of the house was taking this occasion to put his claim publicly on record. He did not enter the house or challenge Quatsia and Leo, who were inside, but he hacked slowly at the weeds. Inside, Leo sat immobile on his heels against the wall, peaceably chewing a leaf. Quatsia, on the other hand, allowed herself to flush. 'It is an insult,' she said to me. 'The man out there knows that Leo is serving as priest this year and he can't get angry. He shames us before the whole village by taking care of our yard.' The interloper finally raked up his wilted weeds, looked proudly at the neat yard, and went home. No words were ever spoken between them." [51]

Aristotle, being a philosopher, was wrong to get angry, but his sudden anger reveals his basic humanity and shows us that in him the human element is much more permeated by the "human collective" idea than in the case of Plato. In short, that Aristotle was very much a "man of the people." The fact is that Aristotle's first arguments in support of the principle of contradiction are neither logical nor dialectic; they are attacks, that is, arguments *hominis ad hominem*, man to man.

51. Verified text in Ruth Benedict, *Patterns of Culture*, New American Library, p. 97 [*Translator's note*].

Aristotle makes this principle a personal question. This is the inevitable result of basing truth on that kind of "evidence." Do not be surprised, moreover, to discover no less lack of balance in the *Metaphysics* books. The great books of philosophy—and I have said that Aristotle's *Metaphysics* is perhaps the greatest—differ from the *Manuals of Philosophy* in that things like this are found in them. In the *Manuals* there are no personal questions; the truth is that there are no questions of any kind.

Aristotle gets angry for the very reason that the "evidence" of his evident principle of contradiction is extremely problematical and quite illusory. It is theoretically arbitrary to start with ontology, through which we will see if we can find out what is the Real or Ens, determining that this cannot simultaneously be and not be, be thus and not be thus. Because we still do not know if we can reach it by our thinking. Even in the best of cases, "evidence" is a subjective passion. The principle of contradiction had to be true for our way of talking, and there was not the slightest guarantee that it has any value for the Real. He is indifferent to what we may think of it. Suárez says it very well: *Nullius rei essentia consistit in aptitudine ut cognoscatur.*[52] At best, the Real consists in being incomprehensible. At least up to now it has always acted this way with mankind.

It is not right, then, to launch the principle of contradiction so lightheartedly and in so confused and equivocal a formula, as the first principle of all. The first urgent thing to do would be to split up that unitary formula into many principles of contradiction, each with a different meaning, according to the kind of subjects to which it refers. It is not said that the structure of the Real coincides with the structure of the intellectual concepts. Plato took on himself the burden of assuming that the exact opposite always happens, contrary to what the mob believes, and thanks to this, already taught by the pre-Socratics, he founded philosophy. To start forthwith, as Aristotle did, from the opposite opinion, which is the popular one,

52. *Disputations,* XL, Section III, 11.

shows to what extent Aristotle was a "man of the people," caught up by antiquated, archaic "public opinion," still inspired by myth. He was not an "Athenian," and compared with Athens, this man, who is going to be the most "modern," had a persistent vein of the "primitive" deep within him. We will speak a little later about the retrogression in *depth of insight* which Aristotle represented as compared with Plato and other men of Attica.

But even within the Real, one would have to distinguish between the structure of physical reality and the structure of "metaphysical" Reality; within physics, between the structure of things and the structure of the human being; within the human being, between the quality of personal life and the quality of society, and so on.

But in the intellectual field one would also have to distinguish between concepts as mere logical "ideas" and concepts insofar as they pretend to be notions; that is, to tell us what things are. The difference is enormous. The first leads us to a logic indifferent to the values called "truth" and "error," to a mere "logic of consequence," while the second obliges us to elaborate a logic of truth.

We could still go on for considerable time making an inventory of distinctions, each of which specifies a different "Universe." The principle of contradiction has a different meaning in each one of them, and in some of them it is not valid. Here I do not treat the matter properly, but show the enormous number of problems in order to contrast them with the simplicity of Aristotle's so-called evidence. It is not enough to say, under the spur of urgency, that Ens cannot at the same time or conjointly both be and not be. It would be enough to warn that not every Ens is temporal. But above all, it is enough to recognize that not this Ens but the Being which functions in that proposition has not only the triequivocal meaning that Saint Thomas discerned—the *esse essentiae,* the *esse existentiae* and the *esse copulativum* [53]—but a great many other meanings as well. The existential *esse* is subdivided into

53. In *I Sent.,* d. 33, q. 1, art. 1, ad 1.

physical, metaphysical, mathematical, logical, cognitive, imaginary, poetic, historical existence. All the enormous riches of the "existential" modality are poured out here.[54]

Nowhere above was it a matter of discussing whether the principle of contradiction is or is not true. It has been essential to concentrate attention on it for the simple reason that, as

---

54. At this point I would not like to imply a suspicion that all this fury, following the allusion to the *anhypóthetos*, in the final analysis is directed against Plato. This attack was inevitable when Aristotle has just been maintaining that opposites could not coexist in the One. This moved him to deal right there with the principle of contradiction, as I observed, but Aristotle could not forget that Plato believed in the possibility of the coexistence of opposites in himself, and therefore, did not believe in the principle of contradiction—at least not in the same way as Aristotle. At the end of the last century Taylor called attention to the fact that the *Parménides* can be understood only if it is interpreted as basically an attack on that so-called law, and in that dialogue an Aristotle appears as interlocutor who, Jaeger assumes, somewhat summarily, does not represent any allusion to ours. Here one sees how, apart from the fact that Plato never came to see the *intellectual function* that we would call "principle," he hated what Aristotle was later going to call principles which were already flourishing in his time; this was due to his scientific precision, which implied extreme caution. It is too often forgotten that he did not serve his first philosophic apprenticeship with Socrates, but in the flock of Heraclitus.

In the matter of the coexistence of opposites Plato refers principally to the nontemporal Being. But let us give another example of positive contradiction in the temporal Ens, and in no less a one than Descartes. I believe that this has not been observed in him, and it is not without interest. In the *Replies to the Second Objections* Descartes resolves to set forth part of his doctrine, *more geometrico,* starting with definitions and axioms. The attempt is not very fortunate, but it is difficult to understand why no one has analyzed it with any care. The second axiom reads: "The present moment does not depend on that which immediately precedes it; therefore, there is as much reason to keep a thing as to produce it in the first place." Heraclitus would have applauded, because it is one of the few ontological theses that has been enunciated where what I call the "principle of ontological inertia," that always triumphant basis of Eleaticism, is denied. But this happens: if a thing has to be recreated at instant 2 this means that it had ceased to be at the "finish" of instant 1. But the thing existed in instant 1. Then that axiom implies that the thing at each instant and during the *continuity* of all its time is and is not. The result is that the Cartesian idea of "continuous creation" coincides with the contradictory Reality of Heraclitus. The reader should note, however, that in Descartes the notions of continuity and contiguity are still confused.

we have seen, the expressions of Aristotle when he speaks in general terms of first principles or axioms are too superficial to give us a clear idea of what he thought concerning so decisive a matter. Only when we confront him with the principle of contradiction [55] does he give us an opportunity to gather from his behavior what a first principle was for him. This is what interested us; not whether the principle of contradiction is true or not, but only how true it is for the Aristotelian way of thinking. That *how* could not be circumscribed if we were not alluding to some problematical aspects which that principle always incorporates. We have left others, even more serious, for the moment when we shall return to find the same principle in Leibnitz.

The result of our analyses is to reveal that, when faced with first principles, there are in Aristotle two attitudes. On the one hand, he calls principle a proposition provided with a truth *sui generis,* different from that possessed by the other propositions whose truth derives from proof. The proposition which is a principle has its own truth, that is, for itself alone. It does not need a preceding truth nor can there be one. Principle is, then, a true isolated and independent proposition. Its truth surges forth continuously from itself, imposes itself on us, invades us, takes possession of us. This characteristic is its "evidence."

But on the other hand, the proposition "from whence" others are derived is a principle. An isolated proposition, however true it may be, is not a principle. To be one it has to initiate a series of truths which are based on it. A principle is a principle of demonstration [56] and, hence, inseparable from the propositions which are its consequences. These latter propositions have need of their predecessor and the predecessor is necessary if the latter and sequential are to be

55. When dealing later with the excluded middle, the discussion is abridged.
56. "I call principles of demonstration the 'common opinions' *from which* it is shown—δεικνύουσιν—all the others derive, e.g., that it is impossible to be and not to be at the same time" (*Metaphysics,* III, 2, 996ᵇ 27).

established. This characteristic of "necessary for" which makes a principle out of a proposition is foreign to the character of evidence.

If we take this point of view by itself and assume the validity of truth in the proposition which is principle, we find that truth here means something very different from evidence, and also different from proof in the Aristotelian sense, for it will mean that "truth" is an assumption from which we start in order to deduce a coherent group of other propositions from it.

Both viewpoints appeared inseparably in Aristotle, each mirroring the other, and when we look at one the other is reflected in it.

At the end of this study it will be obvious why it could not be otherwise; why even in a "way of thinking" like Aristotle's, which carries the evidential character of principle to an extreme, one feels a need to make it a basic "condition of possibility" of the other truths; in short, of the theoretic organism. Beyond the official doctrine of principle as an evident proposition there already appears here, extra-officially, the opposite doctrine of principle as a mere assumption which we must make in order to deduce a body of truths.

We would like to be able to ascertain how this principle was real to Aristotle and how it formed part of his life, what its precise meaning was, and in what manner it illumined his mind with the special character of "evident" truth which he attributes to it.

With respect to the first, the aspect of unlimited generality which his statement presents must not confuse us. Does he want to say simply that everything which is, should be subject to this principle? In his refutation of the followers of Heraclitus who deny it we read this: "One still would have to argue against those who think in such a way that they fix on sense-perceptible things only, and even on the smallest possible number of these, and then assert that the whole firmament behaves this way. But it is only the sense-perceptible world about us that experiences corruption and re-generation. This is merely an evanescent part of the whole, so that it would be better to absolve the sense-perceptible world in favor of the celestial than to condemn the latter because of the former." This indicates that there are things—sublunar, sense-perceptible things—whose composition is contradictory. Therefore, an extension of the validity of the principle appears restricted, and at the same time its character of principle as such is modified, so that it would come to mean something like this: "Not everything there is can be said to *be* if by *being* we understand *Being as Ens.* An Ens is something that has no place for contradictory attributions." But if the principle is so understood it acquires a tinge of the exigent or the postulated and leaves open the problem of "what there is" as compared with "what *is*." This aspect of the postulate is the one which will appear to us in sharper outline in almost all the Leibnitzian principles.

Nothing seems more likely than to assume an Aristotle living with the principle of contradiction having as its dual aspect an expression of Reality and at the same time an intellectual necessity. The whole mental style of the Greeks led to this, but actually the very thing which they called "philosophy" brought it along from its initiation. This starts with Parmenides, the first man who undertook to speak of Ens as against those who spoke of the gods and those who spoke of the *physis*, like the naturalists of Ionia. Men have always sought the genuine Reality behind appearances, illusions, and errors. To the extent that he was starting this inquiry once again, Parmenides was doing nothing new. The novelty was what he thought he had discovered as genuine Reality, namely, the Ens. Parmenides understood by Ens that which properly, truly *is*. But this by itself sheds no new light for us. For the mythologist and for the Orphic theologist the gods are also that which *is*. For the Ionian naturalist water or fire or indeterminate matter is, subject to the multiform appearance of things, what properly *is*. Parmenides rejects all these opinions in a really violent tone; he judges none of this to be proper, but rather improper. If we look for what properly *is*, we will find it only in something which coincides exactly with the meaning *is*. Well now, this in itself rejects everything that manifestly or implicitly means "not to be." There is only that which *is*, and of that which is not we can say only that it is not. In this way we will have spoken and we will have thought exactly. This is the real innovation of Parmenides: the discovery that there is an exact way of thinking in contradistinction to innumerable others which are not exact, although they may be probable, persuasive, plausible or suggestive. This exact thinking consists in turning its back on things and adhering to itself, that is to say, to the meanings, ideas or concepts that words express. The concept or *lógos*—that which is thought, as and how it is thought—has a precise and unique quality: "Being" is Being and nothing more than Being, with no admixture of "not being." It follows from this that relationships between concepts are inflexible, that is, rigid; by the same token they impose themselves on the mind with a character of necessity which none of the other ways of thinking possess.

This exact thinking, which adheres to its own "things thought" or concepts, is the pure or logical thinking which we will call *logicality*. The most impressive thing about it is that in using it man does not feel free to think this or that way, but feels himself forced by a strange and inexorable power to think this way and no other. On the level of Hellenic mythology, in which the most modern parts of the *Iliad* are rooted, there already appears *Anánke*, Necessity, as the highest power which weighs upon and gives orders to the gods themselves. But that mythical *Anánke* was, like everything divine, an invisible, occult, mysterious, and transcendent power. Try to imagine the overpowering emotion which Parmenides felt when he discovered that Necessity manifested itself within him, that it made itself patent in the form of exact thinking, and that, because it was exact, it was also necessitous or *anánkico*. Hence the word *anánke* is one of those which is repeated most often in his poem.[57]

This appearance of necessity in a certain way of using thought made of logicality a phenomenon completely different from popular thinking. This latter is a subjective activity of an individual human being. Everyone has his own opinions, which are different from those of the next man. But logicality, thanks to its necessitous character, is identical in all men. It is not, then, a form of thinking originating in the individual, even when it happens within him. That the *lógos* is "commonal" thinking, as contrasted with private thinking, is one of the few things on which the two great contemporaries and antagonists, Parmenides and Heraclitus, agree. In logicality, the subjectivity of the individual disappears and of it there remains only the pure natural capacity of the receiver. Parmenides sees in logical thinking something like an effective penetration of man by Reality, the authentic reality being understood. Thus he leaves the thinking about Being somewhat subjective, and it is rather a desubjectivization of man because it is the revelation of Reality itself in him. Well now, revelation is one of the words which best translates what he, Plato and Aristotle called *alétheia* or truth. A true thought is true because it ceases to be a thought and is converted into the presence of Reality itself. When Aristotle says that the soul is the form of forms he only states in the best possible way the same relationship between *lógos* and Reality that was evident to Parmenides.

But this question has two sides. One is what I have just expounded: authentic Reality or that which properly *is*, is what logical thinking thinks. Good, but what, then, is that Reality? This is the other side. Reality is Reality only when and insofar as it coincides with concepts. The Ens is *because it is like* a concept, which in this case is the concept Being as it goes into the proposition.[58] Hence, the Ens would have

57. The accumulation of mystical expressions at the beginning of the poem makes that ecstatic emotion evident to us.

58. Up to Aristotle there will continue to be confusion in the propositional *is* with regard to its three meanings of copula, predication and existence.

as its constituent attributes those that are specifics of the concept as such: it will be one, immutable, eternal.

We have, then, the fact that philosophy begins with a surprising tergiversation. Parmenides projects over Reality the characteristics of logical thinking, but he does this for the very reason that for him logical thinking is a projection of Reality over the human mind. Hence, we note a basic duality in the Greek way of thinking which philosophy will inherit later, a duality explained as follows: when one asks oneself what something is, and particularly when asking what is the Real, what is the Ens, one demands in advance that it possess the attributes of the *lógos* or concept, demands of it that it possess the perfection peculiar to the idea that it is—or pretends to be—exactitude. It is, then, at the same time Reality and the Ideal of a reality, and it is the former because it is the latter. When, a century later, the Idea would appear in Plato as that which properly *is*, and this would demonstrate as one of its powers the gift of exemplariness, or being a model for the things of the sense-perceptible world, which properly they are not, he does nothing with it but to cast out its constitutive condition. The Idea, in fact, *is* because it is as it has to be in order to be exemplary—ὄντως ὄν. In the Greek the notion of Being always carries a connotation of the ideal, so that for him to know is, without his realizing it, a form of thinking that idealizes, that invents perfections.[59]

This is enough to show how we must picture to ourselves the strict meaning which the principle of contradiction has for Aristotle. With it, more than making clear the actual non-contradiction of Reality, a Reality is created or constructed which does not contradict itself. Aristotle is heir to Eleatic logicality, but instead of holding himself strictly to it, he mixes it with its direct opposite, sensuality. His concept is rather an inductively generalized sensation, but the fact is

59. Here I hold to the idealization of the Real which logical perfection projects over this, but in the Greek it has, in addition, another ethical and esthetic dimension with which I will deal when I study "The Principle of the Best" in Leibnitz.

that he does not adhere to the characteristics of this—its variability, its imprecision, its approximative validity, in short its illogicality—but he tries, rather, to keep alive the privileges of the pure or exact concept. Not only is this illegitimate, but the result of a hybridization. Aristotle's intention was undoubtedly to make the *lógos* fruitful with all the wealth of particulars which sense-perception offers, and this seems to imply that among the tendencies of his mentality there was one opposed to the Hellenic tradition: an awareness of what was necessary to resist the propensity to perplex, to surmise and to idealize. But this prompting of his individuality was not sufficiently strong or sufficiently clear to overcome the tradition in which he himself had been forged.

The "evidence" of the principle of contradiction, then, has nothing to do with the exigencies of pure theory. It belongs to the *idola fori* and *idola tribus*. Aristotle believed in it wholeheartedly. Hence, the horror and the hatred for those who offered objections to it, who denied it or made it conditional. It is the terror and the fury which the Australian feels when someone touches the "churunga" or little sacred stone with which he believes his destiny to be linked. From time immemorial it is established in his tribe that all men believe in that. For him the "churunga" is the "principle" which may not be contradicted.[60] It is not an intelligible theory, it is a traditional institution, a way of the "city" or collectivity into which he was born and which, since childhood, he has seen respected by everyone.

The "evidence" of this principle is the "churunga" of Occidental society since Parmenides. It is an "unintelligible secret" based on certain crude intellectual experiments made on concepts and transported from them to Reality. But those "unintelligible secrets" are, by definition, gods. The "collective

60. According to Strehlow, the man best informed on primitive Australian culture, this word is composed of *chu-* or *tsu-*, occult, arcane, secret, and *-runga,* which refers to me, pertains to me (*Die Aranda- und Loritjastämme in Zentral-Australien,* Vol. II, p. 58).

soul" is composed only of gods. The gods, mysterious powers, tremendous and all-embracing, inspire terror and love, as everyone knows. Because the gods always have two faces: they are gracious and they are angry, they are with us and against us, they are attractive and they are terrifying. The holy—as Rudolf Otto made us see so clearly—is at once *mysterium fascinans* and *mysterium tremendum*.[61]

As the Hebrews had an "angel of the indirect contributions," so there is in the Occident the "evident" tradition of a god of noncontradiction. Hence, people grow furious when anyone doubts him. They have been like this ever since they were born into that belief. "Evidence" is not a noetic phenomenon. The principle of contradiction does not seem to us "evident" truth because we may have witnessed it, because we have it by intuition, have "demonstrated" or reasoned it but simply because we have been suckled on it. That evidence stems more from lactation than from intellection. In the *Summa contra Gentiles*, I, c. 11, St. Thomas saw this theme in all its clarity: "*Ea quibus a pueritia animus imbuitur, ita firmiter tenentur ac si essent naturaliter et per se nota.*"

61. Referring to God, St. Augustine says: "*Et inhorresco, et inardesco. Inhorresco, in quantum dissimilis ei sum. Inardesco in quantum similis ei sum*" (*Confessions*, II, 9, 1). Otto quotes it to support his doctrine.

20
Parenthetical Note on Scholasticisms

THIS WAS THE "way of thinking" in the exact sciences when the mathematician Descartes appears. We have had to devote several pages to clarifying its bias somewhat, but I do not think that the time was wasted because the understanding of it that we gain is also of value for our consideration of the new "way of thinking" which Descartes initiated. Now we have frequent and intimate traffic with certain points which, whatever the way of thinking, are vitally important in the whole deductive theory. Among other things we have succeeded in penetrating deeply into those vital areas of science which are called "principles." This, remember, is our titular theme, which announced our intention of clarifying Leibnitz' attitude toward the aforesaid vital areas.

It is characteristic of European intellectual history since the new nations began their gestation that they have lived under Aristotle's thumb. To a lesser extent they inherited other influences, but the main body of Western learning is the peripatetic doctrine. Any stirring of scientific and philosophic ideas is confined within it, which means that they scarcely move, and do so with glacial slowness. This scanty progress, achieved over so many centuries, far from diminishing interest in the changes in philosophy and science which occurred during the Middle Ages, makes these even more suggestive to us. Nevertheless in this atmosphere of slow-paced movement, one can see, with what I will now say about it, that the centuries of Scholasticism mean a stabilization in the way of thinking. Hence in expounding this we have to rely heavily on Aristotle, who is the authentic wellspring, the

living and steadily flowing stream which carries all the doctrines floating on it.

To discuss Scholasticism in a manner which would be
honest, fruitful and somewhat discerning is not a task to
undertake by indirection while headed somewhere else. To do
so here would, moreover, be obstructive. But note that it is
one of the most attractive undertakings that can be proposed
in history, especially attractive because it is virgin ground.
To the already rather long list of needed and uncompleted
intellectual enterprises that I am compiling let the reader add
this one—the biography of Scholasticism. I do not remember
any book concerned even remotely with this theme, much
less one that sheds light on it. Which means that everything
which is richly rewarding about scholasticism also remains to
be said.

Nor has even the very first thing been said adequately,
which in turn shows the high rank to which this is entitled
as a historical problem. The historical reality called "Scholastic
philosophy" cannot be understood if a beginning is not made
in framing the idea of "Scholasticism" as a historical category.
That is to say, Scholastic philosophy has to be viewed against
the background of many other scholasticisms. Scholasticism
as such is only one particular European and medieval example
of scholasticism as a historical structure having the generic
character which was given it and is still given it in many
places and at many times.

I use the term "Scholasticism" for all inherited philosophy,
and by inherited I mean all philosophy that pertains to a cultural circle which is distinct and distant—in social disparity or
in historic time—from the cultural circle in which it is
learned and adopted. To inherit a philosophy is not, of
course, to expound it, something which goes back to another
intellectual operation, different from inheriting and limited to
a particular case of the ordinary interpretation of texts.[1]

1. In Christian theology the use of philosophy for the better understanding of dogmas is called Scholasticism. But it has always been
pointed out that that definition of Scholasticism was too vague and

The tragic element in all "inheriting" is not usually understood. Tragic in the most profound sense, for it is an inexorable and irrevocable intervention of Destiny.

Those who do not appreciate the ingredients which go to make up human "ideas" believe that their transference from one people to another and from one epoch to another is easily accomplished. They ignore the fact that what is most vital in "ideas" is not what is thought clearly, and with a burgeoning of consciousness on thinking them, but rather the *subconscious* thinking behind them, which remains underground for their use. These recondite and invisible components are sometimes the life experiences of a people, thousands of years old. This *hidden fund* of "ideas," which sustains, satisfies, and nurtures them, cannot be transferred any more than can anything else which is truly human life. Life is always untransferable. This is historic Destiny.

It follows, then, that any complete transfer of "ideas" is illusory. Only the stem and the flower are transferred, with perhaps last year's fruit hanging from the branches—whatever of them is immediately useful at that moment. But the ever-living "idea," which is its root, stays in the earth of its origin. This is a general historical principle. It is well to note that something similar happens with all the other things that are called human; for example, with the political institutions of a people. Hence an attempt to inject the particular institutions of one people into another and different people is a crime. Every transfer of "ideas" is like cutting a plant above its root or pulling up a radish by its leaves. The human plant differs from the vegetable, in that it cannot be transplanted without considerable losses. This is a very great handicap, but it is inexorable and tragic.

---

comes to be extended over the whole history of theology from its patristic beginnings. On the other hand it is uncertain whether it refers equally to the same activity when Mosaic and Islamic believers practice it. Language has been correcting that imprecise definition until now it gives the word Scholasticism the stronger meaning of a specific philosophy, which is what it has in philosophic history.

Scholasticism is a species of the genus "historic inheritance," and this is equivalent to being a kind of tragedy. But in human affairs tragedy never appears without its shadow, which is comedy. Mankind is tragicomic. Hence in the final analysis there are, and there can only be, two kinds of literature—tragedy or comedy.

The monks of the Middle Ages inherited Greek philosophy, but obviously they did not inherit the assumptions, the historical accidents which constrained the Greeks to create philosophy. Philosophy does not start with any doctrine. To tell the truth, it begins as an assortment of problems. If men really have no problems, the doctrines with which they respond cannot have a genuine and *radical* (here is the "root") meaning for them. But inheritance is a historical phenomenon which is the inverse of creation. The one who inherits begins by having solutions and doctrines spread before him and his problem is to understand them: the problem of understanding ready-made solutions with no opportunity whatever to judge and to look into the original authentic problems to which these solutions apply or claim to apply. Inherited philosophic doctrine acts as a screen *definitively* interposed between authentic philosophic problems and those who inherit them.[2] Hence, the two principal failures of Scholastic philosophy: one is that it could never understand the basis of Greek concepts; the other, more conclusive and ultimately grave, that it could not pose problems by itself, and as that—the posing of problems—is normally the first thing (and who knows if it is not the only thing) that philosophy is, Scholastic philos-

2. The men of the 16th Century were well aware of this derivative aspect of Scholasticism and the petrification of thought which it automatically entailed. See, for example, what Kepler said in 1606. "*Nec sum ignarus, quam haec opinio sit inimica philosophiae Aristotelicae. Verum ut dicam quod res est: sectae magis quam principem est adversa. Da mihi redivivum Aristotelem; ita mihi succedat labor astronomicus, ut ego ipsi persuadere speraverim. Ita fieri solet, gypso, dum recens est fusa, quodlibet impresseris; eadem, ubi induruit, omnem typum respuit. Sic sententiae, dum ex ore fluunt philosophorum, facillime corrigi possunt: ubi receptae fuerint a discipulis quovis lapide magis indurescunt, nec ullis rationibus facile revellentur.*" (*Works*, II, 693 ff.)

ophy can be called philosophy only with a considerable dose
of impropriety. Hence its stability, the slow-paced sluggish-
ness of its development. The marvel of scrupulous tenacity,
acuteness, seriousness, fine perspicacity, and continuity which
the medieval monks put into their preoccupation with philosophy contrasts with this and helps to underline it. In the
whole history of the Occident, including that of Greece itself,
there was never an intellectual effort so serious and sustained
as Scholasticism. The only thing that might be compared with
it is the work of physicists and mathematicians from the 16th
Century up to today.

Unfortunately that exemplary and exceptional effort could
not gravitate toward what was really important—the ultimate
problems themselves. In "inheriting" philosophy the mind re-
verses direction and instead of trying to understand what
things are it tries to understand what someone else has thought
about them and expressed in some way.[3] Hence all Scholasticism is the degradation of science into mere terminology. It
examines in problems only what is strictly necessary in order
to gain a little understanding of their terms, and even what it
examines it sees as problems posed by others, *beyond which
the inheritor can never decide to go.*

I confess that I have never been able to contemplate without
sorrow, without a wave of human compassion, the spectacle
offered by those medieval Christians who lived their religious
creed utterly, who overflowed with faith in God, wearing
themselves out in their effort to think of their God as an
Ens. This is a matter of fatally defective understanding, because the Christian God and the God of every religion is
the opposite of an Ens, however *realissimum* one wants to
consider him.

Ontology is something that happened to the Greeks and
cannot happen again to anyone. It has room only for homol-

3. Sigerio de Brabante (13th Century) was already describing philosophy as "*querendo intentionem philosophorum in hoc magis quam veri-
tatem, cum philosophice procedamus.*" Quoted in Gilson, *La Philosophie
au Moyen Age* (1947, p. 562). Vives in *De disciplinis* said: "*Semper aliis
credunt, numquam ad se ipsi revertuntur*" (*De causis*, Book I, Chap. V).

206 THE IDEA OF PRINCIPLE IN LEIBNITZ

ogies. About 600 years before Christ, some high-ranking Greek minorities began to lose faith in God, in the "God of their fathers." Whereupon the world became for them, a void converted into something empty of vital reality. It was necessary to fill this emptiness with some adequate substitute. Up to about 440 B.C. when Socrates began his new apostolate [4] there was a succession of atheistic generations. Those atheistic generations invented the idea of Ens to fill with reality a world empty of God. The Ens is a reality which is not divine but is nevertheless a basis for the real. There was therefore no better *quid pro quo* than to want to think of God as Ens. As this, according to medieval thinking, is impossible, the God which was compressed into the idea of Ens oozed, leaked out, burst through all the cracks in the concept of Ens. So that this diabolical combination resulted: God, who had absented Himself, returns to install Himself in the emptiness which He Himself had left, but He finds that His emptiness is already occupied by an emptiness of its own. This God inhabiting the emptiness of God is the *ens realissimum*. The result was that they could neither think of the Ens in any suitable way nor could they think properly of their God. This is the tragedy which is entitled "Scholastic philosophy." [5]

This tragedy is presented to us with its corresponding comedy *a latere*. In fact one of the things most typical of the grotesque side of the unavoidable imitativeness which all inheritance brings with it was that Scholastic philosophy manifested itself in the form of *disputatio* to such an extent that at the very last hour its culminating work—and, as I have said, the first treatment of metaphysics which existed—that of Suárez, is called *Disputations*. That is to say, the medieval monks not only inherited the Ens from far away Greece, but

4. As far as I know it has never been pointed out that one of the features characterizing the crisis suffered by "philosophy" in connection with Socrates consists in a change of attitude with respect to religion.

5. Boetius of Dacia, follower of Averroës, distinguished one from the other, the *"ens primum secundum philosophos et secundum sanctos deus benedictus."*

they also inherited the Greek way of talking about it, which was discussion or dialectic.

In Greek life, especially that of the wealthy Athenian, the most important occupation was conversing. The Greek could never stand being alone. For him living was *properly* living with. Existence in Athens was an endless talk-fest. Out of this came the success of the Sophists, who were the technicians of conversation. The mild climate, the pellucid atmosphere, the turquoise beauty of the sky, invited men to live and to live together in the open air. In the public square, in the gymnasiums, men gathered, and without women to carry on their perennial mission of interrupting conversations. In that colloquial activity there was one outstanding figure, a hero of chatter, a Hercules of small talk—Socrates, from the Fox-hole District, or Alopeke. Plato's entire body of work, in which philosophy is established, is an immense epic dedicated to this Achilles of word-power, and therefore it is composed of nothing but dialogues, and for this reason the philosophic "way of thinking" since Plato has been called "dialectic." [6] All this is a unique adventure of Greek man, and one which cannot be exported. Whoever knows how to think in concrete terms cannot think of "Greek philosophy" without seeing a group of men, some young, some old, absorbed in the sport of discussion according to fixed rules of the game.

By way of contrast, let us now imagine a monastery of the

6. This does not mean that the Platonic dialogues, including those called "Socratic"—as well as the dialogues of Xenophon, Antisthenes, and others—were ever intended to set out and transmit thoughts actually enunciated by Socrates. The lack of understanding in the 4th Century of what the literary genus "Socratic dialogue" meant—and had to mean—rendered sterile the painstaking philological effort of the previous century to reconstruct the figure of Socrates. The Socratic dialogue takes the presence of Socrates for granted and does not "repeat" him, just as Thucydides for similar reasons does not reproduce the actual speeches of Pericles, which he almost certainly heard, or of which he at least had faithful transcriptions. If some fact or expression which is historically Socratic appears it turns out to be, for reasons of literary technique, like "local color" or a frame for dialogue.

13th Century in the frozen center of Europe or in the mists of Hibernia, and in the cloister walk where Gothic arches give glimpses of the sky and reveal the well in the center of the sacred courtyard garden where old teaching monks make the youthful novices with purple tonsured heads argue as if they were Plato's young men. It is almost as extraordinary as it was in the 10th Century, in the reign of Otto II, when the nun Hrosvita would write "comedies of Terence," that indecent author, the theme of which was the lives of saintly virgins, and would have them acted by the little sisters of her convent of Gandesheim. The fact is that Hrosvita was a creature of genius and her comedies, read today, still seem delightful to us. Delightful, but of course monstrous.

Do not object to all this on the ground that Aristotle in his doctrine of Ens, or Ontology, is concerned with God, because it is highly debatable, as everyone knows, whether Aristotle was not scientifically inopportune in regard to Being, since it happens that his ontological God had nothing to do with the religious God, nor with the Greek, nor with the Christian God. The God of ontology is a starting point of Aristotelian mechanics, somewhat like Newton's law of gravity. He has no other role than to move the world, to bring it out from afar and place it before him. Much more than the Christian or the Greek god, this one seems like an "eight cylinder" tractor or the handle of a roasting spit that turns the rotisserie of the Universe on which we are the fowl being roasted. In my judgment this does not suggest that Aristotle, at least in his first Platonic period, did not believe piously in a religious God, but this has nothing to do with his *Deus ex machina*, his mechanical God. So that what is found in Aristotle is only an agglutination of two gods out of touch with each other.[7]

Scholasticism, I have said, is a historical category.[8] It is a

7. It is rather shameful that no one has ever studied just how Aristotle lived with that agglutination, that is to say, no one has tried to explain Aristotle's religiosity. This *deficit* is not fortuitous because the truth is that the relationships beween philosophy and religion from Thales up to the Stoics have never been studied.

8. I cannot explain here the purport of the concept "historical cate-

condition of historical categories that they establish a concept representing a scale of magnitude which permits differentiation between degrees of reality itself or, to put it in less precise but plainer terms, which enables us to recognize and to *measure*—for, contrary to all past belief, there are historic measurements—the most and the least intensive degrees of that reality.

Scholastic philosophy inherited Aristotle first in Latin and beyond that principally from the Arab commentators Avicena and Averroës.[9] For these circumcised men the leap from Greece was no feeble hop—in terms of inheritance and hence of Scholasticism. The first "Christian" (!) scholastics are the Arabs. One more reason for learning to view those centuries at the midpoint of the Middle Ages *from* the viewpoint of the world of Islam and the Near East and *not* from that of the Christian and Occidental nations. As long as this is not done, as long as the perspective of medieval history is not oriented *from* the Arab world, it will not fall into place, and our Asín Palacios proved his seriousness, subtlety, and serene devotion to facts by *doing* just that without ever giving any reason for it.

Thus we find that the Scholastic system involves enormous distances *in space and in time* from the cultural circle where Greek philosophy was born and where it is a complete and concrete reality. The distance between Greece and the new Christian nations of the Occident, the distance in time between

---

gory," or even the characteristics of its logical form. About these I only say what follows.

9. Abenjaldún, with the sharp hawk eyes of a great historian, points out that the Greek books lay dead in the libraries for centuries, and that when the Syrian Arabs took possession of them it was they who brought these books back to life. (Ibn Khaldun, *Prolégomenes*, Slane translation, 1863, Vol. III, p. 121.) The Arabs were the first Scholastics of Aristotle and nothing demonstrates better the profundity of the man than their development up to the doctrine of Averroës which gave St. Thomas so much trouble. Now then, Averroësism is materialistic or at least corporalist pantheism, interchangeable with "physics" and the Stoic theory of knowledge which was the *other* wonderfully homogeneous consequence of Aristotelianism.

the 4th Century before Christ and the 12th Century after Christ, the distance between Hellenism and Arabism, and the distance between the Arabs and the monks of Europe. It is, then, a scholasticism of many upward steps and great possibilities.

What this means appears clear when contrasted with another scholasticism, but one of the lowest grade.

Around 1860, the continuity of the serious philosophic tradition had been lost, even in Germany, and up to the point where even the classics of modern and contemporary philosophy were not well understood. In place of philosophy a watered-down intellectual wine called "positivism" was being imbibed. This positivism had scarcely anything to do with that of Comte, who invented the name. The philosophy of Comte is a very great philosophy which is not yet understood. Note this as a matter of justice. The positivism "pervading" Europe around 1860 was that of Stuart Mill and other Englishmen, and the English, who have done such great things in physics and in almost all the humanities, have shown themselves incapable up to now of that form of *fair play* which is philosophy.[10] This is why about that time a new generation, born around 1840, once more experienced philosophic zeal, and seeing that it knew nothing of philosophy, it had to return to "going to school"—to the school of one or another great contemporary philosopher. Hence these are the years of the "*zurück zu*," of the return to Kant, to Fichte, to Hegel. That return was, as I have said, philosophically a *going back*

10. For that reason, among others, there is no talk in this study of the great English empiricists such as Locke and Hume, in spite of the penetrating influence they had on the 18th Century "way of thinking." That influence, which it would be difficult to exaggerate, was not that of a philosophy, but of a series of very acute objections to all philosophy. Considered philosophically they are the *lucus a non lucende* from the 15th Century on. Another reason for disregarding them in this study is that the influence of the first empiricist (chronologically), that of Locke, begins with the death of Leibnitz.

to school and was thus avowedly a form of scholasticism. The most famous of all was the neo-Kantism of Marburg. The Marburg professors belonged to the same cultural circle as Kantism, and chronologically they were only some 70 years away from it. The distance, then, is nothing in social space and minimal in time. The coordination between these two would lead one to think that this was not a phenomenon of inheritance, but of normal continuity and evolution. But there is one thing against that: between 1840 and 1870, there were two generations that busied themselves with politics, made their little revolutions, built railroads, created the first great industrial "plants," played the Napoleon, the Bismarck, the Disraeli and—paid no heed to philosophy. There are two generations which, with a very few feeble exceptions, signify a pause, a break in the historic continuity of philosophic inquiry. In difficult disciplines every break in the continuity of attention is serious. It is enough so that, at least to a minimum extent, an "inheritance" is then produced. Neo-Kantism is therefore an example of Scholasticism in miniature.

Of what I say in this chapter, which tries only to suggest what in my judgment is the fertile take-off point for a study of medieval history, I would like to keep afloat the idea that the most serious deficiency of Scholastic philosophy is its inability to pose philosophic problems for itself, problems which are always fundamental or very far advanced.[11]

11. Contrast with this the vigor, richness, and originality with which theological problems were introduced in those centuries. Unfortunately the Christian monks had to handle them with a tool kit of Greek concepts which were not well adapted to the task. The page and a half in which Dilthey sums up the historical reality of Scholasticism is admirable, as is everything from this author. There one reads: "Among the Scholastics the concepts of the ancients look like the plants in a herbarium, torn from their native soil, of which the location and natural conditions are unknown." [*Introduction to the spiritual Sciences,* translated by Julian Marias (Revista de Occidente, 1956), p. 285.]

Nevertheless Dilthey never came to see clearly the fundamental truth of the autochthonous character of ideas and therefore did not see the origin of philosophy clearly, nor consequently *for what precise reasons* "the concepts of the ancients are plants in the herbarium of the Scholastics." I would not like to leave this theme of "scholasticisms" without suggesting that in my opinion the entire history of the Occident is, in one of its aspects, "inherited." It is truly surprising that the relationship of Europeans with ancient culture has not been interpreted as a tragedy but has been regarded solely as a piece of good fortune and a delight. Provisionally this is due in great part to the fact that European culture has never been a culture of the people, as had been that of the Asiatics, by whose principles both the sage and the man on the street could live.

21
New Revision of the Itinerary

WE HAVE CIRCUMNAVIGATED the Aristotelian-Scholastic or traditional "way of thinking." We had to learn a little more about it in order to understand better the exact way of thinking which modernity sets against it. That has cost us a good many pages. Now we go back to our established trajectory of seeking to understand the attitude of Leibnitz toward principles. As his philosophy, like all modern ones, is oriented in the way of thinking of the exact sciences, it was inescapable that we had to consider what had happened in this field by the time he began to study it. We said that the evolution of the deductive or exact modern method up to Leibnitz could be summarized in three steps: one that Vieta took in creating algebra, another which Descartes took in creating analytical geometry, and a third beyond that, which Descartes also took; here we paused to define this.

We paused because analytical geometry represents the treatment *within* the same science of discontinuous quantity, or number, and of continuous quantity, or extended magnitude. Now this was an enormity, one of the greatest crimes that could be committed in traditional logic and methodology; it was the "passage to another genus." It was the desire to shed a bright light on what this means and on how Aristotle and the Scholastics came to believe in the "incommunicability of genera" that led me to the overlong digression which precedes this.

Now we will see what comprises Descartes' second step, which was the decisive one; so decisive that the present way of thinking in the exact sciences is the same as that of Descartes or, if you wish, it is simply a clarification and reform of the Cartesian mathematical and physical method. Keep in mind the fact that Descartes does not appear to us here as a philosopher, but as a continuator of Vieta and a predecessor of the mathematician Leibnitz. Nor does his method—i.e., his logic and his epistemology—interest us directly, and we need refer to it only to the extent that is essential to a good understanding of his actual thinking when he was working with mathematics. His role in this study, then, is very different from that which we had to assign to Aristotle, because Aristotle formulated a way of thinking which was to become a canon immediately; its undisputed reign in the *lingua franca* of the exact sciences lasted, as I have said, right up to Descartes. On the other hand, the actual mathematical thinking of Descartes is still definitively incorporated in science, but his method, which was his reflection on that thinking, and at the same time what made it possible, after reigning for half a century is replaced by others. Already Leibnitz' method— and, I repeat, his epistemology—is very different from that of Descartes. I think that this defines with sufficient exactness in what measure Cartesianism is a question for us here.

As I have not referred other than incidentally to the philosophy of Aristotle and his sucklings, the Scholastics, so I am not now going to speak of the philosophy of Descartes except occasionally. What is important to us is his exact way of thinking, understanding by this not the "doctrine of method" elaborated by Descartes, but his actual way of using his physio-mathematical creations.

Descartes is the man of method par excellence. I said in the beginning that all philosophers are men of method, but that not all of them explain their methods and this means that they do not carry the title. The fact is that Descartes also did not explain his method formally in any of his writings —books or private letters—which were known to the public in his lifetime. The gist of it, nevertheless, appears in his works and his correspondence. Where it is almost the least visible is in his first publication, the famous *Discourse on Method*, one of the most deservedly popular writings in all philosophic history, and in truth a masterpiece. In it Descartes does not propose to compose a treatise on method, but to speak of what this is as a living function of human life.[1] Hence the paradoxical and never analyzed fact that those pages which open a new epoch for humanity, which initiate the new science and with it a new technical ingredient for life, consist not of a *disputatio*, nor of a treatise, nor of a manual, but of an autobiography.[2]

Descartes explains his method in the *Regulae ad directionem ingenii* which he left in Sweden at the time of his death. He did not finish drafting more than two parts of the contemplated three.[3] And note that to begin with, the *Rules* start directly by accepting as a fundamental error the very doctrine of the "incommunicability of genera" which leads to the separation, multiplication, and dispersal of the sciences. It is an error, he says, "that it should have been believed that the sciences ought to be differentiated because of the diversity of their subjects, and that they must be pursued individually, separated from each other, each one leaving the rest out of consideration." They are nothing else than "human knowledge," which is always one and the same and does not permit of internal "boundaries." That error was the reason why so many things in the Universe were investigated, while, on the other hand, not enough thought had been given to what is "good sense"—*bona mens*, that is to say, "universal knowledge"—*universalis Sapientia*, which is the reason for all those kinds of special knowledge. From this comes the first rule: all

1. In a letter to Mersenne in March of 1637: "*Je ne mets pas Traité de la Méthode mais Discours de la Méthode, ce qui est le même que Préface ou Advis touchant la Méthode, pour montrer que je n'ai pas dessein de l'enseigner, mais seulement d'en parler.*"

2. In 1937, I had prepared a commentary on the *Discourse on Method*, made from this point of view, in order to celebrate his centenary in 1938; but the long illnesses, the comings and goings of those and later days hindered its publication. My students know part of that commentary, which was set forth in various of my university courses, and my listeners in Buenos Aires heard it in my lessons at the Faculty of Philosophy in 1940. [It will be published in *Obras Ineditas*.]

3. It is calculated that the drafting was done around 1628, when Descartes was 32 years old, which in his life's *tempo* (including the physiological) represented full maturity.

the sciences are united and mutually dependent on each other, so that instead of studying each one separately it is much easier—*longe facilis*—to study them all together. They are, in effect, one single science. With this we are reinstalled on the far side of Aristotle, in the purest Platonism.

But this does not mean that we should cease to read Aristotle and set ourselves to read Plato. Descartes proposes with this or that euphemism that we read no one, that is, that we break with the past. On busying ourselves with Plato or Aristotle *"non scientias videremur didicisse, sed historias."* In short, that all this about Plato and Aristotle is pure fiction! And enough of fiction!

Like a very new power which is suddenly incorporated in the historic area, Descartes begins by creating a vacuum in the European cultural tradition, destroying it, annihilating it —acting as though it did not exist. Europe was then reaching its maturity; relatively it was the same age as Descartes, the Modern Age. But in its maturity, as in its youth and its adolescence, Europe carried within itself the "definitive old age" which is antiquity—Greek and Roman. So Descartes will make of that Europe—now very populous and containing this immense historic past—a newly born desert island of which he will be the inspired Robinson Crusoe. Thanks to this—to this rejection of past and present—Europe remains apt for a true rebirth. The Renaissance, unfortunately, so designated by Burckhardt, had ended and now a real renaissance was beginning.[4]

4. Strictly speaking we owe the term Renaissance, as applied to the artistic production which begins at the end of the 14th Century, to a Spanish painter named Diaz, who lived in Paris and there wrote certain articles, if my memory serves me, around 1850. In such a sense, i.e., the artistic sense, the term is all right. The error, as Huizinga would say, lies in the "inflation of that concept" until it is used to designate an era of history. This exaggeration comes from a book by Burckhardt, *Renaissance Culture in Italy* (1860), a book unsatisfactory from every point of view, until now it is a curious historical problem demanding an explanation as to why the book achieved such sweeping success. The fact is that it did, and that with its fame it blanketed another book, published a year earlier, which did not pretend to study the

whole period, but only the humanists, but which in my judgment teaches much more: *The Renaissance of Classical Antiquity or the First Century of Humanism*, 1859, by V. Voigt. There is a good Italian translation. Burckhardt's admirable book—the others are worthless—is his *History of Greek Culture*, a collection of various courses given on the theme which, out of modesty and fear of the dictatorial pedantry of Wilamowitz, he did not venture to publish.

22
Incommunicability of Genera

THE FIRST PARAGRAPH OF the first "rule for the direction of the mind" begins, then, by proclaiming as a norm the unity of science and therefore the communicability of the genera. No more radical and explosive overturn of the traditional "way of thinking" can be imagined. The whole Aristotelian-Scholastic method had come to a head in the dogma of their lack of communicability. The complete abandonment of this means that Descartes has turned that whole method inside out like a sock. And as the traditional way of thinking was as it was and led to the aforesaid conclusion, thanks to many earlier assumptions and previous demonstrations, and thanks to the whole conception of the Real, it is obvious that, although Descartes begins his *Regulae* this way he could not have done so unless those first few words of the Cartesian method postulated the whole Cartesian idea of the Real. Which confirms again the law stated in Paragraph 3 regarding the parallelism betweeen its idea of Being and its idea of thinking which is consubstantial for all philosophy.

Let us see what are the assumptions supporting the dogma of the incommunicability of genera, enumerating them one after another so that there is no escape and we can later compare them with a list of those which support the method of Descartes. In order to facilitate the drawing of conclusions by the reader let us refer to a concrete case of incommunicability —that of arithmetic and geometry—and therefore to the "genera" concerning discontinuity or number and about continuity or extended magnitude. We will then have the following:

(1) Those two "genera" are incommunicable because *in fact* there is no concept common to both which would be concrete

or, which is the same thing, absolute. A concept is concrete or absolute only when it can be thought by itself alone, and this cannot happen unless it is a species which contains something peculiar to itself or *idion* and is therefore integral, complete, and universal. As an example of this let us take the suggestion that Aristotle makes, *lacking his own doctrine*, and which Suárez, as we saw, rebukes euphemistically with good reason: quantity is that which is divisible. We cannot think the divisible through in the Aristotelian way of thinking unless we have in mind subconsciously some species of reality which would be divisible. Therefore *that which* is divisible as such and only that is nothing determinate but a part of something which, unless it is supplemented, is unthinkable as a part and is therefore *a fortiori* unreal. On the other hand, the species which can be subthought in a concept or piece of concept to be "divisibles" are so numerous and unconnected that they have nothing in common among themselves except their aptitude for an abstruse "divisibility." In Aristotle it is not the same thing to divide one number *by another* as it is to divide an extension *within itself*. Nor is it the same thing to divide substance in matter and form, or even to *divide et impera*. Of such a concept, which is valid for many things without having its *own* value, Aristotle will say that it is analogous, as he always says when he does not understand something which, while he does not understand it, continues to make its presence felt in his mind.

(2) The reason for there being no common concept of number and magnitude is that those two concepts—as in principle all of Aristotle's—have been derived, starting from sense-perceptible things, by means of commonal abstraction. The common extract cannot be other than something which was in the sense-perceptible thing; hence it is a "thing" rather than an abstraction. Between the number "thing" and the extension "thing" there is nothing which is both concrete and common. Nothing is gained by generalization of the sense-perceptible. *The "genera" and their incommunicability are an absolute fact*, an empirical determination incompatible with a

theory which claims to be deductive.

(3) This presupposes that "thinking of Being" as a method is understood to start from methodical sensation (i.e., sense-perceptible intuition).

(4) This in turn is believed thus through being persuaded in advance that the senses present Reality to us—which is what "the whole world" believes. Hence Aristotle, in his theory of metaphysical or ontological knowledge, will say that the Real, the Being, is "super-proximate to sensation": ἐγγύτατον τῆς αἰσθήσεως. Note the imprecision in the precision of this sentence. To be the "nearest of all" does not prevent believing that Being *is only* in sensation. In fact, it will also tell us that, on the contrary, Being is the super-remote from sensation: πορρώτατον τῆς αἰσθήσεως.

(5) The thesis according to which we find authentic Reality in sense-perceptible phenomena is, together with the principle of contradiction, Aristotle's other great principle, which he nowhere formulates in detail, much less analyzes and discusses.

(6) But on the other hand, he retains enough Platonism to understand by knowledge the pure relationship between concepts, or logicality. According to this the Real can be attainable only in concept, which seems to contradict the "principle of the senses." How can the one be reconciled with the other? The Platonic concept was a pure, exact concept, not extracted from sense-perceptible phenomena, which are inexact, merely approximate, never adequately correlated with the concept. Hence Platonic concepts can function logically and this functioning is the prototypical science which Plato called *dialectic* but which he could have called *logic,* although not formal logic like ours. Aristotle's solution consists in degrading that which is most essential in the Platonic concept—its exactitude, its logicity—making it emerge from empirical induction applied to sense-perceptible data. Notwithstanding this he will claim that those illogical concepts function logically.

(7) The Aristotelian solution is in structure contradictory, but it has the advantage of coinciding with the way of thinking always practised by the common people. His genuinely

philosophic work was a popularization of the Platonic dialectic, bringing it within reach of every man; this transforms the rigorous, exact and by the same token paradoxical and unpopular method of Plato into the thing-ist, commonistic, empirical, sensual, and "idiotic" way of thinking that we have seen. Renato Descartes, *Peronii Toparcha*,[1] a nobleman like Plato, rebelled against this popular way of thinking, ill-suited to an authentic deductive theory and hence to an effective rationality.

But this, his way of of thinking, played a sorry trick on Aristotle just when he arrived at the concept which meant most of all to him—the concept of Ens. Not for a moment did it occur to him, or to the Scholastics, that so eccentric a concept as this would not originate in some other way of thinking, different from that with which we form the concept of the triangle or the concept of the pig. Being able to predicate Ens of everything which exists, it seems to them that it is simply a matter of commonal abstraction practised on sense-perceptible things to their natural limit. Ens will be superlatively common, the most common of common.

But the fact is that, however many times we turn over a sense-perceptible thing, we cannot find in it any component, any token, any identifiable and controllable, "abstract influence"[2] that would be *the* or *that which is* Ens. We see its whiteness, its spherical or cubic shape, we hear its sonority, we touch its hardness, we perceive its movement, its augmentation or diminution, and so on, but we are not able to conjecture its *entity*, its character as Ens.[3]

Let us agree *provisionally* to the certainty that, as Aristotle and the Scholastics say, the Ens might be the *primum cogitabile*, that which we first think about a thing—first, there-

1. Descartes was of the old nobility. He was *Seigneur du Perron* and one of his contemporaries calls him that with humanistic affectation.

2. For the exact meaning of the term "abstract influence" see Husserl, *Logical Investigations*. [*Investigation* III, No. 17, Vol. III, pp. 49 ff. Spanish translation by the *Revista de Occidente*.]

3. For the terminological value I give to the word "entity" see p. 226, Note 9.

fore, not only in the order or series of scientific concepts
but the first that we know about a thing. So much the first
that we know *that it is* before knowing the least thing about
what it is. Which is not a tentative indication that before we
approach a thing the concept of Ens is already awake in us
and we did not *derive it from the thing,* neither from one
thing nor from an induction involving many things. But then
the result is that it does not consist of anything which is sense-
perceptible; there is no image of it, no *ghost* of it, and Aristotelianism is obliged to explain to us how that "first thought"
manages to be thought.

We must say the same thing of the other concepts that the
Scholastics encounter when they speak of Ens, with which,
like Aristotle himself, they do not know what to do: thing or
res, prâgma, "something," and—they should add—"this" τόδε
τι. These also are most common and are confused with the
Ens. They are not, then, different from it. But then what are
they? They do not know what to say, and in view of this
they say something beside the point. They say that they are
"kinds of Ens." This spontaneous pluralizing of the most
abstract Ens into different "kinds" is unclear and it shows
once more that neither Aristotle nor his disciples—those of the
School—knew what to do with the Ens as a concept any
more than they knew whence it came. But as things impress
themselves on us, however much we may resist, they recognize
—without discussing the consequences—that the concept Ens
has, and alone has, another concept of equal rank which is
like its shadow, to which one must resort in order to detach
the one from the other, to *take it into account*—the non-Ens
or Nothing. As a matter of fact, the history of philosophy
begins with the famous day when Parmenides forged the concept of Ens; but not by common abstraction from sense-perceptible things, rather as an antithesis to Nothing, and by simultaneously disowning, *null*ifying, and an*null*ing sense-perceptible things. It is beyond question historically that Being *was
hatched from Nothing.* But this thinking, which forms a concept not through comparison of some things with others and

the consequent commonal abstraction, but simply by awareness of a contrast between two elements or finite terms, by
virtue of which one of these cannot be thought of without at
the same time thinking of its opposite—in short, this *dialectic
thinking*—is a matter of which Aristotle and the Scholastics
had not the slightest inkling. As for the latter, let it pass, for
they were more "inheritors" than philosophers, but for Aristotle, who had spent 20 years listening to Plato, the thing is
unpardonable. Or is it that Aristotle was already somewhat
Scholastic and *originally posed only to himself the problems
which Plato had not posed or had posed off-hand, or had
frankly posed badly?* This would explain why Aristotle is
deficient in the very questions for which a thorough understanding of Platonic thought would have served him well.

It is well known to us, then, that since Parmenides we cannot derive the Being-of-things from things, and even less from
sense-perceptible things, but that we derive them from
Nothing. Nothing is par excellence the non-sense-perceptible,
but in addition, it is mankind's most original concept. It is
that which least resembles anything—sense-perceptible or not
—so that we cannot derive the concept from things. The
concept of Nothing cannot be derived from anything. It is the
greatest human invention, the triumph of imagination, the
most essentially "poetic" concept of all. It reveals at a serious
juncture that thinking is not—at least it is not only nor
principally—a matter of taking out, but rather of putting in.
Into the Universe man puts the Nothing, which was not in
the Universe. From the shock of this introduction of non-Ens
the Universe of things is transformed into the Universe of
Entia. But enough of that.

We have just seen the very sorry trick which his concept
of Ens *qua* ens played on Aristotle. Its very common character
should have made a very general concept out of it. But here
Aristotle's confusion intervenes, with the unhappy results
which were passed on to the Scholastics. The relationship
between the concept of Being and the things predicated on it
is extraordinarily strange and incomprehensible to them.

If it were true that it had been born of a commonal abstraction applied to the sense-perceptible, it would then be a normal genus which would have its species from which it would be possible to predicate comfortably "for the use of the good worker." But it is not like that; Ens in terms of the pure "general" and the pure "abstract" is neither a genus nor has it species. It is said—positively or negatively—of everything, and this makes it apparently into a thing so empty that it provides no "matter" capable of being established as species.[4]

On the other hand—and said parenthetically—this shows once more how in Aristotle every genus, including this supreme quasi-genus, is already a species, something natural and universal. Then the only manner of thinking about the Ens in this way of thinking, would be to consider it as the species of all the things that are, as opposed to the species of all the things that are not, the nothings. But this would assume a genus common to both, and there is no such genus; at least there is none in Aristotle, nor can there be. For the other species, that of the nothings, there would be no extension. There is no nothing in the same sense as the logicians talk in mathematics of class O, that is to say, a class of individuals containing no individuals of that class.[5] In fact the Nothing is a logical monstrosity; it is a predicate which has no subject. Of course the Ens is another monstrosity because it is a subject which has no real predicate. The appropriate predicate would be that most exuberant genus which Aristotle did not know about. The Moderns believe they have discovered it. The genus would be the *cogitabile* as such. But then we would have emerged from the traditional or realistic way of thinking and would be in the modern or idealistic way of

4. As is well known, Aristotle considers the genus as "intelligible matter" which differences activate to produce species.

5. This is one of the points on which Russell's attempt to found logic on the idea of "class" broke down. This is defined as the elements constituting its extension, an impossible thing when dealing with the concept O. In view of this Russell had to preface the "logic of classes" with a "logic of propositional functions." Leaning on this, he defines class O as the class of all the *x*'s which fulfill any propositional function *phi x* which for all the values of *x* is false.

thinking which starts not with Being (the Ens), but with thinking.[6]

Aristotle recognizes that the very commonal concept Ens is in fact a species, since he recognizes attributes "peculiar" to it ἴδια. But this species, because of its *excessive* generality, is in the devilish state of being included, in turn, in every new species whose *difference* will perforce also be an Ens. Therefore, says Aristotle, the Ens is not a genus of *entia*.[7] Then what the devil is it? If the relationship of this concept with its shadowy companions "this," "something," "thing" is already critical, its relationship with its inferiors is even more extravagant. It is extra-vagance itself! It is "transcendentality." This is what the Scholastics called this kind of concept and its companions, which are forced to belong to no category nor to be attached exclusively to any of them, but flow like all "genera" from all categories. Their unlimited universality hampers their generality. To call these concepts "transcendental" is no more significant than if we were to say they are not called John, but they do not stand in a normal and foreseeable relationship with their inferiors in this way of thinking. But to see what is that singularity or anomaly—this is what we are now discussing.

We already know Aristotle's solution. With exemplary acuteness he had discovered that if we separate all things into broad classes we will find that those things do not differ among themselves, only in *what they are*—hence as one species from another—but also in the way of being what they are.[8]

6. The general character of the Ens as *cogitabile* enabled ontology to be established as a special discipline. A Cartesian, Clauberg, was the first to use that name, which took root above all in the school of Leibnitz. The extensive influence of Wolff's didactical work was the reason why the term was disseminated and became fully accepted.

7. *Metaphysics,* III,3,998ᵇ 22.

8. The natural fashion with which, when we are talking of the different "meaning of Ens," the phrase "kinds of being" or existing is imposed on us as its most obvious name shows how embarrassing is the Scholastic custom of calling forms of the Ens "something" and "thing" or "*res*." This duality of terms which are so similar brings confusion, although in a strict sense they may be different. But their quibble with

Whiteness differs from a horse not only because the one is a color and the other an animal, but also because the existence of whiteness is dependent on another thing without which it cannot exist, whereas existence for the horse is inherent in itself and not dependent on anything else.[9] This most perspicacious observation would have been impossible if Aristotle had not previously made his greatest discovery, which by itself makes up for his other deficiencies and which, with the discovery of the Ens in Parmenides and the discovery of *lógos* or Reason in Plato, constitute the three greatest findings which we owe to Greek philosophy. I refer to the discovery that the basic problem of the Ens is its existence, or in modern terminology, very different from the medieval, that the basic problem of the Real is its reality. But this ontological stroke of genius did not find at its service an appropriate logical and methodological stroke of genius, in a way of thinking able to think out and develop that decisive discovery; this no Greek could do, whether a metropolitan or from the old Greek colonies; for *this* a new man was needed, and it is one of the

---

the modality of Being, which is exactly the modality of the Ens, is more serious, yet it has nothing to do with the relationship of the Ens to "something" and "thing." On the other hand there is nothing to prevent talking on a lower level of "kinds"; "kinds" of a "thing" are understood, whether it be a substance or anything else.

9. The existence of accident is a different matter from the existence of substance, and each category of accidents—being how much, being thus, being experience or being action, *being in* a place or *in* time, habitual being, or being in relation to another—modifies the character of existence and of the term "exist." That the principle of distinguishing the different ways in which things exist may seem most excellent, and one honors its discovery, does not mean that the concrete distinctions established by Aristotle or in general by his very idea of categories need be taken as gospel.

It would be more practical to call "entity" in the strict sense the "way of existing" of the Ens or—what is the same thing—the "way of being" of the Existent, excluding from its meaning the so-called *quidditas* or essence, which I prefer to call "consistence." Remember, then, that I use these terms "entity" and "consistence" with the values that I have indicated. Whoever wants to go on talking about the Ens had better go back to Avicenna. Apart from this practical advantage I have been brought to this terminology by ends too lofty to be pointed out here.

"modern" sides of Aristotle that what was needed was a man fresh from the colonies, a Macedonian.

So it is that Aristotle, without adequate logical equipment for thinking his discovery through, does not know what to do with the concept of Ens which is now the Existent, and—as we wait and hope before every problem which he does not see clearly—he will tell us once more that the relationship of the Existent with things is . . . analogous. The relationship of the Ens with its inferiors—valid for all and not *genuinely* valid for any—will be that of a pseudogenus, an *omnibus* genus, like those "single-class" transatlantic liners of the last days before the war—so typical of the times—on which everyone was accommodated and nobody to his liking.

The difficulties which the "transcendental" character of the Aristotelian concept of Ens posed for the Scholastics was patent in the sterility of their efforts. *"De modo quo ens descendit vel trahitur ad inferiora . . . obscuram habet difficultatem."* [10] Father Urraburu will still say in every dictum, *"Ens contrahitur in inferiora sua per modum expressioris conceptus eiusdem realitas."* [11] So that, while Ens expresses Being as such, other things will *give it expression.* This discovery does not seem very illuminating and would better suggest the superfluity of the concept of Ens since its inferiors express it more and supposedly this "more" is equivalent to "better." The worst thing about this is that Saint Thomas and Suárez say exactly the same thing. Duns Scotus among the old Scholastics and Arriaga among the moderns make a little more of a question out of this strange relationship between the Ens and things. It would not seem a fortunate solution either, but rather a formal declaration of its unsolvability, to say that the concept of Ens relates to concrete *entia* in a confused manner —it is confusing.[12]

10. Suárez, *Disputationes*, II, Sec. II, 36.
11. *Ontology*, p. 156.
12. Suárez, *Disputationes*, II, Sec. I, 6. *Conceptus entis ut sic, si in eo sistatur, semper est confusus respectu particularium entium, ut talia sunt.* Note that the opposite of confused, *distinctus*, "*est qui determinate et*

Nevertheless the "transcendentality" of the concept of Ens is perhaps the most profound, the most fruitful, and the most fertile thing in all ontology. It is enough for it to abandon the method of commonal abstraction, which destroys itself in it, making of the Ens a genus which is not a genus and by euphemism is called "the most common." Its paradoxical relationship with things—to be valid for all of them and not to identify itself in any of them—suggests that it was not extracted from them; furthermore, that it is too early to see each one as like an Ens. Or to put it in more homespun but more vivid language, that the Ens is not in *entia* but the other way round, *entia* are in the Ens. This would be a hypothesis invented by man to interpret both the things around him and his own destiny. The effort to regard things as *entia* began in the first third of the fifth century before Christ, and still goes on. That effort has been called *philosophy*.

In their initial relationship with man things have no Being, but consist of pure practicalities. From a remote past the Greeks preserved an expression which says this very adequately: they called things in this, their first relationship with man *pragmáta*. This word defines things strictly in terms of what we do with them or suffer from them. The electric light beneath the glow of which I write these lines consists in lighting my way or leading me in darkness when I most need it, in my lighting it and putting it out, in my securing its installation, in my paying its cost, and so on. Imagine the entire list of what I can do with it and what I can suffer from it, and call that group of actions and reactions its *pragmatism*. But note that beyond all this pragmatism which constitutes it in the first place and exhausts its practicality there is still something new that I can do with it, namely, to ask myself what *is* light. As regards "doing with it," this is no different from the rest, but it is peculiar in that it does not consist in using the electric

---

expresse repraesentat omnes entitates simplices, quas ens immediate significat" (*Disputationes*, II, Sec. I, 5). This definition of *distinctus* appertains to Fonseca and Suárez, except for their rejection of *simplices*, which does not affect our question.

light or in missing its services; this is rather a way of doing
which detaches the thing and isolates it from the pragmatic
network that made it up and which was characterized by a
series of simple references to the necessities of my life. Actually, in asking myself what is light, I detach this light from
my life and set myself to look at it as if it had nothing to do
with me, therefore, as something foreign and alien to me. I
leave it alone and it leaves me alone.[13] Well now, this means
subjecting it to a basic metamorphosis. Earlier, it was considered only in simple reference to the necessities of my life;
now it is in reference to its own self. The thing is transformed
into an "itself."

Such a metamorphosis of a concrete thing would be impossible if we had not previously had the idea of an *ambit* completely different from that which life creates in its primary
aspect of pure practicality. The new *ambit* is made up of pure
"itself-ness." Everything regarding "itself" that is in it or that
can be in it is there. That ambit is the World. To ask oneself,
then, what light *is* means taking this thing out of our primary
life and projecting it—and ourselves with it—into the World.
And as each thing, although detached from me, appears in
connection with other things also metamorphosed into "themselves" it begins to form part of a network of "self-nesses"
which is the material that makes up the shape of the "World."
Let us say in passing that Leibnitz insists strongly that God
does not solve any single thing without solving all things,
therefore its whole, for His solution of each one turns on its
relation to the whole. For God, according to this, the idea of
World would precede its parts and decree them; or, what is
the same thing, the creative act is directed formally to the
creation of a World and only secondarily to the creation of
the things that make it up. Therefore He created the best
World and not this or that best thing.

When we ask ourselves about the Being of something, and
even more about Being "in general," we eliminate all refer-

13. For Aristotle the most decisive characteristic of the authentic
Being is solitude—μονή—*moné* (*Metaphysics*, VII, 1, 1028ᵃ 34).

ences of the thing to our life which may be regarded as practical—all but one, precisely the one which leads us to ask ourselves about its Being. This question and the attempts to answer it bring knowledge or theory into action. Note the innate paradox which this carries with it. In theorizing we occupy ourselves with or about things to the extent that we refuse to be concerned with or about them in any pragmatic sense. But theory itself is a form of *pragmatism*. What leads us to theorize are vital necessities, and this exercise itself is a practice, a doing something with them, namely, asking ourselves about their Being.

The question about what *is* light implies that we do not know *what* light is, but at the same time it implies that we know what Being is before knowing *what* is *each* thing to the extent that it is. Otherwise the question would be meaningless. But then this means that the idea of Being has not been extracted from things, but rather has been introduced into them by man, that it precedes the Being of each one and makes it possible for them to be *entia*. Hence I said that the *entia* are in the Ens, and not vice versa. Being is certainly the Being *of* things, but the result is that this, the most genuine thing about them, since it is their "itself-ness," is absent by virtue of the fact that they are things, but because it is assumed of them by man. The Ens would in fact be a human hypothesis. It is therefore necessary to define the attributes of Being insofar as we seek it and ask ourselves about it, drawing a distinction between these and those attributes of Being which we think we have found.[14]

In the Aristotelian-Scholastic way of thinking the "transcendentality" of the concept Ens has, as a matter of classification, only trivial significance. It means that it transcends every individual class of concepts, that it is not identified with any and that it soars above them with no obligation to be more specific. That way of thinking had to recognize that it had no means of understanding this strange condition of

14. About this, see my *Annex to Kant*, 1929 (*Obras Completas*, Vol. IV) and *Remarks about Thought* (*Obras Completas*, Vol. V).

the concept Ens, which contravenes all its rules. But what I have just stated—reduced to its simplest terms and lacking any further proposal to suggest—gives us a much richer double meaning of "transcendentality." On the one hand, this signifies that the concept Ens is, in fact, transcendent over every class of things, because it does not originate in them but, on the contrary, is itself the origin of things as *entia*. On the other hand, it means that the hypothesis of the Ens obliges each thing to transcend the primary ambit in which it appears to us and in which it is valid merely in its practical aspect, and to form part of, or become an ingredient in, "something rather like" a World. This transcending is what Plato used to call "Rising to Being." In a world of itself-ness, together with things, man too is like "himself," i.e., in him *"l'uom s'eterna."* But that World is a hypothesis, a postulate, which our life extends from its primary dimension outside of and *beyond* itself, that is to say, it postulates its own projection and metamorphosis into a living *itself*, or shall we say into a living itself-ness of life.

23
Modernity and Primitivism
in Aristotle

ARISTOTLE, who, as I said earlier, appears to be contradictory because his doctrine was not sufficiently systematic, began and ended by relying on analogy for everything decisive, and hence on dialectic or the "desire to talk." He defines analogy nominally as that relationship of a concept to the things conceived which does not imply that the concept expresses the same reality that they do, but rather that their common character consists only in relating all of them, each in its own way, to a single thing.[1] These are not the Aristotelian nor the Scholastic terms, but I think that with these hasty remarks we can contribute to formulating his idea. Aristotle was satisfied with the nominal definition. He does not show us what comprises analogous "reality," which will have to be something, now that he distinguishes analogous unity from mere coincidence in nomenclature. On the other hand, he does not undertake either to show us the particular mental processes by which analogy is established. They will perforce be different from those enumerated in his logic or analytics since its result—the analogous universal—is so different. Let us add finally that, according to Joseph Geyser, a good Aristotelian and disciplined Thomist, analogy is the mental act "which leads to concepts more remote than those which the simple abstraction of concrete existential conditions affords."[2]

This is one of the most curious things that has happened in the history of thought, for we have this:

1. For Aristotle the "way of thinking" by analogy is not

1. *Metaphysics*, IV, 2, 1003^a 33.
2. *Die Erkenntnistheorie des Aristoteles*, 1917, p. 271.

the scientific way, and therefore it does not provide a mental grasp of genuine reality.

2. Nevertheless, we owe to it the discovery of the most important things in science and in Being, which are principles.

3. But this does not induce him to analyze the ontological, methodological, and psychological origin of analogy.

4. Therefore, according to his principle that "he who does not see the knot (the problem) does not know how to untie it," [3] we gather that his failure to resolve the problem of analogy means that he did not see it.

5. Had he taken one more step he would have seen that thinking by analogy differs from his thinking in terms of things in that the former thinks of things only in terms of relationships; therefore, that it was simply a matter of abandoning the category of thing or substance and setting up the category of relationship or πρός τι. *This* Descartes *did* and with this alone he created a whole new exact way of thinking which is now going to be a bit more genuinely so. That step would have placed Aristotle all at once in full and absolute modernity.

6. But as he did not take that step, because he had not seen the problem that analogy posed and grew dizzy when he encountered it within his way of thinking, he revealed that, far from being absolutely modern, he was modern only on one side, only relatively modern, and all the other side of him makes us suspect a certain amount of "primitivism" in him.[4] And now he is formally so classified, because the primitive mentality—what I call "primigenial or magic thinking"—consists in doing the very thinking that Aristotle does when he analogizes.

7. This last, to which previous paragraphs give meaning, is what I consider one of the most curious things in the history of thought, namely that the most modern form of thinking and the most ancient, most primitive form, find themselves

3. *Metaphysics*, III, 1, 995ᵃ 29; λύειν δ'οὐκ ἔστιν ἀγνοοῦντας τὸν δεσμόν.
4. Hence when I called him relatively modern I put this adjective in quotation marks.

separated by no more than a hair. Descartes and Aristotle (when he analogizes) coincide—Aristotle without realizing it —in speaking of things as mere terms of relationship, therefore as correlates. The difference between them lies in that Descartes, recognizing this, accepts correlates as correlates, while Aristotle treats correlates as if they were not relative things but absolutes, independent of relationships, that is to say, formally as "things." Well now, this is what primigenial man did.[5]

5. That the entity of the analogous consists in relativity seems to us so patent a thing that we would judge it improbable that Aristotle did not see and recognize it, chiefly because it is so important a concept in his doctrine. Nevertheless that improbability is the reality. What already gives the clue is that in his dictionary of philosophy—Book V of the *Metaphysics*—the chapter on the *relative* does not allude to it in the slightest. But the fact is that there is not one single text in the entire body of Aristotelian work where one gathers that Aristotle ever knew that analogy is a relationship, despite the fact that whenever he uses that word in an active sense he has no choice but to add to it the grammatical particle which expresses relationship, the πρός. The only one of Aristotle's texts in which a person not warned of that incredible dimness in the great philosopher might find recognition of analogy as a relationship is the *Nicomachean Ethics* (V, 6, 1131ᵃ 30 ff.); τὸ γὰρ ἀνά- λογον οὐ μόνον ἐστὶ μοναδικοῦ ἀριθμοῦ ἴδιον, ἀλλ'ὅλως ἀριθμοῦ ἡ γὰρ ἀναλογία ἰσότης ἐστὶ λόγων, καὶ ἐν τέτταρσιν ἐλαχίστοις, which Dionysius Lambinus translates as: "*Non enim solum sius numeri, quo aliquid numeramus, proprium est proportione constare, sed etiam eius qui universe et omnino numerus est. Proportio enim rationis est aequilitas, quae in quattuor minimum reperetur,*" etc. It was strange that the revelation of what analogy is should emerge there in the *Ethics*, and that it should have been on the occasion of defining justice. But those words convince us definitely—and I say the same of the ὅσα ἔχει ἄλλο πρὸς ἄλλο that Zeller cites without saying where he found it—that Aristotle does not see analogy as consisting *simpliciter* in a relationship, but that here he declares formally that it belongs to the category of quantity, and that if it emerges as a matter of justice this is for the quaint reason that in the struggle for justice *two* men and *two* things intervene; therefore four terms. So it is not for nothing that this is referred to justice itself only through the accidental intervention of numbers.

    This is an excellent example of the *constitutive* blind spots to which mankind is heir. And if Aristotle suffered from them let us not mention those that we carry around! Hence it is very fruitful to devote ourselves from time to time to investigating our own blind spots, not because this rarely enables us to identify them or consequently to eliminate

To regret that Aristotle failed to put himself *d'emblée* into modernity simply by recognizing the relational character of analogy is clearly not to censure him but to express regret and file a just complaint in our own account. Nor can it be taken for granted as a thing obvious in itself that there is any obligation to be modern, or that modernity is always the best; but it does imply demanding of those who think the opposite and who believe that there is a *philosophia perennis*—which is precisely the Aristotelian-Scholastic point of view—that they see clearly, in order to be able *not* to admit them, the ideas which have occurred to moderns and which go on occurring to us who are contemporaries. If this perennial philosophy does not have a good understanding of the philosophy of all times—therefore that of the moderns and of contemporaries —it means that it does not have this perennial character, that it is not present in all periods but has remained in the past, and if it is perennial or perdurable this is because it has been converted into a fossil, has petrified; it is perhaps the "philosopher's stone."

I leave here, firmly planted and waving in the wind, the twice stated diagnostic battle flag according to which there is in Aristotle a surprising mixture of "modernity" (equivalent to relative modernity) and "primitivism." Plato is of a very different makeup. He had about him almost nothing of the "modern" (although his doctrine has become in great part absolutely modern and even contemporary), but neither was he "primitive." On the other hand, it seems to me, looking at the images of him which have been created, that he was typically "archaic" which is something very different from "primi-

---

them, but because it does stretch the elasticity of our mental capacities to the maximum.

The Scholastics, learning it from the Arabs and in low Latin, define analogy as a relationship. So does St. Thomas in his *Commentarium in Metaphysics*, Book IV, Chap. 1, Par. 7 ff. and Book XI, Chap. 3, Par. 4, and in *Summa theologia, Prima pars*, qua. 13, art. 5. But being incapable of posing new basic problems or of reshaping the old ones, everything stays the same and not the slightest result is obtained.

tive." One can glimpse what I mean by this qualification if one remembers those statues from Aegina which historians of art call "archaic." Given the normal anticipation of artistic as compared with doctrinal development Plato would be their contemporary, and one might *a priori* gather that as a writer and a thinker he would exhibit a similar style. Compared with the classic period of sculpture that "archaicism" incorporates certain mannerisms which the classic period eliminated. And Plato was unquestionably quite mannered. For that, his contemporaries charged him with "Asianism." [6]

6. This last stage in archaic Greek art, which is what I refer to, was derived, as is well known, from influences coming from Asia, which is what our Asia Minor was for the Hellenes. Aristotle had this impression of archaicism from Plato, and he points it out expressly in his metaphysical books (1088^b 28 to 1089^a 2) when he says that he saw himself obliged "before everything else" to add the Dyad to the One as a principle "because the questions were posed in the archaic manner": τὸ ἀπορῆσαι ἀρχαικῶς.

24

The New "Way of Thinking" and Aristotelian Demagoguery

WE WERE AT THE POINT WHERE Descartes begins by proclaiming the common character of genera and therefore that there are no individual or plural sciences, as Aristotle argued in opposition to Plato. With this, as 24 uninterrupted centuries have demonstrated, Aristotle dethroned Platonism and arrested the progress of thought. No small part of the blame for this, as I have already said, is due to the fact that Aristotle, one of the greatest philosophers that ever lived, had the temperament of a "man of science" rather than of a philosopher, and this inclined him always toward *specialization*, that is, to interest himself in the specific which, as we saw, is the "genuine," the *idiota*. Specialization has *idiotized* the men of science,[1] those who could not bear to think that one of the greatest philosophers might have had a very faulty philosophical disposition, that he did not try to understand the human, and . . . that he would *study mathematics*, as the Venetian prostitute told young Rousseau to do.

According to the Cartesian, then, there is only one science, unique and integral. Keep in mind that for Descartes, as for Aristotle and for us in this study, "science" is exclusively the deductive theory or theories.[2] According to this all deductive

1. The terrible social consequences which this—together with other things, of course—would bring, and which today are so crudely patent, were announced years ago in the *Revolt of the Masses*, Chap. XII (*Obras Completas*, Vol. IV). [Published in English by W. W. Norton, 1932 and 1957.]

2. "*Je désire que vous remarquièz la différence qu'il y a entre les sciences et les simples connaissances qui s'acquièrent sans aucun discours de raison, comme les langues, l'histoire, la géographie et généralement tout ce qui ne dépend que de l'expérience seule.*" (*Récherche de la vérité. Oeuvres*, Edition Adam et Tannery, Vol. X, pp. 502, 24–29.)

theories form a continuous body, they derive from each other
or are mutually involved, and the names of the different
disciplines merely designate the members of a unitary organism. That Single Science begins with metaphysics and ends
with meteorology, and—God willing—with physiology. That
is the way Descartes sees it and that is how we see it today.
But in Descartes, naturally, it was only a program, which was
a great deal at that time. In our day that program has mostly
been realized.

The continuity of scientific subject-matter does not prevent
us from distinguishing in the whole deductive *corpus* a primary and fundamental area which ties all the rest together:
this is metaphysics. It is concerned with God and with the
soul. How and why to be concerned with these things will
for Descartes be fundamental knowledge—in the sense of
being the foundation for all the rest—is something which we
will see later, although very briefly. But we would already
have had to ask ourselves by means of what way of thinking
we acquired metaphysics. And note that this "man of method"
has never let us know in a clear, articulate, and precise fashion
with what method or what specific use of his general method
he makes inquiries about the soul and about God.[3]

The only treatise on this method which we possess, although
incomplete, is, as I said, the *Rules for the Direction of the
Mind*. There we first find the cry of the provost of Paris:
"The King is dead! Long live the King!" "The incommunicability of genera is over! Long live their communicability!"
It is useful, then, to examine at this point the method which
the rules expound and repeat in the *Discourse*. Then we will
see what happens to metaphysics insofar as his method is
concerned.

If we hold to the *Rules* we would expect to move on to
something concrete after that declaration of the Single Science

3. Many times he calls his own the *méthode générale,* and in the letters of March of 1637, to Mersenne, of the 27th of April of 1637, (?)
to an unknown, and the very important one of the 22nd of February,
1638 (?) to Father Vatier, he points out that it also has value for
metaphysics, but the why and the how remain in doubt (*ibid.* Vol. I).

(which has to be so, as our understanding is single-minded and functions in only one way or, what is the same thing, uses only one method). And the result of this coalescence is that, without warning us and as a natural thing, that Single Science contracts to a Universal Science, or *Mathesis Universalis*. Descartes understands by Universal Science something quite different from Single Science. The *Mathesis Universalis* is the *corpus* of the sciences, including everything from arithmetic and geometry to astronomy, music, optics, mechanics, "*aliaeque complures*"; [4] that is to say, it is extended and kept in the area of those disciplines which could in their time be called mathematical, although in a rather pejorative sense. In the 16th Century it was still normal to call men like Copernicus "mathematicians," which, you will note, carried the connotation that astronomy was not properly a science but only a "keeping up appearances." Aristotle still reigned and the true science of the stars was not the network of hypothesis which the astronomers had woven since Copernicus and Kepler—combining it with geometry to destroy its prestige further—but the "animistic" physics, *soi disant* philosophical, whose principles, the so-called "natures," are first cousins of those that the men of Altamira carried in their minds. Thanks to this, i.e., that it was not a science but the gabble of "mathematicians," the book by Copernicus was allowed to circulate.

The difference between the Single Science and the Universal Science is not really great. The latter takes from the former only metaphysics and logic. But as Descartes does not believe in logic and suppresses it—or thinks he suppresses it—*a limine* and completely, only metaphysics remains. Above the universe of the sciences, and as a preface to them, there is Method.

Let it be said parenthetically that when Descartes, the man of "reason" [5] par excellence, founder and patron of modern

4. *Regulae* IV, *ibid.* X, pp. 377, 15.
5. He tells us (*Discours, ibid.* Vol. VI, p. 27) that he has decided to take as the "occupation of his life" "to use it entirely in cultivating his rational faculties." For how he repudiated logic with infinite disdain

rationalism, turns out not to believe in logic, this is one of
those amusing things which emerge unexpectedly in history
and which *for this very reason are true history*. History is full
of such things as sudden emergencies, or vice versa, of unforeseen trapdoors and devilish tricks. Because of this it is the
opposite of the mathematics which the Venetian prostitute
recommended.

This Universal Science, in whose belly all the sciences except metaphysics find themselves indiscriminately, assumes a
single genus of realities. Already analytical geometry con-fuses
number with extensive magnitude. This second step is evidently reduced to generalizing that con-fusion, extending
it to movement, to stars, to meteors; in sum, to all the sense-
perceptible phenomena or "material things," [6] which is enough
to bring us already to the inescapable problem of the difference between the traditional way of thinking and that which
Descartes initiates.

In the *Discourse on Method* we are presented with the
vertical order of reasons, which is the architectural form of
theory, stretched horizontally in the temporal series of an
autobiography. Descartes insists on showing us that not only
has his thinking been according to method, but that his life
also has been methodical. Because of this the story of the
stages in his life becomes an exposition of his method. This, a
pure sequence of reasoning, is presented to us in the *Discourse*
like a mythological god transposed into a personal destiny.
And we discover that, since all that was thought and said in
his time seemed doubtful to him, he resorts to the only thing
that has the look of being exact knowledge: the mathematical
sciences. "But this did not make me try to learn all these
particular sciences which are commonly called mathematics,

---

see *Discours*, pp. 17–18, because if anyone in this world has been disdainful that was Descartes. And that disdain takes him, as in the case of
logic, to proceeding so summarily that disdain turns into boldness and
boldness comes close to shamelessness. The reader will see later that
this opinion of mine does not stem from any enthusiasm for logic.
6. *Discours*, pp. 41 and 27.

but that, seeing how they do coincide, *in spite of their objects being different,* in referring only to the various relationships or proportions—*rapports ou proportions*—which are in those objects, it seemed to me preferable *to examine only these proportions in general* without thinking about them except in the subjects [7] capable of allowing me to know them more easily, but at the same time *without limiting them at all* so as to be able later to apply them better to *all* the subjects for which they might be suitable." [8]

At one bound we are in a new world. The object of arithmetic is not the quantitative "thing," nor that of geometry the continuous "thing," nor in physics the "thing" which moves with a movement which is also a "thing." The sciences—and except for metaphysics there are no others but the exact ones—do not concern themselves with things. We can understand how cautious Descartes was in publishing his thoughts, and what surprises us is that a doctrine which begins thus did not immediately touch off a tremendous disturbance. Descartes, whose method is precaution added to geometry, and whose life was methodical, had taken good care to start by . . . going away, by going away to what was then the only free country on the Continent and at the same time the one most advanced in the sciences, except for Italy in some respects. He went to Holland, and from there, many years later, he launched into speech.

The sciences do not concern themselves with things as things but with their "relationships or proportions." Let us understand very clearly the newest implications which this encompasses:

1. Science does not speak of things as *entia*

A. to the extent that each one is a *natura solitaria* enclosed in itself or in its essence. Science is not the knowledge of essences but it takes possession of everything that can be useful for our purpose, and in this sense it leads us not to contem-

7. Subject in Scholastic terminology is the thing-essence, at least the thing-essence which is the subject, and it underlies altogether the judgment on which the rest is predicated. Later I will clarify what this enigmatic phrase of Descartes signifies.

8. *Discours,* pp. 19 and 20.

plate their solitary natures, but to compare them between themselves, *so that they can be known to each other.*[9] Therefore, instead of things = essences, things = substrata of relationships.

2. Science does not speak of things as entia:

B. to the extent that they can have a Being of their own, apart from man, except that knowledge is a relationship of anthropological utility. We ask ourselves not for what they may be from their point of view, but for what there is in them which is useful to us; not, for the moment, with a practical or material utility, but useful so as to make possible a deductive theory referring to them.

3. The new way of thinking does not consist only in being a new method of knowing, but it starts from an *idea of what knowledge itself is* which is completely different from the traditional. Theory—θεωρία—is not now meditation about existing but meditation about what is *useful in Being* for a system of deductions.

4. Truth-of-Being is thus reduced in rank by the needs of thinking and will be called truth *à la* truth-in-thinking, which will permit Descartes to burst out with this weighty formula: *"La vérité étant un même chose avec l'Etre."*

5. *Entia* being reduced in rank to mere terms of relationships, scientific knowledge will consist in thinking of the relationships between *entia* and not of them. But relationships cannot be revealed to us by sensation or imagination, and they are discovered rather through *acts of comparison* to which we submit things.

6. Hence the first thing that must be done is to lighten radically the cognitive value of the senses and to put into the pillory the principle from which the Aristotelian-Scholastic method takes off: "There is nothing in the intellect which has not been in the senses first." [10] That must be turned into this:

9. *"Notandum est primo, res omnes, eo sensu quo ad nostrum propositum utiles esse possunt ubi nos illarum naturas solitarias spectamus, sed illas inter se comparamus, ut unae ex aliis cognoscantur"* (*Regulae*, VI, *ibid.*, pp. 381, 17–21).

10. *Discours*, pp. 37, 9–23.

There is nothing in the senses which is real with any surety except for what the intellect decides to put into them.[11] Rationality succeeds the sensuality of the Scholastics. Descartes insists indefatigably on denouncing the senses and dismissing them definitely as a basis for truth. It is basic doctrine with him—because of its decisive importance and its primordiality in the correct order of reasoning which is knowledge—that it is not possible to know or even to understand an authentic truth if we have not previously been able to eliminate within us the belief—in his judgment merely instinctive and animal —in the veracity of the senses or, as he says, without *abducere mentem a sensibus*.[12]

7. In fact there is no *spontaneous* principle which is firmer, more "evident," than this one: The senses bring us face to face with realities or states of being, to such a degree that in order to enunciate the prototype of what should be believed as being the most authentic, "everybody" says: "Seeing is believing." This profession of faith is an expression of the most ancient popular philosophy, which springs, *like all philosophy*, from skepticism—in this case from *the doubt confronting all reasonings*, to which is opposed as a final expression of belief and the only adequate one—seeing, hearing, touching. That, then, is the "public opinion" permanently established in the streets. But philosophy *began and consists*—whatever its other differences between schools may be—precisely in denying the jurisdiction of truth over the senses. Thus it was when it was born with Parmenides, thus it was at its re-birth in Descartes, and in veering toward positivism in Kant[13] and in becoming resolutely positivist with Comte; we will not even mention the others. Thus faced with the commonplace, with "public opinion," *dóxa* or *éndoxon* of belief

11. The expression of Descartes which ends the paragraph is: "*Ni notre imagination ni nos sens ne nous sauraient jamais assurer d'aucune chose, si notre entendement n'y intervient.*"

12. See, for example, (there are numerous passages) the letter to Father Vatier previously quoted, *ibid.*, Vol. I, pp. 560, 16.

13. What shall I say of those who "revert rabble-like" at the instance of "experience" (*die pöbelhafte Berufung auf Erfahrung*).

in the senses, philosophy is essentially, and not by chance, *paradoxa*. To Aristotle was reserved the climacteric honor of taking as the point of departure and starting point of his philosophy this commonplace, this rhetorical *éndoxon*—strictly speaking, one cannot even call it dialectic—this *idolum fori*, this demagoguery of the authentic joined to the senses. His philosophy is the only one—in the whole history of this discipline—which behaves in this way, since the Stoics inherited that dogma from him.

I cannot understand why this popular demagogical character of the Scholastic-Aristotelian way of thinking has not been underlined more strongly. It is not a trait which appears only when, familiar with that philosophy, we wish to understand the psychology, the subjective character which engendered it, which sustains and propagates it. No—it is the doctrine itself which breaks away, in an essential departure from an admission which is truth only for the mob: the ontological "evidence" of the senses. It embraces the criterions of Sancho Panza. Faith in the senses is a traditional dogma, a public *institution*, established in the irresponsible and anonymous opinion of the "people," of the collectivity. Remember what we said about "evidence" in the principle of contradiction. This dogma of ontological sensualism is another "unintelligible" factor, with the force of a myth and of a commonplace or topic in the collective soul. There are neither reasons for it nor is it a reason in itself. It simply has *been there* for millennia, having originated in certain practical and useful experiences in living. No individual forged it deliberately, but, like everything that comes from the people, it has been making *itself* impersonally, little by little, letting time flow over it with its stream of uninterrupted tradition. And this multi-secular and anonymous current has made of it what all "commonplaces" are: a pebble rolled smooth at the bottom of the social stream. To believe in it is not an act of intelligence; nobody actually thinks out its content, its *dictum*, when it is used and trusted. The "commonplace" as a social or collective way which exists is not conscious, not *compos mentis;* it is blind, mechanical. The individual believes in it because from time immemorial *it* has been said all around him, and he repeats this mimetically suggested gesture. The individual adopts it, not through intelligence but through social *suggestion*. It is a "principle" which has nothing to do with theory. It is a mechanical social custom. The ensemble of "suggestive" admissions of this type makes up what since the time of the Stoics has been called "common sense." It is a "common sense truth." Obviously, since "common sense" is not a faculty of the intelligence, it cannot create, have, or contain any truths. It is made up of adages, proverbs. "sayings," i.e., things that say themselves.[14]

If that dogma were not what it is—a social fact, a mere collective "usage," and not a personal mental activity, which alone is capable of theorizing—and if it were not also just that in Aristotle, it would be impossible to understand why, even without laying a foundation for it, he did not at least formulate and *demonstrate* it as a principle, as he does with contradiction and the excluded middle, or even less to understand why he has not even expounded it.[15] It is for him a sort of underground belief, working within him as in any "man of the people," and at the same time latent, subconscious, as are all authentic beliefs—contrary to Philosophy, which is not, nor can be, nor has to be a belief—which he always leaves in the background. "Beliefs" and "commonplaces," since they do not concern our waking and lucid life, always act in us *a tergo*, or, what is the same thing, our lives are driven along by their momentum.

Well then, all that Aristotle does is to say, as if it were the most obvious thing in the world: the real and most authentic Ens is substance, and substance is "this man," "this horse" which I see. Nothing more.

14. About all this, my book *Man and People* [Revista de Occidente, Madrid, 1957, Chaps. XI and XII, "The Talk of the People"]. [Published in English by W. W. Norton, 1963.]

15. Though we were already surprised that he did not analyze, that he did not take permanent possession of his *dictum*.

25
The Cataleptic Imagination
of the Stoics

EARLIER we pursued briefly the evolution of the theory of knowledge and of the noetic psychology connected with it which appears among the immediate disciples of Aristotle. If we had looked farther ahead we would have seen the appearance of Stoicism and, in its theory of knowledge combined with noesis, at the continuation of that development which was the inevitable product of the Aristotelian doctrine.

Within its corporative clumsiness the cognitive doctrine of the Stoics is coherent and not devoid of keen insights. It is the natural consequence of Aristotelianism. We have no more information about Existing or the Real than what the senses provide. But the senses report only the corporeal. The Real, the Ens to be—these are therefore bodies. Here, inevitably joined together, you have extreme cognitive sensualism and extreme ontological corporealism ("materialism"). A straightforward development of peripatetic philosophy had to end inexorably in this. Apart from the moral, this Stoicism is Aristotle's *enfant terrible*. It makes manifest what Aristotelianism really was in the final analysis. This is history. The morning paper *inevitably* shows us the matrix that was pressed yesterday. What was latent and unknown in today's matrix will clearly be public property tomorrow. History is a giant step toward stripping reality completely bare. Hence the idea of the Valley of Jehoshaphat should always be taken as a marvellous symbol: the end of the world as the final stripping to nakedness. It is the visionary expression of a great historiological truth.

According to the Stoics there is no intelligence in man. So

it is not intelligence that fabricates ideas, discovers principles and convinces itself of them. Principles, like concepts, emerge in man little by little, slowly but spontaneously. Sensual experience, dealing with bodies, will *mechanically* leave within him—and this is what is intellectually acute in the doctrine—crystallizations of mental behavior which are concepts and principles. To have them and to make use of them is not, then, what we are accustomed to call "thinking," but rather their mechanical use similar to the reflex with which, as something approaches our eyes, the eyelids close automatically, or like the leap to one side with which we avoid a puddle. These basic experiences of life, which are magnified mechanically into principles (like, I repeat, adages or proverbs), are *common* to all men. Hence *all* men hold to the same principles, up to the point where the criterion for knowing the "truth" of a principle is . . . universal suffrage. Stoicism *declares* that this, undeclared and taciturn, was already present in Aristotle. Principle is not principle *because* its meaning might be clearly expressed; it is not a principle for what it says, but because *everyone* says it, because it *is* said. Listen to Seneca: *"Multum dare solemus praesumptioni omnium hominum et apud nos veritatis argumentum est aliquid omnibus videri."* [1] Consequently, the Stoics do not call principles "principles" or truths, but "presumptions" or "assumptions"—πρόληψις (*prólepsis*). Depending on their content the Stoics called them opinions or "common judgments"—κοιναὶ ἔννοιαι (*koinaì énnoiai*)—which is what Aristotle called axioms or principles. The aggregate of those propositions of universal suffrage or group ruling opinions was called "common feeling" or "common sense." [2] And this is the reality of the Aristotelian-Scholastic philoso-

1. "We place great confidence in what every one *assumes* and for us it is an argument that something is true if we find that it seems so to everyone."

2. The expression itself is not in any of the fragments of the Stoics which we have preserved; but it must perforce have been coined by some one of the Stoic generations (which are many, and very active) as is shown by the fact that it appears in Cicero (*De Oratore*, III, Chap. 1), who was the great transmitter of Stoic gnosticism through the people of the Renaissance, and from them to us.

phy. It is the philosophy of common sense which, take note, is not intelligence but, like everything called "evidence," [3] is *blind assumption through collective suggestion.*

This lets us try a new interpretation of the true character, neither understood nor explained, of what were for the Stoics the criterion of truth and the mental act which together provide the foundation of knowledge: "cataleptic imagination"; that is to say, the "overwhelming or captivating idea." [4] It must be understood that it is man who is overwhelmed and *captivated* by the idea, which imposes itself on us and forces us. But the idea or the conception—*imagination*—which has this hypnotic effect on us is only the survivor of one or many perceptions—*aísthesis.* For the Stoics these are the prototype of a mental phenomenon having cataleptic, suggestive, or hypnotic power. Catalepsy compels us to agree to something —to some perception or proposition. The agreement—*synkatáthesis*—is "free." In the final analysis we can credit it or not to the catalepsy in which we are, but it would cost us great effort to refuse it. [5]

Well now, the Stoics have had to recognize that cataleptic imaginations frequently commit errors. [6] This inevitably brought with it—although they never saw it as a whole—

3. Among the comic things in Spain's unfortunate intellectual life during the past century should be included the fact that Menendez Pelayo would have considered it a great triumph to move in the maturity of Scholasticism to the Scotch philosophy of common sense; this was as though one decided to leave little Málaga in order to move into big Málaga.

4. I suspect, but I have not studied it in sufficient detail to assert it, that our word "percatación" (mature consideration) is the erudite Latin translation of "catalepsy," which in turn is one of Stoicism's technical terms.

5. The Stoics are basically determinists. Their interpretation of Reality as Nature leads them to this. Nature lives and moves and is by itself; it is absolute spontaneity. By the same token each part of Nature, each thing, has its own particular spontaneity, "home-made": οἰκεῖον *(oikeîon).* That spontaneity, which is nothing but determinism, was called "liberty."

6. Now Zeno himself: *"Urgebat Arcesilas Zenonem, cum ipse falsa omnia diceret, quae sensibus viderentur, Zeno autem nonnulla visa esse falsa, non omnia."* (Cicero, *De natura deorum,* I, 25.)

the fact that their persuasive and captivating forces could not proceed on their own, that is to say, under their own power, for this was as well-aimed as it was mistaken. My idea is that the "convincing" or exacting—cataleptic—character of sensations and of certain main propositions came to them and to the Stoics from what was "prevailing opinion," "commonplace," belief in the senses and belief in the principle of contradiction.[7] These two "traditional truths" were two collective usages. Hence they are accepted as "evident" simply because nobody has questioned them. They are "blind and mechanical thinking," generated by collective suggestion and collective "hypnosis"; that is to say, what is literally today, as then, literally understood as *catalepsy*. Insofar as he lives by collective usages, man is an automaton directed by social suggestion; he lives in a perpetual state of catalepsy. This is not a psychic effect of perception, but a sociological effect of society on the individual. It is not, then, this sensation which I now have that induces in me a state of catalepsy, but the general *belief* which I previously held that the senses are authentic which leads me "hypnotized" to them. And Aristotelian-Scholastic philosophy which, without raising any question about it, was starting with the authenticity of sensations and the extraction of concepts by commonal abstraction, becomes a philosophy of cataleptics, psychic slaves of the "commonplace" and victims of commonplaceness.

7. But if they saw very clearly that the *catalepsy* of sensation, image or idea was founded on the *catalepsy* ("evidence") of truth, this does not consist solely in *cataleptic imagination*, but "in the ideas (νοητά) which surround it and have reference to it." (Sextus Empiricus, *Adv. Math.* VIII, 10.) For me this text is decisive, although historians of philosophy do not ordinarily understand it.

As an example of philological inadequacy one may look at the last thing—I think—there is on the Stoics: *Physis und Agathon in der Alten Stoa*, published in the collection of highest scientific rank which there was in Germany before the war. Read in the *Excurs* about πρόληψις (*prólepsis*) what the author says about catalepsy (pp. 74 and 75). To affirm that *prólepsis* is "one and the same thing as what Plato thought" is not an error, it is something worse, which would call for strong language.

For the Stoic, then, truth is given in man with a purely subjective character of "apprehension" which is neither more nor less than the descriptive psychological name for what the Scholastics called "evidence." I find the term admirable. It is impossible to pick a more vivid name for that state in which man is irremediably caught, held, "possessed" by a belief when it is a sincere one. The relationship of man to his belief and in its presence is not freedom. It is an "I can do no less" than believe it. Belief penetrates us and takes possession of our subjectivity before its content is either seen or understood. We do not, then, believe *because* an idea is patent, clearly expressed, well understood, but, on the contrary, it appears to us as patent, lucid, and with an absolute meaning *because* we were already captivated by it, were already its prisoners. This is a matter of a psychic mechanism, not of a genuinely intellectual relationship, and as the psychic for Stoic corporealism is something corporeal, it will be a physical mechanism. Hence they will say that notions—ἔννοιαι (*énnoiai*)—are formed in us physically, that is, naturally; [8] and I referred precisely to this when I said earlier that concepts, according to Stoicism, are formed by spontaneous generation. They go so far as to call concepts "natural notions," physical. Good and evil, for example, are two natural concepts.

The thing that overtakes, *the* thing that seizes or captures is neither sense-perceptible nor intelligible, but a "physical" force which takes possession of men when they try to know them—*vi quadam sua* (of "images" or "notions") *inferunt sese hominibus noscitanda.*[9] That force they call τὸ καταληπτικόν: that which induces catalepsy. Although, I repeat, this appears prototypically in sense-perception, it is not exclusive or peculiar to it: concepts and "evident" maxims are in an identical sense *catalepsy*. All this—sensation and reason—will come together in Stoicism's fundamental term: the "cataleptic imagination." "Imagination" means to them

8. *Doxógrafos,* 400, 17, cited in Zeller, *Die Philosophie der Griechen,* Part III, Sec. 1, No. 2, p. 76.
9. Aulo Gelio, *Noches áticas,* XIX, 1, 15.

equally sensation, notion, and proposition. Cicero translated catalepsis as *comprehendible*, but contemporary philosophers usually understand this term, erroneously in my judgment, as "comprehension," i.e., intellection, when it is just the contrary: it is not the man who "understands the thing," but the thing which "constrains" the man, "fixes itself indelibly" on him, "puts its seal" on him—*phantasía typosis en psychê* (Plutarch, *De communibus notitiis*, 47).[10] Tell me if the *kataleptikón* does not resemble the line of chalk on the billiard table which hypnotizes the rooster rather than an intellectual operation. For the Stoic this is not accidental, since his doctrine—rough, but thought out in grand, magnificent terms—consists in making sure that man is a product of Nature and nothing more, of a Nature composed of bodies, itself the Great Universal Body, endowed in its very corporeality with "sense," with something like a boundless instinct-intelligence or, said the other way round, which governs, which directs its parts, including man, by mechanical means. The soul of this Body is a hot breath, the *pneûma;* therefore something corporeal which is principally in the chest, in the heart and

10. This concept of the "cataleptic imagination" must be made clear once and for all. One need only note that the "evident" contains two counterposed directions, and therefore can be thought and named in two ways or with its two faces. On the one hand, the "evident" is imposed on me, forces and obliges me to recognize it, *convinces* me. This is its action on me. On the other hand, that imposition or conviction is presented as though I am touching, catching, seeing reality itself, therefore the truth. My action toward the object is what I call capturing it, conceiving it, comprehending it. Hence the equivocal aspect of the term "comprehension" and *comprehendibile* which Cicero uses and which means both my catching the thing and being caught by it. In my judgment the question is definitely closed by setting in opposition the two definitions of the "cataleptic imagination" or *visum comprehendibile* which Cicero gives, one in the *Academicos Posteriores* (XI) and the other in the *Academicos Primeros* or *Lucullus* VI. In the former he says "*Visis* (that is to say, 'imaginations') *non omnibus adjungebant fidem sed iis solum quae propriam quamdam haberent declarationem earum rerum, quae viderentur; id autem visum, cum ipsum per se cerneretur, comprehendibile.*" The other says: *Zeno definiret, tale visum igitur impressum effictumque ex eo, unde esset, quale esse non posse ex eo, unde non esset.*" And Cicero adds: "*Id nos a Zenone rectissime definitum dicimus.*"

its surroundings, and manifests itself in the voice, which is at once a corporeal phenomenon and a "sense" or "intellectual" phenomenon. One of the proofs they give for the *pneûma* or soul being in the chest is that on saying "I" we put our hand on our breastbone: τοῖς στερνοῖς ἡμᾶς αὑτοὺς δεικνύντες.[11] It is not by chance that the Stoics avoid speaking of Intelligence or Reason. They prefer to use the word *hegemonikón,* the master principle. Intelligence, insofar as it is the Master Principle, is an ingenious fusion of the elemental clairvoyance of sensation with the sleep-walking awareness that we call instinct. It is a kind of living *radar* with which we are endowed by Nature, which guides us and lets us lead ourselves safely through life: this is *peculiar* to man, it is his particular nature which, like the other, the great and integral one, functions spontaneously.

Another proof that catalepsy is not a function or faculty of the intelligence lies in the fact that it works identically in him who knows and in him who does not know. This was the reason why, when Zeno had barely launched this concept, Arcesilaus, who transformed Platonism into skepticism —he started the "academic" school—opposed him with the objection that then it is something intermediate between knowing and not knowing. We would see in this the definition of instinct. To this objection Arcesilaus added another which clinches the correctness of my interpretation, for he says that *cataleptic imagination* is a contradictory notion, since that imagination is apparently "convincing" and is therefore already an "assent"—*synkatáthesis.* But assent fits only in referring to general propositions, principles and maxims. And in fact, as I have already said, catalepsy, according to the Stoics themselves, acts equally in perception and in judgment, in an axiom. Arcesilaus is right in seeing something contradictory in this. Catalepsy (i.e., "evidence," "conviction") thus comes to mean two things: what happens to us in perception and what happens to us when we encounter a principle or an axiom. But this suggests that one of the two meanings will

11. Galeno, cited in Zeller, 203, note 2.

have to be the originary and effective one. The natural thing would have been that the Stoics, for whom perception is, on the one hand, the prototype of catalepsy, and on the other hand, the noetic function from which the others—concept, judgment, reasoning—are born psychologically, would have considered its specific *kataleptikón* as the origin and basis of all the rest. But the fact is that they did not do so, since their doctrine, at least, makes the catalepsy of judgment and of "evident" principles equally originary. Hence that uncertain wavering of "evidence"-catalepsy over the whole noetic region, in which Arcesilaus sees a contradiction. But this shows that the Stoics did not dare, in spite of the fact that everything encouraged them to do so, to see in perception, in the concrete functioning of the senses, the origin of all catalepsy-"evidence," but rather groped for the versimilitude of the exact opposite, namely, that the "evidence" of principles would be "evidence"-catalepsy, entirely different from the sensory, and especially from that which affirms that we ought to believe the senses to be truly the origin and cause of the pretended "evidence" of perception.

This cataleptic characteristic of what is called "evidence" is of course incompatible with theoretic truth or knowledge; but it comes as a ring to the finger to explain what is the genuine—the most genuine—religious faith, for example, the *fides* of Christian theologians. The concept of belief which I have expounded elsewhere [12] could be extremely effective in theology, because St. Thomas and the other theologians whom I have read, especially Suárez, proceed very awkwardly, it seems to me, in posing the question about the consistency of the *fides* with regard to the *habitus* of man. Then we have the following: St. Thomas does not know in what dimension of man to place faith, with regard to *habitus in nobis*, I repeat. On the one hand faith is the *principium actus intellectus et idea necesse est, quod fides . . . "sit in intellectu sicut in subjecto"* (*Secunda Secundae*, qu. 4, art. 2). But then it turns out that in matters of faith the intellect has no mission

12. "Beliefs and Ideas," *Obras Completas,* Vol. V, pp. 375–489.

to understand—to *inspicere*—but only to give assent in the form of adherence; so that according to the author himself *fides non est virtus intellectualis* (*In III Sent.*, d. 23, qu. 2, art. 3, qu^a 3). With this St. Thomas shows only that he wasted time and a great deal of effort in learning this, because in itself Aristotle's phrase *"virtud dianoética"* is a sufficiently confused notion. From what he makes of the matter, one sees that the role of the intellect in faith is that of the companion of Captain Centellas in the penultimate act of *Don Juan Tenorio* who says only: "I am of the same opinion!" This insistence on locating faith on the genuinely intellectual side of man, useful only to the theoretician, impels him to recognize immediately that faith is less certain than science *"quoad nos,"* which is what we are now dealing with (*Secunda Secundae, ibid.*, art. 8); with this we have crippled faith: first, by making it something like science, and science is problematical in substance; second, by making it as a science one of the worst things in the world, which is quasi-science; and third, by taking from it that which gives it all its strength and beauty, which is its blindness. And all this in the same pages in which he denies the vision, the *inspectio*. But at the same time as faith is less certain *"quoad nos"* than science, it is *certior in nobis* than it (*ibid.*) because, thanks to the *firmitas adhaesionis* its certainty becomes *vehementior* (*In III Sent.*, d. 23, qu. 2, art. 2, qu^a 3). Let anyone who can, tie all these ends together.

The motive for the one and the other—to be less certain and at the same time more vehemently certain than science—is supported by the fact that "the will has the principal role in faith, because the intellect assents through faith to what is proposed to it by virtue of what it wants—*quia vult*—and is not dragged along by the evidence of truth itself" (*Summa contra gentiles*, III, c. 40). But this brings with it the fact that, in spite of being a thing of the intelligence and at the same time what it is, its basis or cause is something *"extra genus cognitionis, in genera affectionis existens"* (*In III Sent.*, d. 23, qu. 2, art. 3, qu^a 1). So that faith, after beginning as an intellectual act, ends by being an emotional disturbance, an intellectual act which is not genuinely intellectual but the effect of an extra-intellectual cause: the effect of the will. Thanks to this, in faith the intellect is *"captivatus, quia tenetur terminis alienis, et non propriis"* (*De veritate,* qu. 14, art. 1; *Secunda Secundae,* qu. 2, art. 9, ad 2). Note that in St. Thomas' description of faith the same expression appears that I used to interpret "evidence" and catalepsy: the captive mind, imprisoned, possessed. Moreover, St. Thomas thinks that in certain eminent cases captivity culminates in *raptus,* as happened to St. Paul. In speaking of the Paulist *raptus* St. Thomas can do no less than record the *éxtasis* which St. Bernard taught, of which *raptus* is the literal translation. Finally, he also alludes to the *prólepsis* of Clement of Alexandria, which is the Stoic term that implies catalepsy. But I would not have been able to understand the basic character of this notion, which is the criterion of truth for Stoicism, if I had not previously seen what is, I feel, "belief" as opposed to "idea" and to intellectuality. See how in the long run all the wild pigeons come into the dovecote together.

I consider this notion of "belief" to be of the highest importance, particularly in Catholic theology. It lends a much more concrete and convincing and, above all, more simple "psychological" meaning, on the one hand, to the intervention in the complete concept of *fides,* of *praedestinatio,* and on the other, to the concept of the *communitas* or church. But, when all is said and done, it is up to the theologians! But I must confess that I cannot understand their attitude—at least in any persuasive way. They were men who had the fabulous luck to live safely entrenched upon a firm subsoil of "beliefs," and nevertheless, they adopted a posture of *snobbism* toward philosophers, that is to say, toward men whose destiny is tragic because, having no beliefs, they *live in an atmosphere of doubt,* as we shall soon see, having to construct with their own individual efforts the makeshift raft, the flimsy life preserver which theory always is, in order not to sink to the bottom. Confronted with such basic confusions in a theme of such great importance, it is well to make it quite clear that philosophy is no more—nor is it less—than theory, and theory is a personal task, while "belief" is not theory nor, when it is true and solid "belief," can it be only personal, but it is collective; even more than that, it is unquestioned by the social milieu. Hence St. Vincente de Lerins was very right when in his *Commonitorium* (of the year 434) he recognizes energetically the character of effective, established "social urgency" which faith must have, when he says that *"magnopere curandum est, ut id teneatur quod semper, quod ubique, quod ab omnitus creditum est."* He launches this formula directly against the interventions of St. Augustine, whom in fact as Father of the Church he greatly surpassed as a philosopher. St. Vincent's work was *"un des livres les plus estimés de l'antiquité chrétienne"* says Monsignor Duchesne in his *Histoire Ancienne de l'Eglise*, III, 283. This book by Cardinal Duchesne is, in turn, one of the most delightful and intelligent works I have ever read.

26
Ideoma—Draoma

FROM THIS ENDEMIC CATALEPSY Descartes awoke—and wakened us.[1] To explain this awakening I have preferred to start from the *Rules for the Direction of the Mind,* the only exposition of method, and a defective one, for the purpose of reducing references to his general philosophy as much as *possible.* The *Rules* begin at once, I said, by affirming the common character of genera, which means a stab to the heart for the traditional "way of thinking." Descartes' affirmation does not appear to be supported by any reasoning, since it cannot pretend to be a simple notice—and at the same time a gratuitous affirmation—that the cognitive power of man—*humana sapientia (Reg.,* I, 2)—is unique and homogeneous. It is likely that it may become this, and also that the immediate inference from it can be reasoned, the inference expressed by Descartes according to which a knowledge that is unique and unitary cannot be diversified according to its objects. But there is not in the whole book of *Rules,* nor need there be, the slightest intention to lay a basis for method. The proposal is reduced

1. The difficulties that people not completely skilled in this discipline encounter in reading philosophic works frequently arise, not from the fact that the author thinks more than the reader, but on the contrary that the reader adds to what the text says ideas that he merely assumes the author *ought* to have. Thus, in the phrase to which I append this note, it is most probable that many readers, losing no time, have already injected the supposition that I set Descartes up as an awakener in contrast to Scholasticism as a hypnosis, because I am not an Aristotelian, but I *ought* to be a rationalist or an idealist. I am not going to say in this note what I am, of course, but I am going to say what I am not, namely, a rationalist and an idealist. If the reader desires to understand me—if not he ought to close the book right away—it will be of much more help to him to turn away from me and entrust himself without reservation, even without compromise, to each line of this study. Otherwise he is in for very frequent tumbles.

to showing this, much as the inventor of a machine exhibits its parts and explains their functioning. As a "man of science" that explanation was enough for Descartes. *In terms of science* the proof of the method consists in testing its use, and if this gives good results there is nothing more to say. I am very sorry that I cannot go on here to describe exactly what Descartes understood by method in the absolute (but not the concrete content of his own). The fact is that I have never seen anywhere that anyone understands what the function is that, in his judgment, competes with him. Method is not a science, any more than the microscope or the telescope is a science. It is an instrument, or *órganon*. That in Aristotle this —logic—cannot be separated from his ontology must be reckoned as a defect. Since method is not a science it need not be tested with reasons but with achievements, with results and accomplishments. The new moldboard plow is tested not by a syllogism, but by a harvest.

After making it as clear as possible that Descartes did not lay a foundation for his method either in the *Rules* or anywhere else it must be underlined with equal clarity that neither did he need to do this.

Whether or not Descartes' methodical contraption could function fully without a real need for a basic support, whether or not he wanted it, is a different matter; this undoubtedly arises out of certain philosophic assumptions, that is, it implies them. This method could occur to Descartes because he had contrived a philosophy for his private use, to use at home, thus making it the most famous "stove" or *poêle*. And what the reader and I have done in earlier pages was to point out its most immediate implications. In listing them we succeed even in taking the Scholastic Bastille, a feat which is the abolition of faith in the senses as a theoretic principle. Here we suffer an interruption of the type that has abounded in this study. It was worthwhile because this is the watershed, the dividing point of scientific waters which flow on the one hand to the Scholastic way of thinking and on the other to the modern way of thinking.

The affirmation that Being manifests itself in the senses is the first principle of Aristotelianism, and it is a plain error on the part of Aristotle and the subsequent Scholasticism to suppose that the first principle is that of contradiction. For Leibnitz it will be, and rightly, for in him this does not mean primarily an ontological principle, but a logical one. But in Aristotle the principle of contradiction presupposes the principle of the presence of the Real. And according to him this presence takes place in the *aísthesis*, in sense-perceptible intuition; let us call it that in order to emphasize our good will, although it is solidly based in the texts and the things to which they refer. What happens is that that principle is so primary, so preferred in Aristotle and among the populace above any other thought, that there is scarcely any consciousness apart from it and even less any theoretic conception of it as principle. Hence it does not occur even remotely to Aristotle to formulate it, any more than anything else which is truly "basic in our life." It belongs to what I call "principles *a tergo*," to "beliefs" and not to "ideas." [2]

Here in this observation, which because of its matter cannot be more fundamental and decisive, and because of the person—Aristotle—cannot be more authoritative, we find ourselves with something which I have not space enough to develop, but which I do want to note. "That the senses are authentic, furthermore, that they give us the Ens with a guarantee" is, I said, a latent and most primary principle in the Aristotelian-Scholastic philosophy. Nevertheless, in its status as principle it is nowhere formulated. This happens simply because it is what it is. It is more principle than all the principles, for example, than that of contradiction. This double observation about *ideoma* [3]—its quality of principle in the

2. See my essay *Ideas and Beliefs* (*Obras Completas*, Vol. V, p. 475).
3. I call *ideoma* all thought (whose expression must have an affirmative or negative, simple or compound proposition) which makes explicit a dogma (opinion, judgment, doctrine) about something; but *insofar* as we state it, without acceptance or refusal. Taking a judgment in this way, it is converted into a pure "idea about something," purely a mental possibility which has no human reality, for the dimension of

highest degree and its uncommunicativeness—results in some confusion, and I am obliged to clarify it since it was mine in the first place.

A philosophy is always two: that which is expressed, made up of what the philosopher "wants" to say, and that which is latent—latent not only because the philosopher is silent and does not tell us about it, but also because he does not even tell himself about it, and he does not tell himself about it because he does not see it. The reason for this strange double reality is that all "telling" is an animate action on the part of man; therefore, the genuine and ultimately real thing in a "saying" is not what is "said" or the *dictum*—what I have called the *ideoma*—but the fact that someone says it, and therefore supports, works with, and is committed (*"s'engage"*) to it. Well now, a philosophy appears to us first as purely a system of ideomas, apart from time and space, with the character of sayings by an anonymous someone who is no one, but only an underlying abstract of the saying. This is how philosophers usually study what has innocently been called the history of philosophy.[4] But if we re-think that system of *ideomas in its entirety* we find that it does not end in itself and that the *ideomas* expressed in it imply, without the author noticing it, others which have never been taken into account but which are the very assumptions that are active in him as a man, and that have led him to "speak

---

being a man's firm opinion, his conviction, a thesis that he supports, has been taken from it. A quarter of a century ago Meinong called this *"Annahme"* (*assumption*) because it interested him from a purely logical point of view. Considered logically, my *"ideoma"* is Meinong's "assumption," but this is the least interesting thing about it. The proof is that in Meinong this means the opposite of logical judgment, whereas for me *ideoma* means the opposite of living action in which man not only "has an idea" but *is* that idea, whether he recognizes it *or* not. When the *ideoma* is put into action, when it functions actively, when it is accepted and upheld, or refused and combatted, it is converted into an effective reality and it is a *draoma* or *drama* (from *drao*, to act).

4. On all this see my "Prologue to the *History of Philosophy* by Brehier" (*Obras Completas,* Vol. VI, p. 377) and "The revival of Painting" (*Papers on Velásquez and Goya,* Vol. VIII, p. 507).

out" and to enunciate his own philosophy and no other. Hence a philosophy, under the stratum of its patent and *ideomatic* principles, has other latent ones which are not *ideomas* apparent to the mind of the author, for the very reason that they are the author himself as a living reality, the *beliefs in which he is,* "in which he exists, lives and moves," like the Christians in Christ according to St. Paul. A "belief" is not an *ideoma* but a *draoma,* a living action or an invisible ingredient in one. Seen from its latent causes a philosophy is not a system of *ideomas* but a "system" of vital actions—of *draomas*—and this has its own principles, different from the obvious ones and essentially latent.

Here, it seems to me, we have clarified the reason why the principle of authenticity in the senses, which is primordial in Aristotle, did not look *that way* to Aristotle himself, but starts from him as something which goes by itself and which he does not notice. The most fundamental reasons why Aristotle should believe that the senses truly show us Being cannot be given here because this matter would take us very far, for they are not in Aristotle, but in the whole of Greek life three centuries before him. When the Scholastics say that they are superior to modern philosophy because they start from an intuition of Being, one feels a sincere regret, not through thinking oneself in turn as possessing a truth superior to the former one—a thing which would always be problematical and disputable—but in seeing in them what is plainly crass ignorance of the very meaning and origins of their opinion, quite aside from whether or not they are right in their judgment. It would be more useful for them if they would for once reconcile themselves—quietly, humanly, with all the conviction and *brio* that is desirable, but without insolence—to the fact that in that mummified philosophy they are completely valueless today.

27
Doubt, the Beginning of Philosophy

THE PRINCIPLE OF sanctioning the senses had, then, a quality and a basic significance much greater than any theoretical principle. While the senses exercise their merely logical function on the surface of our person, which is the narrow region of our *seconsciente* [1] (self-conscious) mentality, principle operates in the secret recesses of our life. Certainly the self-conscious is a part of our life. To theorize is in turn only a part of that part. But it is useless to balance "life" and theory against each other, as though theorizing were not a way of life, even in the sordid sense of often being a way in which men earn their living. Theory is also life, but it is only a small part of our life. What we are while we theorize, and to the extent that we theorize, represents a thin film in comparison with the abysmal depths of our entire life. Barrès was right: "*L'intelligence! Quelle petite chose à la surface de nous!*" So there is no need to preen oneself on being intellectual. To be intellectual is to be very little: first, in comparison with the great number of other men who are not; second, in comparison with the innumerable things of which the most famous intellectual is ignorant, even counting only the things that are knowable; third, in comparison with the totality of himself. Behind the floodlit stage which the intellectual treads

1. As there is a consciousness of a thing, so there is also a consciousness in which I am present as conscious of that thing. This reflected consciousness, whose "thing of which" is always another consciousness, I call *seconciencia* and *seconsciente*, taking advantage of the fact that our Spanish language uses *semoviente* (self-moving) and *sedicente* (self-styled).

within himself when he thinks, is the abyss of how much in our life and our person is invisible but acts *de profundis* on that superficial stage where, playing ourselves, we rehearse our intellectual aria. Everything considered, this quantitative appraisal of the degree of intelligence which is within us does not have the last word, because it could happen that, although it is only a thing of such scanty dimensions, being only a small part of ourselves, it turns out to be *the* small part, the one in which man becomes most himself. In this case intellectuality would lose its appearance of ability, skill, and grace in order to be converted smoothly and simply into man's most fundamental obligation. Then we would discover this diverting situation: that as men are so little intelligent, *all* of them would have the unavoidable obligation to be intellectuals. We will not decide the matter now, but it is useful to note it, even on the wing, for talent is always mentioned as an envied and enviable natural gift when it is, at best, a debt which each man owes to himself.

In any event, one cannot disregard the fact that, as philosophy is an exploration directed toward authentic principles, it is essential or unavoidable for the philosopher to wear himself out in the effort to exhume those pragmatic latent "principles" which operate within his own secret depths and which impose on him—as "evident"—arbitrary assumptions which he disregards, or, if not that, he glorifies them with the pompous title of principles. This task of denouncing presumed principles is not only one of the occupations of the philosopher, it is the alpha and omega of philosophy itself. This sets the philosopher apart from other men, who start forthwith from those beliefs operating in their arcane inner recesses and who do well not to worry about other things. They have the good fortune to believe, at least to believe that they believe. Hence, he is not a philosopher who prefers a ready-made philosophy in order to amuse himself with the accuracy of its analysis, with the very agile acrobatics of its arguments. That is not being a philosopher, but the exact opposite, being curious. Descartes, as contrasted with Aristotle, flatly rejected curiosity as a cause of philosophy.[2] Curiosity is to philosophy, he says, not as water is to the thirsty, but as water to a man with dropsy. Only he can be a philosopher who does not believe, or believes that he does not believe,[3] and hence absolutely needs to search out something like a belief. Philosophy is orthopedics for fractured belief.

But philosophy, which originated as the need of an unbeliever, when once created, becomes a normal dimension of life that shifts its limits from its initial motivation and extends its effectiveness to many other "sides of life." Then *ready-made* philosophy became a need for those who would never by themselves have needed to *make it*. As in law there is a fundamental distinction between *lege lata* and *lege ferenda*, between established law and the new law which it is appropriate to legislate, so philosophy has two very different meanings: the need to imbibe a ready-made philosophy and the need—a genuine and not fictitious, whimsical, or prurient need—to *make another* philosophy, because those that exist seem not to be one.[4] Finally, the same thing happens with philosophy as with other arts or techniques which man created because there was need for them at a certain period, and this is that they end by freeing themselves from their utilitarian origin, lose the character of need, declare themselves autonomous and influential in their own right. Once they reach this point they are transformed from the humble instruments of human urgencies which they were into sumptuary activities, into superfluous elegancies which are a delight to handle and a source of pride to possess. Thus it would be the most normal way of life for philosophy—this is not to incriminate it—to be regarded with affection as a felicitous

2. The theme of what Aristotle thinks about the cause of philosophy is also untouched. I hope not to delay in attacking it. As for Descartes and curiosity, see what he says in the *Recherche de la verité:* "*Le corps des hydropiques n'est pas plus éloigné de son juste tempérament, que l'esprit de ceux-là qui sont perpetuellement travaillés d'une curiosité insatiable*" (*Oeuvres*, Edit. Adam and Tannery, Vol. X, pp. 500, 12-15).

3. Needless to say this nonbelief is even an advantageous virtue within the faith.

4. On this see "On the Races" (*Obras Completas*, Vol. V, p. 167).

occupation[5] which enchants many men and helps them to live out their lives.

Philosophy is reborn in Descartes, and this means two things: that for him philosophizing was a vital necessity, and that earlier philosophies seemed to him not to be philosophizing at all. Descartes believed in the Christian God in the usual way, and in 1600, this meant sincerely but lukewarmly. But he had accepted this Christian God in the guise which Duns Scotus, and above all the genius Ockham, had given it. And this Ockhamist God, more authentically Christian, more Paulist and Augustinian than the somewhat pagan and Aristotelianized God of St. Thomas, was a tremendous Being, magnificent and terrible, whose first attribute is arbitrariness —the most authentic attribute in God when he is truly God and no one has the impertinence to want to domesticate him, as though he were a Lybian lion or Hircanian tiger. God is utter free will, *potentia absoluta*, limited only by the principle of contradiction, and this thanks to an ultimately "rationalist" respect which these men retained for logic, even the most decided of them like Ockham. If we set ourselves to talk about God, we would not retain that respect for logic, which becomes another goddess who coerces God, put at his side in the antipathetic shape of a governess, whose task it is to prevent him from contradicting himself, so that what is left of the idea of God has a lingering flavor of polytheism and paganism. It is useful to note that the founder of rationalism believed in an irrational God, of whose missions one, and not a small one, is not to let professors of logic sleep. Thus they are honest men: problems are not prepared ahead of time, and they do not fight bulls with balls on their horns. The God of Ockham and Descartes had not created a world as did Aristotle's God or the one we shall soon see in Leibnitz, *ad usum delfinis*, assuming men of science to be dolphins. He had not created a world which was intelligible beforehand. He had left man full of faith in God, but full of doubts about the

5. On what the *felicitous* occupations are, see "Twenty Years of Great Hunting" (*Obras Completas*, Vol. VI, p. 419).

world. Ockham and the classic skepticism of Greece were the godfathers of Cartesianism. Descartes began by doubting all human knowledge. When one begins this way he is truly a philosopher. "Every beginner," Herbart says, "is a skeptic, although every skeptic is only a beginner." Now we are at the very beginning, and Descartes' beginning was to doubt all principles and to make of doubt itself the only all-embracing principle.

But note that in this Descartes did not differ from Aristotle or from St. Thomas, at least with regard to the intent to recognize that the philosopher must begin this way. What happens is that those two were not capable of carrying out what they recognized as a mandate. Although everyone knows Aristotle's words with which he defines philosophy in Book III of his *Metaphysics*—knows them but neglects them—or if they are remembered they are robbed of substance—what is lacking is a knowledge, a discipline or a "philosophy" which would be basic to all the others, taken for granted by them, but not implicating them. That discipline will have the right to call itself the "first philosophy." But that science does not yet exist; it is "the sought after"—ξητουμένη ἐπιστήμη (*zetouméne epistéme*). This has always seemed to me one of the most elegant and appropriate names that has been given to philosophy; it has had lexical bad luck. Its official names are all more or less shoddy. So is this one; but . . . it's so pretty! *That which is searched for!* In this dress philosophy looks to us like "La Princesse lointaine" . . .

"But one cannot enter that science which is sought unless one begins by setting forth the doubts that surge around the content of its theme . . . It is inherent in those pretending to investigate to doubt greatly." That is to say, at bottom διαπορῆσαι καλῶς (*diaporêsai kalôs*). Because the resulting good solution does not consist in anything else than in having resolved—λύσις (*lysis*)—the previous doubts. "*The only one who can untie a knot is he who is familiar with the knot.*" The man who is in doubt without managing to resolve it is a man in fetters. Moreover, "those who set themselves to investigate (those who try to know) without previous doubting are on a par with him who starts to walk without knowing where he is going." Because truth being the end—τέλος (*télos*)—of the cognitive effort, although we might find it by chance we would not recognize it, for it consists in the solution of problems, the resolution of doubts. To him who does not first doubt—*prius*—the truth is not made manifest. *Truth is made manifest only to him who doubts. Praedubitanti autem manifestus,* says the version from which St. Thomas starts.

This extract, wonderful for the precision of its content and the unique compactness of its expression, can serve as an example of the Aristotelian style when Aristotle is the good Aristotle, the genius Aristotle. And the commentary of St. Thomas on that text is expressed in this formula, no less vigorous and exact. *"Ista scientia sicut habet universalem considerationem de veritate . . . et ideo non particulariter, sed simul universalem dubitationem prosequitur."* [6]

Good! What are you saying to me? Can Descartes add nothing as a point of departure? Does it make sense to believe that Descartes invented methodic doubt? Because in those phrases of Aristotle, on which St. Thomas puts an acute accent, the *essential connection between doubt and theoretic truth or exact knowledge* is declared. There is no intellectual truth without the *prius* of doubt. This is not just something that happened to Descartes at the end of a very cold winter afternoon, shut up in a stuffy room not far from Ulm. This is the exact opposite of a happening, of a "happy idea." This is . . . philosophy, nothing else. It is philosophy to the extent in which it begins with what St. Thomas so admirably calls "universal doubt." He does it, of course, as a comment on the Aristotelian text; therefore, with the intention of expressing his meaning precisely and forcefully. Faced with these

6. "Given that this science appertains to the universal investigation of the truth—therefore not merely a particular investigation—a universal doubt moves side by side with it."

words of his there is no occasion even to pose the question as to whether he thought that way or not.[7] We are not talking about St. Thomas.

The surprising thing would be rather that it is not considered a platitude that philosophy at first is universal doubt. Then what do people think philosophy is? Do not confuse the thing with the question as to whether this or that philosopher or all philosophers have or have not been incapable of implementing fully that initial and unconditional doubt. This is not a matter of whether there have or have not been philosophers, but of what philosophy is. What is not understood is —I repeat—that one does not fall into the trap of platitudes and believe placidly that to begin with universal doubt is a dogma peculiar to one or to several philosophies. Doubt, in philosophy, is prior to every philosophic dogma or thesis, and it makes them possible. The matter is as simple as saying "good morning." There is no cognitive effort without a previous problem which ignites it. The problem is the *quaestio*, the doubt: that to be *A* or not to be *A* of something. "To be or not to be, that is the question." Therefore Hamlet is the philosophic hero par excellence. He is methodic doubt across the footlights. He is the creature moving with indecisive step who for five acts keeps asking himself for "what is behind it?" which is the doubtful element? what is behind the arras?—he investigates with the dagger and kills Polonius—what is behind life; and he proceeds to find out, he departs from life in order to emerge from doubt.

When the problem is universal, doubt is also universal. If something, even the smallest of things, of which one is absolutely sure can be retained, there is no need for philosophy. In *that security, without previous doubt, which is belief*, however minimal the matter concerned, man can shore up his life. The trouble comes when one has lost belief in this, and in this, and in this, and the mind automatically con-

7. The feats of prestidigitation with which M. Gilson in *Réalisme Thomiste et Critique de la Connaissance* (1939, pp. 54-64) tries to lessen the value of St. Thomas's words are truly lamentable.

cludes that, having been caught in error about those "thises," there is no reason for confidence in the other things in which one still believes. The rupture in our beliefs, the doubt, produces no important effects when it is merely a matter of the normal rectification of whatever or however many opinions seemed true to us. But as that break increases, a point will inevitably be reached where there is automatically produced in us a "functionalization" of that doubting, that is, it becomes generalized. Then one doubts not only what actually is doubted but *is moved* to doubt more. There are periods in history so brimful of belief that even one's doubt about this or that is a form of believing. But there are also periods, on the other hand, in which one doubts even what one believes. Our own is this kind. Cocteau said it delightfully, "What can be hoped of a time like ours which does not even believe in the conjurors?" *Hence*—and against all appearances of the extreme antiphilosophism ruling today—one is assured on this printed page that we are at the dawn of the greatest "philosophic" era. The quotation marks I cannot explain at the moment.

I have said—knowing that I am going to annoy the gallery —that Aristotle, when all is said and done, did not have the vocation of a philosopher, but rather that of a scientist. But— what the devil!—he had one of the most exceptional minds that ever existed. The acuteness of his prodigious mental mechanism made him state those propositions that we have just been reading; but he already knows, *sotto voce*, that he is not going to fulfill them. Aristotle who—perhaps—already did not believe in God, believed deeply in the sciences. *Therefore* he did not need to throw himself personally into carrying out that program of *universale dubitatione de veritate*. Moreover, his "primitive" and popular background is full of faith in the dogma of the streets, in the topics, the "prevailing opinions" or ἔνδοξοι (*éndoxoi*). He believed in prestidigitation because he believed—*sic*, to believe—in the principle of contradiction as the inexorable law of the Real, and so on. His philosophy is full of "evidences," and we have already seen that the Scholastic-Aristotelian evidences are forms of social catalepsy; they are plain and simple prejudices of "common sense." In fact, the Aristotelian doctrine is that which makes least use of primary doubt. This does not surprise us. Without ourselves proposing it the evidence comes at us from all sides that Aristotelianism is one of the least philosophic philosophies that ever existed. But this theme of doubt is decisive, because it is the precise barometer which measures philosophic pressure. So much doubt—precise and clearly evident, it is understood—so much philosophy.

I ask again: but what is philosophy believed to be?

28
The Historical Origin of Philosophy

PHILOSOPHY is a system of basic interpretive, and therefore intellectual, attitudes which man adopts in view of what is, for him, the tremendous event of finding himself alive. This life of his includes not only the event of his own existence but also a whole world of other events which are part of his life. But it would be an error to misunderstand *a limine* that formula of taking it for granted that philosophy—that system of basic opinions—must always be positive, that is, that it consists perforce in a system of affirmative doctrines about the problems that mobilize it in an image of a "complete" world. One forgets that positive philosophy always goes hand in hand with its mongrel brother, skepticism. This too is a philosophy: in it man laboriously constructs for himself—even more laboriously than in the positive or dogmatic philosophies—a basic defensive attitude vis-à-vis possible false worlds, and on being in that negative state toward all knowledge, he feels himself to be in the right, free from all error, neither more nor less than the dogmatic philosopher. Thus we would have in skepticism an essentially *empty* image of the world which leads to *aphasia*—ἀφασία—or abstention from judgment, to *apathy*—ἀπάθεια—or *austerity*—αὐστερία—*austereness*, the dry, cold attitude, severe toward everything. Strictly speaking it is not even possible to make that distinction between dogmatism and skepticism. What was said a moment ago already begins to reveal to us that all authentic philosophy is at once skeptical and dogmatic. We will end by seeing this in what follows.

Man dedicates himself to this strange occupation of philosophizing when, because he has lost his traditional beliefs, he

finds himself lost in life. That consciousness of being fundamentally lost, of not knowing what to cling to, is ignorance.[1]
But this primary ignorance, this fundamental not knowing, is
a not knowing what to do. This is what forces us to frame
for ourselves an idea of things and of ourselves, to find out
"what there is" in reality, so that we may be able, in view of
the image which the Universe presents to us as "being what
in truth it is," to project our conduct with certainty, that is,
with sufficient meaning, and to emerge from that primary
ignorance. Theoretic ignorance, the being surprised at not
knowing what things are, is secondary to the practice which
we can call "perplexity," as we must leave to the theoretic
not-knowing the name of "ignorance."

But if the practical precedes the theoretical in ignorance,
the opposite happens in knowledge; the system of our occupations is secondary to the system of our theories, of our convictions as to what things are; the "knowing what to do" is
founded on "knowing what it is." With more or less adjust-
ment the system of actions in each stage of human progress
is fitted into the system of ideas and oriented by them. A variation of any importance in our opinions has very great repercussions on our actions.

This is the reason why there is no room for perfection in
life—that is, no security and no happiness—if one is confused
and has no clear idea about the Universe. Knowing adds perfection to doing, to pleasure, to pain, but vice versa, these
move and direct or *telekinan* knowing. Hence when philosophy, after its initial stutterings and fortuitous discoveries,
sets forth formally on its historic traverse of millennial continuity, it sets itself up in the Platonic Academy as an occupation primarily concerned with ethics. On this point Plato
never ceased to be Socratic. Publicly or privately, philosophy
always implied the "primacy of practical reason." It was, and
as long as it exists, it will be the *science of doing something*.

1. See *En torno a Galileo* (translated under the English title of *Man
and Crisis*) the chapter "Truth as Coincidence of Man with Himself"
(*Obras Completas,* Vol. V, p. 81). [Published by W. W. Norton, 1962.]

If what I have said is philosophy, it follows immediately that we cannot see in it an occupation which is innate or inborn in man. No, in order that philosophy may emerge, man must previously have been living in other ways that are not philosophic. Adam could not have been a philosopher, or at least he could be one only after he was thrown out of Paradise. Paradise is living in faith, having one's being in it, and philosophy presupposes having lost this and having fallen into universal doubt. A clear indication that our admirable Dilthey, who introduced us to historic thinking, was never sufficiently conversant with "historic reasoning," is that he considers philosophy, together with religions and literature, as an inherent capability of man, and hence *antihistoric*. No, philosophy is a historic capability, like everything human, and consequently, it *is something to which one arrives when coming from something else.* History is "coming from," "arriving at," and "leaving from." Philosophy can spring up only when these two things have happened: that man has lost a traditional faith and has gained a new faith in a new power of which he finds himself possessed: the power of concepts, or reason. Philosophy is doubt directed toward everything traditional; but at the same time it is confidence in a wholly new *way* that man discovers open before him. Doubt, or *aporía*, and *euporeía* or the safe road, *méth-odos*, make up the historical character of that historical occupation which is philosophizing. Doubt with no way in sight is not doubt, it is desperation. *Desperation does not lead one to philosophy,* but to the death leap. The philosopher does not need to leap because he believes he has a way by which he can proceed, go forward, and arrive at Reality by his own means.

Philosophy cannot be something first-born in man. *Primum est vivare, deinde philosophari.* This is to say simply that before he begins to philosophize man "is already there." Then this "being there" is not a lonely state, not a matter of finding oneself in cosmic space, but in a state of being already involved in living, with the rest of the Universe acting on it while it reacts. When the philosophic flute begins to sound, it enters, already predetermined, into a symphony which has previously begun and which animates and conditions it. The first thing is to live; then to philosophize. One philosophizes from within life—in a strange form of being "within" which we will shortly explore—when a living past already exists and in view of a certain situation to which one has arrived. Furthermore, philosophy assumes ontogenetically that the ascendant stage of life, the fullness of living, has already passed. The "child prodigy" is not possible in philosophy.[2] Plato and Aristotle recognized that philosophy—like politics—is a matter for the old men, although Plato concealed this in order not to frighten the young gymnasts who, between two races or two casts of the discus, stretched their necks out toward him, and with their necks their ears.[3] Philogenetically speaking, philosophy was born when traditional Hellenism was breaking down.

Not only is there no *philosophia perennis*, but philosophizing itself does not last forever. It was born on one fine day and it will disappear on another. That day which we optimistically call fine arrived very close to the date 480 B.C. With a startling coincidence in point of time, Heraclitus and Parmenides were then both meditating, nowhere near each other. Perhaps Heraclitus was a bit older than Parmenides. The work of both of them must have taken form about 475 B.C. That adventitious work of two determined men in a specific period of Greek life inaugurated the new human occupation, un-

2. There is only one exception which proves the rule. At eighteen Schelling already had a philosophic system. But the irresponsibility of this *soi-disant* system is demonstrated by the fact that Schelling spent the rest of his life—he died at the age of eighty—creating an uninterrupted succession of *other* philosophic systems, soap bubbles blown by the eternal child genius that he was.

3. The result of this is that the philosopher can only benefit in his lifetime from the philosophy which he created in the form of a marvellous lucidity which irradiates his old age, and that is a special way of "growing young again" which only the philosopher commands; the conclusive reason for all this cannot be given here, because it is rooted in the concept of "experience of life"; but contrary to what it may seem, to say what is "the experience of life" is one of the most difficult things to say that exists, almost as difficult as to acquire it.

known up to that point, which we call by the ridiculous name of "philosophy." At this very moment I am busying myself in the same manner. Between that date and the present moment, men have had their enormous "philosophic experience." I mean by these words not what has been discovered about the Universe through philosophy, but the series of attempts which have been made in these 25 centuries to face up to the Universe by means of the mental process which is philosophizing. Men have experimented with the instrument called "philosophy." In that process of experimentation they have tested various ways of making that instrument work. Each new attempt profited from earlier ones. Most of all it profited from the errors and limitations of former efforts. Thanks to this it can be said that the history of philosophy describes the progress in philosophizing. This progress may consist at the end in the discovery on another fine day that not only was this or that philosophic "way of thinking" limited, and therefore erroneous, but that philosophizing, all philosophizing, is a limitation, an insufficiency, an error, and that man must begin again with a totally new way of facing up to the Universe intellectually, a way which will be neither one of the precursors of philosophy nor philosophy itself. Perhaps we are at the dawn of this other "fine day."

29
The Level of Our Roots

THIS SERIES OF philosophical experiences is on a scale of levels based both on chronology and on intrinsic characteristics. In it there is one *level* which corresponds to the rebirth of philosophizing in Descartes and Leibnitz. But this scale of levels in philosophical experience must be introduced in descending order. Each new level represents a deeper stratum of philosophic problems, with their antecedents always seen from below, from their hidden roots which were invisible to the human plants that were philosophizing on those levels. Man, like the living plant, never sees his own root, but he sees those of his ancestors. This raises for us the question of the order of exposition. As we go on saying a bit more completely what philosophy is, it would be advisable to do so not from our present point of view and at the present altitude of our philosophical experience, but trying—although somewhat loosely—to keep ourselves on the level of experience to which Cartesian and Leibnitzian thinking corresponds. Between then and now many things have happened in the philosophic arena, and it would make no sense for us with our common present-day sapience, to tread too heavily on the initiatives marked by the genius of those two sublime minds, initiatives from which we have benefited and which *to a certain extent* continue to be the base on which we are building.

But, on the other hand, it would be sterile and a sham to appear to be discussing those philosophies in retrospect as if we actually were at their level. They, like all the others, we have been saying, represent thinking in depth. If philosophy did not stand still with Descartes and Leibnitz it was surely because their experience, once developed, revealed that it did not go deep enough. Since this is clearly what must be said

276

about them, it is unavoidable that we, in the briefest possible manner, *establish the level which defines our own sense of what is fundamental.* Let us get on with it, counting the words.

It is not true, as Heidegger claims (he who abandoned his happy visions and turned to engendering general confusion), that philosophy flowers in man when he is *estranged* from the world, when he is disillusioned with the things about him, the chattels (*Zeugen*) which were useful to him. It is not true because man is *a nativitate* estranged from the world; he is a stranger in it, a foreigner—he therefore does not need, all of a sudden and "one fine day," to find out that he is just that—notwithstanding that he has not always been occupied in philosophizing, and moreover, has almost never done it. This initial error proliferates in Heidegger and forces him to maintain that man *is* philosophy and this—one more error—because man, in the face of the world's failure as a combination of *chattels and playthings,* of things-that-are-useful, discovers that these do not really belong to him, while at the same time they have a Being of their own and man's Being consists in asking about them and demanding them. This is a matter of a *katákhresis,* as the ancients called it, of a misuse or exaggeration of concepts to which the *furor teutonicus,* the lack of proportion that is characteristic of German thinkers, has accustomed us. It is not true that man has always been asking himself about Being. On the contrary, he did not ask himself about Being until after 480 B.C., and then it was a matter of a certain number of men in a certain number of places. It is no use to stuff philosophy with illusions. It is now a matter of dispute as to whether—strictly speaking—any one after Plotinus was asking himself about Being. At first the Scholastics did not ask themselves about Being, but asked rather about *what Aristotle understood* by Ens as ens, which is a very different thing. And they did not even ask themselves this question seriously. In general, Scholasticism, as we have seen, is not an urge to question, but on the contrary, an urge to respond. It is therefore preoccupied with solutions to problems

which have never been seen or experienced. It is the prototype of a contra-philosophy or absence of philosophy. But we
will also see that neither Descartes nor Leibnitz, strictly speaking, asked themselves about Being, but about something quite
different. Heidegger's exaggeration of the concept of Being
becomes obvious if one notes that his formula "man has always
asked himself about Being" or "*is* a question about Being"
makes sense only if by Being we understand everything about
which man has asked himself; that is to say, if we make of
Being the great illusion, the "*bonne à tout faire*" and the
omnibus concept. But this is not a doctrine; this inflation of
the concept Being arose precisely when everything favored
the opposite operation: keeping it within bounds, making its
meaning exact.

In the year 1925, I planned a series of publications in which
I proposed formally and by title the "Restating of the Problem
of Being," and I invited my students to organize their university program with special reference to this concept. Perhaps they kept too quiet about that doctrine of mine. The fact
is that in December, 1927, Heidegger's book was published
which carries the word Being on its frontispiece and announces
a "Restatement of the Problem of Being." Without having had
time for more than a glance at it I referred to Heidegger's
work in a note on my essay "Hegel's *Philosophy of History*
and Historiology," which was published in the early days of
January, 1928, the first of those projected studies in which
that restatement was being prepared. In Heidegger's volume—
the only one published—the problem of Being was not re-
stated, *there was nothing said anywhere about Being*, nothing
more was done than to distinguish various meanings of Being,
with a purpose not very different from that which led Aristotle to speak of the "plurality of meanings of Being," the
famous πολλακῶς (*pollakôs*). With my incurable optimism
I nevertheless hoped that Heidegger would attempt it in some
future writing, although my students know that I then announced the nonpublication of the second volume of *Sein
und Zeit* because Heidegger had entered a blind alley. As

usual no one—not even my students—deigned to take into serious consideration what I called the basic approach to the problem of Being in my *Annex to Kant,* published shortly afterward as the second essay in the projected series. It is explained there that this basic approach does not consist in seeking new meanings for the Ens,[1] as Heidegger does when he is busily describing and defining the Ens as though it consists in "being in the there," or *Dasein* or man; nor in inquiring as to which is the *entity* of each class of ens, the Being of the Ens as against the makeup of this ens; but rather in finding out what Being means when we use this word in asking ourselves what something *is*, therefore before knowing what sort of thing, what sort of ens we have before us. This is a question which still has not been posed, and no one therefore has seen clearly how devilish a thing the Ens is. Because he did not know this, Heidegger inflated it, an automatic tendency vis-à-vis every *inherited* concept not created from the ground up, and he extended it to *every last thing* about which man has asked himself questions, with the result that man only *is* the question about Being, if it is understood that Being is all that ultimate thing about which man asks himself, a thing which could be a mere matter of semantics, but which is not what Heidegger affirms and therefore does not have his confirmation.[2]

In 1925, I stated my theme—some of my students may recall it—saying literally: (1) the traditional problem of Being must be reformed from its roots up; (2) this must be accomplished by the phenomenological method insofar, and only insofar, as this means *synthetic* or *intuitive thinking* and not merely the kind of conceptual-abstract thinking which is the traditional way; (3) but it is necessary to integrate the phenomenological method, giving it a dimension of *systematic thinking*

1. Although one must *also* do this.
2. I said long ago that when I also stated—but only as the beginning of a dialectical development—that Being is inquiry, I did not do it without starting (in order to abandon it) from the formula which my teacher Cohen gave me in 1902 (!!) in his *Logik der reinen Erkenntnis,* and in 1904 in his *Ethik des reinen Willen.*

which, as is well known, it does not possess; (4) and finally, so that systematic phenomenological thinking may be possible, it is necessary to start from a phenomenon which might be the *system itself*. This systematic phenomenon is human life and it is necessary to start with its contemplation and analysis.[3] In this way I abandoned phenomenology at the very moment of tasting it.

3. Since 1914 (see my *Meditaciones del Quijote, Obras Completas,* Vol. I) the basis of all my thinking has been contemplation of the phenomenon of "human life." At that time I formulated it—in order to explain Husserl's phenomenology during various courses of lectures—in particular correcting the description of the phenomenon "consciousness of . . ." which, as is well known, at that time constituted the basis of his doctrine. When I became acquainted with the admirable Husserl many years later his age and his infirmities did not permit him to take up difficult themes from his own output, and he had entrusted his manuscripts and the task of developing them to an exceptionally endowed pupil of his, Dr. Fink. Finding myself passing through Freiburg, it was to Dr. Fink, therefore, that I explained my initial objection to phenomenology which, reduced to the simplest terms, is this: consciousness in its character as phenomenon is the arbiter ("*setzend*"), a thing which Husserl recognizes and calls the "natural posture of consciousness." Phenomenology consists in describing that phenomenon of natural consciousness from the viewpoint of a reflexive consciousness which looks upon natural consciousness "without taking it seriously," without adopting its *positions* (*Setzungen*), suspending its operative quality (*epokhé*). To this I object on two counts: (1) that to suspend what I have called the operative quality (*vollziehender Charakter*) of consciousness, its quality as arbiter, is to eliminate what is most basic in it and hence in all *consciousness;* (2) that we are suspending the operative quality of one consciousness from another, the reflexive, which Husserl calls "phenomenological reduction," without its having any superior right to invalidate the primary and reflective consciousness; (3) on the other hand, it is left to the reflexive consciousness to be operative and to establish primary consciousness with the character of *being absolute,* calling it *Erlebnis* or living experience. This shows precisely how *every* consciousness has operative validity and has no meaning insofar as its consciousness invalidates one with another. We will be able to invalidate an act of consciousness by reasoning, as we always do when we correct an error, for example, an optical illusion; but if we contrast "illusory" consciousness with "normal" consciousness without intermediate reasoning, the "normal" cannot invalidate the "illusory." Hallucination and perception have inherently equal rights.

The consequence of these objections was that from 1914 on, I set forth the description of the phenomenon "consciousness of . . ." having pointed out in the face of all philosophic idealism that it is not *simple*

Instead of abandoning consciousness, as has been done since Descartes, we establish ourselves firmly in the basic reality which each man's life is for him. The basic thing about it is not being perhaps the only reality nor even being something absolute. It means simply that in the event of *life* there is

---

description but ultimately hypothesis to say that the act of consciousness is real, but its aim is *only* a matter of intention and therefore unreal. The description which fits the phenomenon closely—I said then—will state that in a phenomenon of consciousness like perception we find the *coexistence of the I and the thing*, hence that this is not a matter of ideas or intentions but reality itself. So that in "fact" perception is what there is: I, on the one hand, being the thing perceived, and on the other, being myself; or, what is the same thing, *that there is no such phenomenon* as "consciousness of . . ." as a general frame of mind. The reality is that I am reaching out and experiencing the reality of my surroundings, and that the presumed description of the phenomenon "consciousness" resolves itself into a description of the phenomenon "real human life," which is the *same thing* as the coexistence of the I with surrounding things or circumstances. *The result, therefore, is that "there is no" such thing as consciousness as a phenomenon, but that consciousness is a hypothesis, precisely the one which we inherited from Descartes.* Thus Husserl comes back to Descartes.

Aside from many times in my writings during those years this interpretation of "consciousness" may be found in my course given in 1916, for the Faculty of Philosophy and Letters in Buenos Aires, from which extracts appeared in *La Prensa*, in addition to which a good stenographic transcript exists in the possession of Dr. Coriolano Alberini, later dean of that Faculty.

There are many reasons why I did not allow those ideas to be put into print at that time, and I would have to recount the life of an idea man who is *independent* and interested in improving the culture of his fellow-countrymen. But I can now state one of those reasons, because it is quickly said, so that the young who tomorrow will *set themselves to thinking* may not commit the same error that I did. This reason for my silence was purely and simply . . . timidity. Because the reader will have seen that the doctrine includes the greatest enormity which, between 1900 and 1925, could be uttered in philosophy, namely, that *there is no consciousness* as a *primary* form of relationship between the so-called "subject" and so-called "objects"; what we have is man in relation to things and things to man, that is, human existence. The young people of Montmartre who today play the guitar of "existentialism" by ear still do not know this fundamental, but without it there is no way to reach the high seas of metaphysics.

This shows why it is stupid to say that Dilthey has influenced my thinking, for Dilthey had no idea of these things, and believed implicitly in "consciousness."

given to each of us, as a presence, an omen, or a symptom a completely different reality comprising that which tries to transcend it. It is, then, the root of every other reality, and only in this is it basic. This being so, the study of human life—*biognosis*—obliges us to investigate everything else in the root which gives it birth and causes it to appear in the area of that universal event which is our living. Then, on asking ourselves what are the great traditional problems of philosophy *at its roots,* we discover that they have always been stated in a way that in the end was secondary, derivative and not primary, already grown tall and no longer in its underground root system.

Not to have done this is what separates me profoundly from Heidegger, although I admire his indisputable genius, which entitles him to be considered as one of the greatest philosophers who have ever lived; and he is fortunately still alive in the fullness of his life and his influence. But I can accept almost none of his positions except those which we hold in common when we approach living human reality. Thus it is not acceptable that he starts forthwith by attributing to man what he calls *Seinverständnis,* "comprehension of Being." Because in none of his books does he take the trouble to try to clarify what he understands by that term. The matter is serious, because it leads him directly to that arbitrary thesis which I encountered on the road along which this study was proceeding, which obliged me to speak of it as the thesis that "man is a question about Being." Now the very word "Being" begins to bother modern philosophers as soon as linguistics comes in sight on the horizon, because it follows that in all languages the words which mean "to be" are characterized by their recent origin and it is a nuisance that, as traditional philosophers—including the modern and contemporary ones—believe that philosophy consists perforce in occupying itself in one way or another, but ultimately, with Being; a concept so fundamental could not have found its *ad hoc* language before the relatively recent stages in human development. Its modernity is made all the more striking because in almost all languages the verb *to be* is formed from roots and stems of the most diverse origin, up to the point where the distortion of its forms is like a piece of darning which proclaims its characteristics of chance and accident.

Thus it happens that in Heidegger's writings we never even know whether we should take the fundamental term "understanding of Being" seriously or as an anomaly; *in modo recto*, like the Being of the Ens which the Greeks invented, or *in modo obliquo*, that is, giving this name to whatever, for any indirect reason *could* with good will be called "Being" in our modern tongue. The difference between the two ways is decisive: because if we understand *being* as formally, terminologically Being, then it is wholly false that "the comprehension of Being" is inborn in man, and if we understand *being* as anything that man has understood, then Heidegger has not said anything at all.

It is inconceivable that in a book entitled *Being and Time* which claims "to destroy the history of Philosophy," in a book, then, composed by a tonsured and furious Samson, not the slightest light is cast on what "Being" means, and on the other hand, this term comes at us modulated in innumerable flute-like variations: such as *Seinssinn*, "sense of Being"; such as *Seinsweise*, "manner of Being"; such as *Sein der Seienden*, "Being of the *entia*" (in this case we also do not know whether these *entia* to which Being belongs are really *entia* or mere things, which would produce two distinct meanings between them) and so on. The fact is that, despite the warning and the back-handed blows which the reader is liable to suffer when he stumbles over this term in the book, Heidegger has not posed the problem of Being to himself in the first place, but rather has tried once again to classify the different types of Ens and has added a new one which he called *Dasein*, profiting by the use in German of the Latin doublet of *Dasein* which is *Existenz;* in fine, directing attention—and this is what is most productive in his work—toward the "way of existing" of this Ens, although forgetting to analyze the way of existing of other types of Ens.

Here is an example. Heidegger distinguishes three types of "Being Ens." Being *as* being useful for something, which is the kind of being of utensils or implements (*Zuhanden-sein*). The Being of the hammer is to give hammer blows.[4] Being *as* "finding oneself there"—what we encounter there—(*Vorhanden-sein*). And Being *as* "being in the there" (*Da-sein*), which is the Being of man; which in Heidegger takes the place of the simple and natural term "life" with that terminological arbitrariness which was always so prevalent among German thinkers; who, not experiencing "loneliness" like every human creature but converting themselves anomalously into "solitaries," shut up in themselves, "auto-ists," invert the usual language in which the individual speaks with his neighbors and start "talking with themselves," inventing a language of which the use is intimate and untransferable.[5] According to Heidegger—this is also in Dilthey—philosophy since the days of Greece has *regarded* only Being as "finding oneself there," and the Ens as "that which is."

Heidegger adopts the popular opinion that the Greeks did not understand Being in any way other than as "that which is," as that which man finds before him. But that does not seem to me either correct or completely honest. The very movement which they invented and which we call philosophizing, consisted in not accepting as Ens simply "that which is," but on the contrary, denying the Being-of-that-which-is and investigating beyond that to "that which truly—is"—the ὄντως ὄν (*óntos ón*). The strange thing about "that which truly is" is

4. See *Meditations on Quijote*, 1914 [*Obras Completas*, Vol. I, p. 311, preliminary pages: "Reader . . . "]. [Published in English by W. W. Norton, 1961.]

5. There is no space here to go into the makeup of the language, but I want to point out that normally the language possesses both dimensions *at the same time* and is always jointly an understanding with oneself and a process of making others understand and, aiming to understand them. The anomaly to which the text alludes consists in the atrophy—greater or less—of this second dimension. On this matter the reader will find adequate development in my Commentary on Plato's "Banquet" (*Obras Completas*, Vol. IX, p. 751) and in *Man and People* (*Obras Completas*, Vol. VII, pp. 79 et seq.). [Latter published in English by W. W. Norton, 1962.]

not only that *it is not,* and no more than that, but rather that it is necessary to discover it *beyond* what there is. There it is necessary at most to say that for the Greeks Ens is "that which is *beyond.*" It is then *a limine* an error to affirm that for them, and through their influence for all their successors up to Kant, the Being of the Ens consists only in that this— the Ens—is "that which is"—*Vorhandkeit.* This is not even true with reference to Positivism because for this the sense-perceptible datum, hence "that which is," has no value as Ens or Reality, but it is necessary to determine with what other data it coexists and which ones it precedes or follows, in short, what is its *law.* The thing = substance, of Positivism, is the law or "general fact" which must be discovered *beyond* the simple facts. This is popular and common Positivism, but in that of Comte which, as I have said, is a great philosophy, what is present in sensation *is* and has *reality* only in relation to man. It is a shame that no one has noted that Comte is the first thinker who has made Being, the Real, consist explicitly *in pure relationship to man,* in a much more basic and profound sense than Kant. And this, precisely this, is what Comte understood by "positivity."

But according to the Greeks, it is not only an error to attribute to Being the character of "that which is there" in the sense of what man finds before him, a presence or something presented, but neither *for* the Ens itself *is there* only its being and nothing else. The Greek conception of Being certainly has a static aspect which derives not so much from being oriented toward the objects before it, which are merely appearances or things seen, but because of the fixation or "crystallization" which the concept imposes on them. The concept, in effect, is immutable (identical with itself); it does not vary, it does not exert itself, it does not *live.* It is what it already is, and nothing more. But Being to the Greeks, although marked by that fixity and paralysis imposed on it by the concept *is*—which is its projection on the plane of "outside existence," τὸ ἐκτός, consists, if I may be permitted the expression, in to be *making* its essence, in to be doing so.

This aspect of Being—vis-à-vis its static aspect—is formulated authoritatively in the Aristotelian idea of Being *as* actuality: ἐνέργεια ὄν (*energeía ón*), the operative Ens. "Being" is the primordial and more authentic operation. "Being horse" is not only presenting man with the visible form "horse" but *being it from within*, making or supporting its "horseness" in the ontological ambit; in short, to be a horse is "horsing," as being a flower is "flowering" and to be a color is "coloring." [6] Being, in Aristotle, has the value of an active verb. It is not enough, then, to establish the special character of man as an Ens whose Being consists in "his own being existing in him," in his own existence being problematical to him, because this also happens to the animal and the plant, although in very different ways in each of the three—plant, animal, and man. It is patent that Being, for the animal, is "to feel itself in danger." If there is an *entity* which consists of a permanent alert it is that of the animal. In its "dormant" form the same thing happens with the plant. We know nothing about the mineral. We know a little about the animal and the vegetable, thanks to the fact that biology is not properly a science. Physics, on the other hand, has taken over the mineral, and this is an intellectual occupation which avoids *knowing* what it is occupied with. The only thing that interests the physicist is finding out on what assumptions a framework of things can be constructed which will enable us *to know* how to use them mechanically. Physics, I have said on another occasion, is the technique of techniques and the *ars combinatoria* for fabricating machines. It is a knowledge which has scarcely anything to do with comprehension.

All this makes it clear to us that Heidegger does not handle the idea of Being with sufficient agility, and that this is because he has not posed his problem with the basic approach which our level of philosophic experience demands.

We shall soon see how Descartes, despite his fantastic gifts,

6. See "Prologue to the *History of Philosophy* of Bréhier" [Section "Thought and Progress toward Oneself in Aristotle" (*Obras Completas*, Vol. VI, p. 409)].

failed because he did not raise the question of the concept
Being and instead started forthwith—he who claimed to
reform philosophy from the roots up—with venerable and
fossilized Scholastic ontology. This was his inadequate sense
of what is fundamental.

Heidegger did the same thing. He starts off with a thing as
inert as Scholastic ontology, worse yet with the distinction
between essence and existence which has been drawn since
St. Thomas—which no one has managed to see clearly. This
also suggests to him arbitrarily that he declare that in man
both dimensions of the Ens stand in a particular relationship,
which, *if* that distinction is accepted, is not true, because
there is not only no type of Ens but no specific ens in which
that relationship would not have a special character. Because
of that such a distinction has no meaning! Color, merely by
being color, already exists in a very different manner from
sound.[7]

There is no need to go into detail in this matter; those who
have read Heidegger will understand what I find lacking in
his treatment of the problem of Being—I only ask them to
compare it with what he has given to the problem of truth.
In this he did go right to the bottom and he got down to
the place where its roots are.[8]

In the present circumstances of Western man there is
nothing for him to do but to don his diving gear again and

7. This led Heidegger to what he considers a "fundamental distinction" between the "ontological" and the "ontic" which, far from being
fundamental, is trivial and worn out, or is an unverifiable distinction
(one never knows where the "ontological" ends and the "ontic" begins)
which can hardly be maintained today. But it has served those little
people in all the crowded lower intellectual quarters of the world so
that they can gargle with it and gain great faith in themselves—being
always disposed like the ostrich to swallow lime, jewels and rough
pieces of marble indiscriminately.

8. Except for ignorance of the essential historical character of the
function "truth" which is common to this with all the other human
ingredients, Heidegger clearly recognizes that, in general, man is
historical, but he does not do this well in his analysis of any individual
theme.

get down under all the problems which keep coming up for discussion, toward the deepest region of their problematical essence. It is not that the inherited solutions are inadequate but rather that problems seem to be inadequately grasped and considered as problems. We must learn to see them with more exasperation, more heat, putting to ourselves the question that would be least anticipated; and this, not out of vanity or for amusement, but because, in fact, a new and deeper and more serious potential arising from their character as problems is now operating—unspoken and ill-defined—in the heart of modern life. Whether we like it or not, whether with the support of the community or under pressure of its hostility, a great philosophic task must be performed immediately because "everything is in crisis," that is to say, everything on the face of the earth and in the minds of men has turned equivocal, questionable, and questioned. The two last centuries have been living on faith in "culture"—science, morality, arts, techniques, money making—above all, on a solid confidence in reason. This cultural rationalist theology has evaporated.[9] Hence the imperative need to develop philosophic fundamentalism to the limit now that the ultimate points of support, which have been firm, are beginning to get shaky. That is to say that once again philosophy must dedicate itself to its inevitable function and obligation—which irritates people so much and makes the philosopher look suspiciously like a marauder, a rascal who comes in through the basement— philosophy must again, I say, "get under the very foundation stones," under the things that have seemed most definitive and unquestionable. And that suspicious and suspected task is, by the grace of God, the occupation called "philosophy," the only human discipline which does not batten on success and on achieving what it attempts; on the contrary, it consists in failing always, because the necessary, the inescapable in it, is not the achievement but the intention. So it happens that we

9. On the present state of "faith in reason" see *Notes on thought: its theurgy and its demiurgy* [Section I: "Crisis of the Intellectual and Crisis of Intelligence" (*Obras Completas,* Vol. V, p. 517)].

must ask ourselves, with regard to truth, not for a new criterion for it, which will be better polished than earlier ones, but,
peremptorily and seizing it by the lapels, "what is truth as
such," and with regard to reality, not what things *are* or what
and how *is* that which is, but for what reason that X which we
call Being is in the Universe, and with regard to knowledge
we must not ask for its bases or its limits—as Plato, Aristotle,
Descartes, Kant did—but for something which comes before
all this: for what reason we concern ourselves with trying to
know.

Our situation is, then, the opposite of what the Greeks
enjoyed. They discovered precise thinking, and to them it
was a delight, a game, a diversion. Theory—Aristotle says—is
τὸ ἥδιστον (*tò hédiston*), the delight of delights. As for us, I
would not say that we are tired of thinking—that would be a
monstrous error of diagnosis—but I will say that it no longer
amuses us, for us *subjectively* it is not a game. We want to
think only as much as necessary. For us thinking has turned
serious.[10]

When one criterion of truth fails we seek another; when
that also fails we seek a third, and so on successively until the
time comes when the accumulation of failures stands between
us and our intention of seeking still another criterion which
will be firmer and more precise than all previous ones. The
errors committed, being so numerous, distill into a general
feeling of frustration which automatically makes us lose confidence in any new effort. This is the situation of skepticism.
But this lack of confidence in the face of every effort of the
kind used in the past, that is, the kind that seeks directly, as
by right, a true criterion more valid than those that failed us,
does not obviate our need for such a criterion. This dual attitude brings with it a need for us to learn finally to distinguish between the problem of discovering a criterion of truth,

10. On how the generation of Unamuno, Bernard Shaw, Barrès,
Ganivet was the last in which writers played with ideas without suspecting the seriousness which thinking might assume, see "Prologue to
the *Finnish Letters* of Ganivet" (*Obras Completas,* Vol. VI, p. 368).

something which will serve as a clue to discerning when an opinion is or is not true—a criterion which always ends in failure—and the problem of truth itself as a necessity which man always feels despite all the failures; therefore, of truth as a function in the organism of human life. Then, and only then, do we realize with surprise that the primary and most basic meaning of the Pilate-like question "What is truth?" is not to be asked for its criterion or clues to its distinctive qualities, but for something that takes precedence over all this, namely, what are the features, the precise characteristics of that special necessity or interest of man in what we are wont to call "truth." As if a curtain had been raised, this warning opens up for us a whole world of new subjects, more elemental, fundamental, with greater priority than those now being given attention and investigated in philosophy. We could say the same thing about the traditional problem of Being.

Man has no right to behave in terms of fundamentals. To say this or the opposite is not, as commonly believed, a matter of temperament which, in the final analysis, becomes a matter of choice as to whether he should or should not behave in terms of fundamentals. Everything in man is problematical, climacteric, partial, inadequate, relative, and approximate. To recognize this is to be, in truth, a man who has come to terms with himself and with humanity. On the other hand, to behave on the basis of fundamentals is to ignore the relativity and uncertainty which are part of man's elemental makeup, and, therefore, such behavior is a sign of appalling blindness and is to drop to a subhuman level. Hence the physiognomy of an emerging semibeast which the fundamental man presents to us.

There is only one activity in which man can get down to fundamentals. This is an activity in which man, whether he likes it or not, has no other choice: that is philosophy. Philosophy is definitely root-deep because it is an effort to discover the roots of all those things which do not show them and in that sense do not have them. Philosophy provides man and the world with the roots that they lack. This is by no means to say that it accomplishes what it sets out to do. As I have shown repeatedly, philosophy is an occupation which does not live on results, which does not justify itself by its achievements. On the contrary, compared to all other human intellectual activities, it is characterized by permanent failure, and nevertheless there is no other choice than always to try again, always to undertake a task which is always aborted but, there you have it, never completely impossible. It is the perennial weariness of a Sisyphus vainly heaving the heavy rock again and again from the valley to the summit. But Nietzsche reminds us that Sisyphus—from *sophós*—again and again means the *sage, Sapiens;* this word like its Greek double does not mean erudite or man of science, but more simply he who distinguishes "flavors" and savors, the taster, he who has a good palate; in short, the man of good taste.

Let us say, then, that in philosophy man starts toward the improbable and steers toward a coast which perhaps does not exist. This in itself would be enough to show that philosophy, if it is knowledge, is not science. The sciences would have no meaning without achieving their purpose, at least in part. It is true that the purpose of the sciences is not to be knowledge in the full meaning of the term but preliminary construction in order to make technique possible. Without going fully into the question it is enough to remember this undeniable fact: the Greeks, who invented sciences, never considered them as authentic knowledge, not even Aristotle. No abstruse notion of knowledge is suspected to be behind this, reached only through complicated lucubrations in which the philosophers would have delighted. On the contrary, it means that what the man in the street understands easily when he hears the word "to know" is not what the sciences propose or what they do. Because the man in the street does not understand the words with any mental reservations but in the frank honesty of their meaning. Thus by knowledge he understands full knowledge of a thing, complete knowledge of what it is; perhaps the only respect in which the philosopher concides with the man in the street. Now then, the sciences neither are, nor do they wish to be this. They do not in the least propose to find out what things are, whatever they may be and whatever the conditions under which they appear, but on the contrary, they set out only toward the probable and explore only things *already* readily available and at the same time useful in a practical way. Therefore it would be an abstruse idea demanding complicated lucubrations to consider what the sciences actually practice as authentic knowledge, for in reference to them the meaning of this word is drastically damaged and placed in splints, becoming strictly a mere hybrid of knowledge and practice. Certainly the sciences also do not accomplish all that they propose and their achievement is only partial. But in philosophy achievement is total or it is nothing. So the sciences are successful operations but they are not properly knowledge, whereas philosophy is an occupation that always fails but is consistent in its effort to achieve authentic knowledge.

Philosophy's built-in failure is what makes of it the most profound activity of which man is capable and—without committing myself to overstatement as Heidegger does—I would say that it is the most human, because man is essentially a failure, or said in another way, man's essence is his inevitable and magnificent failure. What does not fail in man, or fails only *per accidens*, is the animal support in his make up.[11]

This implies that any appreciation or assessment of philosophy must be made with a yardstick which is the inverse of the usual, for it disassociates itself from the statement that all philosophies are an achievement simply because they are philosophies. However erroneous their doctrines may be, they are so in a perspective—the philosophical perspective which is basic in its method and universal in its theme—already truer in itself than any nonphilosophical perspective, that is to say, one which is limited and concerned only with the mundane.

11. See *History as System* and "Prologue to the *History of Philosophy* by Bréhier" (*Obras Completas*, Vol. VI, p. 377). [Former published by W. W. Norton, 1941 and 1961.]

Even more, those philosophies are an achievement from their first step; the initiation of an attitude, the philosophic vision and "abandonment of the inherited and mechanically accepted world," the commonplace world; this is to begin to find one-self in verity. As philosophy is an activity, and activity is movement, and movement has a *terminus a quo* from which it departs and which it leaves behind, and a *terminus ad quem* to which it aspires and which it hopes for, we will say that philosophy, from the moment it sets sail, already succeeds in transcending *a quo* but never has arrived *ad quem*.

Philosophy, we repeat once more, has always failed. But instead of stopping at that, we must ask ourselves if what we call its perennial failure is not philosophy's positive mission. Because the curious thing is that no epoch has regarded *its* philosophy as a failure; it is the subsequent epoch which in retrospect sees it that way. But it sees it that way *because* it has arrived at a more complete, more basic philosophy, and the inferior completeness or integration of the preceding ones is what we call their failure. When we climb a mountain, each step is an aspiration to reach the top, and if we now cast a glance behind, the steps we have taken look like a failure. But each step, like the final one, represented an intention to reach the summit and a belief that we were *almost* there. The man who believes that wherever he may be is the center of the Universe, believes every height where he is to be the top of the world.

Let us then continue to understand philosophy, sapience, and wisdom as a hunger to *know* down to the roots, which implies both the hunger and the need for roots. It fails because the ultimate root for which one hungers is not reached; but it is achievement and success compared with man's other attitudes, with his other opinions. Failure though it be in an absolute sense, it is always firmer and more flavorful, more succulent, than any other form of life or of the world.

Parenthetically, "root" is no more nor less metaphorical than any other term. The whole language is metaphor or, to put it better, every language is in a continual process of being turned into metaphor. It was pure chance that we do not normally say "root" instead of principle, cause, *arkhé, aitía*, foundation, reason. There was a time when the Indo-European tongues, in order to express the meaning of Being, used a word which meant "to put out shoots, to grow as a plant." Thus in Indo-Europe there was the root *bhu;* in Sanscrit *abhut (aorist)* and in Greek ἔφυ (*éphy*). From this our word *ser* (to be) derived the stem of the perfect tense, *fui, fué*. This shows that during a certain period, in order to express the most abstract and profound relationships of the Real, a system of botanical images, "made fashionable" by the invention of agriculture, then recent, was followed. If philosophy had existed at that time, it is most probable that today instead of "principle" we would say "root," and this study would be entitled "The Idea of Root in Leibnitz" instead of "The Idea of Principle in Leibnitz." The philosopher is the specialist in roots; hence he has no other choice than to be root-directed, nor is there a more unsound philosophy than the "philosophy of common sense" which incidentally was that of Menéndez Pelayo.

30
Belief and Truth

FOR SOME TIME we have been marching around philosophy as the Hebrews marched around Jericho. This is a strategy of cycloid approach. As we circle the city the same views appear again and again with stubborn repetition, but each time closer and from a different angle. Let us now take one more turn.

In opposition to Heidegger, I said that philosophy is not born out of the feeling of alienation which the world produces in us when it fails as a system of tools or utensils, a failure which might reveal to us that independence of us which we call its Being. I indicated that this seemed to me an error because there neither was nor could be a moment in which man did not find the world alien, and nevertheless he did not always—in fact scarcely ever—think that things had a Being, or what is the same thing, he almost never engaged in philosophizing. I said that, on the other hand, philosophy is born and reborn when man loses his faith or his system of traditional beliefs, and therefore falls into doubt at the moment when he believes himself to be in possession of a new *way* or method for emerging from this doubt. In faith one is, into doubt one falls, and in philosophy one emerges out of this to the Universe. The first of these two themes is the more intricate. This is reason enough for us to begin with the second.

I pointed out that philosophy cannot be one of man's primary attitudes, but that it always presupposes another earlier one in which man lives on beliefs.[1] It is as shameful that there is no authoritative description of the form that life assumes when existence is a matter of beliefs, as it is that there has

---

1. It is not possible for me to repeat here the exposition of what I understand, *sensu stricto*, by "beliefs." See my essay *Ideas and Beliefs* (*Obras Completas*, Vol. II, p. 381).

never been a persuasive account of the most grave and important event in history, one which has happened so many times: the loss or the dissipation of a faith, that strange and dramatic reversal in which a broad human group moves from believing wholeheartedly in the shape of the world to a state of doubt about it. As long as this is not done there will be no complete clarity either about the origin of philosophy or about what it is.[2] I have always been especially surprised that a man like Dilthey, better equipped than anyone else to clarify this, has never understood how the philosophic attitude was born at a certain moment in Greek life. In his *Introduction to the Sciences of the Spirit* he begins by calmly setting forth the first philosophic doctrines as if creating a philosophy were the most *natural* thing in the world. This is one more indication that Dilthey, whose genius and tenacious effort was directed precisely toward overcoming all *naturalism* in the consideration of man, was in the end always captivated by it and never managed to think of human reality as something absolutely historical, but always fell back afresh into the traditional idea that man has and is a "nature."

If that diagnosis of "life as being in belief" had been made, it would have been apparent that the idea of Truth is not in it. This cannot be formulated except when man finds himself *effectively* confronted with other beliefs, that is to say, the beliefs of others. What would be important to explain is at what precise juncture there must be a "life as belief" so that it may have what I call an effective meeting with other beliefs. The theme is of enormous humanistic interest. The key to the explanation is found where it could, in the abstract, be least imagined, namely, by illustrating the opposite fact, which is that at the present time innumerable small social groups or tribes live together in the Western Sudan and nearby regions in constant traffic with each other, each nevertheless attached

2. We will see if I can publish in 1948, my study *Origin of Philosophy*. I cannot go into the matter here because it is strictly historical, and to clarify it is to write history seriously and all history, if it is to be convincing, takes a long time to recount. [It will be published in *Obras Inéditas*.]

to its traditional beliefs without any dent being made in the solid shell of its faith by the presence and the permanent contact of other peoples which believe just as firmly in their divergent dogmas. The Glidyi-Ewe of Togo say of a man who belongs to another tribe or family: "He dances to another drum." [3] Whoever is truly devoted to the humanities is always delighted when a fact makes clear to him the "undulating and diverse" condition of the human Ens. So it is in this case. The drum is the instrument that symbolizes the system of beliefs and norms for a great many primitive peoples, because the collective ritual dance is the religious and "intellectual" action par excellence which makes it possible to transcend the world. The thing is astounding, and it obliges me to insinuate to my friend Heidegger that for the negroes of Africa philosophizing is dancing and not asking themselves questions about Being. Whoever is incapable of *seeing and understanding* these surprising homologies is unqualified in the humanities. Because the result is that the collective ritual dance, in the enthusiastic presence of the entire group, was what, in believing Greece, constituted the fundamental religious act in which man addressed God and God appeared to man, and therefore that dance and attendance at its public display was the exact homologue of meditation and prayer, was its "spiritual exercises." Now then, look at what happens with this demon of human reality! That

3. Dietrich Westermann: *Die Glidyi-Ewe in Togo* (1935, p. 140). Westermann is one of the greatest masters of the most recent and precise ethnology. It is clear that all of them, including Malinowski, are behind the times in the matter of the humanities. Westermann cites this one among the "sayings" or adages which he heard: "He who has never been away thinks that only his mother knows how to cook." Is this something new, or is it as old as the others? It would be interesting to find out, for if it is new it would have value as a symptom of an initial disbelief, and if not, which for many reasons is the most probable, it would be good datum for the fact—on the whole indisputable— that the coexistence of divergent beliefs next to each other is *ineffective* and has no impact on the faith of these peoples. That these ethnologists have not seen the problems that rise from a fact which leaps to the eye of a mere reader as distant and unimportant as I, shows up to what extent they, like historians and philosophers in general, are not very alert people.

festival of ritual dancing was called *theory* in Greece. Tell me if it is a capricious desire—which for my part I regard as most objectionable and childish—to go seeking data by which to verify that for the African negro to philosophize is to dance. Among the North American Indians it is even more so because their dances, which are also social, arise out of individual invention obtained in dreams, and dreams are the metaphysical "way of thinking" of primitive men. So it is useful to remember that, before the perceptive-conceptual way of thinking which made philosophy possible, for hundreds of thousands of years men made use of other very different ways. Before, in fact, the emotive-imagist or mythological way of thinking predominated in humanity, and even before that, tens of millennia earlier, the visionary way of thinking which these Amerindians and the Chaminist peoples of northern Asia [4] have largely preserved today.

Only when man realizes to what extent other beliefs exist vis-à-vis his own beliefs which, once he is acquainted with them, seem to him more or less as worthy of credence as his own—only then does there arise in man a new need: the ability to discern which of the two complexes of belief is the one that *ultimately* merits being believed. That need, necessity or necessitousness for deciding between two beliefs is what we call "truth." Now, I think, it is obvious why, while one lives fully in belief, it is impossible to feel or even to understand what sort of thing Truth is. As I have shown in another study, the characteristic thing about "beliefs" when contrasted with "ideas" or opinions—including in these the most strictly scientific doctrines—is that reality, complete and genuine reality, is for us simply what we believe and never what we think. It is the same thing in reverse to say that our "beliefs" never appear to us as opinions, personal or collective or universal, but as "reality itself." Furthermore, we are not even conscious of a good part of our beliefs. They take form within us from behind our mental lucidity, and in order to find them

4. See my book *Commentary on the "Banquet" of Plato* (*Obras Completas*, Vol. IX, p. 751).

we must search among "the things on which we count" and not among the "ideas we have." The form of consciousness which "beliefs" take in us is not a "taking into account," a *noésis*, but a simple and direct "counting on."

To recognize a thing without counting on it—as happens to us with the centaur, with mathematical theorems, with the theory of relativity, with our own philosophy—that is an "idea." To count on a thing without thinking of it, without taking account of it—as happens to us with the solidity of the earth on which we are going to take the next step, or with the sun which is going to rise tomorrow—that is a "belief." From this it follows that *we never believe in an idea,* and as theory —science, philosophy, and so on—is nothing but "ideas," it makes no sense to pretend that man believes in theory. As for everyone who, becoming violent about things out of a mania to be heroic or out of a tendency toward histrionics (nothing of this ceases to be that way because at times it costs the life of the maniac, the actor, the mime) has tried to pretend that he *believed* in his *ideas,* his honorable fraud has been apparent in his face. "Ideas" persuade us, convince us, they are "evident" or are "proven"; but they are all this because they are always *mere* ideas and they are never reality itself for us, as is that in which we believe. Thus it is that theory and ideas, even the most consistent and proven ones, have in our lives a spectral, unreal, and imaginary character, not really *serious*. I say this because *we are* never our ideas, we never confuse them with ourselves, but we merely think of them, and all thinking, to put it in concrete terms, is only fantasy. Science is pure exact imagination, and I have already once indicated that this is a truism because it is clear that nothing can be more exact than a fantasy, an act of imagination, something invented *ad hoc* so that it may be exact, as we will see later when we go into the more rigorous method of modern mathematics.

It is curious how Descartes and Leibnitz, whom everything persuaded to make of mathematics "pure understanding," had no choice, (fine as they were at theorizing) but to recognize mathematics as a work of the imagination. One step more, and they would have lost their methodic terror of fantasy, recognizing that all "understanding" is imagination. But the fact is that at the present time, for reasons of persistent and inconceivable superstition no one has yet recognized that thinking is nothing but imagining. Hence we always regard an "idea" as something we *make*, as we made the centaur and the chimera. Hence we *cannot* nor, it is clear, should we take our "ideas" or take theory altogether seriously. By virtue of their taking on a dimension which presents them to us as creations of our own, we automatically recognize that, as we made them, so can we unmake them, that they are therefore *revocable*. Beliefs, on the other hand—everything on which, like it or not, we count—constitute the stratum of formidable and irrevocable seriousness which, after all, is our life.

I express this different aspect by saying that we get hold of and uphold "ideas" but that we depend on "beliefs"; that is to say, it is they which get hold of us, uphold us and keep hold of us. Scientific theory, neither more nor less than poetry, of which it is the twin, belongs to the unreal world of fantasy. The real aspect of science is its application, its practice, and all theory is in principle practicable. But in itself it is unreality and phantasmagoria.

When man realizes that his beliefs are not the only reality but that there are others which are very different, *ipso facto* he loses his virginity, his innocence, and the strength of his beliefs. He recognizes them as *mere* beliefs, i.e., as "ideas." With regard to them he then acquires a freedom which he did not previously possess. They no longer get hold of him and keep hold of him. They become revocable, they lose the absolute weight of their absolute seriousness and come to approximate poetry, forming part of a world which, as compared to that serious aspect, has a playful one. It is clear that this freedom, like all freedom, assuming that this has value, is paid for by exchanging the security of belief for perplexity, insecurity, worry, vacillation, fluctuation, in short for uncertainty in facing "ideas." Uncertainty, which was unknown when he believed, shows him that he "needs to be certain."

If this is genuine, an infinite craving for certainty takes possession of him, he will have no peace and will be upset, in great perturbation, as long as he cannot manage to fabricate for his fractured belief the orthopedic apparatus of certainty. Certitude is the *ersatz* of belief.

Of course, it is unavoidable—although this is not the moment for it—to explain why, when man loses faith and falls into perplexity or uncertainty, he does not stay there quietly, but on the contrary, feels a need to sally forth and attain a "state of certainty." The thing is very far from being obvious or simple. For it happens that most people, including the most believing, spend the greater part of their lives in uncertainty, in perplexity, which proves that it is not impossible to live in a state of perplexity. Nevertheless, why can one not accept it and abandon oneself to it passively? That even the firmest believer passes his life in uncertainty is clear, I repeat, given the primary and principal dimension of our lives as the future: we are continuously in it, from it we live the present and the past. Well now, the future is the uncertain, and perplexity is precisely the essential feature of "being in the future."

Perplexity is not occasional, not experienced now and then but is an "essential feature" of life. We can say categorically that life is perplexity.[5] However firm the system of beliefs in which man is placed may be, the very next instant confronts him as a crossroads of possibilities, of things which occur unexpectedly, against our will and our best foresight, and of things which we may very well do ourselves but which, by the same token, oblige us by their very multiplicity to select one of them without giving the matter much thought. At

5. Life, everyone's life, is always unique. Despite all the difficulties, there are and there have been innumerable unique lives. Those abstract components which make up the *essential* structure of all of them I call "essential features of life." The term, loaded with an Aristotelian meaning which is more than I need, comes from Duns Scotus. That Scholastic philosophy seems to me so bad that it hardly seems a philosophy, does not in the least lessen the fact that as an intellectual effort it may seem to me most admirable from other points of view. The most persuasive proof of this esteem is that I have managed to profit from all of it that is, in my judgment, profitable, which is no small amount.

every moment, facing the more immediate future, our life will usually paw the ground, uncertain which road to take, irresolute as to what to do, while from the secret heart of the universal future it feels itself threatened by innumerable possible developments, some favorable and others adverse. It is well known that *amenazar*, "to threaten," comes from *minari*, a term from pastoral life which entered into the classical language of Rome and means that the shepherd will "throw stones, fling his cudgel from afar, make violent gestures" at his flock. The man withdrawn into the inner corner of his life looks anxiously at the world about him with the meekness of a sheep because he foresees that the stones and blows, or alternatively the caresses and delights, which the atrabilious shepherd named Destiny has flung at him from the other side of the visible, from the other world which is the future, will come whizzing at him and will not be long in reaching him. His firm beliefs serve only to arm him better to endure that eventual hail of stones and keep him from being infatuated with good fortune; but they do not ward off perplexity nor do they relieve his uncertainty. Man, being always in the future, by the same token is always under threat.

When, in this irremediable condition of his life, he comes to lose his beliefs, because he has begun to believe also in those foreign to him and does not know what he can cling to with respect to the world and himself, the reality about him is flooded with uncertainty. "I do not know what to think. . . ." is what we usually say then. Let this be well understood. This is not a matter of having no opinion on the subject, no thoughts about it. It is quite the contrary. It is that we have at least two opinions on the matter before us which are contrary to each other when they are not contradictory; but we believe in both of them, or to put it better, we would believe in them if this nascent double belief did not neutralize our believing. Each one of these attracts our adherence in turn. With this one before me I feel compelled to adopt it, to make myself one with it; but at that moment the other appears and I feel equally disposed to make myself one with that. My being comes and goes, swings back and forth from one to the other like a pendulum. This being able to feel myself one with either of them is precisely what prevents me from being one with any. I am not one, but two, my being is torn apart in a duality of believing; this believing two incompatible things is doubt, uncertainty. It is then erroneous to picture doubting as a negation of believing, like an absence of conviction. Quite on the contrary, doubt cannot possibly exist unless there pre-exist two dogmas, two theses or opinions, both of which I believe, or rather could believe. The doubter believes more than the believer, who is a close prisoner in the monolith of his faith. Doubt is believing in two things at the same time, seeing at the same time two ideas which are disparate and different. This seeing with a double vision, this mental strabis-mus, is doubting. Doubt is the cross-eyed sister of belief.

This is why perplexity, uncertainty cannot be accepted. It can only be endured. It is not possible to stand in doubt be-cause doubt is a coming and going from one opinion to an-other, an inability to stay in any one of them. This is the reason why the idiom says that "one falls into doubt." When doubt is strong one exaggerates the situation by saying yes, that is so, but "one is all at sea." Being in the sea is not stand-ing, it is floating to and fro, coming and going on the restless waves and suffering the anguish of sinking, of going to the bottom. The doubtful thing is not the solid ground on which one can stand, it is the liquid element in which one can only float, sink, and be submerged.

These expressions of the language into which humanity has been decanting its millenary "experience of life" must be taken seriously. These expressions are metaphors, but *the metaphor is the authentic naming of things,* and not the tech-nical term of terminology. The term—in this sense not of concept but of the word that expresses it—the technical term is a dead word, sterilized, aseptic, which by the same token has been converted into a symbol and has ceased to be actively naming, that is, carrying out by itself that operation and func-tion which is "saying the thing" that we call *naming.* The true meaning of *name* is "that which serves to *call* someone." The word *calls* to a thing that is not there before us, and the thing runs to us like a dog, makes itself more or less apparent to us, comes to us, responds, makes itself manifest. Therefore the notion that the name *calls* to things arises from the primitive "animist" thinking in which everything has a soul, an innermost center, from which it hears, understands the call, responds and comes forth.

The moment that a name is converted into a technical term, a change comes over it, and over our use of it. Far from telling us what the thing is, bringing it to us and making it visible, we must now seek the thing that the term expresses by other means, observing it closely, and only then do we understand the term. A terminology is the exact opposite of a language.[6]

6. To think that for more than 30 years—it is quickly said—I had, day after day, to endure *in silence, never broken*, when many pseudo-intellectuals of my country disqualified my ideas because I "wrote only in metaphors," they said. This made them conclude and proclaim triumphantly that my writings were not philosophy. It is clear that fortunately they were not, if philosophy is something that they have the capacity to set aside. Certainly, I carried to an extreme the hiding of the definitive dialectic musculature of my thought, as nature takes care to cover fiber, nerve and tendon with the ectodermic literature of the skin where it took great pains in placing the *stratum lucidum*. It seems impossible that concerning my writings—whose importance, apart from this question, I recognize as scant—no one had made the generous observation, which is also irrefutable, that in them it is not a matter of something given as philosophy which turns out to be literature, but on the contrary, of something presented as literature which results in philosophy. But those people who have no understanding of anything understand less than nothing of beauty of style, and do not conceive that a life and a work can cherish this virtue. Nor do they have the least suspicion for what *grave and essential reasons* man is an animal with style. *Dies irae, dies illa.*

31
The Dramatic Side of Philosophy

PHILOSOPHY is explicitly the movement which leads to emergence from doubt. Without doubt there is no philosophy. Hence it cannot consist in wondering at things near at hand and in its ambit or its world. From the start philosophy is not a direct concern with the world but with certain preexisting opinions or "ways of thinking" about it. Hence philosophy is not a uniform method in man, not ubiquitous and timeless. It is born and reborn at certain definite junctures in history which are characterized by a breakdown in faith, in a whole repertory of "ruling opinions," in traditional intellectual attitudes. This is why the attitude of the philosopher in his term *a quo* is so dramatic. No preexisting idea, no commonplace among those that he "finds there" established in his social sphere *means* enough to him. All of them seem to him crippled, or vague, or flimsy. Consequently, he gets into a state of hyperaesthesia in which he cannot believe, use, even live with any inherited idea about any theme of any important subject. Hence the bad temper toward the crowd which is characteristic of the philosophers—Parmenides, Heraclitus, Xenophon, Socrates, Plato, Bacon, Descartes, Kant, Hegel, Comte. The only one who is angry with nobody is the meek Dilthey, but this for the strangest reason: because Dilthey—educated in what was then called "Positivism"—was appalled at the strong suspicion stirring in the hidden depths of his mind that he had discovered a new philosophy, he who, on the other hand, was imbued with the idea that philosophies had already come to an end like a display of fireworks.

If philosophy were alienation from the world, it would

begin by being an absolute nonknowing—the nonknowing of one who does not know what has been, or that there could be something like knowing. Well now, the essential thing for philosophic first steps is to realize that *man has believed that he knew,* and that this belief has been revealed as an error.

The first knowing appears as such at the precise moment when doubt of it—the doubt of "belief"—invalidates it and it is rejected. It is like health, which has no shape except when it fails and shines . . . by its absence. Let us look at this dramatic side of philosophizing.

In Greece, if ever, philosophy was in one sense a question about Being.[1] Clearly, this means that what was called Being was postulated in order to fill the void of what had gone: a world in which the decisive reality was the gods. Note what this attitude of seeking anxiously for Being assumes. It is a matter of examining all of "what there is" with respect to its entity or its reality, which implies a judgment that it is not enough that there "should be" something for which it may have reality, for which it would have a genuine Being. Or to put it another way, that Being, if "all there is" be included in it, has different values, different qualities with respect to its "being it": that which properly is, that which seems to be, that which almost is, that which almost is not, that which is and is not, and so on. All this, in turn, implies that the world which simply "is there" and in which we live, as and how we live, that is to say, according to how inherited opinions made us see it, is a deceit, a mirage, a fraud. The "natural" thing would be that the world in which man is—his surroundings, his circumstances—would be something completely clear and in no way doubtful. Philosophy's point of departure was the contrary impression which originated in the discovery that "ruling opinions" and traditions were erroneous, and above all, that there were no gods to be the support and set standards for the world, an impression of living amid deceit and fraud. This is alienation from the habitual or traditional world. The

1. We will now see that not even in Greece was it properly this, *because Being is not a question* but already begins by being an answer.

terrible thing is that the universe in which we live and of which we are, seems no longer what it most definitely has to be: firm. It turns formless, insecure, problematical, fluid. To find oneself in it is the opposite of being—it is to fall, to lose oneself, to drown. It is painful enough to suffer deceit in life, but imagine that this deception is generalized and that we find our whole life to be entirely a fraud. It is enough to drive one mad! It is to feel that we are demented—that nothing is or really is, that nothing is what it is, but, in turn, the opposite of what it is, something quite otherwise—and that we are demented not through some defect in our minds but through that of the world, which is essentially deceit and delirium; it drives us mad! It is lunacy, insanity, and in it we are submerged.

The World as deception is a most unpleasant reality which we can describe only by calling it—and feeling it as—a Nothing-being, being so for us. Pure Nothing is better because one is satisfied with an absolute non-being and only its self is reduced to nothing. But to be in Nothing, as we are in basic doubt, is to find ourselves subdued and given over to an operating, active Nothing which exercises its terrible crushing, annihilating power on us. To live in an atmosphere of substantial deceit is to witness moment by moment the destruction of every one of our actions and our conditions, the ruination of our enjoyment of life.

The anxiety, the deep uneasiness which must have been felt by these first men who did not believe in the gods, for whom the world had collapsed as "security" and had become a deception for them, must have been terrible. Hence the heroic reaction with which they sought to emerge into something firm and to find certainty for themselves. Hence the tone of the cry of salvation, the gesturing exuberance of people saved from shipwreck, with which they speak to us while clinging fast to the providential rock which they have found—their philosophy. It is a cry at once exultant and irritated. Irritated against tradition, the commonplace, which had created a deceitful world from which they had found it necessary and dangerous to free themselves. These first philosophers represent optimism in the "tragic epoch of the Greeks." They were optimists since they attributed the deception which was the World to the erroneous opinions of the men who had gone before them, because when there is deceit it is essential to detect the deceiver.

Now then, we can react in two ways to the consciousness that we are amid that deception which we call the World: one by seeing that deception immediately as willfully produced by some superior power; another, by taking it as an unexpected result for which no one is responsible. In this latter case deception is weakened into mere enigma. It is obvious that Heraclitus was within a hair's breadth of the first when he says: "Reality enjoys hiding itself." Nevertheless, that was not the road which his philosophy took. It seemed to him that in thinking of a latent power concerned with deceiving us—Descartes' *esprit malin,* an idea so very profound and so little understood—they were retreating to the myth, and those men hated mythology because it was so palpably fraud. They sought a way out by seeing the Real as mere enigma, as a riddle, and hence the style which the philosophers adopted of being decipherers of riddles.

But it is clear that we lack a "science" which tries to explain the World and find its true Being by starting to consider the deception in which we live, and that the World is to us like someone's doing. *Someone has wanted men to live amid deceit.* There is a "malign spirit" about. Christianity, Mazdaism, Manicheism, Cartesianism, the Hindus, Schopenhauer, all have been an attempt at that "*epistéme.*"

This is philosophy's dramatic side, in which there is reflected with matchless clarity the essentially plaintive ingredient which is at the very root of the human being and his way of life—that consciousness of the dog that has lost his master, of the disoriented animal which does not know either where it is or what it ought to do. But it is wrong to define the phenomenon which is life as though at bottom it consisted only of this. Heidegger claims that philosophy consists in making it patent that life is Nothing, not noticing that when he does this he is already demonstrating that what he says is not true, because the Nothing which is life has the special quality of generating a tireless capacity to *enjoy oneself* in elaborating the great game of creating a theory—a philosophy which makes it patent that life is Nothing. If life were in fact only Nothing, the only appropriate and inevitable action would be suicide. But this is not what happens; instead of committing suicide, life is busy philosophizing, which is inevitably to experience fruition in juggling ideas, in playing at getting concepts exact. In the far reaches of this study the reader will see with what radical means I turn against the traditional optimism of philosophy. Do not, then, suspect me of any affected piety and humility before the frightful negativism of Being. But even supposing that philosophic dogma, in order to coincide with Reality, had to be an extreme pessimism, it is evident that philosophizing in this way reveals that at the root of life— that is to say, on the most basic and profound level of the phenomenon life—there is, together with the Nothing and the "anguish," an infinitely sportive gaiety which leads, among other things, to the great game which is theory, and especially to its superlative, which is philosophy. As at the starting point of phenomenology—which is a description of the phenomenon "consciousness of . . ."—a huge error was committed, so also in the description of the phenomenon life which serves as point of departure for what is called "existentialism." Hence it is fitting that we should not be confused by all those things which we start from, because immediately on setting forth, we part and re-part one from the other. Heidegger always failed to perceive that life as a reality *obviously* has the surprising character of what is not only "possible death" at any moment, and therefore absolute danger, but that death is in the hands of life, that is to say, that *life can give itself death.* But if it were only that death would be not *possible,* but *inevitable*— that is that life, man, would not live longer than the precise moment of committing suicide. Even admitting—with reservations that it is inopportune to set forth here—that life is a phenomenon of the mortal Ens, and therefore a living danger and an existing Nothing, the result is that it can only be thus if *in addition* it is acceptance of danger, a happy and fruitful consecration of death. Life is precisely the basic and antagonistic uniting of these two Ens-like dimensions: death and resurrection or the will to exist *malgré tout*, danger and gay defiance of danger, "desperation" and fiesta, in short "anguish" and "sport." [2] Hence from my earliest writings I have opposed the exclusiveness of a "tragic sense of life" which Unamuno rhetorically proclaimed, preferring a "sportive and festive sense" of existence which my readers of course take as merely a literary phrase.[3] Before us, although for certain reasons we could not take note of it,[4] Dilthey had already discovered that life is *eben mehrseitig*, that life is "definitely multilateral," that it is always "the one or the other," that is to say, what is most basic in the phenomenon life is its equivocal character, its substantially problematical quality. Everything comes out

2. This formula is the greatest concession to "existentialism" that could be made, but it should not be understood as if the other side of life which is not sport were only anguish. Not for a hundred thousand leagues! Life is anguish and enthusiasm and delight and bitterness and innumerable other things. Precisely because it is so many things at once and from the root up, we do not know what it is. In the syncretic religions of imperial Rome they talked of Isis Mirionima. Life, too, is a reality with a thousand names, and it is so because, consisting originally in a certain *flavor* or temperament—what Dilthey calls *Lebensgefühl* and Heidegger *Befindlichkeit*—that property is not single but definitely a thousandfold. For this whole life it continues to *flavor* every man's existence with the most varied and antagonistic essences. Otherwise life, that basic phenomenon, would not be the enigma it is.

3. Literature is read without thinking what is read, and therefore it makes literature of everything that is read. All writing can be transformed into literature by anyone who makes reading a superficial operation, a skating figure, gliding down the printed page. The reader, then, is the effective *litterateur*, rather than the writer. If infinitesmal calculus or the theory of groups could be read, readers would convert them into a kind of royal octave.

4. See what I say in my essay *Wilhelm Dilthey and the Idea of Life* (*Obras Completas*, Vol. VI, p. 165) on the strange condition of Dilthey's work which has prevented others, not only me, from profiting by it at the proper time.

of this, but very especially philosophy. Hence philosophy has its solid and inescapable problem. Heidegger went further back than Dilthey, and has turned to "simplifying" things in their content and the style of treating them. Because the so-called "existentialism" is also a deplorable retrogression in terms of style. With Husserl and Dilthey we had—at last!—reached a temperament in making philosophy which was quietly preoccupied only with "seeing" how things properly are, or better, which things we see clearly and which we do not, without fuss, without phraseology, without tragedy or comedy, *pari passu*. Now it comes at us again with pathos, with gesticulations, with phrases of terror, with losses of courage, with a freeing from their cages of all the words in the dictionary denoting seizure—anguish, uneasiness (*Unheimlichkeit*), decision, abysmal (*Abgrund*), Nothing. The "existentialist" starts out resolved that it is not possible to know what man is and what the world is. Anything that is not abysmal, an irreducible mystery, a black chasm, unknowable and loathsome, does not "pay its way" with him. He begins by deciding not to "understand" because "understanding" seems to the typical "self-satisfied young gentleman" [5] who is the existentialist as a thing for anyone, and he—a great *snob* before the All Highest—is not concerned with anyone, that is to say, with those who understand and who, like Goethe

from the obscure aspire to the light.

As the morphine addict needs his drug, so does the existentialist need darkness, death, and Nothingness. This is enough to make one want to laugh; it recalls *The Despair* of Espronceda which still sells in the Puerta del Sol for a penny.

"I like a cemetery
Stuffed with the dead
Oozing blood and mire
Which chokes the breath;
And in it a grave-digger

5. *The Revolt of the Masses*, Chap. XI (*Obras Completas*, Vol. IV). [Published in English by W. W. Norton, 1932 and 1957.]

With sullen gaze
And impious hand
To crush the skulls.

"I like the open fields
Carpeted in snow
Stripped of their flowers,
No fruit or verdure,
No birds that sing
And no sun that lightens;
So that only Death
Can be sensed around me."

Note, then, that a scrupulous description of the phenomenon of human life certainly reveals a basic anguish in it, but at the same time a no less basic and incredible "devotion to anguish" of which Heidegger is the most famous example, for he is, *sensu stricto*, an "amateur of anguish" in the sense in which there are also amateurs of the bulls. It may be as paradoxical as you like, but the fundamental truth is that man "loves to suffer" and this is the definition of sport. Sport is a very crude effort, fatal at times, which men seek instinctively. Nietzsche was right! "Is that Life? Good, let it come again!" Life is to feel oneself dying and to shout at the same time: *da capo!*

On whichever side one takes existentialism, one sees that the other side, the opposite, is equally true and basic. For example, the World as the *unheimlich*, the "strange" and disquieting. Good, already in Dilthey the World is proclaimed as *resistance*, but one does not stop there. On resisting the World, I discover myself as "another than I" and as being that other. But on rejecting this, I discover that in that World there is also something "good," favorable, useful, pleasant. A shipwrecked man, I yearn for that wonderful feeling which is the "resistance" of solid ground. Because the World is not only a great sea in which I am drowning, but also a beach that I can reach. In short, the World as resistance to me, shows

me the World as "assistance." If it were only *unheimlich*, disquieting, unfamiliar, I would already have left it, and the sentiment of "unfamiliarity or disquiet" would not exist unless its
opposite—the cozy [6] and restful—were also existing. So the
World is equally rough weather and warm hearth.

I do not, then, believe in the "tragic sense of life" as the
ultimate form of human existence. Life is not, cannot be a
tragedy. It is within life that tragedies are produced and are
possible.

That idea of the tragic sense of life is the product of a
romantic imagination, and as such it is arbitrary and crudely
melodramatic. Romanticism poisoned the Christianity of a
born actor who lived in Copenhagen: Kierkegaard, and from
him the refrain went first to Unamuno and then to Heidegger.

Christianity carries within itself not a sentiment, not a vague
"sense," but a direct and essentially precise *idea*, an almost
tragic *interpretation* of life; but that is precisely why it does
not stop to contemplate the phenomenon of life as such, but
is an obvious solution to the problem of life through salvation.
Therefore I say that it is a conception which is only *almost*
tragic: everything finally ends well and things sort themselves
out. Christianity *obviously* sees life in its relation to God, and
this means that it presents itself to Him *a limine*, before con-
templating life, without relation to it, as something infinitely
distant from God, the *Ens realissimum* and absolute, that
which absolutely and completely *is*. At the same time life
seems to be automatically almost, almost Nothing, as almost
being the Nothing, the non-Being.

One of the most profound minds of German Romanticism,
the Catholic theosophist of Munich, Franz von Baader,[7] who

6. This Asturian word (*atopizado*) is the only one that provides an
exact translation of the German *heimlich, gemütlich*, and the English
cozy.

7. 1765–1845, almost the same dates as Chateaubriand. This is the great
creative generation of romanticism. The others are only tenants. On the
distinction between the "creators of a land" and the "tenants," watch
for my *Dawn of Historic Reason*. Descartes, for example, is the "creator
of a land" in which Señorito Pascal, whom all the señoritos like so
much, is already a comfortable tenant.

had great influence on Schelling, as the latter recognized, and on Hegel who, an unheard-of case, is not slow to recognize it,[8] sets forth a phantasmagoric doctrine of the origin of matter which, because it expresses the Christian idea of "that World" very well in its almost mythological form, and because it is very little known, even in Germany, deserves being mentioned here. God—Baader states—is first of all the Creator, substratum of an eternal *Fiat*. Of Himself He is incapable of creating anything which is not perfect, including beings which are completely so. Hence He carried out a primary creation, the original, authentic one in which there was no matter. It was the good World of the first man before the Fall and of the "original hierarchies" of the angels whose principals are Michael, Lucifer, and Uriel. But Lucifer wanted to "stand up against God," to be for himself, and, denying the original cause of his Being, to become an original cause himself, that is to say, to become an absolute Being. God, irritated, thundered forth against him an order for his destruction and annihilation. He who wanted to be a complete Being is going to be Nothing. But in one instant of Eternity, indiscernibly later, God felt pity and thundered forth a new decree suspending the first one: Lucifer must remain in existence. But the first decree was already being fulfilled; Lucifer was becoming Nothing, and when the second order arrived there was little left of Being for him except the ultimate and exact minimum for still being something, that is, for being almost Nothing. This Being which is full of non-being, which has nothing of itself save that which is needed for carrying its substantive Nothing— which never becomes more than a ruined nonBeing and an interrupted annihilation—this is the Being of matter, is "this World" and we in it. According to von Baader it is, then, false to say that God created matter. In his judgment nothing

8. No less than in his *Encyclopedia of the Philosophic Sciences*, of 1827, did he extend himself to saying no less than this: "On a great part, and perhaps on everything" that Baader upholds "it would not be difficult for me to come to agreement with him, that is, to show that my doctrine does not differ from his opinions" (Lasson edition, p. 20).

is more profoundly antireligious than to confuse matter and creature. The creature, authentic creation and child of God, was made perfect but he failed, and when he failed it was right that he be annihilated. Matter is the limitation on this annihilation; it is, we might say, the ontological differential in which the complete "abyssing" of the creature is stayed. Whence it ensues that the existence of matter or Nothing-Ens is due, not to an act of creation but to a divine act of justified destruction which was curbed by an act of mercy. Thanks to this, the Nothing which is the material World, and in it man, can, from its evanescent entity, from its near nullity, redeem itself and return fully to Being, therefore, from the life which is Nothing to success in doing something. The idea is a magnificent and notable example of the way in which it is possible to weave together dialectic and the myth.[9]

This affinity of the Baaderian vocabulary with "existentialism" reveals how the latter has imbibed romantic philters. Above all the raw spirits of that provincial romanticism which Kierkegaard embodied have gone to his head. He was the typical provincial "genius." In the narrow environment of Copenhagen, where everything is small, absurdly crowded, where every man automatically becomes a "type," a "bonhomme," a public marionette, and a byword, Kierkegaard, superlative at dramatizing himself, a very frequent occurrence in those last two romantic generations (the other, the later one, is that of Baudelaire)—a marionette of Hegel who wants to "act" the antiHegel—needs to make and be made a spectacle of himself and to be a great "type," an "original," at whom children laugh in the street and point with a finger when he turns the corner, in the little town where all the corners are familiar. With this swollen ostentation, this moral tumescence which usually afflicts the intellectual tied to the provincial

9. As the men of those days created romanticism, above all with electricity—the word "electric" is one of the most frequent—and with chemistry, von Baader calls this a possibility which materialism finally offers us—our eventual "de-Tartarization."

THE IDEA OF PRINCIPLE IN LEIBNITZ

clay which he knows he can never leave, Kierkegaard absolutely must be "the exception," "the extraordinary." [10] At times he feels dissatisfied with his limited public and, without realizing it, with the provincial dimensions of his world. "In human terms it is not a happy situation to be extraordinary in circumstances as restricted as those of Denmark. It is a veritable martyrdom." [11] I have known another man singularly like Kierkegaard in this, and hence I know the latter well. In order to explain his profession of extraordinariness, everything is good material and a convenient tool. But in these cases the best thing is to get to the most important point, to what most concerns the public, and to make a great fuss about it. In Copenhagen religion is always the only thing that is *talked about*. Kierkegaard without blinking will create a scandal in Christianity. This is customary strategy in a town that is out of the way. Hence, and in view of the fact that St. Paul said, among innumerable other things, that Christianity was a scandal, Kierkegaard will make religion a real scandal and with *that* scandal will create *his* scandal. "Scandal," Jean Wahl said piously, "exercised a great attraction for him." "Only an instrument chosen by God can produce an enormous scandal," and his going to the cemetery to insult in his grave the most respected and famous theologian, Mynster, will in fact create the enormous scandal, "the third great scandal since the

10. See the texts gathered in Jean Wahl: *Etudes Kierkegaardiennes,* 1938, p. 29: *"A la fin de janvier, 1847"*—we know it because these bulging provincials fatten their vanity by writing minute and cynical diaries in which they secretly monumentalize themselves—"he took cognizance of what he ought to be, he will be extraordinary in the service of God" (VII, A 221, 229). "He—the vagrant in the streets of Copenhagen—because he had so much wanted to seem like the rest," he is "the penitent chosen to be the extraordinary one." "I had been accorded the role of the extraordinary" (X, 70). In fact, only the exceptional has value, and only the extraordinary possesses genuine reality, but the surest sign that some one is truly exceptional and not a festival number or a ship's figurehead is that he has no occasion to perceive it, he does not see himself as such a one. He is too immured in what he is creating to be able to contemplate himself. For that one needs that typical "excess time" which those who are not in the least exceptional have to spare.

11. *Ibid.* p. 35 (1849, p. 45).

preaching of Christ, since the marriage of Luther." [12] In the same way this man thinks that the grotesque mischief which he wrought in his village will resound throughout the cosmos. Here is a laboratory example for anyone who wants to see what the great defect of "localitis" is, a thing which is almost the opposite of the good kind of provincialism in which every nation sinks its roots and from which it is nourished. The provincial believes that his province is his province, but the "localist" believes that his province is the Universe and his village a galaxy. In this fashion the factions of the small hamlet are absurdly enlarged to ecumenical size. On the other hand, it must be emphasized that a man capable of thinking up the stupid business which I have just recounted has the best press today, and remember that I said earlier, in passing, that experience had taught me that everything which enjoys a good press is suspect. It can happen that something has outstanding quality, but this would be rather the reason for its having a bad press. A good press does not exist unless one is also an intriguer or an irresponsible person charged with so many faults that his fame does not bother anyone.

In the provinces no one can pass for intelligent or feel himself so if he does not play a part. The reason for this is that in the provinces there is no real "public" before which to be what one truly is. The true "public" is abstract because it is composed of so many individuals, so far off and indistinguishable that their individuality, their personality is no longer evident. Such a public, which is the real one, also does not know the personality of the writer on topics of public interest; it is directly interested only in the "themes in themselves," and the intelligent man must manifest his "personality," his "genius" by applying it to the matter at hand and disappearing into that application. But in the provinces there is no other matter, no other subject than other people "well known to everyone," which means known within the province. Provincial life is all directed inward, it reabsorbs its own secretions and consists in a continual return to the within-ness of

12. *Etudes Kierkegaardiennes*, p. 37 (c. X², A 219, 1830).

the within. Hence the "intelligent" provincial must create, not thematic doctrines for unpredictable fellow creatures, but a role for himself, a "well-known" figure adopting, for example, the *dramatis persona* of being the titular, official, and quotidian enemy of the respectable "Don What's His Name." In the Casino, when one wishes to speak badly of Don What's His Name, one waits for the drinking hour of the "original" and "intelligent" man whose specialty is speaking badly of Don What's His Name. Thus Kierkegaard in Copenhagen. The great provincial personality there was the theologian Mynster. So Kierkegaard will make it his business to be "he who attacks and insults the theologian Mynster."

I do not believe that a writer exists who stands apart from Christianity as much as Kierkegaard does, because in this he is provincial to such a degree that he managed to make of this religion a matter than can be of interest only in the neighbor-hoods of Copenhagen. He manages to convert the question of God and the Devil into something like the question of whether the lion or the tiger is the king of the wilderness, a question which the "lively element" of the village discusses in the Casino every evening.

Do not think it strange that I stopped to discuss this theme of provincialism. Actually we should have spoken of it much more, for it is one of the greatest infirmities from which the Occident suffers. Europe is not only de-capitalized by the Socialists—a matter which leaves me only lukewarm, although I do not consider it trivial—but, which is much worse, it is de-capitalized by the provinces and by the provincials. A quarter of a century ago, in the *Revolt of the Masses*, I called attention to this phenomenon which was already quite obvious. Since then the process has advanced in a way that is frightening. Some time ago I gave a cry of alarm in the *Revista de Occidente*, warning that the world was turning stupid, as it did in the 80 years before Christ. One of the causes of this is universal provincialism.

The level of intellectual life has deteriorated seriously everywhere, but in countries where it was never normal and healthy the degeneration of understanding is excessive, and the level is now as far below sea level as the Asphalt Lake.[13]

Philosophy in particular is the opposite of all provincialism because, like it or not, it consists of a basic perspective through its method and a great universality through its theme. All other human perspectives are limited, and their way of thinking or feeling or being is a provincialism of thinking, feeling, Being. Philosophy detests whatever is part, partiality, and party-ness. The philosopher never belonged to any one party, and all of them try to appropriate him for themselves.

13. Madrid has lost the bit of alertness to ideas which was once roused in it; it has gone back to being the eternal Manchegan (provincial) town which it always was at heart, and its inescapable Madridism shows in its face. Madrid has been handed over, as one turns a good sheep over to carnivores, to the provincial "intellectuals" and the amateurs. The amateur is the localist of whatever he is amateur of.

32
The Jovial Side of Philosophy

ALL THIS goes to show that the tone which philosophy adopts today is wrong. Because while it is certain that its theme and content, being theoretical and a combination of ideas, have an immensely dramatic and emotional character, its proper temper is as jovial as though it were a game. Philosophy is, in fact, a playing with ideas, and hence in Greece, where it was born, after the trauma occasioned by its discovery in pre-Socratic men, it set up its manner of speech definitely in an agreeable style suited to agonistic discussion and disputation. As one plays at the pancratium and at hurling the discus so one *plays at philosophizing*.

If our beliefs are reality itself to us this means that the level of our life on which they function and which obeys them is profoundly serious, up to the point in which everything else is in comparison a more or less imaginary life, that is, not serious. What I am trying to suggest by this is clearly evident if we remember our situation in poetry. While we read a novel we are outside our real life and have almost been carried away into the unreal life of the novel. During this short space of time we have almost been not living seriously; on the contrary, we have succeeded in escaping from the onerous and irrevocable seriousness which in the final analysis constitutes the act of living. It costs us no effort to recognize that poetry, in this sense, is not a serious thing. When we say this, only the poets are irritated; they are, as everybody knows, a *genus irritabile* and moreover by custom divinely incapable, by the express and beneficient will of God, of understanding anything. Because if they are irritated by that observation they fail to perceive that their lack of seriousness, their essential irresponsibility, is the marvellous mission and the prodigious gift

320

which has been granted them, thanks to which they make possible for the rest of mortals an hour of metaphysical holiday and freedom from the onerous seriousness which is life. But the fact is that, just as in the case of poetry, so we can say the same thing to only a lesser degree of the world of the true sciences, its theories, its ideas. If scientific truth seems serious in comparison with poetry, ideas are not a serious matter in comparison with the believing life, the credulous life. Thus we place theory nearer to poetry than it has customarily been put, I do not know why, and we avoid confusing it with the inevitable reality of living. This wise placing of philosophy on the level of humoral tonality which is proper to it is very important. We are lost if we take it emotionally, as we would a religion, because then we lose the "freedom of spirit," the audacity and the acrobatic exhilaration without which it is not possible to theorize. My idea then is that the tone proper to philosophizing is not that of the overwhelming seriousness of life but the halcyonic gaiety of sport, of a game. Do not put on disapproving faces, do not make gestures of offended alienation. Do not be foolish or pedantic toward me. At least do not be ignorant. Read Plato in the *Laws* (p. 820 c–d) when, at the end of his long life, he surveyed his immense philosophic and scientific experience and said: "Who knows? Perhaps backgammon (*petteía*) and the sciences are not so very different." The incredible genius concentrated and concealed in these few words will be made patent later when we see that Descartes and Leibnitz were devoted to chess and card games and inspired their mathematical followers to work *very seriously at games*.

To ask that one believe in the theory of relativity or in quantum mechanics seems to me a distraction or a piece of uncommon nonsense. Those theories can only persuade us, which is an effect produced entirely in our intellect, and only with this have they anything to do. They persuade us because "they are true," and they are true not for any emotional reason but because in them the theoretical "rules of the game" are complied with, those peculiar requirements which theory imposes on itself in order to be perfect within its own method. Neither more nor less. A few pages further we will come up against the tremendous fact that the most modern mathematics defines itself as a game, and this, with a very slight modification, confirms Poincaré's thesis which makes of mathematics a conventional entity, hence with a playful rather than an emotional nature.

In theory it is only a question of whether certain ideas which someone keeps propounding to us fit with each other or not, and when dealing with realistic theories such as physics whether they also fit the facts to which they refer. It is not then a question of *s'engager* or of *ne pas s'engager* or of all the other confusions of provincial "existentialism." [1]

But once we have recognized that theory has in it *something* of a game we have seen the light, as it were, saying to ourselves: "Yes, that's it!"—then we should go back a bit. The concept "game," encountered suddenly and in its entirety, contains an extraordinary wealth of styles, of ingredients, of dimensions. The first we see of it, almost deluging it with our attention, is that it breaks into the plural: games, the very different forms which go from children's games—and even those of baby animals—to the mortal effort of those who try to scale the Himalayas or of the bullfighter who dances with dedication and courage in the face of death. Halfway between these extremes are the scientific games of epic tension and skill, as in the case of the great chess players. I knew Capablanca and he seemed to me as serious in his dedication as Einstein, if not

1. The reader will note that by its mere *facies*, by its physiognomy, existentialism belongs to a style of life *prevailing* a quarter of a century ago. In fact Heidegger's book—which was a work of genius—was published just 20 years ago. But it has taken all this time to reach the province that Paris has been since the beginning of the century—a most curious case in which a "world capital" has evolved into a village and consequently has now *exploited* it. What I have called "low intellectual quarters" of the planet continue to be ascribed to Montmartre. This is most regrettable, for the world needs a capital and it is difficult to see how there could be any other capital unless Paris returns to that status—a Paris new "in form" without the *fête foraine* of the disgraceful Picasso, of pederasty and existentialism.

more so. The game is certainly one that cannot exist without particular seriousness in "sticking to its rules."

There is in the theorizer, above all in that outstanding form of theorizer which is the philosopher, a certain gratification common to the "decipherer of enigmas" in which the enigma momentarily loses all the zealous devotion which may *per accidens* envelop it and put it on a par with hieroglyphs, charades and crossword puzzles. This skill of players with the enigma, which the Greeks adored to a supreme degree, was well expressed in the legend about Homer when it says that he died of rage because he had not been able to solve the famous riddle of the lice which some fisher lads put to him. From the Sophists and Socrates until its end in Plotinus the whole of Greek philosophy moves in an atmosphere crowded with . . . crossword puzzles. In this sense Parmenides and Heraclitus themselves, despite their austerity, are "Homeric," men capable of dying because of an insoluble enigma.[2] Zenon was a Capablanca, but with a sense of humor which the latter lacked. He played at philosophy in a much stronger sense of the verb "to play" than Capablanca played at chess.

In this game of deciphering enigmas the philosopher creates an appearance of the Universe—like the poet, the painter, the creator of illusions.

2. In my *Origin of Philosophy*, I will show why this first generation of philosophers and *only this one* was somber and bad-tempered. Nietzsche, who, as I said before, wrote his essay—a splendid essay on "The Tragic Philosophy of the Greeks,"—did not know how to explore things thoroughly in their basic structure, although as always he had brilliant flashes of vision. He did not know how to explore them because, as the last romantic, he did not know how to be truthful. For him, as for so many thinkers of the 19th Century, to think was to juggle with ideas whether or not they matched reality. Nietzsche never came to know what tragedy was, or what philosophy was. He took up both subjects like a maniac—with the mania of Schopenhauer and Wagner and the "strong men" and other *fin de siècle* trifles. Not for one moment did he believe that thinking was as simple as opening the eyes and seeing. While he gesticulated, the humble Dilthey, hidden and quiet, without a murmur, looked . . . and saw. But Dilthey has never had a good press and now, posthumously, the saddest fate has overtaken him; the "pseudointellectuals" have fallen on him like a plague of cultural locusts.

Given the aspect of extravagance which at first glance the philosophies offer us—an aspect which we should not look down upon but should emphasize and let it influence our concept of the reality which is "philosophy"—we must first assimilate them (the philosophies) into art because of what art also has in it of play, of its lavish and exuberant "all or nothing" attitude. But we are not satisfied with accepting this accentuation of the side which we see as philosophy's "lack of seriousness."

In fact that very warning spurs us to ask ourselves, Good! But why does man do that? The best way of answering such a question begins by assaying the presumed suppression of what is asked for and then seeing how things would seem to have been at that time. If that which is suppressed is truly something real, its supposed absence will work again on the rest, on what remains, modifying it, and this will put us on the track of why the thing that was thought to be suppressed still exists. Well then, we have eradicated philosophy from Western history. What happens now? *Ipso facto* other human occupations come out to meet us and try to fill by expansion the spaces from which we have dislodged philosophy.

If for 26 centuries there had been no philosophy Western man would have fought to continue concerning himself only with religion, with mythology, with "experience of life," or with prudence (*sagesse*). On the other hand, poetry, which for those same centuries is *only* poetry, would have tried automatically, without anyone needing to propose it, to recover the meaning, equivocal to us, which it still had in Homer. For the Greeks of 750 B.C. to 500 B.C. (the probable period of time in which it flourished) the Homeric poems were not simply what we call poetry, but they *believed* in what they said, with a believing which turns like a sunflower to nonbelieving, but which was more, much more than mere complacency toward a legend as such. Our presumed suppression brings together those three "ways of thinking"—religion, myth, and poetry—so as to form a common front to capture human conviction. Poetry as a legend in which one quasi-believes is already a quasi-myth because this is formally *fabula*, which is what *mythos*—μῦθος—means, and a fable is what *is* fabled, *is* talked about, *is* recounted. The myth alternates between being a story and being a truthful account of a metaphysical, transcendental happening. One step more and we are in religion, which is believing tenaciously in a *certain idea of the Universe*. So poetry (in the sense of "Homeric poetry"), myth, and religion are three forms of believing, with different gradations, but among which there exists a perfect continuity, so that their reciprocal frontiers are indistinguishable. This continuity I call their "common front."

The myth is not a literary genre. *Mitopoeia* is an intellectual method which forges the World in which a people live for thousands of years. This method or mythic way of thinking consists in pure imaginative invention inspired by an extraordinary object, an outstanding deed, an event or a form that triggers emotion in men.[3] The mind reacts to this by inventing a narrative, recounting a "story" which is then accepted at face value. It needs no proof because no one subjects it to criticism, and no one subjects it to criticism for the simple reason that it does not encounter other inventions *different from and contrary* to it. It is the first "explanatory" interpretation.[4] Contrary to philosophy, mythology is a first type of thinking and does not start by opposing other preexistent opinions. Hence it is "ingenuous," paradisaic, and credulous. A first invention which "makes clear" to man something which is surprising is automatically "true," so much so that, as I said earlier, in mythological truth the distinction between truth and error is not yet even known. One knows only the intramundane

3. One of the things which most stands out and is most startling to archaic man is precisely the regularity in certain processes of nature, such as the regular rhythm of day and night and the seasons, the orderly reappearance of the sun, the moon, and the stars, and so on.

4. Before it there is the absolutely primogenitive, but this is not "explanatory" but merely practical: magic. Man has not known how to distinguish with precision these two successive strata of human mentality —primogenitive thinking, or magic, and visionary or mythological thinking.

contraposition of frankness and falsehood. The whole mythic invention works on those that are already there; it does not pretend to invalidate or contradict the earlier ones, but joins hands with tradition, develops it, and is rather a vegetative supergrowth on the initial invention like the unrestrained proliferation of a polyp, of a living piece of coral. Thus the mythic World goes on enriching itself, extending itself, and even becoming hypertrophic.

The "mythic" in its primary general character is *that* originary World or World of origins—the *Alcheringa* or *Alterta* of the Australians—a pre-World or first-born World, born before this one in which we live and characterized by the fact that things were possible in it which are now impossible; a definitely marvellous World, then, in which all the things that are now in our World, which is a post-World, a succeeding World, could be created, could be originated. Every important new, notable, and sensational event is referred to that World of marvels—that is to say, the myth absorbs the reality which *is there*, including the merely human and normal legend, the story, and by this the human hero is transformed and fused with God.

The myth which, as an intermediate link in the religion-mythology-poetry continuity, we can take as a key to clarify for us the other two ends of the triad, is on all sides, in the way it was received and produced and in its own content, the complete opposite of theory.

In its creation and its reception the myth assumes a type of man incapable of doubting—except in the practice of his own life—and completely indifferent to criticism with respect to the interpretation of the World with which he is provided. The myth is that which is "believable in itself," the "unquestioned." Its "truth" is not truth because of the particular content of what it states, but simply *because* it is tradition, because it is fabled and is anonymous. Like every collective usage it is irrational and is received, divulged, and transmitted mechanically. Hence the impersonality of its propagation. A myth which is personally created, a myth which bears the signature of its author at its foot, is as contradictory as would be, on the other hand, a scientific truth which does not have a personal origin.

As for its content, it is so opposed to the theoretically true that, as I have said, it consists essentially in the marvellous, in improbability itself. In it one tries to "explain" the realities that surround man, and what he is, assuming that at a moment different from all our historic times, or as the extremely primitive Hottentots say so admirably, in a "time which is at the back of time"—the mythic age—all the impossible things were entirely possible. In our time, when only the possible is possible, rocks cannot be created, nor plants, animals, men. The mythic time, on the contrary, is the season for all the creations, is the original age. In this substantial sense it is the World of the marvellous as such. Therefore the content of the myth is "poetic" par excellence, and one would have to ask oneself if there is, if there can be, other "things poetic in themselves" besides the mythological. Hence the emotional power which all its images retain. I have experienced it many times. When speaking in public, if I notice that my audience is slack, cold, insensitive, I resort to the great *Deus ex machina* of mythology and, opening the stable door, launch my centaur colts at a gallop. It is very difficult for an audience, confronted with the mythical galloping of these profoundly enigmatic and beautiful beings with flashing human eyes and trampling equine hoofs which make the earth resound, not to shudder to its very marrow. It is true that these constitute one of the most ancient imaginings of the Indo-European mind. The centaurs or *kentauros* are the Gandharva of Hindu culture.

What the Greeks properly caled "poetry" was concerned with mythical material in the same sense in which the poets of the French *gestes* in the 13th and 14th Centuries said they treated *la matière de Bretagne*, that is to say, the marvellous cycle of King Arthur and his twelve knights. This consisted in recounting or inventing mythical narratives. When doubt and criticism, "ideas" and theories, began in Greece the poets were contaminated, even those of the most traditional vocation, and there began that elegaic lyricism in which the poet expresses opinions, babbles, theorizes. That theory, practised by men not gifted for it, produced as a result something like that which, derived from other roots, would become the terrible rhetoric that ended by devouring the whole of Greco-Roman culture and becoming its last floating survivor. The humanists reabsorbed it and left the Occident infected *in aeternum* with rhetoricism. There is an anecdote of great interest from Plutarch referring to the moment when Corina, the old traditional poetess of Boeotia, threw in the face of her countryman Pindar—he being still young—the charge that he "made petulant use of logomachy" and was "amusical," unfaithful to the Muses, not managing instead "to make myths"— ποιοῦντα μύθους—*poioûnta mythous*, "which is the proper work of poetry. Locutions, figures of speech, metaphors, periphrases, numerosity, and rhythm are enchanting, but subordinated to the actions which are narrated." [5] And this in spite of Pindar having proclaimed his willingness to be a "reactionary" as compared with the other poets of his time who had turned into thinkers (gnomic poetry)!

The religion-myth-poetry common front *sensu Homerico* consists then in a purely imaginary interpretation of the World, and man would finally have had to take refuge in it had philosophy not existed. This confirms to us that man has no alternative but to believe, and if this fails him, to quasi-believe— with the most varied degrees of credulity—in the shape of what the World is, what he with his way of life is. Later all these serve in diverse forms the same inescapable function in the economy of human life.

The game does not oblige us to ask ourselves so peremptorily about its necessity because it seems superfluous by *antonomasia*. Perhaps it is not so, but *prima facie* there is no doubt that it is presented to us as something the absence of which would not be impossible. Hence, while we have seen its somewhat playful side, it did not appear to us as something which *in addition* is a

5. Plutarch, *De Gloria Atheniensium*, 4. See on this Wilamowitz-Moellendorf, *Pindaros*, 1922, p. 113.

serious thing, i.e., indispensable.

Now we see that there is in human life an indispensable function—that of having ready for man's use a repertory of "ideas" about what there is, of interpretations of his existence, and that philosophy is one way of building up that repertory along lines different from that common front.

Now then, philosophy reappears to us, after it was thought to be suppressed, affirming its genuine method—and again ousts its emulators, reoccupying the spaces from which we removed it and affirming its strong opposition to poetry, myth, and religion—which means that it represents unconditional hostility. Its attitude is negative in the inevitable measure in which it—philosophy—must affirm itself strongly in the face of these and other affirmations.

Because in the dialectic fantasy which we have just pictured, one essential note was lacking when we asked ourselves what would have happened if philosophy did not eixst. An attempt by that common front—religion-myth-poetry—to reoccupy the field of man's convictions would have failed lamentably, because philosophy, as we said, is born in view of the fact that man had lost all of his healthy faith in those things. Philosophy does not create doubt, but on the contrary, is engendered by doubt. It is folly to accuse Voltairianism of having caused disbelief when it is the opposite that is true. The poorest, most miserable thing is that when all is said and done Voltairianism appeared and performed those vain and formal posturings of which it consists, because men had ceased to believe. A hundred Voltaires compressed into a single pastille are not enough to create the slightest doubt in a man who is truly a believer. Hence I complained earlier that the continuing history of the "losses of faith" which have overwhelmed men so often in the human past has never been told in sufficient detail. That history would convince us that it is only ineluctable fate for every belief to expect a time to come when it will corrode and destroy itself.

It is then illusory to admit that, if philosophy had been suppressed, man would have gone back to believing with a normal and healthy credulity in religion, myth, and dogmatic poetry, as he did up to certain dates. What probably would have happened—and in many cases did happen in part—is that, having lost his ancient faith, and there being no real substitute for philosophy, man would have faced the Universe without any certainty; that is to say, faced with the enigmatic and equivocal facts of his life he would have been stupefied, without any adequate reaction to them. Well now, prolonged *stupe*faction engenders *stup*idity; hence, those periods of general imbecility in which history makes us participate. There would have followed a general degeneration of the human mind in which neither religion nor living myth nor luminous poetry would exist, but those voids in human conviction would have been stuffed with superstition, which is the form of mental life characteristic of the *mente capto*. It remains to be seen whether contemporary primitive man, rather than authentically primitive man, is not a degenerate fallen into atrocious stupidity and inert superstition.

The theme of the relation between philosophy and its fellows—religion, myth, and dogmatic poetry—would demand that certain far-reaching developments which are now hidden from me should be treated in similar fashion. I have already said that it was a capital and antihistorical error of Dilthey to see in those four things "permanent possibilities" for man, so that he could jump from one to another at any moment and be completely free to be religious or mythological, to be a "Homeric man" or a philosopher. Far from that, those four things constitute an inexorable sequence through which man passes at predetermined dates. The inescapable movement from one to another is part of human Destiny.

Now it becomes patent to us that what the philosophic occupation deals with is a very precise thing concerning which each individual would have to make his own decision, namely, as the need to interpret *what there is* is inexorable, does another way exist, when certain dates are reached, a better qualified way of confronting the enigma of living which is more *serious* and *authentic*, more *responsible* than philosophy? Subterfuges are of no use. Here we touch on the fact that the philosophic way of thinking is not one among many, nor is it just any one which we are free to adopt or not. Here we get a glimpse—though only a glimpse—of the fact that to be a philosopher, or to be "reason," or something like both things, is perhaps the human Destiny, because at a certain level in human experience it is the only suitable way of reaching the state of being genuinely oneself. But this is not to recognize that man *has been* and *is* philosophy, but on the contrary, it is to say that perhaps he *must be it*. Thus Reason appears, not as a gift which man possesses of himself—certainly he does not possess it of himself but goes slowly and lazily about acquiring it without having ever yet managed to possess it—but vice versa, a compromise that man makes with himself. To define man as a rational animal is a stupidity because he undoubtedly is an animal but—also undoubtedly—he has not arrived at being rational. He is simply on the way to it. Reason, far from being a gift which is possessed, is an obligation which one has, and like every utopian intention, very difficult to fulfill, because reason is in fact an admirable utopia and nothing more.

We see then that philosophy is neither a gift nor is it a permanent possibility, but rather an inescapable duty which we have toward ourselves, and, hence, it is of no use to say that philosophy also fails in trying to serve that essential function of life which is interpreting the Universe. As long as there is no other and superior new form, as long as man does not discover the ultraphilosophy, he must, whether he likes it or not and although he perpetually fails, keep on repeating his effort without pause, and this must be recognized as an effort which is necessarily perpetual and perpetually necessary.

But it is so essential to the real to "take sides" that man spends his life, and not by accident, saying to himself: "On the one hand . . . ," "on the other hand . . . ." Our mind, when it is what it should be, is a pendulum of meditation, and everything which is not this can be defined as brutish. Thus, turning once more to see what philosophy is, we cannot leave the last word on the side of inescapable duty, of necessary occu-

pation, of passionate seriousness, because it is theory, and theory breathes *velis nolis* in the halcyonic and laughing air of
sport and play. Hence, there would be nothing more alien to
the true face of philosophizing than to talk melodramatically
about its trying to *engager l'homme* in a doctrine. This would
be possible and would make some sense only if philosophy
were a "belief." But it is precisely the contrary, a theory, and
therefore something which is born of doubt and which, as we
shall see shortly, persists in it permanently. The verifying per-
suasion of truth is permanently nourished on uncertainty up
to the point at which truth, understood as it should be, in its
effective reality and therefore dynamically, consists in a cease-
less effort to overcome every possible doubt, which is equivalent to saying that doubt is the living core of truth.

Certainly philosophy is a most personal matter. In philosophy the philosopher stakes his life. He puts his life in play.
I just finished saying so. Philosophy and reason are two com-
mitments which man—the man which each one of us is—has
with himself.[6] But this does not mean in the least that when
man philosophizes he *s'engage*. *Quite the contrary*. The basic
obligation of the philosopher is to concern himself with the
substantially constituent doubtfulness of everything human,
and therefore the pledge that man makes to himself is *ne pas
s'engager*. The *engagement* is the most basic contradiction
which there could be in the very essence of the *theory which
is permanent revocability*. Following this, we are going to see
how theory is authentically exact, and the most rigorous philosophy has always been Platonism, and this because of its
core of skepticism. That it has not been made apparent how
Plato's teaching had perforce to be made up of exemplary
skepticism, and that Academic philosophy meant skeptical
philosophy, shows that there has been a very vague idea of
what theory is, of what philosophy is, and of what the history
of philosophy is. Because the matter is, we will see, as clear
and simple as "good morning." The term that best expresses

6. See *The Theme of our Time*, 1923 (*Obras Completas*, Vol. III,
p. 143).

the core of knowledge, insofar as exact thinking is concerned, is "skepticism"; man has no right to more, and he has an obligation to be skeptical. This is the level proper to the human being, a hypothetical animal who, as Plato taught for the ages, lives on hypothesis. When he ceases to be this, or does not achieve it, that stupidity and brutishness which are his most prominent tendencies begin to function automatically.

Hence an "existential philosophy" would be *a limine* impossible and a basic tergiversation. After the false step of letting it be influenced by Kierkegaard this has not been understood, because in Kierkegaard what is "existential" is not philosophy but religion, and in this he is completely right. Otherwise the result will be that the flow of water is reversed and the idea that the philosopher is obliged to *s'engager* in the truth in order to be a philosopher will bring with it—it already has—the implication that he will make of the fact of *engagement* the criterion of truth; then there will be given out as "philosophic truths"—there already are—the most exuberant and prolific idiocies and stupidities, like the glorification of the commonplace, and so on.

Philosophy is not a demonstrating with life what truth is, but the exact opposite, a showing what truth is so that, thanks to this, man can live genuinely. The rest is pretending to prove that two and two are four by dint of betraying confidence or letting oneself be betrayed. No, no, the philosopher cannot usurp the office of the martyr and leave him unemployed. The martyr is witness to the fact which is "belief," but not to that most subtle utopia which is Truth.

Let us then have done with intemperate melodramas and philosophize gayly, as is right and proper. Nor is there any reason why this demand should evoke attitudes of astonishment or offended dignity. That state of mind, that temper which I propose as appropriate to philosophy, the ancients—who knew more of these matters than we do—called joviality, that is, the vital tone proper to Jove, to Jupiter, to God the Father. Thus philosophy becomes an "imitation of Jove."

33
The Cartesian "Way of Thinking"[1]

WE LEFT OFF where Descartes was beginning his youthful *Rules for the Direction of the Mind* by proclaiming the communication of the genera in his denial that sciences exist individually or in the plural, as Aristotle claimed in opposition to Plato. According to the Cartesian doctrine there is then only one science, unique and integral. The first effect of this affirmation, coming as we do from Aristotle, is that we fail to understand it, or rather that we understand it only as the announcement of a "way of thinking" and an idea of knowledge in which traditional doctrines will be turned upside down. Consequently, we must prepare to witness a basic reform in the most fundamental of our inherited ideas. This is always a serious intellectual situation in which we run the risk of not understanding what new thing is said to us because it seems to us that the proposed innovation will not affect the deepest strata which we consider unchangeable. Hence it would be well for us to take certain precautions. The chief one will be to open wide the horizon of possibilities so as not to close our minds to ideas, considering them impossible *a limine*, ideas which, when they violate our habits of thought excessively, present an appearance which is extraordinarily paradoxical. As it can also happen that the innovator, in this case Descartes, may not develop his idea initially with all the fullness and maturity which is required if he is to make his point clearly and successfully, we are exposed to the danger of being caught in the tangle of an inadequate exposition

1. The paging of this chapter of the manuscript does not follow the preceding ones, so there is some doubt as to its place in the book as a new chapter; or whether, although written later, Ortega thought to interpolate it among the preceding ones. (*Compilers' note.*)

and being so seriously blinded that we cannot understand the initial idea, which is the truly important one.

The best way to avoid all this is to pause a moment before following Descartes into the exposition of his epistemological doctrine and see what we can with our own means extract from this simple statement: there is only one science instead of many which are distinguished by the variety of their subjects—*pro diversitate objectorum ad invicem distinguentas*.[2] After a little reflection, we will come to realize the following: it is unquestionable that objects present themselves to us as being different in kind and condition. If nevertheless there is a single science, this means that it does not derive its principles from the contemplation of things, because this would lead to a variety of principles and therefore to a plurality of sciences. But then principles can only originate in understanding itself, as and how it is previous to, or apart from, all contemplation of things. From those principles which are purely intellectual and chary of things, consequences can be deduced which will form a whole world of intellectual determinations, that is to say, of ideal subjects which are constructed by starting from them. This would be the kind of task of which science must consist if it is to be unitary. But this represents a most exaggerated tergiversation of what was believed to be knowledge. Cognitive activity once seemed to consist in an attempt to reflect, to mirror or to copy the world of real things in our own minds; and now it would appear to be the complete contrary, namely, the invention, construction or fabrication of an unreal world. Once science was developed, the relation of knowledge to real things would be reduced to looking at them through a network of fabricated ideal subjects and verifying whether they coincided with those real things to a sufficiently approximate degree.

The basic consequence to which this simple reflection has led us will give our march forward the dose of warning necessary for our understanding (despite the inadequacies of exposi-

2. *Regulae, Oeuvres,* Edition Adam et Tannery, Vol. X, pp. 360, 4–5.

tion) of what in the Cartesian reform of the way of thinking could resemble it.

The science that Descartes seeks must not contain *probable opinions* but must be a *perfecta scientia.*[3] This is characterized by its intolerance of doubt. Among the sciences "already invented" only arithmetic and geometry boast this privilege. To what do they owe it? We have only two paths to knowing: one is experience, the other deduction, or *inferentia pura unius ab altero.* Deduction never fails. When this seems to happen, it is due not to deduction itself, but to the fact that it has been based on false empirical assumptions. The error always originates when we assume as true something which experience, inadequately understood, suggests to us. Well now, this is what arithmetic and geometry avoid, because "they alone are occupied with an end so pure and simple that it allows them to assume nothing that might be subject to the uncertain character of the empirical, but which consists entirely in consequences that are deduced rationally." [4] By science, then, Descartes understands the deductive theory exclusively and he attempts to define the only way of thinking which makes it possible. This first formula is not very lucid. Nevertheless, what he follows it with will make his meaning a little clearer for us: science is made up of a body of propositions deduced rationally, i.e., strictly, the ones from the others. Such strict deduction is possible because the judgments or propositions which take place in it are "pure and simple." [5] The text that is cited makes this purity and this simplicity negative in character: that the judgments contain (*supponant*) nothing originating in the senses and, by the same token, imprecise and confused. To this note is immediately added another: indubitability. Judgment pure and simple "does not derive from the vacillating testimony that characterizes the senses,

3. *Ibid.*, X, 363.
4. *Ibid.*, X, 365.
5. Keep in mind that Descartes frequently uses the terms "objectum," concept, idea as equivalents among themselves, but also as meaning what we call judgment, proposition, statement or maxim, therefore, that which can be true or false.

nor from the fallacious criterion characteristic of our imagination which contrives stupid combinations, but it is a pure and
attentive conception of our mind, so easy and intelligible that
it should leave no room for doubt, or what is the same thing,
it is an indubitable conception of our pure and attentive mind
which has its origin only in the light of reason." That mental
action in which such a conception arises Descartes calls *intuition*. We could hardly explain what these expressions and
formulas are, for they themselves declare their inadequacy as
they are multiplied one by another, trying to correct themselves, if Descartes did not proceed with some examples. *In-
tuitio* is "that I exist, that I think, that the triangle is limited
only by three lines and the globe only by an outer surface." [6]
This is a matter, then, of a connection between two somethings—I and existence, a sphere and limitation to a single surface. To know by intuition (to intuit) is to *see* that connection, to understand it or take it into account and at the same
time to see it as necessary or beyond doubt. This necessity
does not have its basis outside the simple mental presence of
the connection. It is one and the same thing to think it and to
perceive that it cannot be anything else. This is what Descartes
calls "evidence." To intuit is to observe the necessary connections and therefore to think truths that are evident or *per se
notae*. For Descartes this is the intelligent act par excellence,
which he represents as a flash of light, an instantaneous illumination in which a truth as such is presented to us.

It is beyond question that some of the basic ideas of Descartes
coincide *one by one* with others of St. Augustine. But the
truth is that it has not been possible to prove persuasively
the Augustinian origin of Descartes' ideas because whatever
obvious coincidences they show, when taken one by one,
vanish when we take them as articulated together in terms of
their intentions, their movements, designs and results. It seems,
then, as fruitless to play down recognition of the coincidence
as it is to disregard the different emphasis given to each of
those ideas by both thinkers. I judge it more interesting to

6. Regulae, *Oeuvres*, Edition Adam et Tannery, Vol. X, p. 368.

try to define how the intellectual style of one of them resembles the other, because this would lead not only to explaining those coincidences, but also to greatly broadening the parallelism between them, i.e., to showing how they also "coincide" in not a few other things in which they appear not to coincide, and finally to illustrating the well known fact that the Cartesian school would turn out to be nourished in ensuing generations precisely by the Augustinians.

An example of what I have called coinciding in the non-coincident can be found in this same decisive point of man's acquisition of truth. St. Augustine and Descartes call the action in which it is acquired "illumination." But in St. Augustine the illumination which is the intelligent act proceeds not from man but is an operation of God in man (*De Civitate Dei*, VIII, c. 5), while according to Descartes intellective illumination is an action of the *lumen naturale*, if at the same time *nescio quid divini* [7] that man possesses, even more that it is man in his very self-ness. *Lumen naturale* is an expression handed down to moderns by Cicero, which he must have found in the Stoics for whom it had a full and juicy meaning, while in Descartes it has no such meaning, for his mechanical world is not properly "nature," and moreover man insofar as he is intelligent does not belong to it. With the same idea of shedding light they enunciate, then, two contradictory things. Nevertheless, on this same point of man's acquisition of truth we see that Descartes attributes to God the most fundamental intervention that can be imagined. In fact, according to St. Augustine, man sees truth through divine illumination, but that truth is truth in itself because it is rational—*rationes aeternae*. For Descartes, on the other hand, truth is not true in itself, or to put it another way, truth is not truth because it is rational, but on the contrary, it is rational because God wished to create that connection which is the substance of truth, as that which it necessarily is. The result is that the divine intervention rejected by Descartes as an act of illumination comes out even more basically in the object which that illumination

7. *Regulae, Oeuvres,* Edition Adam et Tannery, Vol. X, p. 373.

reveals. Note, by the way, how strange this is: for the man who initiated modern rationalism, rationality is in origin irrational and even necessity ends up as the great contingency.

Consequently, it would seem that we follow in the Aristotelian tradition, that the *intuito* is only the *noûs* of the Stagyrite, and that the basis of first truths is the evidence or characteristic of *per se notae*. But this is not certain. In Descartes all this has a very different significance. In the first place, the operation of the Aristotelian *Noûs* when fully understood consists primarily in capturing, touching, θιγγάνειν, (*thingánein*) the very Reality of a thing, or a thing as real. The truth of a thought as such, a thought, for example, of a proposition, follows truth as the capture of Reality itself by intelligence. Hence, the true proposition in Aristotle always transcends itself, it speaks of real things and defends them. The principle of contradiction proclaims that Reality itself cannot be contradictory. But in Descartes the connection which *intuito* observes and recognizes is a connection between ideas as such. Here truth is primarily a characteristic proper to the relation between ideas. In the second place—a consequence of the first—although evident or *per se nota* truth does not have an external source or reason, its evidence does not lack an internal basis. In fact, the consciousness of necessity in the connection of two ideas is based on the fact that these are simple. The simple idea does not permit error, just because of its lack of all internal multiplicity. Thus the relation between two simple ideas is always simple. We could say that the simplicity of the ideas when connection is studied does not give the mind much "play" nor much option in choosing between various observations, and in making a mistake.

Between two simple connections we discover, in turn, a new connection. This as connection is no less simple than the things connected, and the *intuito* which discovers it for us is also a simple act of intellection. But by the same token, this new act is found in a situation different from the primary ones. It sees the new connection, but its very simplicity keeps it from seeing each one of the two simple connections linked in it or through it at the same time. Its evidence refers only to the secondary connection. The two primary connections are not clear to it through actual evidence, but the truth of them is received by means of memory. This *intuito,* which starts from supposed truths and on the basis of them recognizes a new one, is therefore a function of knowledge different from the primary *intuito:* it is called *deduction.* Thanks to this we move some truths to others which form a "chain" of evident connections. The movement of the mind, which produces this "chain" and moves along it, is reasoning. The image of the chain appears in Descartes again and again. It expresses with imaginative force the relationship of evident connection between each two truths, the continuity of the whole series in deductive theory, and the methodic principle of which science consists in so ordering our ideas that it is passed from one to the other in an evident manner.

All this appeared to Descartes when in his inquiring youth he was obsessed with the way of thinking or method which the ancient mathematicians used to create arithmetic and geometry, particularly the latter, the prototype of the deductive theory for so many centuries, and equally so for him. In his judgment it was not possible that those doctrinal bodies would have been forming by chance through an accumulation of happy accidents. He believed firmly that the old mathematicians possessed a method, but he suspected that they hid it deliberately like a trade secret.[8] Only in periods which are

8. A good example of the deficient attitude in which historians exercise their commitment is that they have never thought seriously about this accusation of Descartes which attributes to Greek mathematicians nothing less than "culpable deceit"—*pernitiosâ quadam astutiâ.* This is not a matter of momentary bad temper, but it corresponds to the spirit with which Descartes always talks of the Greeks and not only of the mathematicians. In the Preface to his *Principles of Philosophy* he says that Plato "confessed frankly not having been able to find anything certain, and he contented himself with writing the things that seemed true to him, imagining for this some principles by which he tried to give reason for other things; whereas Aristotle was less sincere, and although he was Plato's disciple for twenty years and had no other principles than those he got from Plato, he completely changed the manner of stating them and set them forth as sure and certain without

very advanced does one find in Pappus and in Diofonto some indications of the mental process of which mathematics consists.[9]

According to Pappus there are two paths to follow in science: analysis and synthesis. Analysis starts from what is sought—(Getoŭmenon)—i.e., the problem itself, and, giving it as resolved in one sense, γεγονός (gegonós) takes it apart by following a certain order in the things which may be already known to us, and as a last resort in propositions which may have the value or rank of principles. In synthesis we proceed inversely: we start with these ultimate truths, and by ordering and combining them according to their nature we arrive at what we propose, namely, the substance of what is sought.[10]

Descartes had studied Pappus very attentively, notwithstanding his dislike of reading. It is most probable that he also knew Proclus' commentary on Euclid's work in which the latter insists on both methods. But, let it be said in passing, the invention of the analytic method is attributed to Plato, who taught Leodomas, his mathematical pupil. Leibnitz certifies that the famous problem which carries the name of Pappus had been proposed by Golius in 1631.[11] Well now, the meditations dedicated to solving it were the occasion when the idea of analytical geometry came to full fruition in Descartes.[12]

The statement by Pappus is very sober. It does not even try to be a theory, much less philosophical. It is a simple reflection

giving the slightest inkling that he never esteemed them as such." The thing is highly important. Descartes was not content with declaring Aristotle's doctrines erroneous, but classed him formally as a falsifier and disingenuous. How can one help pausing at such an enormity? If it is anything, history is an effort to understand human deeds and events. Here is a human occurrence of the highest rank, because of him who says it, because of him of whom it is said, and because of what is said.

9. Regulae, Oeuvres, Edition Adam et Tannery, Vol. X, p. 376.

10. Altenburg, Die Methode der Hypothesis bei Platon, Aristoteles und Proclus, 1905, pp. 23 ff.

11. Philosophie Schriften, IV, 316.

12. It is known that from earliest youth the mathematical production of Descartes changed in this direction, as on another side Desargues precedes him in the geometric-analytic treatment of certain problems. See Gaston Milhaud, Descartes Savant, 1921.

by a mathematical creator on what he finds himself surprised to be doing. In it he tells us neither which are the conditions of that which is "sought," whether it be problem or question, nor which are the requisites of the principles.

Science undoubtedly proposes to know things, but these as such do not enter into science. They must first be converted into questions. These are the points of departure of the cognitive operation. Hence it would be of the highest importance to determine precisely what a scientific question is. This is not simply something of which we are ignorant. There is in the question something clearly unknown and this moves us to exercise the effort to know. But that something which is unknown must appear determined in some manner, and that determination must consist in something which is already known to us. Every question, then, breaks down into two parts: the unknown, and the data which determine that it is in fact unknown. If a question does not have these characteristics, no matter how interesting it may seem, science will have nothing to do with it. For the deductive theory, then, there are no absolute problems but only those relative to certain data. These apportion continuity between what we know and what we do not know but can know.

They are, then, compound questions, and their solution will consist in taking them apart until their ultimate simple ingredients are reached. These cannot be a question because they are evident or *per se notae*.

The relation between genus and species which made the Aristotelian-Scholastic way of thinking function was replaced by the relation between composite and simple ideas.

Appendix 1: Concerning Optimism in Leibnitz

THE TERCENTENARY of the birth of Leibnitz occurred last year [1] and the Spanish Association for the Advancement of the Sciences wanted the inaugural address, given when its members met, to pay honor to so famous a figure in Western thought. Although the planned reunion had to be postponed until this year, and the date of the homage was not that of the actual tercentenary, it nevertheless seemed to them that the initial plan should be carried out. It was not right that this Association should fail to devote one of its meetings to the memory of one of the most powerful minds with which the destiny of Europe has been inspired. It has been said many times, and not without reason, that if Aristotle's was the intellect having the most universal capacity in the ancient world, so was the mind of Leibnitz in the modern world. Of the basic disciplines of the "intellectual sphere" there is none which Leibnitz did not possess and, what is more surprising, none on which he did not leave a creative imprint. He renews logic in a most original form, he broadens the domain of mathematics in a fabulous manner, he reforms the principles of physics, fertilizes biology with new hypotheses, purifies juridical theory, modernizes historical studies and gives linguistics new horizons by proposing the great theme of comparative grammar. On top of all this, he constructs a philosophic doctrine which in its details is one of the most complete and most beautiful that has ever existed.

There would have been more than ample reason for considering Leibnitz as the man who symbolizes the intellectual

1. Leibnitz was born in 1646 [*Translator's note*].

destiny of Europe in the most intense, complete, and refined form. But by the same token, as every destiny is determinate and has its limits or deficiencies, Leibnitz also symbolizes the limitations and defects of our culture. Apart from his personal gifts of an almost mythological quantity there were also circumstances which contributed to making Leibnitz that symbol of faults. In fact it was in his time that the civilization of Europe attained its maximum integration. A civilization is a gigantic welding together of principles and standards, of usages and illusions, at the same time that it is a social integration of human beings living together within boundaries, within nations, into an ultranational area over which certain ways of being a man hold sway, with consequent solidarity. The process of achieving a civilizing integration is extremely slow, difficult, and full of problems. It is always in danger of not being achieved, and when it is achieved it is always in danger of falling short of complete achievement. Many centuries are needed for a civilization to organize itself, and three or four generations are enough for a civilization to disappear. One can say that around 1700, the European way of human existence attained its *maximum in form*, that is to say, a greater number of men living within the territorial limits of our continent and its islands were reached by a greater number of principles reduced to organic unity than before or since.

The mind of Leibnitz is the most perfect and complete expression of that fortunate hour. In it the heritage of classical antiquity converged with the rehabilitation of the medieval past and the highly potent innovating effect of the sciences which characterize modernity. In that millenary movement of European integration there had, however, been one seriously disintegrating event, the division of Christianity into divergent professions of faith which occurred during the 16th Century; this was accompanied by a growth, unimaginable until then, of what were called "Libertines," that is, men freed from religious faith. A secondary manifestation of this event was that the link between religion and reason does not usually appear clearly among the men of science who were active during the second half of the 16th and first part of the 17th Centuries, although personally they were not "Libertines" and even more they personally held to a living faith. Men like Bacon, Galileo, Descartes managed in their scientific work to disregard anything that might infringe the themes of dogma. It would be a mistake to attribute this to any latent irreligiosity there might be in them. Among those three men attitudes toward religion are undoubtedly different, but the most cautious of them, who was Descartes, makes his religious fervor clear to us.

We are dealing, then, with an imperative of the period. The change that was soon produced confirms it. As a matter of fact the two generations born around 1626 and 1641—which includes a Malebranche and a Leibnitz—are, perhaps, those that most effectively united religious inspiration with rational thought. A curious expression of this, in terms of light caricature if you like, is the physician and biologist Dodart—born in 1634—who, as Fontenelle tells us in his *Elogio,* takes advantage of the Lenten fast to study its effects on the organism and weighs himself, only to find that in 46 days he has lost eight pounds and six ounces, or the fourteenth part of his substance, and that later he had gained back four pounds in four days. I cite this anecdote only to make clear, in the briefest and therefore most pointed form, how the person of Leibnitz coincides with a new impulse toward integration in European life, an impulse so mature and so full of energy that it proposed to correct that single disintegrating event which our civilization suffered in its upward progress toward unity. For it was then that Europe came—I will not say nearest to but certainly the least far from—achieving a reunion of the Christian professions of faith. To this undertaking Leibnitz, as is well known, dedicated a great part of his effort and his enthusiasm.

In the old manuals of the history of philosophy the Leibnitz doctrine was called "eclecticism." As philosophy, among all human undertakings, is that which most essentially demands a unitary inspiration, to say of a philosophy that it is eclectic is equivalent to saying that it is no philosophy at all.

The doctrine qualified by that word presents itself to us as a patchwork of heterogeneous fragments held together by an intention outside themselves; there could be no image less faithful to Leibnitzian thought. Leibnitz was not an eclectic, but quite the contrary, an integrator of genius, that is to say, a mind which succeeds in transforming that which is multiple and in appearance divergent into genuine unity. The error which that charge of "eclecticism" implies arises from attributing the great enterprise of theoretic unification which Leibnitz achieved to a personal bent which led him more to affirming than to denying, more to conciliation than to polemic. Hence it was right to make it clear, although as concisely as possible, that the movement of integration does not spring from the psychology of Leibnitz, but vice versa; Leibnitz is an integrator because the whole history of Europe, having reached the culmination of its progress, determined that magnificent project and made it possible. Of himself, Leibnitz put into it the capacity to raise it to a peak with his exceptional gifts and the circumstances of his education which allowed him to absorb almost all the principal disciplines when still an adolescent. Nevertheless it is well to remember the odd fact that Leibnitz, who was one of the greatest mathematicians that ever lived, had no acquaintance with anything more than elementary mathematical science until after he was twenty-six years old, when he made a trip to Paris and lived there with contemporary men of science. This is a symptom of the state in which the devastating Thirty Years War had left the intellectual life of Germany.

But I do not think that the most fruitful way of filling the brief space at my disposal would be to devote it to making a vain attempt to draw the historic figure of Leibnitz in full, or even to outline the structure of his philosophic system, whose refinement, ingenuity, and precision would be obscured for us if we were to compress it unnaturally. I think that it might be somewhat more fruitful to do just the opposite: to take from his doctrines one particular thesis which would tolerate, without too much violence, being separated from the others, although not from all of them, and because time does not permit more, to announce the subjects of some new investigations to which this invites us. To this end nothing would seem to me more fitting than the most famous, most popular of his pronouncements: the doctrine of optimism.

If we could take for granted an acquaintance with this doctrine, we could begin at once to state the points of view about it which I consider basically new, and which, moreover, are in my judgment decisive for the future of philosophy. But I cannot accept that assumption. In spite of the fact that Leibnitz is not a thinker with an obscure style, but on the contrary, has the most pellucid one that ever existed, it happens that this style is very seldom practised and therefore is very little known. One symptom of this is the incredible scarcity of books about his work and his person which makes him, of all the great philosophic figures, the one who has been least studied. Even more striking is the lack of new editions of his published treatises and letters, and the scandalous fact that a good part of his manuscripts continue unpublished. So I see myself obliged to spend the best part of the time allotted me in a brief development of what is strictly necessary so that the Leibnitzian doctrine of optimism may be transparently clear and powerful. Here is the proof that this is necessary. For my own part I would limit myself to citing the following paragraph, in which Leibnitz sets this doctrine forth:

"From the Supreme Perfection of God it follows that in producing the Universe He chose the best possible Plan, in which the greatest variety is given in the best possible order; in which the terrain, the place, and the time remain best arranged; in which the greatest effect is produced in the simplest way; in which there is the maximum of power, of knowledge, of happiness and of goodness that the Universe can absorb. Because all these possibles, pretending to an existence in God's understanding which is proportionate to His perfections give as a result of all these pretensions the most perfect actual

World which is possible. Without this it would not be possible to give the reason why things are as they are, and not otherwise."

Let us not deceive ourselves. Whoever reads or hears those phrases today without previously knowing Leibnitz's thought cannot realize what they mean. As they speak of God and Supreme Perfection he will think that they deal with theological statements, or with those that are merely mystical. Nevertheless, all their expressions designate concepts of such strict rationality that, combined as they are with the greatest theoretical precision, they constitute an admirable doctrinal edifice. Let us then try briefly to make this explicit.

Man needs to understand what is important to him. What is important to him is his actual situation, what we are accustomed to call reality, that which exists, the world in which we are. Man would not need to comprehend reality or, what is the same thing, there would be no question for him, aside from reality, if man were—as is the stone—only one reality within the great reality which is the world. But not only must we cope with reality, but we also find ourselves at the same time with possibilities. For example, we think that there *could* very well be no reality, that it *could* very well be that nothing exists. We also think that there *could* be a real world which is very different from the one that now exists. On the basis of these possibilities the reality of the world loses its firmness, becomes questionable, is converted into an enigma. Why is there something and not simply nothing? Why is the something that is, this and no other? As one sees, the presence of mere possibilities is more decisive for man than the very reality in which he is prisoner. They interpose themselves between us and the real world. Leibnitz was the one who first saw clearly that man is not, as is the stone, inside reality in a direct or immediate way. The fact of our being in reality is extremely strange: we are always arriving at it from the outside, from possibilities. The matter is much simpler in the concrete than when said this way in the abstract. Those who are now here, in the reality which is this room and this assembly, have not just happened to come here from their homes or from the hotel, or from the street, but have come out of a combination of possibilities which was offered to them for occupying this hour of their lives. Being here was only one of those possibilities. In preferring this one and coming here they have in fact abandoned, have refused the other possibilities, among them that of remaining at home, or in the hotel, or in the street. These three things, these three different possibilities of the situation in which they are, were possibilities from which, in brief, those who came here had retired or retreated.[2]

This very trivial example will enable us to understand how Leibnitz recognizes that reality is a problem to us and obliges us to exert ourselves to understand it when it arises as one possibility among other possibilities,[3] or to put it differently, that the real is, first of all, possible. This leads Leibnitz to construct an ontology of the possible being. It is customary to

2. The "being here now" has passed from being only one possibility among several to being a reality. The change was produced because it was preferred, and it was preferred for some motive, what we commonly call "some reason." The reality of our being here now does not appear isolated and casual, to put it that way, or in the air, but it is motivated. Its basis, its foundation goes with it, inseparably. If we should examine with an analytical microscope the motive, reason, basis, or foundation which made each one prefer to come here, we could find ourselves with a most various casuistry, but despite all that variety we would find that in all of them there was the same element, namely, that to do this seemed to them the *best*, that is, the best way to spend this hour of their lives. Let us remember, without insisting on it, that the hours of our lives are numbered, that therefore it is not a matter of indifference how they are utilized, that this is what obliges us to spend them in the best possible way, and that, in this order, we understand by "best" doing that which most adequately realizes among our possibilities the I which each one feels that he must be. Thus our reality emerges with the character of being the best possibility.

[The notes of this speech, which appear in the original manuscript, were not included in the text as read.]

3. Among these the most surprising, most paradoxical, most disquieting is that in place of reality there would have been only Nothing. Nothing is without question man's most original idea. All the others can spring more or less indirectly out of the things there are, but the idea of Nothing could never have been suggested by anything. Nothing is precisely no thing.

believe mistakenly that "ontology" is a Scholastic term, when it was actually created by the first philosophy which managed to win an advantage over Scholasticism, namely, Cartesianism. The Cartesian Clauberg was the first to give that name to the discipline which is concerned with the *Ens* as *Ens*. Christian Wolff, a disciple of Leibnitz, popularized the name, thanks to the extensive influence which his didactic work achieved all over Europe. The possible is not simply nothing, it has a consistency and therefore it *exists*. The possibility of the possible consists in not including contradiction or, to turn it around, all that does not include contradiction *is*. The proof of this lies in the fact that everything which does not include contradiction can be stated in propositions from which theorems and entire systems of truth can be derived. Because of this it has been possible to construct innumerable geometries starting simply from axioms that do not include contradiction. The being of the possible is a diminished being, but it is a being. To use the term employed by certain Scholastics of the 13th and 14th Centuries we might call it the *Ens diminutum*. Leibnitz calls the possibles "essences." 4

4. Well now, although possibility as such possesses no complete being, but only one which is diminished or weakened, it should be understood that possibility is, in itself and always, the possibility of a full being. This is a point of Leibnitzian thought which is insufficiently clarified, but there is no doubt that he saw the possible as something which possesses a tendency to be real. To show this it is enough to remember that he defines existence—hence reality—as *exigentia essentiae*. What does this mean but that the essences insist upon being made real, that *omne possibile exigit existere?* The being of the essences or possibles is eternal. They never began to be. They were not created. Their way of being is to be eternally present in the divine understanding, which can be said to consist of them themselves insofar as they are eternally present. But they are not content with being there but exercise pressure "claiming to exist." Leibnitz had a dynamic conception of being in all its gradations. It is not strange, then, that even in the mere possibility, in spite of the fact that its makeup is nothing more than not including contradiction, there should be a tendency, an effort, a pretension, all terms which he uses for this purpose. What is there about possibility in itself that we must picture to ourselves as inert and static this dynamic characteristic which compels it to exist? We will soon find out.

Meanwhile let us underline these two things: first, that the possible includes all Being, while the real being is only one of the possibles;

Parallel to the doctrine of the possible or essential being, there marches in Leibnitz the doctrine of the true or logical. Truth, according to our philosopher, is the truth of the proposition. But while Descartes makes the truth of the proposition consist in the evidence by which two concepts appear to us as linked—what he called the method of clear and different ideas—Leibnitz distrusted the individual subjective factor which is active in all evidence, and considered it indispensable to find, as the criterion of truth, a formal character which guarantees it with the automatic efficiency proper to all formalism. Thanks to its simple form a proposition is false when it states a contradiction. Contradiction is falsehood because it destroys the meaning of a proposition, making it say nothing. The form of a true proposition will then be the form capable of declaring that it excludes contradiction. This is the form of the identical proposition: *A* is *A*. In it the predicate appears clearly as included in the subject or, to put it another way, there is nothing in the predicate except what was already in the subject. This is what the term *is* [5] states, in its pure form as a copula, therefore in its strictly logical significance: it means *to be* in the sense of in-being, *inesse*, inclusion, "being in"—

---

second, that the possible being, we would say, composed of noncontradiction and therefore of identity, coincides in structure with the structure of concepts or, what is the same thing, is wholly logical, coinciding in its constitutive law with the laws of thinking, and is left therefore to penetrate totally into this; in sum, that Being is basically intelligible. In Leibnitz, in fact, the rationalism which since then has done nothing but shorten sail reaches its most extreme form.

But what, for Leibnitz, is it to "understand"? Simply this—to perceive something as identical. Intelligence is advance warning of the truth, and truth is identity: *A* is *A*. Here is the prototype of all the "eternal truths" which are such because something appears in them that excludes contradiction. The propositions which are not identities have the character of eternal truths when they can be reduced by analysis to a mere complication of identities. That operation of reducing the nonidentical to identity is what constitutes reason, because the proof consists in this. Reason is giving the reason for something, proving it.

5. English readers may have trouble here because the two Spanish verbs, *ser* and *estar*, both carry *to be* as their English equivalents. *Ser* means "to be" in the permanent sense of existence, *estar* is a verb of temporary location—to be here, to be ill, and so on [*Translator's note*].

one concept in another. Identities are the true prototypes or, as Leibnitz calls them, the *vérités premières*. There are no evident truths, because nothing is without reason. Every truth must be proved. The special privilege of identical propositions is that one need not go beyond them to prove them. Their form as identities demonstrates them, that is, gives the reason why we join the predicate to the subject, namely, because it was already joined, included in it. Truths that are not identical must be proved by showing that they can be reduced to identical propositions. How can this be done? By means of what Leibnitz calls the "analysis of concepts." Breaking the concept of a subject and a predicate into its elements we can, by a series of intermediary identities, establish a continuity of identification between concepts which at first sight appeared to be different. In this operation in which the nonidentical is reduced to the identical lies what Leibnitz most accurately calls "reason."

Let us pause here a moment and underline what all this represents. The possible being includes all Being since the real being is no more than one case of the possible being. But the possible, we would say, includes noncontradiction and therefore identity, which in turn are the principles of thought in form or logic. The result is that Being is completely logical, coincident in its constituent laws with the laws of thinking; therefore, that the one lets itself be totally penetrated by the other; in short, that Being is fully intelligible. Man's understanding is limited, but intelligibility is unlimited to the extent that it exists. In Leibnitz rationalism reaches its culmination.

But does not a tendency to wishful thinking underlie all this? Is it certain that the form of identity guarantees the truth of a proposition? Let us cite an example, and instead of adducing just any one let us make the most of the occasion by taking a sidewise glance at the attitude of Leibnitz toward the ontological proof of the existence of God which St. Anselm put forth and which Descartes had renewed a short time before Leibnitz. If there is one thinker whose mental style would lean toward accepting that proof it is certainly Leibnitz. Ontological proof actually consists in showing that predicated existence is already included in the concept of God, of the *Ens perfectissimum,* since existence is the most typical perfection. Nevertheless we see Leibnitz vacillate before it, and the closer he comes to admitting it the more he does this with distinctions and reservations and additions. Here is the reason why. In order for it to be true that the most perfect Ens exists, it is necessary that the most perfect Ens be most perfect. We would have an identical proposition, and therefore a *vérité première.* But Leibnitz, who comes from handling the most intricate mathematical problems, above all that of the infinite and the continuum, approaches ontological proof as the singed cat approaches the fire. He has learned in mathematics to distrust superlatives. Mathematical concepts which *prima facie* seem obvious turn out to be impossible when they involve contradiction; for example, the concept of maximum velocity or that of the greatest number of all the numbers. The rationalist enthusiasm of Leibnitz, his faith in intelligibility, in the logical character of being, must have suffered an enormous trauma when, in a region as close to pure logic as numbers and magnitude, he discovered an abyss of irrationality. Again and again he is heard to complain of what he calls the *labyrinthus difficultatum de compositione continui.* The continuum is an ens which is essentially contradictory; it is, yet nevertheless, it is irrational. The continuum is at the same time divisible and indivisible. It can be divided, but from each division it is always born newly undivided. (Because of its continuity, space and everything spatial does not, according to Leibnitz, have "real existence" but is a "phenomenon." What makes it a phenomenon is the appearance of genuine reality which the subject has. That appearance is confused, and hence at the end is not reducible to the character of logic. It is the "perspective" in which reality is presented and as "perspective", at once subjective and *well founded,* it is motivated in reality itself.) Well then, before a proposition like this: the most perfect Ens is most perfect, Leibnitz becomes aware—and he makes it clear that this concept leads him to it—that for a proposition to be true it is not enough that it be identical. It is necessary first to be sure that the concept of the subject is possible, that it involves no contradiction such as is involved in the concept of a greatest number. Therefore he will say that the ontological proofs of St. Anselm and Descartes—disregarding their differences—are insufficient, and that the only thing they prove is something conditional, namely, that *if* the concept of the most perfect Ens is possible it is indubitable that it includes existence. (It would be an error to cling to the formulation of the ontological proof which Leibnitz gives in the *Monadology*, Chapter 45. What he expressed there is not compatible with the many places where the philosopher makes a formal question of it and discusses it with care. The best course is to keep in view all those steps in which Leibnitz is concerned with this proof. Then what in fact was his opinion is seen clearly, and at the same time the indecision and the caution that he introduced into his statements are acknowledged. Keep in mind that the formulas of the *Monadology*, although often the most impressive, are in many cases the least faithful to the author's authentic thought.)

If Leibnitz had attentively followed this road, or, as he himself called it, the *filum meditandi*, he would have come to the precise situation in which we find ourselves today when facing all logicism and even logic itself, a situation which is strictly opposed to the movement that he initiated in logic and in mathematics, and which, in an ascending and apparently triumphant march, continued until the second decade of this century.

It is not enough, then, to reduce the nonidentical to pure identities so that thought may be logical. It is necessary to be sure that the concepts themselves are individually possible, that is to say, that they do not involve contradiction. For this, one of these two things would be necessary: first, to arrive at concepts that are absolutely simple, although the fact of arriving at them does not prove that they are simple. Second, to prove that a concept does not involve contradiction in any of its consequences. Note that when in recent times an attempt has been truly made to construct a body of logic, which up to now was a mere project, a *desideratum*, and as I said before in a trivial phrase, but very deliberately, a bit of wishful thinking, it has been found that it is not possible to demonstrate of a concept that it will not imply contradiction.

Here is one of those points which I would have liked to develop on this occasion, one of those themes which, as I stated, basically affect the future of philosophy as well as the future of sciences, and therefore the destiny of Western man. To commemorate the intellectual figure of Leibnitz leads inevitably to facing up to this tremendous question. Because Leibnitz and the trend which he initiated—a trend, I repeat, which remained dominant until the beginning of this century —represent the golden moment in which man believed most fervently that he in fact possessed an infallible instrument with which to interpret reality and to know what to cling to with respect to it: logic. I do not wish to frighten anyone, much less so when penalties of so many sorts and kinds vex all the living, until it seems not exorbitant to doubt that anyone in this world today is happy. But in an "Association for the Advancement of the Sciences," and on an occasion set aside to render homage to Leibnitz, a homage which obliges one to note his limitations, it seems to me inescapable to declare the following:

When wars and social conflicts interrupted scientific work the two exemplary disciplines—logic and mathematics—had entered into what was called a "crisis of principle." This means, plainly and frankly, that logic, the court of last resort to which was referred everything that was questionable, had itself been questioned. I want to keep within this euphemism. Therefore, when those conflicts lapse and that calm returns which Aristotle called *skolé* and Descartes called *loisir*, but which both coincided in considering indispensable for scientific work, there will be no choice but to submerge oneself resolutely in the abyss which the questionability of logic proclaims. The problem is terrifying, but if philosophy is to continue as a human occupation there will be no choice but to confront it, because philosophy was born precisely as a resolution to maintain serenity in the face of the most terrifying problems. Its initiators, those men who for the first time found themselves exercising a way of thinking which later would be called philosophy, and which disclosed to them the first visions of the real which are reached only by means of pure concepts, did not know how to master the very thing that they surprised themselves doing. Not to have a name is a sign that something is new. In relation to creative thought the language is always archaic. One should have paid more attention to the efforts which those men employed in order to put a name to what they were doing. It took a series of agitated efforts to say the new with old words which therefore meant other things already known. Parmenides above all, the first man who philosophized, searches in his poem for expressions with which to make clear to others what constitutes the new mental path which he has discovered, and among them there is one which seems to me magnificent. In order to state, on the one hand, the unheard of character of universality or totality proper to the theses which men later called philosophic, and on the other hand, the paradoxical character of those theses which makes them fly in the face of all inherited opinions and, by the same token, assume courage in whoever decides to accept them, and even more in those who decide to proclaim them, Parmenides will call his discipline "the rounded truth of the intrepid heart." [6] Hence, I said that philosophy cannot evade a resolute confrontation of terrible problems.

But from the rapid glance which we have cast at the logic of Leibnitz—without which his optimistic doctrine would not be clear to us—let us return to his ontology of possible Being which, as I said, includes all Being. The possibles or essences consist in not implying contradiction, that is to say, in not being impossible. But at the same time possibility means the possibility of "real existence." For a reason that will emerge later I hold to the terminology of Leibnitz himself. In the brief

6. Diels, Fragment I, v. 29: ἀληθείης εὐκυκλέος ἀτρεμὲς ἦτορ.

treatise *De rerum originatione radicali* [7] he calls essence *realitas possibilis*. For Leibnitz the possible is its option to exist. Right there he gathers together the expressions which designate, on the part of all that is possible, this propensity to exist. Thus we read: "Given that something actually exists, and not simply nothing, it is essential that in possible things, there be in the possibility or essence itself, a requirement to exist, or to put it another way, a claim to existence, and to express it in a single turn of speech, that the essence in itself tends to existence." At first this is not understood. Applying Leibnitz's most characteristic principle, which in his judgment is the principle of all thinking, namely, the *principium rationios reddendae*, the intellectual imperative that it is necessary to give a reason for everything, we do not see why it would be enough that something is not impossible for it to have a claim, and therefore some right to exist. Possibles are eternal. They have no beginning. They are not, as Descartes thought with the Nominalists of the 14th and 15th Centuries, arbitrary productions of the divine will. The being of the possibles is rooted in being eternally present before God's understanding: strictly speaking they are the perennial act of that understanding. Well now, God is for philosophy strictly the cause of Existence prevailing over nonExistence, or in other words, of there being something rather than nothing. God is *Existentificans*. But as no one possible shows any reason for existing more than and before any other possible, the source of existence which is God is extended equally over all, of them and this is the reason why *omne possibile habeat conatum ad Existentiam* or, as he will say, with an expression of the most bearded Scholastic Gothicism, that "*omne possibile Existiturire*"—that everything possible is in the future of existing.[8]

But this does not carry with it that all the possibles attain existence, because while each possible excludes its internal contradiction and hence is possible, this is not to say that there

7. *Philosophische Schriften*, Hg. C. J. Gerhardt, VII, 302.
8. *Philosophische Schriftsn*, VII, 289.

is no contradiction between them. In order to exist together it is essential that they be compatible or, as Leibnitz says, *compossibiles*. Many of the possibles, then, mutually obstruct each other in achieving existence. Even within the same sphere of possibility, they turn out to be inept in forming the unity of multiplicity which is a world. This represents a first selection among the possibilities for attaining existence. What is left are the groups of "compatibles." Each one of these aggregates is a possible world. Why is it that of all those possible worlds our own is the actual world which actually exists? Our world is a fact or, if you wish, an immense aggregate of facts. But among all those facts there is none which grants our world the right to exist. Its existence is unjustified, of itself it has no reason to exist. Hence it is something irrational. Let it suffice to consider that while the contrary of the possible is impossible—and this is why the possible is homogeneous with the logical, rational, and intelligible—the contrary of the real world is not impossible: many other worlds could exist which are therefore possible; even more, it is not impossible that no other should exist, that there might be nothing. This possibility of its contradiction is what makes the existent world *prima facie* irrational, and what Leibnitz understands by being a fact. Scholastic terminology called this *contingentia*. But Leibnitz does not surrender his rationality before the opacity of the fact which is the world. Following the intellectual style which his logic revealed to us, a style that consists in a Utopian and idealizing form of thinking, he will tell us that the irrationality of the fact is only apparent and related to our limited intelligence. If we, like God, could have in mind all that this world contains, and in addition all the other possible worlds, it would appear to us as a strictly logical consequence just why it is this world which exists and not the others. What makes the fact, the existent reality opaque to pure logicality is the accumulation—excessive to us—of reasons. There would be so many reasons with which to deal in order to deduce this world —as a mathematical theorem is deduced or a syllogism concluded—that these reasons are stacked and compacted like the

coral polyps in the sea, and as these form the islands in which
the individual coral ceases to be visible, so from pure rational
being reality is made impenetrable, unintelligible to us.

The possible being constitutes a luminous sphere into which
our reason penetrates in order to obtain the "eternal truths"
of logic and mathematics, although in this last the pellucid
zones begin. Before the fact of the world, on the other hand,
we must descend to a second form of rationality which contains the *vérités de fait* or contingent truths. It is not enough
for us to reach these and hence make the existent intelligible
to us, with the principle of contradiction directing our steps
in a purely logical sphere. We need another principle which
gives rise to another type of reason, of intellection, different
from that which consists of mere awareness of identities.

For Leibnitz a world is an aggregate of essences. Let us note
in passing that his idea of the world is his least refined idea
because deeper reflection would lead him to see that the world
does not result from the aggregate of its parts but that, inversely, in order that a thing may be there must have been a
world in relation to which the thing is. But let us now leave
this difficult matter. Worlds would be collections of possibilities compatible or compossible with each other. Some would
contain a greater quantity of possibles than others. Since the
possible is, as we said, *realitas possibilis* where *reality* means, as
with the Scholastics, not existence but positive being as opposed to deprivation and negation, we would have a world
among the possibles which would contain a *maximum* of realities, hence a maximum of positivity. But for this purpose that
world must also be organized with a *maximum* of order, otherwise the realities would hinder each other, that is to say, some
of them would render each other impossible. But, in turn, a
maximum of order implies that it be obtained through a *maximum* of simplicity in the way it is ordered. All those characteristics derive, then, through the very assumption of maximum reality.[9]

9. If anyone should assure us beforehand that our world is that which,
among the possibles, has more realities that anyone can think of, with

We have now reached the crucial point of the Leibnitzian doctrine and it is appropriate that we make an effort to understand it precisely.

In the sphere of possibility there is no room for a more or a less; I mean to say that one thing cannot be more or less possible than another. It is either possible or it is impossible, *tertium non datur*. Therefore that possible world which contains maximum reality or possibility and, so far as possible, maximum order and maximum simplicity, is no different from that which may contain fewer of these qualities. Which means that the step from possibility to existence is an absolute step.

But the world exists. That is the fact. Therefore that absolute step was taken. There was, then, an absolute power that took it. This permits us to reason that something exists, and not nothing. But it does not tell us the reason why that exists which exists, and no other possible thing. That absolute power which, says Leibnitz, *uno vocabulo solet appellari Deus* had to choose between the possibles. This basically modifies their ontological condition. In exercising upon them the operation of choosing, of preferring, they cease to be merely and simply possibles. Although being equally possibles, they cease to be equals but are placed in an order which is not primarily ontological if by "being" we understand bare "being" without qualification. They cease to be equals in an estimative order in which we do not talk of "being" and "not being," but of

---

the greatest order and the greatest simplicity, it is evident that the world would be more intelligible. We would, in fact, be able to construct *a priori*, by pure concepts, a system of general laws that would rule things and their opposites. For example, a world where a phenomenon can emerge by itself, independent of every other phenomenon, would be unintelligible, but if every phenomenon unfailingly follows the previous one in such a fashion that, given the latter, we can affirm the appearance of the former, or vice versa, if starting from its appearance we affirm that before this thing there had to be an earlier one, and so on successively, we will have an intelligible world. Well now, this admission of ours is simply the law of causality: every fact has its cause. But in addition to this, that confidence which has been given us allows us to affirm no less *a priori* that the cause of a fact will be the simplest that can be thought of, with which we will have "the law of minimum effort," and so on.

good, better, best. It is certainly difficult to pass from possibility to existence; but is it by chance easier to pass from plain being to the notion of what is good, from the entitative order to the estimative? Let us see what Leibnitz has to say on such a difficult matter: "As soon as God has resolved to create something there is a struggle among all the possibles, since all of them claim the right to exist. Those will triumph which together produce more reality, more perfection, more intelligibility. It is clear that this whole struggle can only be one of ideas, that is to say, that it can only consist in a conflict of reasons within the most perfect understanding, that it cannot cease to comport itself in the most perfect form, and consequently, to choose the best." Leibnitz makes it clear that God is not needed in this out of any metaphysical need but out of a moral necessity. Leibnitz calls a metaphysical necessity one of pure logicality. "If God," he tells us, "felt it necessary to produce what He does by metaphysical necessity He would produce all the possibles, or none." [10] This is what I expressed before in a formula that Leibnitz does not use, saying that in their being all possibles are equals.

To make sense out of the existing world one has to have recourse to a principle alien to logic; one must admit what Leibnitz calls "the principle of the best or of the most advantageous." While the possible being exists because it contains no contradiction the existent being, the actual world, *is* because it is the best, because it is optimum.

The optimism of Leibnitz is not, then, a question of state of mind or temperament. It is not the optimism that someone feels but optimism that something is. It represents an ontological dimension. It is the optimism of being. It is not that, observing what the world is composed of, we make a comparative appraisal of the doses of good and evil which both show in order to conclude which of them predominates. Such an appraisal is illusory. It was Schopenhauer's error to try it, and to believe that by empirical considerations one could decide whether the world is good or bad. This led him to con-

10. *Philosophische Schriften*, VI, 603.

sider reasoning as being effective, to invite us to compare the pleasure of the fox when it eats a hare with the suffering of the hare when the fox eats it. One cannot in this way found an ontological pessimism. In Leibnitz, on the contrary, the optimistic character of the world takes precedence over any contemplation of its content. The world, in his judgment, is not the best because it is as it is, but vice versa, it is as it is, it was chosen to exist because it was the best. It is, then, an *a priori* optimism. Our world, before becoming existent, was already the best and because of this it came into existence.

Looking at this doctrine of Leibnitz the first thing that surprises us is that it should be surprising, because the whole of philosophy's past from its very beginning is a continual affirmation of the same thing. Prior to Leibnitz, medieval philosophy set forth the doctrine of the transcendental predicates, that is to say, of those characteristics which Being possesses simply because it is. One of these is goodness. The Ens and the good are reciprocal. This doctrine of the transcendentals appears, I believe, in the 12th Century. Alexander de Hales seems to have been the first to state it. He had taken it from the Arabs, who were the first Scholastics, and who in upholding it did no more than make Aristotle's thoughts scholastic. In the latter's book *On the Parts of Animals* one reads that "among all that is possible, nature does the best." [11] But in the last book of *Metaphysics* he will maintain more basically that substance, therefore what by itself and ultimately is, *is* because of the fact that it possesses what it needs, thanks to its *autarchy* or self-sufficiency. This permits it to sustain itself in being, to persevere in it, to save itself, *soteria*. And all this, in turn, because it is good.[12] Although on this occasion Aristotle argues with his master for other reasons, in saying this he is only professing the purest Platonism. In the *Timeus* we read that in shaping the world God or the Demiurge wanted it to be the best that was possible.[13] In the *Republic* Plato will give the most extreme

11. De Partibus Animalium, 687ª 16.
12. *Metaphysics*, XIV, 4, 1091ᵇ 18.
13. *Op. cit.*, 29 a; 30 b.

expression to this thought, which is apparently deep-rooted. He will say that there is something "above being, superior to it in power and dignity." This something which takes precedence over Being is the Good, *Agathón*. To which the interlocutor replies: "What a hyperbole Socrates proposes to us!"

I do not think that this Platonic paradox has ever been clarified suitably; on the other hand, we see it as constituting the root of all early or ontological philosophy up to Leibnitz. Why, when we are thinking of Being, do we always stumble over the good? Going even further back we would find that Heraclitus asserts: "To God all things are beautiful, good and just. To men, on the other hand, some appear just and others unjust." [14] God in Heraclitus signifies the point of view from which the authentic Being is seen. With this we have reached the birth of philosophy.

Thus the famous optimism of Leibnitz is rather the perennial optimism of philosophy and it is difficult to understand why the Leibnitzian idea caused so much surprise, so much talk and, thanks to Voltaire, so much laughter. Voltaire, if he had paid more attention to the whole of his own ideas, would have seen his own coincidence with what seemed to him laughable when said by Leibnitz.

Certainly there is a difference between what Leibnitz asserts and what philosophy always upheld, and this difference deserves to be studied as a whole. Leibnitz does not say, as do the others, that Being is good. He does not seem to be satisfied with that. He needs to say that it is the best, and that it is the optimum. This makes us realize that he talks in comparative terms, and now he does surprise us, because we find that Leibnitz, for all his famous optimism, does not affirm that the world is good *simpliciter*, but only that it is the best of the possibles, which means that the rest are less good, therefore that they include greater evil, therefore that they are worse. Here is how, on affirming that our world is the best possible, he recognizes only that—strictly speaking—it is the best of those that are not good, therefore of the bad. This makes us

14. *Op. cit.*, Fragment 102.

infer what we least suspected: that the world is not only not good, but that any world *simpliciter* good, therefore without evil, is impossible. Otherwise that world and not our own would be the world which exists.

The thing is less paradoxical and extravagant than it would seem at first sight. On every peak a climb culminates, but on the other side a descent begins. In the history of philosophy the mind of Leibnitz is a watershed. Up to him the basic optimism in thinking, which began with philosophy in Greece and has its prehistory in Hellenic mythology and even in more remote zones before that mythology, advanced in *crescendo*. But all at once pessimism begins in Leibnitz. This ultimately appears in his great disciple Kant. This embryonic pessimism which we encounter within Leibnitzian optimism is found in almost all the dimensions of his system, but above all in what is the peak of his metaphysics, the doctrine of the monads, which we have not been able to consider in this brief discussion. In Leibnitz the idea of monad plays the role of giving a reason and serving as a basis for the second "truth of primary fact" which becomes the Cartesian *cogito*. In effect it is not only true that I exist as a thinking being but that I think an unlimited multitude of thoughts, *plura a me cogitantur*. This demands a limitless multitude of realities to which that mental multitude corresponds, although with a correspondence which need not be close. There is not one monad, then, if there is not an infinite number of monads, and there is not an infinite number of monads if they are not discernible, and they are not discernible if each one does not possess a separate degree of reality, i.e., of perfection, since for Leibnitz "perfection" is *quantitas realitatis*. Therefore there are no monads if there is not relative imperfection. This consists of confused perception, which is evil. From whence it results that without this intrinsic evil, ascribed to the root of whatever is—except God—there could not be anything. An ens—except God—which was not imperfect would be a "deserter from the general order." Plato's optimism is also Utopian. In the *Republic* we read that the good things of this world are not entirely good but ἀγαθοειδῆ, *agathoeides,* "goodish," i.e., quasi-good.[15]

Here, gentlemen, is the theme on which I would have liked to talk to those present: what do optimism and pessimism finally mean in ontology? what does it mean at bottom to say that Being is good, and what does it mean to think that Being, as Being, is evil? Although, gentlemen, it may seem to be something else, it is this that is being dealt with today, more actively than theoretically, in all the dimensions of the human world.

Leibnitz himself came close to posing this tremendous problem to himself. He saw God as *sagesse et bonté,* struggling against the evil of being which His *entendement* laid before Him. Reading the *Theodicea* leaves us with this conclusion floating in the mind: Being is evil in such a way that not even God Himself has been able to check its evilness fully, and He had to make a pact with it in order to escape a worse evil.[16] It leads to statements which are like a kind of Manicheism within God. *"Il y a véritablement deux principes, mais ils sont tous deux en Dieu, savoir son Entendement et sa Volonté. L'entendement fournit le principe du mal, sans en être terni, sans être mauvais; et représente les natures comme elles sont dans les vérités éternelles; il contient en lui la raison pour laquelle le mal est permis, mais la volonté ne va qu'au bien."* [17] On the other hand, he recognizes that a concrete justification of the actual evils which our world contains *"nous est impossible dans l'état òu nous sommes; il nous suffit de faire remarquer que rien n'empêche qu'un certain mal particulier no soit lié avec ce qui est meilleur en général. Cette explication imparfaite et qui laisse quelque chose à découvrir dans l'autre vie, est suffisante pour la solution des objections, mais non pour une compréhension de la chose."*

All this is an example of the peculiar euphemistic style of Leibnitz because, stated in his own precise terms, it means that

15. *Republic,* 509 a.
16. See, for example, *ibid.,* VI, 182–183.
17. *Ibid.,* VI, 198–199.

actually optimism is irrational.

Resolved not to enter into a theme which I have limited myself to suggesting, I can nevertheless let its exact shape appear imperfectly by adding these two single observations: one is that if actual evil is justified as an avoidance of another greater evil we are obliged to attempt a metaphysical *disteleology*, that is, to try to take for ourselves the measure of this "even greater" possible evil, of which the lesser existing evil is a symptom, so to speak. The other is that as the optimistic system of Leibnitz shows us a panorama of being in which a dimension of evil, an imperfection, appears as part of it, we realize that among the intellectual disciplines there has been lacking up to now an empirical *disteleology* which ought to investigate, define, and analyze the imperfection of nature. Only this corrective entry vis-à-vis the deep-rooted teleology of thought can readjust the mind of man to his destiny.

But homage must be rendered to one of the loftiest minds which has appeared on the planet, and it has seemed to me that the most sincere and respectful homage should consist in ceasing to argue and bowing out from his imaginary presence.

The most important and most fertile angle from which Leibnitz should be studied is the analysis of the structure of his ontology, and it seems wrong to abandon this brief contemplation of some of his most characteristic doctrines without a fleeting glance at a question which it is rather bold of me to include in a lecture. The ontology of Leibnitz was the only one centered on the modality of Being. The others focus only on the way of being which common speech today calls "reality." Possibility, necessity, contingency remain on a lower plane. Unfortunately the doctrine of modality is difficult to elucidate and moreover it suffers from deficiencies of terminology which it is not feasible to correct. As a matter of fact, there is no philosophic word in our Romance languages which is fully adequate to express exactly what the populace calls "reality." In Leibnitz what is possible is real, and by this there is understood a possible reality. What people of today ordinarily call "reality" Leibnitz calls "real existence." It is not a good designation, because what is possible has, of course, a manner of existence—for example, what the mathematicians call "mathematical existence"—and in general the ways of being are clearly ways of existing. The Germans, thanks to the linguistic doublets so frequent in their language, can distinguish between *Realität* and *Wirklichkeit*. We can translate this last term as "effectiveness" or "actuality," and thus designate the way of being of the thing which surrounds us, and the way of each one of us, but even while doing so we know that these are not satisfactory terms.

If we compare that which is possible and necessary, on the one hand, with the "real" on the other, a strange difference leaps to the eye. Nothing can seem possible or necessary to us except by virtue of a previous reason. Both ways of being are presented to us, then, carrying with them their reason for being, and hence they are eminently rational. Thus the possible "exists" *because* it is not contradictory. With the effective or the actual, with "reality," this does not happen. The true existence of things is at first set before us devoid of reason or source which may make it intelligible. It is an irrational *crude fact*. Being so, it irritates our rational processes and moves us to seek its reason for being, a proof that this is not immediately made apparent by the thing. In principle the true or "real" could exist without any reason. It would then be an irrational world, unintelligible and without foundation. This characteristic of being without reason for being, of pure happening, is *contingentia*.

In comparison with the possible and the necessary, the contingent is so strange a way of being that the mind on observing it is actually left without knowing whether this is to be treated as an authentic way of being for the Ens, or is rather a deficient way for the Ens to manifest itself to us. In Leibnitz, as we shall soon see, this dual and equivocal aspect of the contingent is always formalized. He makes clear several times the effort he has made to elucidate this way of being, and in turn he lets us see his satisfaction in the result obtained.

With what does Leibnitz show himself satisfied? In his letter to Jacques Bernouilli of December 2, 1695,[18] he declares: "*Sed contingentiae sua jura conservo.*" What lies at the bottom of this whole question? What are those laws of the contingent?

This touches one of the greatest internal struggles through which Leibnitz must have passed during his youth. Rationalsim cannot admit that anything may be without a determining reason for its being: it is determinism. This imposes on rationalism a modal doctrine rendered tyrannical by a kind of necessity. If nothing is without reason, everything which exists is made necessary by the reason that determines it. Rationalist that he was, Leibnitz could not think in any other manner, and his disciple Wolff does no more than formulate the Leibnitzian attitude when, in his *Philosophia prima*, Chapter 288, he says: "*Quodlibet, dum est, necessario est.*" This is also valid for the possible. Since its reason for being is non-contradiction, given this the possible necessarily exists as possible. Hence the truths about possibles are *nécessaires, éternelles, de raison.*

But it was as a boy that Leibnitz encountered this rationalism, this determinism, in the fundamental form which Spinoza had given it. That influence did not consist in the fact that he would never be a Spinozan but, on the contrary, in the efforts to which Spinoza forced him in order not to be one. Spinoza revives the extreme determinism which has its most pointed expression in its *kurieyon* or principal argument of Diodorus Kronos. This is exactly contrary to the distinction between the possible and the real. Compared with the real, which is absolutely determined, the possible is something more or less determined, that which can be or not be. But such indeterminacy is not intelligible. If something can be it is inconceivable that it not be, and if it is not this means that it lacks something. But then one would not say that it is possible, but that it is impossible. Nothing is possible unless it has been, is, or will be real or actual.

This famous argument, which reappears in Spinoza leads

18. *Mathematische Schriftsn*, III, 27.

Leibnitz to a profound reform of the doctrine of modality. He never set this reform down in any orderly and complete manner but I believe that its reconstruction can be attempted.

For Leibnitz, the possible is not counterposed to the real as the least determined to the most determined. The possible always has its determining reason. It is possible that A is, and possible that A is not, but it is impossible that both be true at the same time. Starting from one or the other we can derive a whole series of necessary consequences; or vice versa, starting from other possibilities, we can show the necessity for each one of those possibilities. Every possibility begins, then, by disassociating itself from a duality or plurality which is internally incompatible, but having terms of which each one is in fact possible, and it coexists with others that are compatible with it or, as Leibnitz says, are compossible. The indeterminacy as to whether A is or is not—therefore the duplication of possibility—is eliminated when each one of its extremes is considered to be included in an organism of compossibles which are mutually determined. This means that every possible postulates a "world" of compossibles, even more an infinity of "possible worlds." The plural with which the idea of "possible world" always appears in Leibnitz is not accidental, but proceeds inevitably from the disassociative character of possibility. The "possible worlds" constitute a system, a group which is ordered though infinite. The law of its arrangement is the more or less of compossibility and therefore of better and greater intelligibility. Each one of those worlds possesses its complete internal determination and it is an error on the part of Nicolai Hartmann to call them "incomplete worlds," that is, worlds insufficiently determined in their internal consistence. They are so much so that for this very reason they cannot be real worlds. This is the Leibnitzian inversion of tradition in modal ontology. There is no lack of internal determination among the possible worlds for being real. There is no sufficient reason within them for them to become real, but on the other hand, there is not sufficient reason in any one of them to make itself real over and above others. Hence the possibles remain always possible. That there is a real or actual world in addition to the possible worlds cannot be derived from the element of possibility, but is something new and different. Reality or actual being is not a final degree of determination in the possible but requires another type of determination or necessity. Take into account the fact that "necessary" meant, until the time of Leibnitz, *absolutely* necessary, that is, with *nécessité logique métaphysique*.

The modes called "possibility" and "necessity" are characterized, as we said before, by the fact that in them being is at the same time reason for being, because in them what is, is by virtue of an implicit reason. Hence knowledge of the possible and the necessary proceeds by means of pure analytic thinking in deductive theories or systems which start from definitions and from the principles of identity and contradiction. In the case of the Real the situation is different. The Real, *insofar as it is a way of being* is purely artificial. It does not exist by virtue of an implicit reason; otherwise it would be necessary in the aforesaid meaning. But the Real is real in such a manner that its opposites, for example, its nonbeing or its other-being, are possible. The Real being is characterized, then, by not being necessary, and this is what a contingent being means. It is not for a reason but for a bare happening or fact.

What should be the mental attitude toward what is like this, therefore toward what is without reason? Evidently it cannot consist of pure deductive theories of an analytical system of "eternal truths" dowered with absolute necessity, but it will start from a simple recognition of fact, that is to say, of *vérités de fait*. But this imposes on thought the task of discovering the reason for the fact. This reason is not implicit in it as in the possible and the necessary, but will be outside the fact, namely, in another fact. This reason, external to a thing, is what is called cause. Causal theory must be substituted for pure analytical theory. In the possible and the necessary the reason for being is previous to being. From here on it might go by itself, automatically, to put into practice the principle of reason, the principle that nothing is without reason. But vis-à-vis the real, the perspective is inverted: what is, is without reason. Hence it may be necessary to formulate specially an imperative of intellectual behavior which might be stated thus: Whatever is presented without reason or basis must be provided with one. Hence Leibnitz refers his principle of sufficient reason mainly to knowledge of the real notwithstanding the fact that this is valid *a posteriori* in the sphere of the possible and the necessary. But it should be noted meanwhile that in this the principle of reason is analytical and constitutive—while nothing is presented as possible or necessary without previously showing its reason for being so, toward the real the principle of reason acquires the meaning of a postulate whose truth is not its own, but which, on the contrary, comes from the theory that by supposing it one reaches—if one reaches—the explanation of the fact. This, then, is what verifies the principle and not vice versa.

In this manner the discovery of cause, which in turn is a fact, a contingency, gives reason and basis for fact. But cause requires another fact, another cause, which explains it, and thus a chain of cause and effect is built in which the real acquires a structure of reason. Within that chain the relation between cause and effect is necessary. But it is a matter of a necessity between one thing and another which is merely relative. The cause which is the reason for the effect is, in its turn, a simple fact without reason. So that, while within the causal chain we find the mode of necessity, the integrity of the chain is contingent.

It would be absolute only if the first link in the chain were not only a necessary Ens, but also needed so that element in it would inescapably be followed by all the rest. This is the opinion of the Megareans, of Spinoza, of the absolute determinism which is inspired by the idea of *Fatum* and is in fact fatalism. In this ontology the mode Reality is the necessary consequence of the necessary Ens—*Natura sive Deus*. This means that in it necessity absorbs or rather eliminates the other modal forms. The "real" is not characterized as what it simply is but as what it has to be, therefore as necessary. This is due to the fact that no other possibility is admitted, that there was no Real, or none as it is. With this its contingency disappears from the Real.

For Leibnitz the chain of cause and effect does not end in a cause which is necesary and not contingent. Without doubt God is for Leibnitz the necessary Ens, although like everything referring to His concept His necessity is far from precise. But what is limiting in Leibnitz is that, although God is the necessary Ens, His role as creator is not necessary in the same sense. Creation is not an automatic emanation of divinity. It is also a contingency. God *could* create, or not create, another world different from the actual one. This implies that He has at hand a plurality of possible worlds or, what is the same thing, contrary to Megareanism and Spinoza, the possible way of being is different from the real way of being. The principle of the contingent is in turn contingent. It is a choice among the possibles which God exercises. This choice is not without reason, but this reason is not implicit or analytical. It is not a reason operating from His understanding—a logical, metaphysical reason—but a reason of another kind which springs from His goodness: it is a divine determination of what is best. This sparks the creative decision, the causal principle of the contingent. The contingent is the "necessary" consequence of divine goodness. Its necessity, according to Leibnitz, is then a "contingent" or moral necessity. There will be no need to underline up to what point so paradoxical a concept is problematical.

But from the point of view of God the contingent shows another characteristic. He has before Him an infinite number of possible worlds, among which ours remains *absolutely determined* as the best. His will having freely resolved to create the best, He finds in His understanding an infinite number of reasons, that is, absolute reason for choosing the actual world. In God, then, the Real is deduced with logical necessity from pure possibilities and therefore, given His resolution to create, it is not contingent. We cannot know the infinite reasons implied in the Creator's decision in favor of the Real, but we can be sure that they exist—hence that the "real" is a product of rationality—and this imposes on us an intellectual obligation to discover those reasons by means of a "progress toward limitless" knowledge. We will never succeed in making the sufficient reason for the Real manifest to ourselves, but in our unlimited advance we can always approach it. This possibility of limitless progress is the rationalization of the Real, *habet ipse rationis locum,* and it has for us the value of sufficient reason, since we can always discover more reasons for being insofar as it is Real. In the principle of sufficient reason, then, Leibnitz includes his principle of continuity, which will give him such excellent results in mathematics, leading him to the invention of differential calculus. At this juncture it could be stated thus: every explanation (rationalization) of the Real world is deficient, but the final one is never possible in that behind it there is always available another and better one. Let it be said in passing, as I have never seen it noted, that the Leibnitzian principle of continuity, if one thinks it through to the end, leads to a continuity between truth and error in that it considers as truth an error less erroneous than any other. Let us sum up: in the sight of God, given His resolution to create, the contingent is absolutely necessary. In comparison with that characteristic the "contingent necessity," which always represents the Real for man, would give to this contingency the value of a mere deficient aspect produced by our finite perception. Leibnitz called the infinite number of reasons implied in the real but unavailable to us the *radix contingentiae.*[19]

It was important for us to show why Leibnitz makes ontology gravitate toward the mode called "possibility." It is not enough to attribute this to his propensity for logic, formalism, and mathematics. In a specific manner he makes us see that "*Si on voulait rejeter absolument les purs possibles, on détruirait la contingence; car si rien n'est possible que ce que Dieu a créé effectivement, ce que Dieu a créé serait nécessaire en cas*

19. *Philosophische Schriften,* VII, 200.

que Dieu ait résolu de créer quelque chose." [20]

Now we see what comprised the laws of the contingencies, those laws that Leibnitz seems so pleased to have saved. The contingency of the real is no mere deficient aspect with which this is presented to the limited human mind, as Spinoza contended, but a formal way of being different from possibility and from absolute necessity. This distinction or profound differentiation between the forms of modality brings with it the fact that in Leibnitz the "ways of being" are congealed or condensed into spheres of *entia*. The possible is not only a modality of the Ens but it is a class of *entia*.

Nevertheless, in what is said above there remains one point which it is useful to clear up. When we said that the Real is an irrational way of being and that therefore we must search beyond it for that foundation which it does not show in itself, and that this leads Leibnitz to establish the principle of sufficient or determining reason, the motivation for this is not apparent. Why do we not leave the Real in all its nakedness as a bare fact without foundation and without reason? Why do we assume that reason which *prima facie* it does not have?

Leibnitz leans on one of the most enduring opinions of traditional ontology, namely, that the Real insofar as it is real is *a fortiori* possible. Well now, this implies that it is intelligible, that it is by virtue of reasons. Well now, it can be said truthfully of something that it is possible only when it has been possible to demonstrate that it does not involve contradictions. According to Leibnitz there are two possible ways of making this demonstration. *La marque d'une idée vraie et réelle est lorsqu'on peut démonstrer la possibilité, soit a priori en donnant ses réquisits, soit a posteriori par l'expérience, car ce qui existe actuellement ne saurait manquer d'être possible.*[21] The first form of demonstration is based on "giving the requisites" of the idea, that is, in breaking down the composite idea into the simple ones which make it up. Simple ideas do not involve contradiction, and keeping them in mind one

20. *Ibid.,* II, 45.
21. *Ibid.,* III, 257.

can discover if they contradict each other. We saw in the text of the present discourse that this is Utopian, as Leibnitz' thought customarily is, because there is no guaranteed way of arriving at simple ideas. But let us suppose that it was not like this, and ask ourselves for the meaning of the second form of demonstration. Experience is proof of reality or actuality. This leads to admitting abstractly and blindly that such a reality is possible, but we do not see what specifically constitutes its possibility. This remains as a problem to solve concretely if starting from its abstract certainty: that ambivalent mental situation in which something with no reason for being is in turn conviction and problem, is stated in the principle of sufficient reason which for it is at once axiomatic and postulated. Everything rests, then, on an assumption that the thesis "the real is possible" may be true. In the whole philosophic past we do not find, at least in express form, that such a proposition has been doubted. How is there room for doubt that what is can be? To declare it problematical, questionable, would be to invite a basic reform of the very idea of Being, and to turn traditional ontology upside down from top to bottom. The result is that by this road we have come back to the great question which this discourse announces, and at the same time we put it off because this is not the proper occasion to present it. In fact to affirm that the Real is possible is founded on the idea of being with which Plato and Aristotle innoculated all subsequent philosophy. According to this the Ens is autarchic, is sufficient, is its own achievement. This is what they called "perfection" or the goodness of the Being, and it has given all later ontology an ultimate basis of unshakeable optimism. In that tradition a way of being which consists in a mere attempt or effort at being, which does not include any guarantee that it will not go astray, that is to say, that its attempt at being will not serve only to demonstrate that it is impossible—all this is incomprehensible. But, I repeat, these days are not a good time for discussing whether such an unheard of enigma has meaning.

Appendix 2: Renaissance, Humanism, and Counter Reformation

THE OTHER RENAISSANCE, that of Erasmus and the humanists, was nine-tenths the complete opposite of a renaissance, namely, one that we will do better to call a return to the womb. It was a *retrogression*, further back than the Middle Ages, to the ancients *insofar as they were primitives*. Hence it was not merely a return to the Greeks and Romans, but also to Hebraic primitivism; in religion, bypassing the Church with all its history, a return to the primogenial gospel. Nietzsche saw clearly that Luther and Protestantism were, above all, "primitivism." [1] In all that, there was no will to go forward and grow but rather a desire to contract, to become primitive, to make oneself as a child, in short, a deliberate involution of the adult organism toward the foetus. Hence my name for it. Up to the time of Vives humanism contains hardly any substantial gestures toward the future. The *humanists* are merely grammarians of dead languages. They were traffickers in mummies, and in their persons many of them were hardly to be recommended.

At the end of the last century and in the first quarter of this one the "ruling opinion" in Europe was to indulge in such blind worship of the Renaissance and of humanism that it prevented one from seeing clearly just what these had been. Blind worship is essentially obfuscation. With the most arbitrary lack of sophistication the marvel of 14th and 15th century art—architecture, painting, sculpture, and the decorative arts—was confounded with the useless rhetoric of writers and the

---

1. See *En torno a Galileo*, Lesson VI (*Obras Completas*, Vol. V). [Translated as *Man and Crisis* (W. W. Norton and Company, 1958 and 1962).]

ornamental but slovenly poetry of the rhymesters, with the misery and mob rule of politics without grandeur or vision.

It is true that in thought the men of the Renaissance broke with Scholasticism, but they did this deviously, angrily, without knowing why, without any reason or with the mere reason of "because we do." In the final analysis, and for the only reason which was at all justified, they did it out of satiety and boredom. The philosophy of the Renaissance is not philosophy as such but a make-believe pretense to be "doing what is done," and a pure fake. Menendez Pelayo, who is usually not right, gets hold of a piece of it when he considers the Renaissance a subversive movement and certainly more than a little frivolous. Of course this is not true. One cannot sum up the Renaissance by reducing it to a mere rebellion, nor is it even adequate to treat it as a revolution. A revolution, if we do not call insurrections and pronouncements by that name, is a definitely serious phenomenon in a society which it leaves forever weakened because it leaves that society forever in discord. On the other hand, it is undeniable that a genuine revolutionary phenomenon is typically inspired by what is called an "ideal" which moreover is apt to be very much needed. But I do not know what happens to the "ideals" which—for one reason or another—initiate a series of assassinations, spoliations and bestialities of every kind as occurs whenever an "ideal" is exploited on this planet, as though it were under an evil spell.

The Renaissance is a historic reality of a very different caliber. It is not a phenomenon of collective pathology, it is not inspired by any precisely identifiable "ideal," and what we call the Renaissance lasted strangely enough for two and a half centuries, a length of time which revolutions cannot achieve, for they cannot spend two and a half centuries in the uninterrupted killing of men. It must be filed in the drawer where we have collected "historic crises." But that there was one facet of pure and simple subversion in the enormous polyhedron of desires and integrating tendencies in the Renaissance is indicated by the fact that the fragment of reason which Menendez

Pelayo found wore a revolutionoid face. An accusing symptom of every period, however little of revolution it may have in it, is that the man who takes the floor is not the thinker nor the man of science nor the true poet—these must keep silent—but the pamphleteer, or as we say today the journalist, because things in Europe reached such an extreme some time ago that we accept as normal the probability that the journalist will become professionally and constitutionally a pamphleteer. Humanism, above all in its first generation, coalesced into an immense pamphlet of so little interest that it no longer endures in man's memory, and only the erudite know about it. It is not without significance that its most popular figure, and the one now most favored in the memory of the semicultured is Pietro Aretino; and Aretino was a giant of insolence, a profligate scribbler, a monumental blackmailer. The French Revolution brought with it the same phenomenon, though on a much greater scale and with a definite Western character. Ideas are strangled by verbiage. Pico della Mirandola, with the enchanting sincerity of a young prince in a story book who is to vanish quickly in the pure grace of a premature death, declares in his famous letter to Ermolao Barbaro that the humanists have substituted their tongues for their souls.

To say that the Renaissance is this, or something like it, does not imply, however, that what made it up was right. Scholasticism, Gothicism, the medieval Church were already corpses. That something else was needed was indubitable. But humanism was not a thing but the mere scarecrow look of a thing. What the real thing would be appeared when Galileo burst out on one side and Descartes on the other. *That* was the real Renaissance. In the case of Descartes particularly the phenomenon appears in peerless clarity. Think back to the infinite confusion of minds between 1450 and 1600, the heap of empty mental gestures, of attempts at ideas, of chaotic doctrines, and compare this with the sobriety, the steely acuteness, the radiant clarity, the simplicity of style, the efficacy of each phrase with which Descartes in a trice founds a truly new and responsible concept of the Universe. He was one of the old nobility, a fine swordsman, and with a single thrust he pinned the Middle Ages to the wall. In the Renaissance there had been only one real philosopher, Giordano Bruno, the magnificent friar. Therefore everybody was against him.[2]

This does not pretend to say what the Renaissance was, but on the contrary to say what it was not, and to refuse to see in it a movement that was unitary and on the whole valuable. The truth is the opposite: it was an efflorescence of sprouts that were very different in direction and in quality. There are no more than two general notes to be found in it: its subversive or at least insolent character, and the predominance of an unauthentic tonality in what is said, is done, and is desired to be.[3] Hence this new aspect of the Renaissance forces us also to rectify the idea about the Counter Reformation prevailing for about a century. The very name makes clear the partial character of the judgment. It appears that the Reform was the positive and that the other was merely "counter." The truth is the opposite. The movement of the Counter Reformation

2. To give only one example, although a solid one, of the disingenuous and unauthentic cajolery which predominated in the humanist period, I will cite—taking it from Toffanini's *Storia dell' Umanesimo,* 1941—the case of Pope Leo X who, giving thanks in a letter dedicating a book written by a certain humanist, recognized how much his spirit was lifted and strengthened by the "immortality" which that book of rhetoric assured him, an "immortality" which he both desired and enjoyed. On this point the Pope was reminded that there is another kind of immortality, that which *"post discessum ex hac vita, in illa altera vita felici et sempeterna nos cum Deo ipso collacat."* Thank goodness that he does not forget to distinguish between the immortality of worldly fame—which is clearly neither immortality nor anything resembling it, but a mere *modus dicendi* like almost all humanism—and the other, which is hidden problematically behind our personal and inescapable death! But the reader errs if he believes that the joke ends here. After making this distinction the Pope returns to comparing both immortalities, to fusing them by making the fame of this world the symbol and outline of fame in the other. *"Est enim profecto haec famae et laudis ad commemorationem hominum celebritas, imago illius verae immortalitatis, quae eximio dono omnipotentis Dei, uni Christiano generi, per Dominum nostrum Jesum Christum proposita est, ad quam potissimum aspirare debemus."*

3. The feature which has been considered most salient—the study of the Ancients—is the least easily fixed, because since the 6th Century the intellectual life of the West is a progressive absorption of the classics.

was never anything but the most natural thing in the world. The lack of faith of the 15th Century and up to 1530, was socially and therefore historically false. It was a "game," as was almost all of the Renaissance. One played at being this or the other.[4]

Nor did that decline of faith correspond to the actual state of the spirit in the social *depths*, nor even to what was basic and real in the beliefs of the visible minorities themselves—which in this sense formed the superficial or apparent face of the period—"representatives" of the aforesaid decline of faith.[5]

The Counter Reformation was the tightening up of the loose screws in the European soul which obliged everyone to make contact with their obscure authenticity. One of the most illuminating things in both movements is the study of the backlash which the Counter Reformation produced in Protestantism itself. Without this, it would have been dissipated and lost in an absolute dispersal of persons and doctrines. Another proof of the same thing is to note where and in what measure the Counter Reformation caused injury, because then we see that where it was harmful it was not so of itself but because it coincided with some other national vice. Thus it caused some injury in Italy where a few vestiges of creative energy in science and technique still remained. Italian art was already moribund of itself, and political life was debased. Where the Counter Reformation did cause definite injury was among the people who began and directed it, that is to say, in Spain. But it would be not only unjust but also lacking in understanding to make it guilty of the damage done to that country since in other countries—in France, for example—it not only caused no harm but made possible that nation's great epoch. That in Spain it should have originated an impairment from which we have not been able to recover was due to the combining of what was both the virtue and the great effect of the Counter Reformation—namely, the skill to prepare quickly

4. Here I speak of the Renaissance as if it connoted humanism.
5. On all this see, for the moment, *En torno a Galileo* (*Obras Completas*, Vol. V). [Translated as *Man and Crisis* (W. W. Norton, 1958 and 1962).]

a strict regimentation of minds and in this sense a discipline which held those minds within themselves, thus preventing them from being converted into an edifice composed only of doors and windows—with a terrible illness produced in our country, and coinciding in a surprising manner with the timing of the Council of Trent, organ of the Counter Reformation. This sickness was the isolation of our people as against the rest of the world, a phenomenon which does not refer especially to religion or to theology, nor to ideas, but to the whole of life, a phenomenon which, by the same token, has an origin that is completely foreign to ecclesiastical questions and that was the true cause of the loss of our empire. This I call the "Tibetanization" of Spain. The height of this process came between 1600 and 1650. The effect was disastrous, fatal. Spain was the only country that not only had no need of counter-reform, but that had an excess of it. In Spain there had been no true Renaissance, and hence no subversion. Renaissance does not consist in imitating Petrarch, Ariosto, or Tasso, but rather in being them.[6]

6. In my book on Velasquez I try to describe this phenomenon of "Tibetanization." In outline it is like this: around 1600 the European nations reached a first stage in their differential formation which made them, for the first time, feel themselves different from each other. This, also for the first time in the history of the Occident, caused a tendency in each nation to withdraw within itself, a characteristic symptom in the collective as in the individual, and even in the merely zoological, on approaching adulthood. Well now, this withdrawal, which is only a "concentration toward that which is within" of attention and the collective forces, assumed a different character in each European country which can be formulated with some precision. What predominated in Spain was a basic process of isolating itself from everything foreign, including the periphery of Spain itself, that is to say, its colonies and its Empire. This was the real reason why the Empire was ruined. All the others are only secondary causes in comparison. Here is the sad mechanism which I call the "Tibetanization" of Spain. (*Obras Completas*, Vol. VIII, p. 457 et seq).